Loyola's Acts

The New Historicism: Studies in Cultural Poetics
Stephen Greenblatt, General Editor

1. *Holy Feast and Holy Fast: The Religious Significance of Food to Medieval Women*, by Caroline Walker Bynum

2. *The Gold Standard and the Logic of Naturalism: American Literature at the Turn of the Century*, by Walter Benn Michaels

3. *Nationalism and Minor Literature: James Clarence Mangan and the Emergence of Irish Cultural Nationalism*, by David Lloyd

4. *Shakespearean Negotiations: The Circulation of Social Energy in Renaissance England*, by Stephen Greenblatt

5. *The Mirror of Herodotus: The Representation of the Other in the Writing of History*, by François Hartog, translated by Janet Lloyd

6. *Puzzling Shakespeare: Local Reading and Its Discontents*, by Leah S. Marcus

7. *The Rites of Knighthood: The Literature and Politics of Elizabethan Chivalry*, by Richard C. McCoy

8. *Literary Practice and Social Change in Britain, 1380–1530*, edited by Lee Patterson

9. *Trials of Authorship: Anterior Forms and Poetic Reconstruction from Wyatt to Shakespeare*, by Jonathan Crewe

10. *Rabelais's Carnival: Text, Context, Metatext*, by Samuel Kinser

11. *Behind the Scenes: Yeats, Horniman, and the Struggle for the Abbey Theatre*, by Adrian Frazier

12. *Literature, Politics, and Culture in Postwar Britain*, by Alan Sinfield

13. *Habits of Thought in the English Renaissance: Religion, Politics, and the Dominant Culture*, by Debora Kuller Shuger

14. *Domestic Individualism: Imagining Self in Nineteenth-Century America*, by Gillian Brown

15. *The Widening Gate: Bristol and the Atlantic Economy, 1450–1700*, by David Harris Sacks

16. *An Empire Nowhere: England, America, and Literature from Utopia to The Tempest*, by Jeffrey Knapp

17. *Mexican Ballads, Chicano Poems: History and Influence in Mexican-American Social Poetics*, by José E. Limón

18. *The Eloquence of Color: Rhetoric and Painting in the French Classical Age*, by Jacqueline Lichtenstein, translated by Emily McVarish

19. *Arts of Power: Three Halls of State in Italy, 1300–1600*, by Randolph Starn and Loren Partridge

20. *Expositions: Literature and Architecture in Nineteenth-Century France*, by Philippe Hamon, translated by Katia Sainson-Frank and Lisa Maguire

21. *The Imaginary Puritan: Literature, Intellectual Labor, and the Origins of Personal Life*, by Nancy Armstrong and Leonard Tennenhouse

22. *Fifteen Jugglers, Five Believers: Literary Politics and the Poetics of American Social Movements*, by T. V. Reed

23. *Romancing the Past: The Rise of Vernacular Prose Historiography in Thirteenth-Century France*, by Gabrielle M. Spiegel

24. *Dearest Beloved: The Hawthornes and the Making of the Middle-Class Family*, by T. Walter Herbert

25. *Carnal Israel: Reading Sex in Talmudic Culture*, by Daniel Boyarin

26. *Dilemmas of Enlightenment: Studies in the Rhetoric and Logic of Ideology*, by Oscar Kenshur

27. *Writing and Rebellion: England in 1381*, by Steven Justice

28. *Roads to Rome: The Antebellum Protestant Encounter with Catholicism*, by Jenny Franchot

29. *The Renaissance Bible: Scholarship, Sacrifice, and Subjectivity*, by Debora Kuller Shuger

30. *Another Kind of Love: Male Homosexual Desire in English Discourse, 1850–1920*, by Christopher Craft

31. *Nobody's Story: The Vanishing Acts of Women Writers in the Marketplace, 1670–1820*, by Catherine Gallagher

32. *Mapping the Renaissance World: The Geographical Imagination in the Age of Discovery*, by Frank Lestringant, translated by David Fausett, with a Foreword by Stephen Greenblatt

33. *Inscribing the Time: Shakespeare and the End of Elizabethan England*, by Eric S. Mallin

34. *Resistant Structures: Particularity, Radicalism, and Renaissance Texts*, by Richard Strier

35. *Mexico at the World's Fairs: Crafting a Modern Nation*, by Mauricio Tenorio-Trillo

36. *Loyola's Acts: The Rhetoric of the Self*, by Marjorie O'Rourke Boyle, with a Foreword by William J. Bouwsma

37. *Cannibals: The Discovery and Representation of the Cannibal from Columbus to Jules Verne*, by Frank Lestringant

Loyola's Acts

The Rhetoric of the Self

Marjorie O'Rourke Boyle

University of California Press
Berkeley · Los Angeles · London

The publisher gratefully acknowledges the contribution provided by the General Endowment fund, which is supported by generous gifts from the members of the Associates of the University of California Press.

University of California Press
Berkeley and Los Angeles, California

University of California Press, Ltd.
London, England

© 1997 by the Regents of the University of California

Library of Congress Cataloging-in-Publication Data

Boyle, Marjorie O'Rourke, 1943–
    Loyola's acts : the rhetoric of the self / Marjorie O'Rourke Boyle.
      p.   cm. — (The new historicism ; 36)
    Includes bibliographical references and index.
    ISBN 0-520-20937-0 (cloth : alk. paper)
    1. Ignatius, of Loyola, Saint, 1491–1556. Autobiografía.
2. Christian saints—Spain—Biography. 3. Rhetoric, Renaissance—Spain.
I. Title. II. Series.
BX4700.L7A3   1997
271'.5302—dc21
[B]
                                  97-2132
                                      CIP

9 8 7 6 5 4 3 2 1

We are as ignorant of the meaning of the dragon as we are of the meaning of the universe, but there is something in the dragon's image that corresponds to the human imagination.

Jorge Luis Borges, *The Book of Imaginary Beasts*

Contents

Foreword	xi
Acknowledgments	xv
Introduction	1
1. The Knight Errant	22
2. The Ascetic	53
3. The Flying Serpent	100
4. The Pilgrim	147
Notes	185
Primary Sources	255
Index of Subjects	267
Index of Persons	271

Foreword

A major achievement of recent scholarship has been the demonstration that, alongside scholasticism and partly in reaction against it, there emerged, with Renaissance humanism, a major alternative to it. Among the distinguished scholars who have variously participated in this work have been P. O. Kristeller, Charles Trinkaus, and Salvatore Camporeale. They have demonstrated that, following the Bible, Saint Paul, and Saint Augustine, the humanists of the Renaissance discovered in rhetoric, as they saw it, a vehicle of communication, Christian but also secular, vastly superior to scholastic discourse because of its ability to speak to the human heart. But while these scholars have chiefly described the emergence of this movement, Marjorie O'Rourke Boyle has shown in precise detail how rhetoric empowered the writings of major figures of the time. In addition to her remarkable empathy and imagination, she has brought to this project a training in philosophy and a deep knowledge of the classical and medieval sources of Renaissance culture, both learned and popular.

Her first book, *Erasmus on Language and Method in Theology* (Toronto: University of Toronto Press, 1977), dealt generally with the devotion of Erasmus to the rhetorical theology of the church fathers; in this connection it emphasized the significance of Erasmus's translation of the *logos* of the Fourth Gospel. For the *verbum* (*word*) of Origen and Jerome, Erasmus substituted *sermo* (*speech* or *discourse*). Indeed, she tells us, Erasmus would have preferred to translate *logos* as *oratio* but was too fastidious to designate the Son with a feminine word (p. 33).

Her interest in rhetorical analysis figured even more directly in *Rhetoric and Reform: Erasmus's Civil Dispute with Luther* (Cambridge: Harvard Historical Monographs LXXI, 1983). This work dealt with the debate between Luther ("the elephant") and Erasmus ("the fly") over freedom of the will. In Boyle's treatment the two sides represented two kinds of rhetoric: Luther's was juridical, Erasmus's deliberative. In his dogmatism and his love of "assertions," however, Luther plays somewhat the same role as Erasmus's scholastic opponents in Boyle's earlier book. This book also was more general in its sense of historical context, noting the effect of the so-called Peasants War on Luther's mood at the time.

With *Petrarch's Genius: Pentimento and Prophecy* (Berkeley: University of California Press, 1991), Boyle struck out in another new direction; Luther was recognized on all sides as a theologian, and the significance of Erasmus for religious thought had been well established. But Petrarch has often been regarded chiefly as a figure in the history of secular literature, his poetry isolated from such pious works as the *Secretum*. Boyle now demonstrated that the Augustinianism of the *Secretum* was not the product of a momentary crisis but an essential element in a career that had to be understood as a whole. Underlying this argument was a general insistence on the affinity in the Renaissance between theology and poetry, and again on the religious significance of rhetoric. One of Boyle's individual articles also made her point with particular effectiveness. Entitled "Rhetorical Theology: Charity Seeking Charity" (Berkeley: Center for Hermeneutical Studies Colloquy 54, 1987, pp. 22-30), it argued that charity, which, alone among the traditional theological virtues, is clearly directed out from the self to others, is "the greatest" among them, in accordance with the familiar Pauline formula.

The rhetorical reading of a text recognizes, as other readings may not, that linguistic communication has many purposes, especially in ordinary life, and that the communication of information or systematic argument is, for most human beings most of the time, one of its least important—and indeed least effective—functions. For language accomplishes a host of human purposes, and notably the communication to others of needs, directions, love and other feelings, the insights of imagination, and a multitude of singularly powerful impulses that often operate among us below the level of consciousness. Rhetoric is also aware of the importance of genre, so that it tries to avoid reading in one genre what was composed in another: to avoid, for example, extracting from a poem a "meaning" in prose or an argument or moral.

All of this is brought to bear in *Loyola's Acts*, now Boyle's most sustained work of rhetorical analysis; it is also, in the best sense, a tour de force. It interprets the so-called autobiography of Ignatius of Loyola as a work of epideictic rhetoric rather than, in the accepted sense, either a biography or an autobiography; there is no direct evidence of its authorship. It seems, in fact, to belong to the genre of saints' lives, the function of which is to induce pious admiration and emulation. Boyle demonstrates how it does this by a detailed analysis of the text, making each detail the occasion for an illuminating essay on its artful incorporation of materials drawn from iconography, folklore, bestiaries, and the personal experience of its subject, as well as the Scriptures and classical and patristic literature. The result, however, is far more than a dazzling display of erudition. Boyle intends it as a model for the reading and interpretation of numerous other texts in European culture that have never been analyzed in this way. Some of the detail in the book may not survive the scrutiny of other scholars; but its general method, however shocking its novelties at first sight, should stimulate other "rhetorical" readings. Such readings promise to make familiar texts, like the "autobiography" of Ignatius of Loyola, once again rich and strange.

William J. Bouwsma
Department of History
University of California, Berkeley

Acknowledgments

I wish to thank William J. Bouwsma, who supported this manuscript steadfastly from its initial draft to its final publication, and who has graciously written its foreword. Also, Stephen Greenblatt, who enthusiastically accepted it for his series The New Historicism. Thanks are also owed to the readers appointed by the Press for their endorsement; my sponsoring editor, William Murphy; and the Press staff. And to my patiently loving family.

Introduction

Once upon a place: A man out for a walk sat down on the bank of a deeply coursing river and, with his face toward its surface, experienced his supreme understanding. What did he, Iñigo López de Loyola, see reflected in that natural mirror? Although from there he went on to found the Society of Jesus, renowned in the sixteenth century for its reformatory and missionary endeavors, and in the twentieth century the largest religious order in the Roman Catholic Church, his climactic experience is virtually unknown. This obscurity even after his quincentennial (1491–1556) is arresting in comparison with the celebrity of the historically parallel experience in the Protestant tradition, Martin Luther's illumination in the tower about justification by faith.

This book is about the renaissance rhetoric of the self, as focused on a character tempted by fame. Autobiography has attained status as a genre only within the past several decades, with criticism concentrated on texts of the seventeenth through twentieth centuries. There is a commonsense definition of autobiography as writing about the self by the self,[1] with the paradigm as Augustine's *Confessions*. Yet that text eludes that norm, for it was not autobiographical but epideictic: rhetoric invented *from* the self *about* God. "The thirteen books of my *Confessions* praise the just and good God from my evils and from my goods and they arouse the human intellect and affection toward him." The self was not the object of the text but a source from which Augustine invented those divine praises. Augustine was not an autobiographer; God was the Creator. The author of the text was ultimately the creative indwelling

Spirit, who formed and stimulated his tongue to confess. As an epideictic rhetorician, Augustine was a confessor in prudence, the parts of which virtue formally structured his text: memory, intelligence, and foresight.[2]

Prudence, the virtue that classically elected between good and evil, governed the medieval and renaissance literature since then mislabeled "autobiography" by a historiographic zeal to assert a modern empirical self. The virtuous structure of this imitative literature may be less formal than in Augustine's prudential paradigm, or in the triple-headed Prudence of art;[3] but prudential conventions such as the choice of Hercules, which informed Augustine's conversion,[4] still prevailed. In a sophistic parable Hercules, that most popular of Greek heroes, was adapted to idealize the human faculty of deliberation and its power of decision. Hercules in his passage to youth also went, like Loyola, to a quiet place and sat down pondering which path of life to choose. Two contrasting female figures appeared and addressed his doubts with the divergent attractions and promises of vice and virtue.[5] From that exemplar, the classical ancestor of medieval and renaissance masters of choice, a character was typically plotted as a traveler on the path of life, confronted at crossroads with moral decisions. Although autobiography has been dated to the invention of the silvered mirrors of Venetian technique,[6] in which an individual could accurately examine himself, even late in renaissance literature that visionary mirror could still be the exemplary mirror of medieval morality. As in Guillaume de Deguileville's *Pelèrinage de vie humaine*:

> In thys boke, yf they rede yerne,
> ....
> Ther they may, as in a merovr se
> holsom thynges, & thynges full notable;
> What ys prevyd, & what thyng ys dampnable,
> What ys holsom, the solve for to save,
> Whan the body ys leyd in hys grave.[7]

Loyola's experiences are related in a text titled *Acta*, to which modern translations into English have insinuated the novel title "Autobiography."[8] The critical edition states that "this *Acta* contains his life (*vita*)," from the time of his wounding at Pamplona in 1521 to the favorable opinion given of him and his companions by the pope to the governor at Rome in 1538.[9] The premise of modern interpretation is that this "life" is an autobiographical narrative as a factually historical document. *Loyola's Acts* will not convert such an "autobiography" into a biography. Other authors have essayed that, even as a literal foundation for psychoanalysis.[10] This book intends to argue that the text is not an autobiography, to question the validity of treating it as a historical document on the modern empiricist model, and to offer a heuristic for the interpretation of similar texts in the Christian tradition composed in the epideictic genre. It proposes an alternative to historical literalism.

Loyola indicated to the Society of Jesus in 1553 his decision "to declare whatever had passed through his soul until then."[11] He acceded to its explicit request "to explain how from the beginning of his conversion the Lord had governed him."[12] The title *Acta* might be hagiographic; the text of St. Francis of Assisi translated into Italian as *Fioretti* was originally titled *Actus*. The title more probably derives from the scriptural Acts of the Apostles, in which "they gathered the church together and *declared* all that God had done with them" (Acts 14:27; 15:4). The text of Loyola's recital was occasioned by such a spiritual accounting (*dar cuenta*) by its Jesuit author, Luis Gonçalves da Câmara, to the Society's founder, which Loyola reciprocated. The Jesuits had petitioned an explanation from Loyola of how the Lord had governed him. Like Augustine he responded as a prudent confessor of values. The text is epideictic rhetoric, in conformity with Loyola's determination in his *Exercitia spiritualia* of the primary purpose of life as epideictic: "to praise" God.[13] Epideictic rhetoric was the genre that classically treated praise or censure, from panegyric to invective, as derived from the personal topics and as aimed at the honorable. It was distinguished from the deliberative rhetoric of the forum, which debated an issue for the civic moral good, and from the juridical rhetoric of the court, which defended or prosecuted a legal case. Although epideictic rhetoric assumed the matters for praise or blame to be true, it could by the rules exploit the techniques of fiction, so that every detail was not necessarily factual. Even when the matter was factual, it was not factual qua factuality but factual qua evaluation. The intent was not on the conveyance of information but on the persuasion of judgment. Its import was moral not empirical.[14] *Loyola's Acts* will explore that moral sense of the text. It will do so by situating the morality in its cultural context. Venturing beyond a close literary reading of the text, this book will research its milieu to expose its values as cultural conventions. The very exposure of its conventionality—popular piety—will also allow the disclosure of its rare but important countercultural innovations.

Acta is not autobiography. Loyola, unlike Augustine, did not even compose the text. It was five times removed from his lips: after recital were audition, memorization, notation, composition, transcription. Erasmus complained of a devotion that preserved the dirty handkerchiefs of saints in gilt reliquaries, while "the books into which they put so much work, and in which we have the best part of them still living and breathing, we abandon to be gnawed at will by bug, worm, and cockroach."[15] There remains not even an infested exemplar of Loyola's recital. The original manuscript is reported by the modern editors as lost, with the critical edition compiled from partial versions.[16] Until that publication in 1943, even a Latin translation was used, rather than the Spanish and Italian copies of the lost original. Loyola speaks with the hollow voice of medieval texts, for which the original was anonymous, lost, forgotten, disappeared, with only copies of copies extant.[17] That factor of distance between self and text will necessarily figure in its interpretation; the function of memory in its invention will be emphatic.

The text was invented by imitation. The imitation of models was a pancultural precept and activity that flourished in the sixteenth century as both focal and diffuse theory and technique in literature.[18] In humanist aspirations imitation was not a crude reproduction but an elegant resemblance of texts. An author was not an ape. Imitation was in the superior theory of Erasmus not mimicry but emulation, a transcendence of the style of the ancient master by cultivating one's own native beauty in harmony with the persons and conditions of contemporaneous life. The author reflected the individuality of his own mind as in a natural mirror. Any mimicry of another's gifts distorted the reflection, as if the author were masquerading.[19]

Renaissance literature thus requires for its interpretation a discernment of the latent texts of tradition, or intertextual allusions. Of the metaphors for imitation that were commonplace since early in the period—the apian, the digestive, the filial, the echoic, and the choral[20]—it is the filial that governs this text. The metaphor derived from Seneca's theory of imitation, which advised a resemblance to the original without an exactness, much as a son might resemble his father.[21] As Petrarch explained, "While often very different in their individual features, they have a certain something that our painters call an 'air,' especially noticeable about the face and eyes, that produces a resemblance." Imitation consists of concept and style, not exact words, so that its art is concealed rather than blatant. The similarity of copy to exemplar is so profound that it can only be extricated by a quiet meditation.[22] Gonçalves da Câmara refers deferentially to Loyola as "the Father,"[23] although as a priest he himself was entitled to that appellation. Just as he identifies himself spiritually as a son, so is his composition literarily a filial imitation of Loyola's discourse.

The initial sentence of the preface of *Acta* signals the elision of history into morality: it begins with a date but ends with a vice. "The year of 53 one Friday morning, 4 August, the vigil of Our Lady of the Snows, while the Father was in the garden adjoining the house or apartment which is called the Duke's, I began to give him an account of some intimacies of my soul and among other things I spoke to him about vainglory." He details the circumstances of its composition. At dinner after their intimate conversation in the garden about vainglory, Loyola mentions how often Jerónimo Nadal and others of the Society have especially requested something of him, about which he has never decided.[24] This matter proves to be, as Nadal's preface reveals, "something after the manner of a testament, to give them advice that they might be assisted in the perfection of virtue," such as "the holy fathers, authors of some monastic institutes, confided to posterity."[25] As Gonçalves da Câmara relates, Loyola explains at dinner how after the conversation in the garden, having retired to his room, "he had quite a devotion and inclination to do that; and (speaking in a manner that showed that God had given him great clarity that he ought to do that) that he was wholly determined. That matter was to declare whatever had passed in his soul until now. He had also determined that it was I to whom he would expose these matters." Although Loyola is quite ill and unaccustomed to promise himself even a day of life, he expresses the hope of survival for three or four months to complete the affair.[26]

Gonçalves da Câmara reports their collaboration. Although Loyola requires a daily reminder of this duty, he postpones it daily for many days, until because of other commitments he asks only for a reminder every Sunday. In September on an unremembered date Loyola summons him and "begins to tell his entire life and the lively fancies or antics of youth clearly and distinctly in all their circumstances." There are three or four more meetings in the same month that bring the account up to the first days in Manresa, as indicated by the difference in the penmanship. Although Gonçalves da Câmara dates their causative conversation, he cannot recall the dates of the recitals and he is vague about the number of early encounters as "three or four." There is no vagueness in the original discourse, however, as he reports it. "The Father's manner of narration is as in everything; that is, with such clarity that it seems to render a man present to the entire past."[27]

Clarity of style was a classical virtue of rhetoric. A clarity so vivid as to render the absent present was *enargeia*. This was the rhetorical term for the representation of reality that evoked a physical—primarily visual—scene in all its line, texture, and color. It was a stylistic effect that appealed to the senses and so described the scene that the listener became a spectator. With emphasis on the sense of sight, it thrust itself upon his notice by displaying facts in living truth to the eye of the mind. This vivid pictorial description penetrated to the very emotions. Although the comparison of writing to painting was a humanist habit, *enargeia* was the essential painterly skill. As an ornament its achievement was the greatest of all rhetorical gifts. It displayed this excellence in historiography and poetry.[28] Erasmus, whose popular textbook on style was included in this very year of Loyola's recital in the regulations governing all Jesuit colleges,[29] instructed on *enargeia*. It was employed "whenever, for the sake of amplifying or decorating our passage, or giving pleasure to our readers, instead of setting out the subject in bare simplicity, we fill in the colours and set it up like a picture to look at, so that we seem to have painted the scene rather than read." Vividness derived from a mental review of the entire subject and its associations, which was then given substance with apt words and figures.[30] Unlike medieval description, which prescribed a set of techniques, the renaissance revival of *enargeia* suggested a creative approach to composition. There was a shift of categories of formal thought to an intuitive domain of vast potentiality.[31]

The mental visualizations of *enargeia* resulted from *phantasiai* or *visiones*. The term was almost synonymous in later classicism with *ekphrasis*; while Latin translations were *demonstratio, evidentia, illustratio, repraesentatio*, and *sub oculos subiecto*.[32] The common equivalents, *evidentia* and *illustratio*, were often synonymous among rhetoricians. Yet *illustratio* was the most exact rendering, since *en-argeia* means a "bringing into light." To bring things into the light is also to bring things into a field of visual perception. From *enargeia* derived Argos of a hundred eyes,[33] the mythological monster who will serve as an interpreter of Loyola's morality. *Acta* is a text that proves the later maxim "The style is the man."[34] A style was classically *illustris* if the words were selected for their gravity and applied metaphorically, exaggeratedly, adjectivally, in duplication, synonymously, and in harmony with the actual action and representation of facts. Dante used it as his term for the high vernacular style corresponding to the grand Latin style of epic, tragedy, and *canzone*.[35] The vividly representative style of *Acta* is integral with

Loyola's vividly representative piety. Its climax on the riverbank in his life and in the text he will precisely term *enargeia: illustración*.

The collaboration of Gonçalves da Câmara and Loyola coincides with the cultural change from orality to literacy, which from the mid-sixteenth century experienced the complex relationships of writing and speaking.[36] Their situation is secondary orality, an orality influenced by the printing press, as distinguished from the primary orality of a society before print. In the twentieth century the Iberian Peninsula still affords the richest examples of vigorous poetic traditions maintained without writing.[37] Oral delivery may thus have been Loyola's native habit. Perhaps in continuity with the humble theme of his recital, however, its delivery was a conscious attempt to evade the fame the printing press would ensure.[38] The text is not an original composition or a dictated transcription but a memorization and an imitation. Gonçalves da Câmara is in the clerkly tradition of the translator-adaptor, whose witness was fundamental to hagiography.[39] He states that he listened, memorized, "then went immediately to write, without saying anything to the Father, first in point-form in my hand and then more copiously as it is now written."[40] This immediacy displays a culture of literacy, in which postponement weakens recall. In an oral society the teller of the tale would have delayed his repetition to assimilate it into his store of themes and formulas.[41] Quintilian observed that rapid memory as a rule usually failed to endure, but that whatever could not be recalled on the spot was easily coordinated the following day. Time traditionally strengthened memory.[42]

Memory was the mother of the Muses.[43] Although but one of the five parts of rhetoric,[44] it was "the guardian of all the parts of rhetoric"[45] and "the treasure-house of eloquence."[46] The ancient art of memory derived from the poet Simonides, who was able to identify for burial the corpses of guests in a banquet hall that had tragically collapsed by remembering their locations at table. By inference, the orator training his memory for the accurate delivery of a lengthy speech should mentally form images of the facts and select places for their storage. The most complete pictures were formed by sensory impression, especially sight. As Cicero instructed, "The keenest of all our senses is the sense of sight, and that consequently perceptions received by the ears or by reflexion can most easily be retained if they are also conveyed to our minds by the mediation of the eyes." The mnemonic process was like an interior writing that placed the images on the places, like inscribing the alphabet on a papyrus, tablet, or parchment. The placement was serial, with markers for every so many images, usually five, so that the orator could summon his speech by progressing through the model.⁴⁷

There was a memory for things and a memory for words. Although the rhetorical ideal urged a firm perception of both, the difficulty of allotting an image to a place for every word was acknowledged. And so memory for things—the subject matter—was allowed as sufficient.⁴⁸ As Quintilian advised, the rhetorical model was not to memorize verbatim but "to secure a good grasp of the facts (*res*) themselves and to leave ourselves free to speak as we will."⁴⁹ This is what Gonçalves da Câmara means when he explains that he retired immediately after Loyola's recitation to write it down "in point-form" (*en puntos*): the rhetorical matters. He would not have memorized by rote Loyola's words, although certain diction may be original; rather, he concentrated mentally on his subjects. The text is a filial imitation of the paternal speech, in which by Seneca's theory there is a resemblance to the original without an exactness, much as a son might resemble a father.

In mnemonic theory and practice ordinary images easily slipped the memory, while novel ones stimulated it. A solar eclipse was a better mnemonic image than the daily sunrise. Images were to be active, not vague. The classical recommendation was for images that were base, dishonorable, unusual, great, unbelievable, ridiculous, or comic. Exceptional aesthetic qualities of beauty or ugliness, whether ornamental or disfigured, were advised. The medieval scholastic practice, which shifted memory as the first part of the virtue of prudence from rhetoric to ethics, acknowledged that gross and sensible things were more easily remembered than subtle and spiritual ones. For the easier remembrance of intelligible notions, Thomas Aquinas advised their linkage in Ciceronian method with some kind of phantasms. Since human cognition was stronger in regard to the sensible, corporeal likenesses and images were to be invented lest simple and spiritual intentions slip from the soul.⁵⁰

The visual imagery of the text, derived from Loyola's vivid recollection, is thus required by its memorial nature. Recollection was the recovery of knowledge or its base in sensation by a deliberate hunt through the corridors of memory according to principles of association and of order. The common mnemonic model was architectural, such as palaces and churches. Thoughts were assigned and arranged sequentially in rooms, even entrusted to its furnishings or statues, then recalled at will from their custodians.⁵¹ Another mnemonic device, which Quintilian recommended, was "a long journey."⁵² Loyola and Gonçalves da Câmara may each be imagined as plotting the memorial pilgrimage that structures the recitation and the text.

Not only was the rhetorical skill of memory derived from places, so also was the rhetorical art of invention. Places were fundamental to recall and to argumentation. The topical art indicated the location to search and develop, as Cicero explained. Topics were seats and domiciles of arguments, like cubicles from which the oratorical themes must be tracked down or dug out. They were the sources of speech. Rhetoric was developed from such "places," then entrusted for memory to other "places," so that place was fundamental to its interpretation. The practice implied a classical association of mental and physical realms in which intellectual apprehension depended upon sensory grasp. To understand an idea was to locate and recall its position.[53]

Loyola's piety is established in the renaissance revival of that rhetorical culture. The *Exercitia spiritualia* begins with a comparison to the physical exercises of moving in place, by strolling, walking, and running. These three speeds of travel allude to the three traditional "ways" (*viae*) of religion—purgative, illuminative, unitive. The person making the Exercises is even advised to retreat from home to another dwelling. The prelude of each meditation is "artful structure seeing the place" (*composición viendo el lugar*). He is to note where the object to be contemplated or meditated is situated. For a visible object such as Christ, the artful structure imaginatively pictures the corporeal place where his house may be located, since he may be in the temple or on the mount. For an invisible object such as sins, the artful structure imaginatively pictures and considers the soul imprisoned in a corruptible body, while the total composite of body and soul in this valley is exiled among brute animals. The meditator is instructed to use the sense of touch to embrace and kiss the places where holy persons are positioned. In the examination of conscience the penitent is to recall his sins after a lapse of time by locating the place and house where he lived, his conversations with others, and his occupations. The meditations depend on recalling and retaining in memory.[54]

The journey of chivalric literature also employed geography as a mnemonic device. By connecting events with their background, an atmosphere was developed through a technique of linking emotion with scenery.[55] Loyola's habit before his conversion to asceticism was to fantasize from such romances.[56] They influenced not only certain scenes in his *Exercitia spiritualia*—such as imagining oneself a knight in the presence of the king and court, ashamed and confused for grievous offenses against a generous benefactor[57]—but its very concept of mnemonic movement through places. This concept was also literarily indebted to accounts of pilgrimage, the paradigm for which was Jerome's description of Paula in Palestine: how at the stable of the Nativity she meditated with the eyes of faith the infant wailing, the magi adoring, the star shining, Mary nursing, the shepherds arriving—all the details vividly and affectively. And she kissed those places.[58] Meditation in movement proved too arduous for some late medieval pilgrims, who took to their beds; but others, like the friar Felix Fabri, relished their devotional exercise from place to place. Loyola's own pilgrimage to Jerusalem influenced his conception of the *Exercitia spiritualia*, as is evident from a detail like the apparition of Jesus first to Mary after his resurrection. Although the incident is unscriptural, it was included in the processional of pilgrims, at the chapel of the Virgin in the church of the Holy Sepulchre where they knelt, sang, prayed, and received plenary indulgences. The instruction of the *Exercitia spiritualia* to kiss the mnemonic places imitates the actual practice of pilgrims at the holy sites.[59] The setting of *Acta* is not mere scenic backdrop for its protagonist; it invents and informs the plot. Setting is structural.

Quintilian argued against the contention that language in the rough is more natural and virile for artistic structure (*compositio*). Art depended on discipline and cultivation. Structure gave force and direction to thoughts as the bowstring did to the arrow. "All the best scholars are convinced," he wrote, "that the study of structure is of the utmost value, not merely for charming the ear, but for stirring the soul." The qualities of composition were decorum, pleasure, and variation. Its parts were order, connection, and rhythm. Since composition was the counterpart in prose to versification in poetry, it virtually equalled rhythm. The triads extended to the parts of a sentence, the comma, the colon, and the period.[60] And they were applied to the parts of rhetoric itself: invention or discovery, disposition or arrangement, elocution or performance. In Leon Battista Alberti's seminal theory of art they explained circumscription or the drawing of figures in outline; composition or the indication of planes within the outline; and reception of light or the rendering of color.[61] Similarly the meditations of Loyola's *Exercitia spiritualia* are all punctually triadic: first point, second point, third point.[62] The methods of meditation are also rhetorically rhythmic. Each word of a composed prayer, such as the Lord's Prayer, is to be considered serially, then coordinated with breathing. In such measured praying a word is aligned with a thought and with a forced respiration or loud breath.[63] The *Ex-*

ercitia spiritualia is in method rhetorical. So is Loyola's recital as imitated in the text *Acta*.

The onset of this oral and literary pilgrimage is marked by procrastination. Delay was typically a female wile, as in the quip from the favorite military comedy, "Woman is certainly the daughter of Delay personified! Why, any other delay, even one of equal length, seems shorter than what a woman lets you in for. I really do believe they do it just out of habit."[64] The procrastination of Loyola culturally reverts to a female character in another tale of quest, the sagacious Penelope, who nightly undid her weaving to postpone the deadlines of her amorous suitors until Odysseus might return.[65] Morally his antecedent is another lover, Augustine, who in contradiction of her virtue implored, "Give me chastity and self-restraint, but not just yet."[66] In performance delay was associated with the temperament of Quintus Roscius Gallus, the consummate Roman actor. He was introduced in Cicero's *De oratore* in the context of the profound disturbance of even first-rate speakers, for the greater the orator's talent the more nervous he could be. Such an orator could be "out of the humour or hindered by indisposition (people say, 'Roscius was not in the mood for acting today,' or 'He was a little out of sorts')."[67] A renaissance painter who delayed the delivery of his portraits was imitatively called "a humorist," because he worked when he pleased, inventing excuses.[68]

It is to obviate any allegation that Loyola postpones his promise of delivery from the vice of sloth that both prefaces, in detailing his procrastination, explicate the reasons for it. The preface by Gonçalves da Câmara is almost consumed with procrastinations. He relates how, immediately after Loyola's determination and revelation of this duty, he fails it. The excuse is illness. Although Loyola never expects a single day of life, ironically when others voice their own procrastinations—"I'll do that in five days from now or in eight days from now"—he chides them. "The Father ever astonished says, 'What! so do you think you will live so long?' "[69] This chastisement echoes a scriptural lesson against pride. Those who are talkative about their plans for the future are admonished, "You do not know about tomorrow. What is your life? For you are a mist that appears for a little time and then vanishes. Instead you ought to say, 'If the Lord wills, we shall live and we shall do this or that.' As it is, you boast in your arrogance. All such boasting is evil" (James 4:13–16).

Although Loyola humbly expresses the hope that he will live to complete the recital, the project is desultory. When Gonçalves da Câmara questions him about beginning it, Loyola replies that he should be reminded daily until he feels ready to do it. "I cannot remember how many days!" cries Gonçalves da Câmara, in a feigned lapse of memory that is hyperbolic. The excuse is illness, then business. Loyola is then to be reminded only every Sunday (the day of leisure).[70] The recitation commences on some unremembered date in September 1553, followed by three or four more sessions during that month. Then the procrastinations resume. "The Father was always making excuses, with some illness or various affairs that occurred, telling me, 'When that business is finished, remind me'; only, when it was finished and I did remind him, to say 'Just now we are involved in this other business; when it is finished, remind me of it.' " Upon the arrival of Nadal (who will write yet another preface) on 18 October of the following year, Gonçalves da Câmara is ordered by him to "importune the Father, telling me many times that in no matter could the Father do more good for the Society than in doing this; and that this would be to have founded the Society truly."[71] This statement replicates a favorite topic of the exordium, the belief that the possession of knowledge or virtue required its dispensation.[72]

Nadal himself many times speaks to Loyola, as amply recorded in his preface. At the opportune moment he asks him for a "testament" and "paternal instruction." Loyola offers business matters as an excuse for refusal, stating that he has neither the time nor the inclination for it. He indicates, nevertheless, that three of the Jesuits are to offer Mass for this intention and after prayer to report to him their thoughts. Loyola promises to comply with them. The following year when Nadal returns he asks Loyola if he has done anything about the promise. " 'Nothing,' he said." After return from yet another journey, he inquires once more. Loyola has not yet undertaken the recital. Nadal insists that for almost four years the Jesuits have implored as a benefit to their Society an explanation of his instruction since the beginning of his conversion. He adds boldly that, if the request is granted, the Society will put it to its best use; but that, if not, it will maintain the same confidence in the Lord "as if you had written everything." There is no reply.[73]

Yet, perhaps the same day, Loyola summons Gonçalves da Câmara and begins his recital. Nadal remarks that "this Father, as he is of excellent memory, afterwards wrote it."[74] The *Constitutiones* of the Society of Jesus require of candidates an aptitude for memory to learn and to retain. Lack of memory is an impediment to membership in the Society. Mnemonic skills were a fundamental part of the curriculum in rhetoric and ethics at the Jesuit College in Rome; scholastics were instructed to commit their studies to memory.⁷⁵ One avid student of the system would be the Jesuit missionary Matteo Ricci, who notably constructed for the Chinese nobility a memory palace.⁷⁶

The commendation of the memory of Gonçalves da Câmara does not establish his accuracy but his ethics, however, since the faculty was not one of rote communication but of familiarized understanding. Memory distinguished moral character. It was common in the process for canonization to praise the prodigious memory of the saint as an indicator of his fundamental humanity.⁷⁷ The credentials of Gonçalves da Câmara are stated: elector at the General Congregation and assistant to Father General Diego Laínez; later, tutor in letters and Christian manners to Sebastian, king of Portugal—in sum, "a Father distinguished in religion and virtue." The preface is noted as written partly in Spanish, partly in Italian, depending on the availability of amanuenses. Another "learned and pious" priest, Annibal de Codretto, translated the text into Latin. Nadal concludes by stating that "both the author and the translator are living." Although this testimony is for authentication, Gonçalves da Câmara, not Loyola, is credited as the "author" (*auctor*) of the text.⁷⁸ This designation departs from medieval practice, which considered the initiator the author (*auctor*) and the guarantor the authority (*auctoritas*).⁷⁹

When with Nadal's encouragement Gonçalves da Câmara persists, Loyola tells him to remind him of his commitment after the business of securing an endowment for the Jesuit College at Rome is arranged. The next excuse becomes "the question of Prester," the issue of supplying Jesuit missionaries to Abyssinia. Loyola will not meet with him until the courier has departed. The continuation of the recital begins on 9 March, only to be interrupted on the 23rd by the death of Pope Julius III. Loyola refuses to meet again until the election of a new pope, but that successor, Pope Marcellus, soon falls ill and dies. The tale is yet again postponed until the election of Pope Paul IV. Then there are "too many hot spells and too many occupations" that summer, so that Loyola keeps delaying until 21 September, when Gonçalves da Câmara is about to be ordered to Spain. With his departure impending, Gonçalves da Câmara urges Loyola to fulfill his promise.⁸⁰

A meeting is arranged for the morning of the 22nd. After Mass (and here the Spanish copy ends, with the remainder of the preface only extant in the Latin translation), Gonçalves da Câmara inquires if this is indeed the time. Loyola instructs him to go and wait for him in the Red Tower and to be there upon his arrival. Since Gonçalves da Câmara assumes from experience that he will have to wait for quite a while, he engages in conversation with a brother in the hall. Loyola reprimands him for failing in obedience, since he has not been waiting in the appointed place. The meeting is cancelled. "He wished to do nothing that day." A delegation of Jesuits urges Loyola to continue. Loyola returns to recital in the tower but breaks it off abruptly when Gonçalves da Câmara's disobedient and rude behavior again provokes him. He returns after some time to complete the recitation, as written.

Gonçalves da Câmara's preparations for his journey to Spain disallow him the leisure to write everything out in detail. The very eve of his departure is the final occasion of conference with Loyola. So he is left to dictate from his notes to an Italian scribe in Genoa and to put the finishing touches on the composition there in December 1555, two years and four months after the original conversation in the garden.[81] The unfinished manuscript shares the fate of the medieval fragment[82] and the renaissance epic, that peerless genre with the scope for the heroes of its journeys, crusades, wanderings, pilgrimages, and explorations—of which ambitious projects few were ever finished.[83]

Classical rhetoric emphasized the importance of the introduction as paramount. Aristotle tersely explained that "the most essential and special function of the exordium is to make clear what is the end and purpose of a speech."[84] Gonçalves da Câmara complies with this in exposing the vice of vainglory. In Ciceronian rhetoric, which influenced him even more, the introduction was designed to dispose the listeners to regard the argumentation of the speech with benevolence. Because an audience desires to hear first just what is within its competence and judgment, Cicero advised against bounding emotionally into a subject, arousing passion rather than understanding. He recommended an unhurried style.[85] Gonçalves da Câmara's preface with its tedious tale of procrastinations obeys this law of languor. It serves classically to capture the benevolence of the reader.

By another favorite topic of the exordium, the promise to relate news,[86] the difficulty of obtaining the recital establishes Gonçalves da Câmara's authority to transcribe it. This authorization originates from the personal conversation in the garden, during which he filially imitates and repents the sin of the Father. As Gonçalves da Câmara discloses of his confession of vainglory, "The Father gave me as a remedy that I should often refer to God all my affairs, endeavoring to offer him all the good that I might find in myself, recognizing it as his and giving thanks for it. And in this matter he spoke to me in a manner that greatly consoled me, so that I could not restrain my tears." He relates how Loyola confided to him particulars of his own struggle with vainglory and the peace of its solution.[87] Gonçalves da Câmara's tears of consolation at Loyola's speech are models of the affective response to be evoked in the reader of the text. His authority to write is further established in an explicit decision of Loyola to recite to him, a decision stated as a divinely inspired duty and shared with the Society at its communal supper. Readers are finally disposed toward him by his undaunted perseverance in the trials of obtaining the substance of the text, despite rejection and reproof. His integrity is reinforced in the preface of Nadal, who states what the convention of modesty would disallow Gonçalves da Câmara himself to mention: that he is learned and pious, of excellent memory, of service to church and state, and (should anyone wish to verify his testimony) still living.[88]

The preface is especially intended to capture the benevolence of readers toward Loyola in filial piety. Loyola's procrastinations are ambiguous. If he is postponing a humble confession of vice, he is not being humble but vain. The excuses that are cited, however—illness, business, mourning, and even the weather—are designed to obviate this accusation. So it is the rhetorical topic of modesty that governs the preface and its interpretation. Since classical antiquity the principal device for the capture of benevolence was a modest manner. The modesty of the author became the model for eliciting the modesty of the audience: to listen, to lean, to assimilate, to assent. It was an affected modesty, a necessary convention of the author as the condition of a favorable response from the reader. The concept depended, before Christian humility, on Ciceronian humility. The classical orator protested his inadequacy to the task. The theme was projected as beyond his talent; he feared the criticism of learned men; he dared not hope to accomplish it successfully; but he resigned himself only because the request was justified. It was conventional to emphasize that the work was undertaken only at the beseeching of others. A form of affected modesty was fear and trembling at the venture: literary trepidation. There were various formulas of this disparagement of the self as a mite and the text as a trifle. Loyola's illnesses mimic the most common affected modesty, which was a protestation of feebleness (*infirmitas*).[89]

Gonçalves da Câmara's introduction complies with conventional affected modesty. The self-abasement implied in his deference to Loyola as "the Father" echoes formulas of submission to a literary patron.[90] The acknowledgment that his memory may be faulty, although he promises to tell as well as he can, is stylistic hesitancy.[91] The topic of modesty was often conveyed in a declaration that the author dared to write only at the request or command of a friend, patron, or superior.[92] This is true of both Gonçalves da Câmara and Loyola. Gonçalves da Câmara initiates the task only at the command of his religious superior, who is Loyola, and persists only at his command and with the repeated urgings of the Society. Loyola initiates the recital and persists in it only by divine inspiration and at the insistences, pleadings, and exhortations of the Society. The device of delay in the topic of modesty introduced texts from Cicero's *Orator* to Castiglione's *Il libro del cortegiano*: "For a long time I debated earnestly with myself, Brutus, as to which course would be more difficult or more serious—to deny your oft repeated request, or to do what you ask";[93] and, "I have spent a long time wondering, my dear Alfonso, which of two things was the more difficult for me: either to refuse what you have asked me so often and so insistently, or to do it."[94]

The detailing of the desultory project is required by the nature of the text as a mirror of vainglory. It is because Loyola characterizes himself shamefully as vainglorious that Gonçalves da Câmara and Nadal must emphasize, even exaggerate, his character as unvainglorious. This rhetorical device is imperative to capture benevolence toward the founder of the Society and to legitimate as moral their own imitative vocations and vows as its filial members. Loyola must be introduced as decisively converted from vainglory, so as to exonerate the father, if not the sons, from the capital vice. This is hagiographic. While Loyola as father would exaggerate their similarity, the Jesuits as sons must exaggerate their difference.

The prefaces even contradict the text. The subversion of Loyola's intentions is patent in the preface by Nadal, who exploits Loyola's grace as the very occasion for inviting the oral recitation and written text. As he relates, once when they were together Loyola remarked, "'Just now I was higher than heaven.' He had experienced (I think) for a while an ecstasy or rapture, as he was frequently accustomed. Reverentially I inquired, 'What of that place, Father?' He changed the conversation to other matters. Judging this the opportune moment, I therefore asked and beseeched the Father to set forth for us how from the beginning of his conversion the Lord had governed him, so that that relation would be for us in the manner of a testament and paternal institute."[95] Nadal infers a sublime interpretation of Loyola's remark, buttresses it with mention of the frequency of his raptures, questions him with reverence, and seizes this odd occasion as the "opportune moment" for petitioning a recital for the Society. Loyola does not comply. It is not Nadal's reverence that elicits his response but Gonçalves da Câmara's weakness. The intentions of Loyola may, nevertheless, be inferred from his preface and text. As a hermeneutic principle, where the text blames the sinner it is authentic to Loyola's recitation, where it praises the saint it is Gonçalves da Câmara's intervention.

The preface establishes the text as a mirror of vainglory for repentance and consolation. It captures the benevolence of the reader toward Loyola by justifying him as unvainglorious through the emphatic modesty of his procrastination. In recommending a remedy for vainglory, Loyola confesses to Gonçalves da Câmara how he himself struggled with the vice. His counsel to refer everything good in oneself to God imitates the epideictic conclusion of Augustine's *Confessions*, in which the author praised himself as good in the divine image and referred that praise to its Creator.[96] The weeping of Gonçalves da Câmara in response also imitates that exemplar, the contrite Augustine in the garden of conversion. Yet although Augustine's tears had streamed in the aqueous imagery of the Neoplatonist topic of departure and return,[97] here they have no such metaphysical import. They are moral tears. Gonçalves da Câmara becomes the model for the reader of the text, who is to respond to it by weeping.

Crying was classically recommended as an oratorical practice. Cicero advised that the speaker must feel the emotions he wishes to excite, so as to be reduced to "tears of compassion."[98] Preachers like Bernardino of Siena, or in Catalonia, Vincent Ferrer, were renowned for their ability to incite their listeners to weeping.[99] A certain preacher, much admired by the humanist Angelo Politziano, would collect his falling tears in his cupped hands and throw them at the congregation for effect.[100] The weeping of Gonçalves da Câmara indicates his spontaneity toward morality and thus establishes his sincerity of character. The inclusion of this personal detail is also conventional, well within the rhetorical purpose of an introduction: to gain the reader's confidence. Weeping presumes a naive belief that emotional spontaneity is more sincere, thus more credible, than literary artifice. The eyes were the most important physical feature for oratorical expression since they revealed the temper of the mind, either twinkling with merriment or clouded with grief. As Quintilian instructed, "Nature has given them tears to serve as interpreters of our feelings, tears that will break forth for sorrow or stream for very joy."[101] Weeping is also appropriate penitence for the vice of vainglory, which is sensuously ocular.

Tension about eyes mars the recital, however. As Loyola paces in recital, Gonçalves da Câmara relates, "I, so that I might observe his face, kept approaching steadily a little at a time, while the Father said to me, 'Observe the rule.' And when, neglecting this, I approached another time and relapsed in the same matter two or three times, he said this to me and went off."[102] It was classical theory that sight impressed the memory better than the other senses. Heraclitus attested that "the eyes are more exact witnesses than the ears," and Quintilian repeated that "the perception of the eye is quicker than that of the ear."[103] Since sight was the keenest sense, Cicero instructed that the perceptions received by the ear were most easily remembered if they were also conveyed to the mind by the mediation of the eyes. Cicero also signaled the importance of the eyes for expressing feeling in delivery, "for this is the only part of the body capable of producing as many indications and variations as there are emotions, and there is nobody who can produce the same effect with the eyes shut."[104] Quintilian agreed that in the expression of the emotions the greatest influence was exercised by the glance. "It is on this that our audience hang, on this that they rivet their attention and their gaze, even before we begin to speak. It is this that inspires the hearer with affection or dislike, this that conveys a world of meaning and is often more eloquent than all our words."[105]

Gonçalves da Câmara thus has a legitimate basis for desiring to observe Loyola's facial expressions, the better to understand and remember his delivery. Yet Loyola rebuffs his advances. The memorization that Gonçalves da Câmara would reinforce by close-up observation is explicitly negated by his forgetfulness of Loyola's reminder of the rule. Since Gonçalves da Camara fails to avert his eyes, Loyola protests, then quits the scene. Such intrusion of personal boundaries is commonly met with defensive gestures, postural shifts, even attempts to move away.[106] Aversion of the eyes is among the psychological techniques for establishing distance,[107] especially during intimate conversation. In most cultures staring is taboo.[108] Courtesy, as traditionally instructed at the courts, monasteries, and schools, assumed a certain alliance of inner virtue and outer gesture.[109] Courtesy was believed ordained by God as a perfection. There was a coherent pattern in which even small mannerly acts were meaningful, as informed by the divine courtesy that desired to assist and please people. It was not mere nicety. By the concept of just measure God's vengeance on the erectors of the tower of Babel could be termed "courtesy."[110]

So it is that Loyola's rebuke is not discourteous. Beyond social convention, monastic rule expressly forbade staring at others.¹¹¹ The Rule of St. Benedict stated the final twelfth step of humility as the monk's exterior manifestation of interior virtue. "Whether he sits, walks, or stands, his head must be bowed and his eyes cast down."¹¹² The *Constitutiones* of the Society of Jesus also regulate comportment. "All should take special care to guard with great diligence the gates of their senses (especially the eyes, ears, and tongue) from all disorder, to preserve themselves in peace and true humility of their souls . . . the modesty of their countenance, the maturity of their walk, and all their movements, without giving any sign of impatience or pride."¹¹³ During the *Exercitia spiritualia* the penitent is to observe restraint of the eyes, even to experience the sensory deprivation of light by closing the doors and shutters of his room.¹¹⁴

Unrestraint of the eyes, or curiosity, was in classical and Christian cultures pejorative. Curiosity was the appetite to know what was beyond the essential and it could penetrate into forbidden areas. It was not only vain and illicit but even sacrilegious. Curiosity, which dallied with the occult, the heretical, and the speculative, opposed the knowledge of faith as ordained to the proper human end of salvation.¹¹⁵ Plutarch specified curiosity as the desire to know the evil in another.¹¹⁶ The physical advances of Gonçalves da Câmara move beyond his legitimate sphere of knowledge; he is curious about Loyola's vainglory. Bernard of Clairvaux chastised such vain curiosity as a frivolous consolation.¹¹⁷ Gonçalves da Câmara errs by choosing a superficial good—literally, facial appearance.

Curiosity is allied with vainglory. As Michel de Montaigne would explain, "Glory and Curiosity are the two scourges of our soul. The one prompts us to stick our noses everywhere, the other undoes us by leaving nothing unresolved or undecided."¹¹⁸ Both are social sins and both are ocular in origin: curiosity as the inordinate desire to peer into others; vainglory as the inordinate desire to be observed by others. The consolation Loyola would offer requires a penetration beyond corporeal appearances to spiritual realities. Gonçalves da Câmara's curiosity involves him in disobedience to the rule of the Society. His sin repeats Adam's primal sin of appetite for the fruit of the tree of the knowledge of good and evil. He portrays himself as fallen man. By this employment of the topic of modesty he confesses his unworthiness to be the recipient of Loyola's recital. He is a sinner who forgets a rule of the Society while striving to memorize the face of its founder.

Loyola's concern for manners reflects the social regrouping from the decline of the nobility of feudal knights to the transition to courtly aristocracy. Yet for the Society of Jesus the medieval rule about comportment of the eyes is anachronistic to its active apostolate, with its need to know the social conventions and to behave with the civility characteristic of renaissance culture. With the increase of sensibility, emotional restraint began to replace moral simplicity, as revealed in an altered tone about manners. Observation from experience replaced the impersonality of tradition. This observation of self and others was reflected in a more deliberate molding of character and a more emphatic demand for civility. As the code of behavior became stricter, the imperative not to offend became more subtle and more coercive. The problem of social behavior was so important in renaissance culture that even celebrated persons like Erasmus were concerned with it. It was his treatise *De civilitate morum puerilium* that marked the transition from medieval courtesy to modern civility as a symptom and composition of social processes.[119] Of enormous circulation in texts, translations, imitations, adaptations, and sequels, it was unexcelled in force, clarity, and personality. As the most esteemed schoolbook in the sixteenth century, from it generations of children in the intermediate grades learned to read and write Latin, for it was used not only to teach mores and manners but also grammar and style. Dedicated to the eleven-year-old son of a prince who did not attend school but was instructed by a tutor, it was likely the manual that would soon be used by Gonçalves da Câmara to tutor young Sebastian, king of Portugal, in letters and manners.[120]

Its premise was that, while decorum was the crudest part of philosophy, in the current climate of opinion it was very conducive to securing good will and to commending intellectual gifts. In the conviction that a well-ordered mind was most strongly displayed in the face, Erasmus began with the deportment of the eyes. "The eyes should be calm, respectful, and steady; not grim, which is a mark of truculence; not shameless, the hallmark of insolence; nor darting and rolling, a feature of insanity; nor furtive, like those of suspects and plotters of treachery; nor gaping like those of idiots; nor should the eyes and eyelids be constantly blinking, a mark of the fickle; nor gaping as in astonishment—a characteristic observed in Socrates; nor too narrowed, a sign of bad temper; nor bold and inquisitive, which indicates impertinence; but such as reflects a mind composed, respectful, and friendly." He repeated the adage "The seat of the soul is in the eyes." Well-composed ocular gesture, even to the comportment of eyebrows, rendered what was naturally decorous even more attractive.

This new civility contradicted the monastic aversion of the eyes. "The eyes should be directed at the person to whom you are speaking, but should be calm and frank, with no trace of boldness or insolence. Looking down at the ground as the catoblepas does gives the impression of a bad conscience. Looking sideways at someone gives the impression of being an embezzler. Turning the face this way and that is a sign of inconstancy."[121] A *catoblepas*, meaning "down-looking," was a gnu, known from ancient natural history for its grim expression and narrow, bloodshot eyes.[122] Leonardo da Vinci recorded in his notebooks that a catoblepas was a small, sluggish animal, its head so large that it carried it with difficulty, so that it always drooped toward the ground. This was a blessing, he decided, because anyone on whom it fixed its eyes died immediately.[123] That observer of customs Erasmus provided the probable rationale for Loyola's retention of the monastic custody of the eyes. "Old pictures tell us that is was once a mark of singular modesty to observe with eyes half-closed, just as among certain Spaniards to avoid looking at people is taken as a sign of politeness and friendship."[124] Loyola reverts to a native Spanish habit.

Gonçalves da Câmara is reduced to the status of an auditor. He is forbidden by the Jesuit rule, and reprimanded by Loyola on this very point, to observe his face closely. For the interpretation of oral delivery the observation of the speaker, especially his facial expressions, but also the comportment of hand and arm, foot and leg, was essential. As Quintilian epitomized, "The temper of the mind can be inferred from the glance and gait."[125] Although Gonçalves da Câmara praises Loyola's delivery for its clarity, he remains deprived of the primary sensory aid for its comprehension—sight.

What he does not lose vision of is Loyola's focus on vainglory, a moral in a milieu that is literally fascinating.

ONE

The Knight Errant

Loyola swaggers onto the scene like the stock comedic character of the glorious soldier. "Until the age of twenty-six he was a man given to worldly vanities and he principally delighted in military exercises, with a great and vain desire to acquire reputation" (*honra*). He is situated in a fortress under siege. While the entire garrison clearly perceives that resistance against the invading French army is impossible, and surrender the only chance of survival, Loyola singularly persuades the governor to its futile defense. During the attack a cannonball hits him in one leg, shattering it, and in passing through his legs severely wounds the other. At his injury the garrison surrenders the fortress to the enemy.[1]

As with the preface, the text begins with a historical date but ends with a moral vice: vainglory. Although there is a discrepancy of this dating with a later statement,[2] sixteenth-century society was not fixed by the calendar and clock. Spaniards particularly disregarded time. Almanacs were rare, even measuring instruments were scarce, so that it was exceptional for a watch to be included in an inventory of goods.[3] Most persons were ordinarily unaware of the year of their birth.[4] Even that of the most distinguished scholar, Erasmus, varied by several years, either forgotten or feigned.[5] Epideictic rhetoric is invented from good and evil toward praise or blame, so that the time of importance is not Loyola's chronological age but his moral experience. This comprises twenty-six years of vainglory, which as coincident with his youth as a soldier underscores his immaturity.

Here begins the confession of "the fantasies and antics of youth" (*travesuras de mancebo*) that Gonçalves da Câmara declared in the preface Loyola had related to him clearly and distinctly.⁶ The ages of man were differently defined in classical, medieval, and renaissance cultures than in the modern. Augustine in his *Confessions* only became a "youth" at age thirty. Youth was a period that extended classically into the forties because of the economic dominance of fathers over sons.⁷ The fourth or middle age was the period of military service, in ancient descriptions sometimes called *iuvenilitas*, with the individual as *iuvenis*; and it was cognate in the romance vernaculars with *caballero, chevalier, cavaliere*, and in the northern vernaculars with *cnicht* and *Knecht*. Both the primary meaning of "youth" and a secondary meaning of "service" or "attendancy" were consistently maintained. *Iuvenis* and *miles* were interchangeable, and by extension so were *mancebo* and *caballero*. According to Isidore of Seville's etymology, a knight was called *iuvenis* because he was beginning to be able to assist (*iuvare posse incipit*). The connotation of "youth" was virility in strength but immaturity in judgment: a junior, not a senior—typically lacking in wisdom. Chronologically that age ranged from twenty or twenty-five years of age to forty, or even fifty-five.⁸ In the poetry of the troubadours "youth" usually expressed something different from biological age: an ensemble of moral or aesthetic qualities, the sum of the virtues that defined courtesy.⁹

A well-born youth was a warrior in a defined stage of his military career, armed and dubbed as a knight. Although in modern society he would be considered an adult, he was historically called "youth" until his marriage, and perhaps even after that until he fathered children. Then he became a "man" as a head of household with a family. The social situation was caused by the rules for the management of patrimony, which the father tenaciously held even while he had grown sons. Excluded by social prohibitions from the body of settled men, the youth lived on an unstable margin. The period between entry into active military service and fatherhood could be of long duration, so that youths composed the chivalric culture not only by numbers but also by behavior. In epics and tales youth was a phase of impatience, turbulence, instability, as reflecting its interim status between the fixed stations of childhood in the house of the father or patron and of adulthood in his own household. In that interval the youth was a roamer. The fundamental characteristic of all descriptions of youth was the roving life: the refusal of place. The youth was in departure, or en route. He traveled through many provinces and regions, throughout the earth even, in quest of adventure and its prize of honor. Vagabondage was regarded as a necessary stage of male development, the study of military matters.[10]

Military service did not terminate for Loyola with his wounding at Pamplona, since he is introduced while a pilgrim at Manresa as a new recruit for Christ, still a soldier in active service but with a different master.[11] Pilgrimage was conventionally compared with combat.[12] Since Loyola died at sixty-five, the designation "youth" comprises most of his recital, which ends at about age fifty-one. Perhaps the papal approbation of the Society of Jesus, father-to-father, is his rite of passage to the age of manhood. The preface by Gonçalves da Câmara portrays him as an elder, from whom his young companions, typically vainglorious, may benefit morally. *Acta* is an admonitory mirror,[13] designed to deter them from that vice by the vivid depiction of Loyola's youthful indulgence in its "fantasies and antics." The choice of Hercules between virtue and vice was essentially the choice of youth. The virtue of the classical parable was not Christian conduct, however, but *aretē*,[14] defined as "a proud and courtly morality with warlike valour."[15] This is the ideal in its Basque descent that Loyola rejects as the social and moral norm, exchanging his weaponry for Hercules' club[16] as the symbol of prudence.

The confessional nature of the text is proclaimed in his very act at the prospect of siege: he makes his confession to a comrade in arms.[17] Loyola in battle imitates the typical braggart soldier, a stock theatrical character played most popularly on the sixteenth-century stage as a Spaniard, since that nationality was ridiculed as the haughtiest.[18] The role devolved to "the one and only Pyrgopolinices on earth, peerless in valour, in aspect, and in doughty deeds." That protagonist of the most successful of all Roman comedies, *Miles gloriosus*, was "a bragging, brazen, stercoraceous fellow, full of lies and lechery." A rival to Mars, he puffed away legions with his boastful breath—he computed killing seven thousand in a day—and even toppled an elephant with a tap. In Plautus's comedy Pyrgopolinices was duped by a lover and a courtesan, both in disguise, so that he did not recognize their plot to convict him of his vainglorious vice.[19] Like Pyrgopolinices, Loyola does not judge the situation correctly because he does not see it, even though all the other soldiers on the scene do. Loyola does not see what every other man in the fortress sees because he is blinded by the vice to be seen. This personal vice becomes socialized when he persuades the governor to collaborate in his vainglory by defending the fortress. Even the caballeros are said to admire Loyola's firmness and fearlessness, although these apparent virtues will prove to be mere stubbornness and recklessness. By manipulating the other characters toward admiration of himself, his vainglory endangers the garrison and, by implication, the city. Like all vice it portends death.

The literary spareness of this opening displays its subject as typological. Here is agonistic man universally at war. This archetype is symbolized by Loyola's opposition not only to the inimical French but also to his compatriot Basques. The fortress, which is his typical place, is an enclosure. It is the antithetical enclosure to the garden of the preface, the classical and renaissance place for the choice of Hercules,[20] since war was classically the absence of leisure.[21] The city under siege on the geographical map may be Pamplona but on the rhetorical map it is Dis. The very detail that the fortress under siege is in Pamplona is delayed until Loyola leaves the place, bound for home,[22] so that its factuality is typical. Pamplona was on the road of pilgrimage to the famous shrine at Santiago da Compostela;[23] thus it serves as the point of departure for Loyola's pilgrimage as the narrative plot. Loyola is there in an architectural fortress but also in that moral "fortress" of enormous walls and battlements that another pilgrim, Dante, named the metropolis of hell, capital of sorrow, kingdom of the dead.[24] It was commonplace of epic to begin, as Horace said, "in the midst of things."[25] So Dante discovered himself: "Midway in the journey of our life I found myself in a dark wood, for the straight way was lost."[26] So Loyola in his vainglory finds himself in the midst of war. And both pilgrims find hell. The imitation of Dante's *Commedia* as a device for framing Loyola's recital will be patent from their identical closures on a vision of the sun.

Remarkable about this scene is the absence of ekphrastic description, whose epitome was Homer on Achilles' shield.[27] Even the braggart Prygopolinices began his comedy with a command to polish his enormous shield to rival the sunbeams and dazzle his foes.[28] In his treatment of the vivid style Quintilian acknowledged that the mere report of war included everything that such a fate involved. He argued, however, that to elicit the full emotional effect of commiseration the writer must expose all its horrifying details. From the sack of Troy the topic of the captured city was early established in epic, tragedy, and historiography. As the stock in trade of the rhetorician, the cruelty and terror of the scene especially allowed the historian a display of skill at vividness in the description of suffering. The staple items in describing the capture of the city were the shouts of the enemy, the wailing of the women and children, the rapid movement of advancing troops and fleeing citizens, fire and sword, the crash of buildings, and the slaughter of the defeated.[29] There is no employment of the topic in this text, however, because the reader is not to be aroused to pity for Loyola. There is nothing in him of the magnanimity or skill that distinguished the chivalric code, only brute violence. Loyola is the type of choleric temperament, whose wrath was emblematized by a knight in arms.[30] It is the acknowledged role of the inimical French to treat him "courteously and amiably."[31]

The focus is on Loyola's vainglorious visibility and its ruinous consequences. "He" is in a fortress under attack, "he" persuades the governor to its defense, the other caballeros all admire "his" virtues, "he" confesses, "he" is wounded, and, to aggrandize his role as protagonist, "as soon as *he* fell wounded the others in the fortress surrendered."[32] This is no idealized Christian warrior but, like the pilgrim from another tale, a profane professional soldier pretending to the dignity of chivalry. In the "Knight's Tale" from the road to Canterbury, Geoffrey Chaucer best satirized the new soldier. With the late medieval breakdown of military honor and social order, the feudal host became a mercenary army. Autonomous companies terrorized and lorded all over Europe, obeying only the law of profit. Whether Loyola's role is patriotic or profiteering is undeclared. What he does share with the lawless brigands and nefarious knights is vainglory, an obsession with pomp and display amid vicious and brutal reality.[33] A tome that defined the social ideal for the sixteenth-century noble, Baldassare Castiglione's *Il libro del cortegiano*, frankly admitted that "in war what really spurs men on to bold deeds is the desire for glory." Its advice against ostentation and vainglory in arms only underscored their prevalence.[34] The Spanish kingdoms were no exception to the phenomenon. Although the most notorious of mercenaries, Sir John Hawkwood, could rise to the position of captain-general to the pope,[35] moralists criticized the vainglory of war. As Ramon Lull complained, these alleged knights were "the devil's ministers"; and he questioned rhetorically, "Who is there in the world who does as much harm as knights?"[36]

Loyola introduces himself as vain and rapacious for honor, reveling in military exercises. As Francisco Guicciardini observed of the Spaniards, "In war they have a high regard for honor, and would rather suffer death than dishonor."[37] The ideal was as ancient as a Greek society based on competitive, not cooperative, activities and excellences. The virtue of the warrior was *aretē*, which embraced goodness, bravery, success, and prosperity. It meant holding firm in the face of bloody carnage and thrusting close-up at the enemy. The successful defense of the city-state demanded complete success in battle to maintain stability and prosperity. It was a culture of results, with an absolute demand for the attainment of certain goals as determining its values. The norm was "'what people will say.'" Although winning was the good, it was also good to die fighting bravely for the common benefit of one's city. If it should fall, the lot of each citizen would become terrible; while, if the warrior were killed in its defense, his recompense was still a good. That was fame, fame for himself and for his posterity, undying fame. Although he might lie in the grave, the warrior was immortal in memory. If he was not killed, he was assured of honor by society.[38]

The Greek value of "what people will say" itself became the enemy when Christian faith strove to supplant the drive for human glory with the worship of divine glory. A neat example was Lull's juxtaposition of courtly and clerical ideals, in which a character named Quemdería hom, or "what people will say," usurped the divine prerogatives, while Pochme preu personified "little do I matter."[39] It will be Loyola's conversional task to exchange for himself these roles, from Quemdiría hom to Pochme preu. Glory was defined in Ciceronian rhetoric as "fame with praise," a great good second only to good itself, to which men since the Homeric heroes had aspired. Its desire was classically a native instinct that likened humans to gods. It was a stimulant to action that would yield virtue, and virtue in turn would be rewarded with glory. Glory was morally neutral itself, however, an ambiguous concept that could be real or illusory, durable or fugitive, objective or subjective. Christianity aggravated these conflicts into Augustine's condemnation of glory, with the fall of Rome as his proof. Yet the desire for glory prevailed among the troubadours and heroes of the chivalric romances. Medieval authors accorded glory to the individual who avoided excess and inordinateness and maintained the difficult equilibrium between fortitude and wisdom. In the literature called courtly these qualities were possessed by the good prince, who united personal merit with noble blood. The chivalric ideal comprised largesse, pity, bravery, and courtesy. Glory was the attribute of the adventurous, and between two paths the valorous knight would choose the more difficult. The ideal was in decline by the fifteenth century, however, with a decadent chivalry attacked by many authors. Glory proved unsustained by morality: debased into the glamour of luxury; satisfied with ceremony, pride, and a spirit of class.[40]

Although there was a renaissance revival of the cult of glory, the theologians of the sixteenth century, like their predecessors, distinguished between divine and human glory. Divine glory was the knowledge God has of his absolute perfection; human glory, the fame a man might acquire through the eyes of others. While divine glory was established on a real perfection, human glory was more or less illusory. Its inherent dangers especially included its insatiability. The unregulated love of self that substituted for the final good of God was an egotism that the appetite for glory revealed. Theologians supported the argument with Augustine's topic of the two cities: love of self to the disdain of God, love of God to the disdain of self.[41] As he distinguished these, "Worldly society has flowered from a selfish love which dared to despise even God, whereas the communion of saints is rooted in a love of God that is ready to trample on self. In a word, this latter relies on the Lord, whereas the other boasts that it can get along by itself. The city of man seeks the praise of men, whereas the height of glory for the other is to hear God in the witness of conscience. The one lifts up its head in its own boasting; the other says to God: 'Thou art my glory, thou liftest up my head.' "[42] The itinerary of Loyola's pilgrimage is plotted rhetorically by similar extremes between two cities of man and God, from Pamplona to Rome.

After an interval Loyola is transported on a litter from the scene of siege to his native province. (Hercules, the protagonist of *aretē*, although usually a comedic figure, made his appearance on the tragic stage in such a litter.)[43] With this journey home the epic hero at the center of the massed encounter—the pitched battle—becomes the hero of the romance with its solitary adventures. At his familial castle Loyola is in serious condition. The many consulted physicians and surgeons agree that his fractured leg should be broken again and the bones reset, since either the original job was poorly done or the mend became dislocated during the journey. The bones are out of joint and beyond healing. During this repetition of the conventional "butchery"[44] Loyola remains silent, only displaying the pain of the operation by tightly clenching his fists. Yet his condition badly deteriorates until he is unable even to eat. The signs of death are upon him. Since the physicians expect his demise, on the feast of St. John the Baptist (24 June) they advise him to make his confession. By the vigil of the feast of SS. Peter and Paul only four days later, he is informed that, unless he improves, by midnight he will surely die. His recovery begins that very hour, a blessing attributed to the invalid's devotion to St. Peter. Within a few days he is pronounced out of danger.[45]

As this begins Loyola's recovery, thus begins the Petrine motif that will culminate historically in the vow of the Society of Jesus to the papacy. The cure of the man lame from birth was the original Petrine miracle in the Acts of the Apostles. He had begged alms from Peter at the gate to the temple only to be better rewarded. "But Peter said, 'I have no silver and gold, but I give you what I have; in the name of Jesus Christ of Nazareth, walk.' And he took him by the right hand and raised him up; and immediately his feet and ankles were made strong." The man entered the temple walking, leaping, and praising God to the amazement of the crowd (Acts 3:1–10). The incident also adumbrated Loyola's decision to be penurious—a beggar like the lame man and penniless like St. Peter. Neither is St. John's feast negligible, for its celebration in Basque lands reflected an ancient cult of the sun, which peasants claimed they could see at dawn on that day dancing on the horizon. Its emblem was the bonfires around which they danced and over which they leaped ritually, reciting poetic formulas to solicit preservation from or cure for ailments. Taking the waters was a feature of the feast in some locales, while in those lacking famous springs there was aspersion or bathing in fountains and brooks. Houses were decorated with branches of white hawthorn and medicinal plants, and there were traditional vegetable offerings. The feast was medicinal,[46] yet for Loyola it forebode death and not cure. Only the chief of the apostles, St. Peter, possesses the power of intervention in his case.

When his bones knit, the tibia overlaps the femur to produce an ugly bump and foreshorten the entire leg. Loyola cannot tolerate this deformity since he is determined to "pursue the world." He informs the surgeons to cut off the bump, which they agree to do, although they warn him that the pain will exceed any he has so far suffered and that the operation will be of some duration. In response he is "determined to martyr himself for his own taste." He bears the pain with his usual patience. The physicians, having cut the flesh and the protruding bone, apply various ointments and mechanical devices to stretch the leg, lest it prove too short. Loyola endures for many days even this "martyrdom," until the Lord restores his health. Yet, because he cannot easily stand on that leg he is forced to remain convalescent in bed.[47]

This description might be real but it is rhetorical. Warfare was classically memorized for recital by imagining some weapon.[48] Here the effects of the cannonball are recorded. With the mnemonic preference for exceptional aesthetic qualities, for ready remembrance the orator might introduce his personage as ugly and deformed, as "stained with blood" (or even for effect as "smeared with red paint").[49] Rhetoric did not shrink from gore. Since actions as well as words might be employed to move the court to tears, the orator could present as evidence "blood-stained swords, fragments of bone taken from the wound, and garments spotted with blood, displayed by the accusers, wounds stripped of their dressings, and scourged bodies bared to view." Such exhibitions produced an enormous impression since they brought the spectators face-to-face with the cruel facts.[50] With the imitative description of Loyola's suffering, a sympathy is evoked, although only superficially for his physical condition.

His spiritual state is hardly heroic. There is but a conventional Christian piety that confesses on the verge of death and appeals for recovery to saints, and a conventional Stoic morality of indifferent endurance in the grip of pain. Even this morality is fired by vainglory. He seeks Herculean pain as glory.[51] It is because of his determination for worldly success that abhorrence of his physical deformity—his appearance to others—provokes him to demand further surgery. This "self-martyrdom," twice named, parodies the stretching of the limbs of real Christians on the racks. Illness played a prominent role in the lives of holy penitents, who turned its commonplace assault on society into a triumphant sign of personal election. They bore its burdens not with resignation but with joy, as a share in Christ's passion that would conform the human body to the divine will.[52] Loyola's prone posture is a travesty of sanctity.

The customary "patience" with which he endures the surgical suffering is not virtue but vice. Some persons so admired their lack of arousal or disturbance by external causes as to lose their very humanity. It did not follow, argued Augustine, that difficulty must be right or insensibility, healthy.[53] Although the endurance of pain was considered virtuous, some victories were judged morally not worth suffering. Suffering was to be for righteousness, as in the beatitude (Matt. 5:10). Medieval homilists elaborated on Augustine's dictum that a good cause, not suffering, made a martyr. Suffering for a cause less than divine was sinful. The term for this fictive patience of the "martyr of Satan" was *duritia*, a hardness to pain that allowed the worldly person to pursue a base goal without reckoning the costs of his effort.[54] Such "savage hardness as endurance" was among Cicero's catalogue of vices parading as virtues, such as pride masquerading as over-valuing honors or audacity pretending at bravery.[55] "Martyrdom" was also attributed to the militant and the lewd. The knight who died on the road to Compostela in the most extravagant medieval defense and challenge was known as "the martyr of chivalry"; while the death of Trotaconventos (Convent-trotter), the old bawd of Juan Ruiz's *Libro de buen amor*, was celebrated as a "martyrdom" of love that promiscuously merited her salvation in the glorious company of the saints.[56]

Theologians would not have admired Loyola's self-induced pain. They invented spiritual consolations for all manner of distressing conditions. As compiled by John of Dambach in his influential *Liber de consolatione theologiae*, there was even counsel for people who were too short. There were scriptural examples of short persons like David and Zacheus, and there was scriptural proof that one could do nothing to affect one's stature (Matt. 6:27), so that God evidently meant for short people to be that way.[57] Brunetto Latini's moralistic *Il tesoretto* considered among the sins for repentance taking pride in "beautiful limbs."[58] So did Spanish confessional manuals. To be boastful about a fine body and its strong and elegant members was "vainglory" and a sin. To be sad about one's body and its small or ugly members God had given; to desire a different body; to try to remedy it with cosmetics or other means—all were "pride" and a sin. To desire beauty intensely as "a very honorable thing" was false, vain, and deceitful.[59]

Loyola is absorbed with both divine and human observation and judgment: vainglory. Diminution in physical stature meant humiliation in social status. Lameness was a defect. In the medical opinion: "the lame man, an imperfect man."[60] There would occur in the decade after Loyola's recital a notable parallel to his injury that well displayed its courtly consequences. The left leg of Don Carlos, son of the Spanish monarch Philip II, was notably longer than his right, so that it was bent and splayed. When his prospective bride received a description of his physique that was both flattering and devastating, followed by a portrait that could not conceal his defect, she married his father instead.[61] Character was classically inferred from the gait.[62] In the convention physical erectness signified moral rectitude.[63] Renaissance manuals on courtesy prescribed very precisely on straight walking. Erasmus instructed in *De civilitate* that a man's gait should be neither effeminate mincing nor headlong raging. The foolish half-halting gait should be left to Swiss soldiers and to those who considered it decorative to sport feathers in their caps.[64] Giovanni della Casa in his manual on courtesy taught men neither to run in the streets nor to pace slowly like brides. They should not lift their legs prancingly, or stamp their feet on the ground, or bend at every step to pull up their stockings, or wiggle their behinds excessively, or strut like peacocks.[65] The ideal of *Il cortegione* was to be of moderate build "with finely proportioned members," so as to be good at all the physical exercises befitting a warrior. The legs were not be languid in their gait, looking as if they were about to fall off. One of the conversationalists in this famous book thought he possessed such grace and beauty of countenance that many women fell passionately in love with him; but he expressed reservations about his legs, which did not seem to him as fair as he wished.[66] As to courtly dancing, the seminal treatise by Domenico de Piacenza, *De arte saltandi et choreas discendi*, declared it useless for a person handicapped by any deformity to become a dancer, since beauty and physical aptitude were prerequisites.[67] So did Guglielmo Ebreo reject as dancers persons of faulty and feeble limbs "like the lame, the hunchbacked, the crippled."[68] The soldier was, of all classes, expected to be the most attentive to his body for stamina. A disabled knight, once the strongest and most valiant of men, plunged to the nadir of public esteem.[69]

Loyola's chivalric aspirations are shattered as surely as the cannonball fractured his leg, although he struggles to maintain the ideal by a spiritual transference. He is displaced by his vainglory from the civic fortress to the familial castle. His place in a castle allegorizes the fallen human condition. Humanity was commonly compared to a castle besieged by temptations and guarded by the wardens of his soul. The allegory was a type of the psychomachy of the virtues and vices, and on a pilgrimage a castle could be an abode or goal of them.[70] In the medieval *Songe du castel* the human edifice rested on two slender pillars, its legs, only to be attacked by the seven capital vices until it lay prone on the ground, a desolate ruin.[71] In Loyola's castle of cure and convalescence his agonistic attitude, externalized in belligerence toward others, becomes internalized. The arena of conflict becomes his own will. Chivalry was commonly tested at a castle, as Parzival at Munsalvæsche.[72] Castles, palaces, and temples of virtue were in the sixteenth century all rhetorical places in the quest for immortality.[73] A famous mountainous castle was the very house of Fame, in the classical description of Ovid's *Metamorphoses*, an open house with brass walls to echo the merest whisper.[74]

Loyola's vice of vainglory, concerned with "what people will say," debases him morally, as does his disability physically. It was a classical topic that punishment was peg-leg. "But rarely does Vengeance, albeit of halting gait, fail to o'ertake the guilty, though he gain the start."[75] The description concluded Horace's ode with a memorable verse, which epitomizes Loyola's ideal at Pamplona, "'Tis sweet and glorious to die for the fatherland." The ode exhorted youths hardened by active service to bear difficulties with patience and to spend life with a dreadful lance amid stirring deeds, so that foe and maiden might sigh at the sight. "True worth that never knows ignoble defeat, shines with undimmed glory . . . True worth, opening Heaven wide for those deserving not to die, essays its course by a path denied to others, and spurns the vulgar crowd and damp earth on fleeting pinion."[76] By implication of punishment as a limper, lameness is punishment allegorized. This is the fallen human condition.

Still unsteady on his legs, Loyola is bedridden. Since he is very fond of reading chivalric books, he asks for some to pass the time; but, as there are none in the house, he is given the life of Christ and the lives of the saints in romance.[77] The selection was typical. The popularity of reading had increased in the fifteenth century when Spanish nobles began to collect books as fashionable, and in the sixteenth century literacy spread to the lower classes. Males typically learned to read from the primary schoolmaster or from the village priest or sacristan. Diocesan and Inquisitional records manifest an interest in learning that extended beyond urban centers to small towns and villages, which hired schoolmasters or freelance teachers. There were book owners among laborers, especially farmers. The rural population read from inexpensive chapbooks or broadsheets, but a Latin book was not beyond the expense of a determined reader of whatever financial circumstances. Printing was dominated by prose nonfiction: devotional, moral, and historical. Readers were less interested in advancement in high culture than in the salvation of their immortal souls. The human condition reflected in an exemplary mirror or in a saintly life was topical, and the most common use of a book was as a devotional aid.[78]

Reading was traditionally formative of the self,[79] and the opening of a book could signal rhetorically a moral conversion. While reading and re-reading these books Loyola fancies them some. Yet, when he pauses, his musings vacillate between such subjects and the worldly affairs to which he was accustomed. Of these inanities one so possesses his heart that he is absorbed in thinking about it for two and three and four hours unaware. This is his fantasy of the obligations in the service of a lady: how he would travel to her land; then the signals, the words, the exercises at arms he would perform in her service.[80] Loyola portrays himself as the person "gifted with a vivid imagination" (*euphantasiōtos*) of whom Quintilian wrote in his discussion of *enargeia*, the vivid style. The person sensitive to the imaginative impressions (*phantasiai, visiones*) that produced vividness had the greatest sway over the emotions. As the possessor of a mind absorbed in fantastic hopes and daydreams, he was so haunted by such visions that he imagined them very realistically, as if he were not dreaming but acting.[81] The classical gift was prominent in sixteenth-century culture in fantasy, the inner capacity of the artist to fashion vivid, if fictive, images through the transformation of remembered sensory experience.[82] Leonardo da Vinci noted that "I myself have proved it to be of no small use, when in bed in the dark, to recall in fancy the outlines of forms previously studied, or other noteworthy things conceived by subtle speculation; and this is certainly an admirable exercise, and useful for impressing things on the memory."[83] Loyola repeats in his fantasy about the lady of his dreams several of Quintilian's examples of this faculty: traveling, addressing people, and fighting. Imagination was a power all might acquire at will, thought Quintilian, and he urged the orator to turn this form of hallucination to a profit.

Loyola's fiction is what the troubadours lamented as *amor de lonh*, the male lover's aspiration of service in verse and in valor toward a beautiful and virtuous, but inaccessible, woman. Since the love was unrequited, its adoration from a distance echoed Augustine's confession of "loving to love."[84] Loyola confesses that in dallying with this fancy he did not consider its impossibility, since his lady was not of the common nobility (such as himself), neither a countess nor a duchess, but of much higher station.[85] Such social discrepancy typified the "courtly" literature of amatory discontent. Its culture arose in periods of demographical imbalance in the ratio of the sexes, causing a shortage of marriageable women for the upper classes and male anxiety regarding marrying upwards.[86] Although it was promoted by the Provençal troubadours and German minnesingers, its greatest influence was Hispano-Arabic poetry. This culture of *cortezia* Loyola derives from the chivalric romances, which he denounces as "worldly and false books" that promote "vain things."[87]

Books on Christian living, or dying, outsold in sixteenth-century Spain the novels and dramas. Although the chivalric *Amadís de Gaula*, which Loyola favored, was the best-seller in fiction, it was second to Friar Luis de Granada's *Libro de la oración*.[88] Ecclesiastical attitudes toward the chivalric novels that Loyola requested for reading during convalescence differed. Most clergy were preoccupied with their danger to the moral conduct of the faithful, but those who fulminated against them censured all secular literature, not only that genre. Some cultured critics thought they merely fell below acceptable literary standards; some recognized exemplary value in them; some applauded certain titles like *Amadís de Gaula*. Their criticism originated not with a moralist but with a publisher, who was hostile toward their circulation because his religious tracts were not competitive in popularity of sales. That criticism dated only to near mid-century,[89] so that Loyola's rejection of chivalric books is either historically precocious or epideictically retrospective. His denunciation, as issued from his place in bed, imitates the conversional crisis of the ascetic St. Jerome, who in bed famously dreamed that Christ judged him a pagan for reading secular literature.[90] It also reflects moral judgment of the peril of the amatory page, dramatized in Dante's infernal tale of Paolo and Francesca, who imitated the acts of Lancelot and Guinevere they read.[91]

Loyola blames his imagination for so "idling in inanities" that he is unable to see the impossibility of his courtly performance, just as he was unable to see the impossibility of the civic defense. This blame of self is countered with praise of God, who assists him by succeeding these thoughts with others originating from his spiritual readings. In reading the lives of Christ and his saints Loyola begins to wonder to himself, "'What if I should do what St. Francis did and what St. Dominic did?'" He rambles like this through many good matters, always proposing to himself difficult and serious ones, which he seems to find in himself a facility to perform. His entire reasoning, he says, went like this: "'St. Francis did this, so must I. St. Dominic did this, so must I.'" Although such thoughts linger, they are only to be interrupted by worldly musings, which also linger. And so a succession of competitive fancies persists, detaining him always in the thought of the hour, whether the worldly exploits he desires or the spiritual ones suggested to his imagination. Wearily he drops both and attends to other matters.[92]

His reasoning imitates the divine accusations Augustine catalogued in a commentary on the psalms: You can not? how can that man: how could the other? Are you more delicate than that senator? Are you weaker than this man or that in health? Are you weaker than women? Women have been able; are not men able? Delicate, wealthy men have been able; are poor men not able?[93] In medieval hagiography the saint was weakly individualized, morally vague, without psychological characterization of tastes, feelings, dreams, or wishes.[94] Although Loyola's deliberation is imitative, his interior reflection and discourse also typifies the new renaissance emphasis on the delineation of personality and the revelation of character. As derived from classical models, it distinguished humanist from medieval hagiography in aesthetic sensibility. With the social change from monastic to mendicant rule, personified by Loyola's examples of Francis and Dominic, there emerged a piety of personal commitment. The institutionalized discipline and formalized almsgiving of the monastic rule were replaced by private asceticism and public charity. Personal conscience became the principal theme of the quest for holiness, and saints' lives were enriched with such details of inner discourse.[95]

Yet Loyola's mental vacillation between the secular and the sacred remains under the sway of the chivalric ideal. He is entertaining the exchange of one kingdom for another, not deliberating the abandonment of kingdoms. A historical factor in conversion, especially among the young, was the holy preacher, of which type his examples of SS. Francis and Dominic were the luminaries. They inspired a romance of the gospel in which evangelizing the public proved more attractive than contemplating in solitude.[96] The hagiography of Francis even portrayed him chivalrously as a troubadour, playing a stick across his arm like the bow of a violin and singing in French verse about his Lord.[97] His friars were commissioned publicly to sing the divine praises and to proclaim, "'We are the jongleurs of God, and the only reward we want is to see you lead a truly penitent life.' "[98] While their vocation complemented Loyola's chivalric ideal, there was no guarantee of sanctity in the exchange of allegiances from a secular to a spiritual lord. The very visibility of those religious orders in their mendicant ministry exposed them to vainglory and venality.

The questions Loyola poses to himself coincide with the self-accusation of Augustine in his *Confessions* when confronted with the tale of the conversion of two military acquaintances. Their report mirrored Augustine's own ugly deformity, his abhorrence for "the disease of concupiscence," in which he "walked the crooked ways." He was distraught with questions about his inability to follow their example.[99] Loyola's questions, "'Can I not do what Francis did? Can I not do what Dominic did?' " are projections of the neophyte whose imitation is mimicry rather than emulation. He supposes that what SS. Francis and Dominic actually did he must literally do. The assumption trespasses on hagiographic tradition, which well distinguished between the admiration and the imitation of the saints. As one hagiographer stated, he had written not to recommend excess but to manifest the saint's fervor. The privileges of a few did not constitute a law for all.[100] A maturer question for Loyola would have been: Can I not do what Iñigo can do?

Loyola's musings are "rambles" in the lesser faculties of the imagination and reason. They are base groping, inferior to the contemplation of the intellect or the compliance of the will. Yet, even at this ingress to spiritual pilgrimage he discerns a difference in their vacillations. Although he greatly enjoys thoughts of worldly affairs, when he dismisses them he finds himself "dry and discontent." But when he thinks of traveling to Jerusalem barefoot, and of eating only vegetables, and of performing all the rest of the rigors of the saints, not only is he consoled during these thoughts but even afterward their effect is to leave him "content and happy." He neither notices nor ponders these experiences, however, until once when his eyes are opened a little he begins to wonder at their different emotional effects of sadness and happiness. Reflecting on this, he gradually perceives the difference between the spirits that agitate him, the one demonic, the other divine. Gathering not a little light from this lesson, he begins to think more earnestly on his past life and how great a need he has to do penance for it. Desires to imitate the saints present themselves to him, and, without further regarding his circumstances, he promises himself with the grace of God to do what they have done. Especially he desires, upon recovery, the affair of Jerusalem, with as many scourges and such abstinences as a noble valor kindled by God usually desires to do.[101]

This ideal of the "generous" spirit is chivalric. Loyola is flat on his back. He has not even ventured to swing his legs out of bed onto the floor for the first tentative steps of pilgrimage. He has only entertained fantasies in his imagination, as promoting affective states. These emotional extremes he naively identifies with Satan and God. Loyola's affective self-examination, derived from heterodox notions and popular devotion, is the Achilles' heel of his personality and spirituality. The norm departs from the wisdom of Augustine's argument for the moral neutrality of the emotions, since the intention of the will matters.[102] The affective fallibility was a fault Loyola shared with holy multitudes in the late medieval to baroque ages. As John of the Cross, surveying the popular indulgence in sensationalism rather than the exercise of the liberty of faith, would define the vice, it was "spiritual gluttony."[103] Loyola himself suspected it as a personal fault, although he did not relinquish his dependence on sensibility. He confided this much in his diary: "Also considering if I ought to proceed forward, because one part of me seems to desire seeking too many signs, and in times and in Masses past for my satisfaction, when the matter in itself was clear and I was not seeking the certitude of it, but only that the relish was entirely to my taste."[104]

It was not the discernment of spirits but the disposition of the will that traditionally mattered, and emotion was not theologically equatable with love. The end of the Christian life was not consolation but charity; and charity, as every lover knows, is not necessarily consoling. Loyola's discernment of dualistic spirits from affective states was not in origin even Christian. It derived ultimately from the Zoroastrian hymns, mediated to Judaic asceticism through the Essene *Manual of Discipline*, and transmitted to Christian tradition in the eleventh mandate of *Pastor Hermae*, an early treatise on repentance after baptism. Published by the humanist Jacques Lefevre d'Etaples in a collection of spiritual treatises, it enjoyed in the sixteenth century quasicanonical status.[105]

Neither spirit, divine nor demonic, is moving Loyola forward or backward as on pilgrimage. Both spirits are indiscriminately "agitating" him (*agito*), stirring him, shaking him up. In the seminal *Vita Antonii* that disturbance producing instability of character had been the role of the evil spirit, while the good spirit was so quiet and gentle that it induced joy and confidence in a calm soul.[106] Loyola is roaming about in his imagination, fantasizing a personal facility to imitate glorious saints in difficult and daring deeds. Going barefoot to Jerusalem on a vegetarian diet in imitation of saintly rigors is not necessarily progress beyond going shod to Pamplona beefed up in imitation of knightly rigors. Loyola has not yet experienced a true conversion of interior disposition. He is merely exchanging one set of appearances and allegiances for another. Whether in arms or in asceticism, his values remain agonistic. His object is to be observed and praised for excellence: vainglory.

Although he is now motivated by the recognition of a need "to do penance" (*hacer penitenzia*), this was a testy term in sixteenth-century religion. As Erasmus corrected the Vulgate translation of *poenitentiam agite* ("do penance") to *poeniteat vos* ("repent"), *metanoeite* meant a conversion of heart, not an exercise of deeds, to be penitent, not to do penance.[107] Loyola does not disclose the affair of Jerusalem as a pilgrimage: neither as a *romería*, such as a processional to a local shrine, nor as a *peregrinación*, a journey to a distant site. He consistently terms it an *ida*, which can mean "departure" or "trip out" but more pejoratively means "impetuosity," "rash proceeding," "sally." This pejorative connotation will be reinforced by another *ida*, his enforced walk to military headquarters under arrest as a suspected spy, which incident he compares to his great consolation with Christ arrested for his passion.[108] Although Loyola's penitential exercise is voluntary rather than judicial, as were most pilgrimages since the fourteenth century,[109] he promises it to himself, not to God. He does so "without seeing" his circumstances, employing the very philology (*non mirar*) that has already marked his misperceptions in the fortress and in the castle. The light (*lumbre*) he has gathered from his ruminations[110] is not "light" (*luz*) but "firelight," or better, "matchlight" struck feebly in the dark.

Yet its affective connotation of warmth is reinforced by Loyola's belief in being "kindled by God." He begins to forget his past thoughts with his saintly desires. These are confirmed to him in a "visitation" (*visitación*). Awake one night he clearly sees an image of the Madonna, or Mary with the child Jesus. With this sight (*vista*) he receives for a long time extreme consolation. He remains with such loathing for his entire past life, especially carnal affairs, that it seems to him that all the species previously painted on his soul are erased from it. Here intervenes the author Luis Gonçalves da Câmara: "From that hour until the August of 53 that this is written, never again did he have even minimal consent in carnal affairs. From this effect it can be judged to have been the work of God, although he did not dare to determine that, nor to say more than to affirm the aforesaid." Loyola's brother and the whole household are summoned to witness from this exterior change the transformation he has undergone interiorly.[111]

Such incidents were related literarily according to the classification of Macrobius's *Commentariorum in somnium Scipionis* on dreams. Loyola's *vista* might translate *visio*, the prophetic dream, or *visum*, the apparition in the drowsy moment between wakefulness and sleepiness.[112] There was no strict distinction between dreams and apparitions.[113] The designation "visitation" (*visitación*) recurs later during Loyola's travel as "great supernatural visitations" (*grandi visitationi sopranaturali*), comparable to those experienced early at Manresa. Yet that description does not square with Loyola's deprecation of his early experiences as rough tutorials, nor with his confession that in Manresa he was spiritually "blind."[114] The designation "great supernatural visitations" is Gonçalves da Câmara's hagiographic flourish. Although the phenomenology of the visions is vague, what matters in epideictic rhetoric is not fact but function. Loyola habitually practiced and promoted imaginative prayer, so that "image" (*imagen*) was his ordinary experience. The noun also designates the statue or painting (*imagen*) of the Virgin on which he will spend his final wages. The usual place for a Marian image in a late medieval or renaissance home was the bedroom, where it was hung in a gilt frame with a candle attached. Paintings of the Madonna were sometimes even attached to the headboard of the bed. Display of her small and intimate image in a domestic setting invited her presence and protection.[115] Loyola's visitation may have been a heightened spiritual awareness of such a statue or painting of the Madonna he physically viewed in his chamber. The verbal phrase "to see clearly" (*ver claramente*) had occurred in the second sentence of the text, where all the soldiers in the fortress except Loyola clearly saw that its defense was futile. The expression encompasses intellectual understanding and judgment.

Loyola habitually described affective states not as welling from within the self, as in modern psychology, but as invading it from without. During this convalescence desires to imitate the saints are "offered" to him. The more common verb is that various states "come" (*venir*) to him. Accusatory stirrings about failure of duty "come" to him; the temptation to sloth "comes" to him, its relief "comes" to him; even the assent of his own will to resume eating meat "comes" to him; a temptation concerning righteousness "comes" to him; a great impulse to protest an attempted rape "comes" to him.[116] This tendency to externalize spiritual influences, as originating from agonistic spirits of good and evil, complicates interpretation if modern empirical evidence is normative. Yet in medieval culture sensory evidence was so blended with spiritual conviction that the concept of the real included much that modern science would term imaginary.[117] The incident demonstrates how indifferent even a renaissance person could be to the empirical nature of his own most important, salvational experiences. Loyola believed that the divine was apprehended through the imaginative faculty—the *Exercitia spiritualia* is based on that principle—and it mattered not for the result whether he created the good image in his soul or if God imprinted it. What did matter was pragmatic not theoretical: the moral effect. From the moral effect Gonçalves da Câmara judges that the visitation was "the work of God," although he states that Loyola himself did not dare to determine even that much or to explicate it.

The dominant period for reported apparitions in the Spanish kingdoms was from about 1400 to 1525, when the Inquisition assumed control over ecclesiastical institutions and popular initiatives. Seers with stereotypical revelations of pious remedies for local crises who were once revered were now whipped, even when their testimony was orthodox. The cultural form of the public, lay vision as a mediation between society and divinity waned.[118] Yet the visitation of virtuous ladies was a commonplace of visionary literature developed from personifications into personages. There was Lady Church in *Pastor Hermae*, Lady Philosophy in *Consolatio philosophiae*, Virgin Truth in *De secreto conflicto curarum animarum*. In Petrarch's dialogue she appeared to the poet in a waking dream.[119] To Boethius's consolation Philosophy even drove the

Muses from his bed.[120] In courtly literature ladies also entered bedchambers, especially in trials of sexual temptation, as in the courteous exchange with erotic innuendoes in the castle of *Sir Gawain and the Green Knight*.

In Loyola's recital the visitor is the Madonna. A castle is her ideal rhetorical place. The most complete and distinctive of the many medieval allegories of the castle was that of the Virgin as the castle of love. It developed from a verse about Jesus' ministry, "He entered a village; and a woman named Martha received him into her house" (Luke 10:38). In the Vulgate translation "village" was *castellum*, so that the transition to Jesus entering the castle of Mary at the Incarnation was simple. The genre culminated in Robert Grosseteste's *Le château d'amour*, which detailed every feature of that castle, to which a Christian fled for refuge from the three temptations allied with the seven capital sins. Since the Lukan pericope was common as a liturgical reading and homiletic topic on the feast of the assumption (15 August),[121] there is an association of Loyola's experience with it, although he does not explicitly so date it. The fundamental theme of his recital is glory. The specific concept in this scene is the glorified body. Loyola enjoys through the visitation of the Madonna the liberation from concupiscence that was her singular privilege. Other mortals were believed to share it only in the body of resurrection. Her bodily assumption into heaven, like her immaculate conception, are the archetypes. Although Loyola has not like Mary been immaculately conceived or celestially assumed, he is by her intercession restored to the preternatural and advanced to the eschatological state of innocence.

The norm even among practiced ascetics was incessant struggle against concupiscence. Loyola's instantaneous cure by the visitation of the Madonna recalls hagiographic claims of marvelous chastity. An abbot called Serene was so gifted that he was no longer disturbed, even in sleep, by natural sexual arousal. Then there was a monk who fled from a convent of women he had founded and dreamed of castration by a trio of angels, so that for forty years he felt no more desire. Another prayed to be made a eunuch, then dreamed of an angel opening his body to remove a tumor. A voice pronounced that God had given him perfect chastity.[122] Loyola's nocturnal cure of concupiscence is ascribed to the Madonna in the oxymoron of her virginal-maternal role, which merited her bodily incorruption assumed into heaven. Belief in her assumption was also theologically important in relating Mary to his pilgrimage, for she was revered as possessing the "fullness of glory" pilgrims sought.

The assumption justified in folklore her manifestation in bodily, visible apparitions. Because her body vanished from this world at the assumption, she was supposed capable of reappearing in it in a more corporeal way than were other saints, whose bodies remained interred or whose relics were geographically scattered.[123]

The Madonna of Loyola's sight imitates Lady Continence, who appeared to Augustine in his *Confessions*. "The chaste dignity of continence began to manifest itself: tranquil and joyful, but not in a lascivious way, inviting me in an upright fashion to come ahead and not hesitate; stretching forth to receive and embrace me holy hands filled with a multitude of good examples." These exemplars were the souls in which continence was the pregnant mother of the joys of divine espousal. And, "with mocking encouragement, she mocked me, as if saying: 'Can you not live as these men and women do?' " Continence assured Augustine that they lived not by their own powers but by the Lord's commendation to virtue. She reproached him as if he were spiritually without legs. " 'Why do you stand upon yourself and so have naught to stand on? Throw yourself upon Him, fear not; He will not pull himself away and let you fall. Throw yourself confidently; He will take you up and heal you.' "[124]

The imaginative cure of Loyola's concupiscence, rather than the physical healing of his wounds, is not miraculously odd but rhetorically coherent. Just as Continence appeared to exhort Augustine about the spiritual instability of his legs, so does the Madonna appear to Loyola in the same debility. Among legendary visions of the Virgin there had indeed been miracles to heal physical legs. There was the case of a certain nun, told in Caesarius of Hiesterbach's *Dialogus miraculorum*, who had injured her leg by overzealous genuflection at prayer. The mother of God appeared in a vision in the infirmary at high noon and anointed her leg with unguent from a vial to effect its cure.[125] Then there was the miracle, notably preserved in Alfonso X the Wise's *Cantigas*, of the man suffering from a cancer of the foot. In a moment of despair at the pain he cut it off, only to be cured on pilgrimage during a dream in which the Virgin immaculate descended from her altar to tend it.[126] In Loyola's recital there is no such physical healing, because the wounds to his legs function as symbolic of the wounds to his soul. Although his injuries may have been real rather than legendary, they were still rhetorically exploitable for spiritual malady. Legs was the rhetorical topic for lust.

The limping hero or anti-hero had an ancient lineage whose significance centered in sexuality, whether generative or impotent. The concept may have derived from a Near Eastern mythology of sacral kingship that demanded death for fertility. For death was substituted castration and laming, by hamstringing or dislocation of the thigh; and for these acts, circumcision and the wearing of buskins. Although most of the ancient limpers were wounded in the foot rather than the leg, the scriptural Jacob and the classical Aeneas[127] were analogues to Loyola's patrimonial status as founder of the Society of Jesus. In his mysterious folkloric wrestling with the demon at the ford Jacob was struck in the socket of his hip. It became dislocated, so that at sunrise he left the site limping. Yet he had won the match face-to-face with God and survived. This ancient animistic narrative was associated etiologically with the Judaic taboo against eating the sciatic muscle, since the thigh was the seat of life. Most important, it established Jacob as a patriarch. He wrestled from the spirit a blessing, and his name was changed to Israel as progenitor of the chosen people (Gen. 32:4–33:17).[128] Aeneas was lamed in the Trojan war when a rock thrown by the enemy crushed a cupbone. He was rescued and healed by his mother Venus to become father of Rome,[129] as Jacob had been of Israel. This classical example of an injury in war to the leg, miraculously healed by a heavenly mother, is analogous to Loyola's vision; so is the scriptural example, as his test at crossing the river will prove.

Christian morality and literature commonly employed limping for the antihero, however. A notable figure of sterility was the maimed Fisher King who appeared throughout the Grail legends. By transference of this attribute another lame protagonist was the devil.[130] Yet limping was an attribute of fallen Adam, and so of Everyman, as in the lament of the most popular of all medieval spiritual authors, Bernard of Clairvaux. As he wrote in his *Sermones super Cantica canticorum*, with original sin humanity lost its "uprightness," although the soul retained by its greatness a divine image. "But he limps, as it were, on one foot, and has become an estranged son." In this weak condition a person even limped away from the path. In this disabled uprightness the human limper was disturbed and he was wrenched away from the divine image. He bent to the ground and brooded over the earth.[131] The metaphor was current as late as John Donne's universal anatomy:

> Then, as mankinde, so is the worlds whole frame
> Quite out of oiynt, almost created lame.

As the poet exclaimed, "How lame a cripple this world is."[132]

Limping on pilgrimage was the fate of Dante as he initiated his journey, glancing back in confusion at the perilous pass he had barely escaped, yet hobbling toward the summit like a man wounded in the left foot. There developed a medieval tradition about lameness from Aristotelian physics, in which all movement originated from the right, so that the left was the stationary position. The analogy of walking was applied scholastically to the faculties of the soul: to the intellect as to the right foot, which struck out, while to the will as the left foot, which dragged behind. This limping symbolized the imbalance of intellect and will, in which humanity was disabled toward its divine destiny. From original sin the right leg, or intellect, suffered the wound of ignorance; the left leg, or will, the wound of concupiscence. Adam's progeny was afflicted with this limping, unable to order appetite to mind.[133] The ascetic accusation in Petrarch's *Secretum* that the poet was dragging his feet in renouncing his art implied such weakness of the will to accomplish what the intellect perceived as the good.[134]

Loyola is disabled by the cannonball in both legs, the one completely fractured, the other severely wounded. The analogy is patent: Loyola the limper is an Adam. When *he* "falls," the other men in the fortress surrender to the enemy.[135] The accident of war in the fall of Pamplona is perfectly symbolic of the human condition after the fall of Adam. Physical erectness was since classical antiquity a vast topic in philosophy and rhetoric for moral rectitude.[136] The fall was thus developed in the patristic tradition as a physical metaphor for debasement from the erect stature of contemplation. Gregory the Great moralized about Adam moving the foot of his will from a firm contemplative stance toward guilt, so that he fell immediately from the love of God to love of self. Since he had collapsed below himself, he could no longer stand up by himself.[137] In Loyola's imitation of the scholastic analogy of legs and faculties the intellect is badly injured, but still able to grope while dragging the destroyed limb behind it. The will is shattered and immobile, however, in need of redemption, as his leg bones are of resetting. The wound of concupiscence to the will requires for healing a spiritual intervention, like the visitation of the Virgin with the child Jesus.

Although her iconography is unspecified, if she may be portrayed as the Madonna of Montserrat before whom Loyola will keep vigil as a spiritual knight, then she is like the scriptural woman who is black but beautiful (Song 1:5). The child enthroned in her lap would also be dark. Jesus would function in Loyola's visitation as the antithesis to the figure who in the ascetic lives of the saints, from *Vita Antonii* to Teresa of

Avila's *Vida*, personified the demon of fornication: the little black boy (*negrillo*). He appeared to the anchorite in the desert, he appeared to the nun in the cloister, to tempt and torment them with carnal images.[138] Here the sight of the little black Jesus would erase them from Loyola's soul. Mere vision impresses his will with absolute effectivity, in an ascent from the sensory to the volitional, as in his *Exercitia spiritualia*.

The process was established on the renaissance theory that the imaginative power retains the images seen and imprints them in mind and body. Art involved *costume* or the virtual life of the image, its psychic presence. Among the many examples of the power of fantasy to affect the body was that of the white woman who gave birth to a black child who perfectly resembled an Abyssinian painting in her bedroom on which she had gazed.[139] In his analysis of vision Augustine taught that in animals "the fetus usually show some traces of the passionate desires of the mother, whatever it was they gazed upon with great delight." The more tenderly formative the original seeds were, the more effectively they followed the inclination of the maternal soul and the phantasm that arose in it through the body that passionately gazed at it. He cited the example of the patriarch Jacob placing streaked rods in the watering troughs for his sheep, so that in viewing them when they bred there they would conceive striped, speckled, and spotted lambs (Gen. 30:37–42).[140] That scriptural verse was discussed among the medieval scientific questions.[141] And that actual practice of husbandry was current in sixteenth-century Spain for the breeding of mares, as testified by the physician Laurent Joubert.[142] Albert the Great among the scientists thought the interrelationship of soul and body so intimate that daydreaming about a desirable image elicited physical stirrings in the body.[143] Fantasy was believed efficacious for human conception. Augustine traced the concept to the ancient authority of the most expert physician Hippocrates. In an exegesis of Jacob's breeding practice Augustine told the story of a woman about to be punished for adultery because she had given birth to a beautiful boy who resembled neither of his parents nor any other member of the family. Hippocrates suggested searching her bedroom for a picture resembling the child. It was found, and the woman freed from suspicion.[144]

In the principal text on gynecology Soranus taught that various states of the soul produced changes in the form of the fetus. If a woman during sexual intercourse saw a monkey she would conceive its likeness. He cited the case of a deformed tyrant who forced his wife to look at beautiful statues during sex; she indeed bore him well-formed children.[145]

The ancient fear that the maternal imagination would conceive monsters from vision of some aberrant object or from a fantastic dream was rehearsed by Ambroise Paré, among the most excellent of renaissance surgeons. He cited the scriptural and classical authorities; and he told tales, such as the social expulsion of the girl with two heads, lest she impress on pregnant women images that would similarly deform their fetuses. Detailing such horrors in *De monstres*, he warned women at the hour of conception and during the formative period not to look at or to imagine monsters. He articulated the common belief in "the force of the imagination being joined with the conformational power, the softness of the embryo, ready like soft wax to receive any form." It was dangerous to show a pregnant woman even a picture of deformity.[146] Leon Battista Alberti urged the husband about to decorate the bedchamber he would share with his wife not to paint anything on the walls except "the most comely and beautiful faces." That choice would be "of no small consequence to the conception of the lady and the beauty of the children."[147]

In Quintilian's discussion of the effectiveness of gestures he wrote that "pictures, which are silent and motionless, penetrate into our innermost feelings with such power that at times they seem more eloquent than language itself."[148] Augustine's *Confessions* rued the example for rhetorical exercise from Terence's *Eunuchus* of the youth inflamed by a lascivious painting of Danae and the shower of gold.[149] Gazing on a religious image was no guarantee of consequent beauty and virtue, however. Montaigne related in his essays the fate of a woman who conceived a daughter as furry as a bear because she had gazed during conception on a picture attached to the foot of her bed of the hirsute John the Baptist in his animal skins. Montaigne confessed himself to be very impressionable. "A strong imagination creates the event, say the scholars. I am one of those who are very much influenced by the imagination. Everyone feels its import, but some are overthrown by it. Its impression on me is piercing." He considered miracles, visions, enchantments, and other such extraordinary effects as the power of the imagination in common people.[150] Loyola also confessed himself a classic enthusiast—highly imaginative—and his visionary experience of the Madonna is consistent with the psychosomatic belief about conceptions from images. In his imagination the Madonna impresses his soul with her likeness, whose dazzling purity renders his very body asexual.

Loyola's brother, indeed the entire household, recognizes from his exterior change an interior change.[151] Such conversion was the interest in the sixteenth century, whose historiography introduced the onset of maturity as the crucial phase in the quest for identity. That introduction substituted for the significance in medieval hagiography of a birth heralded by portents and a childhood guided by visions. Although the sign of Loyola's change is unspecified, it is not negligible, since sexual inactivity among the nobility was extraordinary. The rule was an aggression linked with the violence of the class. The necessary condition of an ascetic life, therefore, was sexual renunciation. Folk wisdom and religious ideal both identified intercourse as the fundamental division between innocence and worldliness. It was an absolute norm, allowing no degrees or compromises, since there could be no almost-virginal saint. Chastity was the mark universally understood as the rejection of the flesh; thus it was considered the initial and important step toward spiritual perfection.[152]

It was a virtue for whose aspiration the Spanish clergy, to which estate Loyola already belonged, provided little example. Concubinage was their rule. Newly ordained priests celebrated the first Mass by dancing in the streets with their mistresses and their chief interest was in the acquisition of benefices.[153] In Loyola's province of Guizpúcoa the large number of illegitimate children of priests in the first half of the sixteenth century was an equally great problem for the ecclesiastical authorities.[154] Loyola's lameness would not have been any incentive to chastity either. On the contrary, folk wisdom believed that sex with a cripple was the best sex. There was the common proverb "He does not know Venus in her perfect sweetness who has not lain with a cripple." It probably derived from a Greek adage in which the queen of the Amazons declared "The lame man does it best!" In Amazon society the legs of the males were deliberately disabled from childhood so that the females might better exploit them sexually. The lore was circulated in Erasmus's *Adagia*, from which Loyola likely studied Latin, and in Montaigne's *Essais*.[155]

While the healing of his lame will required the imaginative intervention of the Madonna, the wound of ignorance to the intellect might be healed more naturally by reading devout literature. The arts and sciences were believed remedies for the wounds of original sin.[156] Loyola likens his exercise of reading in bed to striking a match in the dark,[157] analogous to the doctrine of the "spark" in the soul that is not extinguished even by original sin.[158] The "kindling" of an ascetic conversion during his pious reading is invented from the rhetorical topic of the opening of the book. A dramatic example was the abrupt conversion of Giovanni

Colombini, founder of the mendicant order of the Gesuati, while reading about Mary the Egyptian in the lives of the saints. His wife had thrust the book at him when he screamed and cursed at her because dinner was not ready. (She lived to regret her pious deed: he became so penitent that he demanded of her celibacy in marriage.)[159] The topic was celebratory from Augustine's *Confessions*, from the scene in the garden in which the voice commanded, "'Take it, read it! Take it, read it!'" Augustine's opening of the book of Romans imitated his friend Pontici-anus's chance finding of a Pauline volume; that served as a pretext for relating the conversion of the two military agents who had read of the conversion of Anthony, the ascetic archetype to whose life these tales-within-tales regressed.[160] The humanist imitation was Petrarch's epistolary ascent of Mont Ventoux, in which he happened to open Augustine's *Confessions* to the accusation, "'And they go to admire the summits of mountains and the vast billows of the sea and the broadest rivers and the expanses of the ocean and the revolution of the stars and they overlook themselves.'"[161]

Loyola perseveres in his own reading and in his good intentions and he converses with the household to its benefit. Since he greatly enjoys these pious books he decides to excerpt from them the essentials of the lives of Christ and of the saints. He begins a copybook industriously, for he is just beginning to get about the castle. He transcribes the words of Christ in red ink, those of his Lady in blue, on shiny lined paper in a good hand, for his penmanship is quite fine. Thus he spends part of his time in writing, part in prayer.[162] These pastimes parody the monastic exercises of transcription and prayer. In the art of memory it was a practice to visualize the color, shape, position and placement of letters on a manuscript.[163] Yet Loyola is fascinated by the surface of the spiritual: the polished paper, the striking colors, the fine script. Sheen, color, shape are the matter of the letter, not the spirit. He is playing a comedic role like Polyphemus, the liar and rake. A character in Erasmus's *Colloquia*, Polyphemus was based on the author's amanuensis and messenger, Felix Rex. Erasmus introduced him in "Cyclopes sive evangeliophorus" as an ass carrying a copy of the gospels he had painted bright red and blue. As Erasmus explained in correspondence, "Polyphemus used to carry with him a beautifully decorated volume of the Gospels, though nothing could be more soiled than his own life." And as his colloquy accused him, "'But it would be well if, as you've decorated the Gospel with various ornaments, the Gospels in turn adorned you. You've decorated them with colors; I wish they might embellish you with good morals.' "¹⁶⁴

Even in his alternative pastime of prayer Loyola is bedazzled. The greatest consolation he receives from it is "to look at the sky and the stars," which he often does for hours, because from this exterior vision he feels interiorly a magnanimous courage to serve the Lord.¹⁶⁵ The saint at the open window considering creation was a detail of medieval hagiography.¹⁶⁶ Yet stargazing was also a philosophical topic exploited in epideictic rhetoric for praise or for blame. For Plato, since only sight could regard the heavens and incite wonder at the celestial movements and laws, vision penetrated philosophically from sensation through intellection to the ultimate good, beauty, and truth.¹⁶⁷ The erect posture able to behold the stars distinguished humans from other animals (like the gnu) with their earthbound stare, in a popular topic repeated by classical, patristic, and scholastic authors.¹⁶⁸ Seneca specifically contrasted stargazing with warring, which he likened to a file of ants scurrying in a small plot. The mind engaging the celestial regions expanded and, bursting its chains, returned to its origin. Stargazing was a Stoic proof of human divinity, for in it one was pleased with divine affairs and inhabited this realm intellectually, not as an alien but as a kindred spirit. "Here, finally the mind learns what it long sought; here it begins to know god."¹⁶⁹

This human excellence inferred from an erect anatomy was a much criticized doctrine. There was from Plato the exemplar of Thales the natural philosopher, who tumbled into a well, so eager to explore the heavens that he could not see what was before his feet.¹⁷⁰ The astronomer in *The Canterbury Tales* was typically portrayed:

> He walked the fields stargazing, to foresee
> What might befall; and suddenly fell in
> A clay pit—something that he'd not foreseen.¹⁷¹

Erasmus in his *Moria* ridiculed cosmologists as touched by "a pleasant form of madness, which sets them building countless universes and measuring the sun, moon, stars and planets by rule of thumb or a bit of string, and producing reasons for thunderbolts, winds, eclipses and other inexplicable phenomena." Although they were too purblind to notice the plainest manifestations of nature—a stone in the path, a ditch in the road—they claimed to see such insubstantial forms as ideas, universals, quiddities, even prime matter itself. This variation on the topic of Thales lampooned the alliance of nominalist logic with natural philosophy at the Collège de Montaigù in Paris, renowned as a center for dynamics and kinematics. Erasmus matriculated there only to acquire more lice than learning,[172] and it is in that very college that Loyola will enroll in arts toward philosophy.[173]

It was influentially Augustine who enlarged this astral topic for spiritual blame. In *De beata vita* he charted the courses of voyagers to the port of philosophy. The confused pilot, who was moored at sea while he gazed at the sinking stars, was typical of Augustine the procrastinator, who postponed his conversion to the safe haven of the Catholic faith.[174] He accused himself in his *Confessions* of stargazing rather than self-examination in the sentence famously cited by Petrarch, "'And they go to admire the summits of mountains and the vast billows of the sea and the broadest rivers and the expanses of the ocean and the revolution of the stars and they overlook themselves.' "[175] This topic of human dignity focused on introspection rather than extrospection—self rather than stars—was the norm. As Montaigne would moralize in concluding his essay on experience: "It is an absolute perfection and virtually divine to know how to enjoy our being rightfully. We seek other conditions because we do not understand the use of our own, and go outside of ourselves because we do not know what it is like inside. Yet there is no use our mounting on stilts, for on stilts we must still walk on our own legs."[176]

Loyola as wobbly-legged and starry-eyed is the novice at divine science. At prayer he seeks consolation from the revolution of the heavens rather than the reform of the self. In his celestial aspirations he is vainglorious. Glory as an elevation to the stars was a renaissance rhetorical topic to exalt the fame of personages as piercing the heavens. The poet himself was an archer toward the skies; his pen lent the wings on which to fly.[177] Such vainglorious stargazing so encourages Loyola toward divine service that he is eager to be on the road. Yet for the moment he must content himself with dispatching a servant sixty miles to Burgos to inquire about his destination. In anticipating his future beyond the pilgrimage to Jerusalem, so that he might live in perpetual penitence, the idea occurs to him of enclosure in the charterhouse at Seville. He thinks of doing this without divulging his identity, so that he may be less regarded. He also plans to eat nothing there but vegetables. When he reconsiders the penances he desires to perform at large in the world, however, the desire for the charterhouse abates. He fears that he will not be permitted to exercise there the self-disdain he has aroused. Although the servant returns from Burgos with information about the Carthusian rule that seems satisfactory, Loyola's reservations about its laxity and his preoccupation with the sally to Jerusalem persuade him to postpone a decision about enclosure. Although he does not reconsider the matter,[178] Carthusian profession would have been an appropriate moral choice, since the order was founded for the vigilance of the eye against all diabolical ambushes, especially as arms against vainglory.[179]

The soldier and the Carthusian was a comparison of vocations Erasmus explored in a colloquy of that very title. The Carthusian exemplified the humanist ideal of virtue and learning, while the soldier was a glutton, lecher, and gambler. He was also portrayed as a cripple, which accident he attributed to " 'the chances of war,' " while the monk rejoined, " 'No, it's your own folly.' "[180] The protagonist of Erasmus's colloquy "Militaria" was also lame:

HANNO:	How is it you come back a Vulcan when you left here a Mercury?
THRASYMACHUS:	What Vulcans or Mercuries are you talking about?
HANNO:	You left as though wing-footed; now you're limping.
THRASYMACHUS:	The usual way to come back from war.

(To tell the truth he was wounded when he fled fearfully from battle, fell, and banged his leg on a stone.)[181] In "Militis et Cartusiani" the soldier criticized the monk for exactly the loss of liberty Loyola fancies for himself, even as a penitent. "'You're not free to walk about wherever you like.'"[182] It is Loyola's reconsideration of the penances he expects to perform while "walking about through the world" that cools his interest in Carthusian enclosure. The Carthusian of the colloquy would have rejoined that regret for entering an order only came to those who "throw themselves into this mode of life as if into a well."[183] Loyola may be starry-eyed in his religious ambitions but he is not about to trip like Thales into that well. There is a certain measure of practical deliberation, as in his resolve to postpone a decision about enclosure until his return from the outing to Jerusalem.

Since he has regained some strength, it seems time to leave the castle. Loyola approaches his brother with the ruse that, since the duke of Nájara, whom he serves, knows that he has recovered, it would be good to join him at Navarrete. His brother tours him through the castle from room to room and with flatteries begs him not to ruin himself, to consider how much hope the family has for him, how much he is able to accomplish, and pleads similar arguments—all contrived to detach him from his good desire. Loyola replies evasively and slips off.[184] The usual precipitants of an adult conversion were the death of a loved one, serious illness, the preaching of a holy evangelist, an acute sense of worldliness, and the sudden intervention of the supernatural. Its consequences were difficult, because an adult was already involved in an established network of comforts and demands. The vocation to holiness was experienced typically in a social setting in which parents, siblings, spouses, and children were affected by the penitent's decision for a change of life. They could be protagonists or antagonists, but not bystanders.

Conversion in adulthood, which tended in medieval hagiography to be sudden, involved enormous difficulties of extrication from secular attachments and responsibilities. Lay saints were usually urban patricians, with many more canonized from the upper than the lower classes. It was a phenomenon of the landed elite, not the tenant laborer. The saintly aristocracy largely coincided with the social aristocracy, for the institutional Church protected and rewarded the class of its hierarchy. Canonization supposed cult; cult, visibility; visibility, social status. The gospel may have blessed the poor and the meek with the kingdom of heaven, but few were the canonized who embodied those beatitudes by station of birth. The lower class lived the apostolic life by necessity. The marvel of conversion was that the upper class could live it by choice. The act of conversion mirrored these elitist social values, with the dominant image as the prince or merchant—like SS. Francis and Dominic, those nobles Loyola so admired—who renounced a patrimony with its wealth and power.[185]

Social position entailed family obligation, whether to progeny or to property.[186] Loyola's elder brother intervenes in this crisis of conversion. He has already been noted as daunted by the pain of Loyola's operation on his legs, which he himself would not dare suffer. He has also interpreted Loyola's exterior change after the Madonna's "visitation" as a sign of an interior change.[187] Now in touring him through the rooms of the castle he is cast in a diabolical role. He is like Satan tempting Jesus in the wilderness with a panorama of the glorious kingdoms of the world (Matt. 4:8-10). Although his part is dialectical and does not extend to the shocking details of abuse, even murder, which could intrude in hagiography, the temptation is real enough. Loyola does not rebuke but evades him, much as Jesus outwitted his enemies by verbal parry or avoided them by slipping into the crowd.

TWO

The Ascetic

The family was the initial context in which religious desire was manifested. The vocation then broadened to the streets of the village or city, the road of pilgrimage, the monastery, or even to civil and ecclesiastical palaces.[1] From on his feet in the fortress to on his back in the castle Loyola secures a new place and position: "on a mule."[2] Loyola begins his pilgrimage humanly half-erect astride this symbolic beast. Most pilgrims walked on foot, from devotion or from penury, with the aid of a staff. Only the rich afforded horses or mules or, through perilous regions of banditry, enclosed carriages[3]—an inequitable practice about which moralists complained as a pretense of devotion.[4] The posture of Loyola as Jerusalem-bound mimics the triumphal entry of Jesus into that city. It was an elected sign of humility, as in the scriptural prophecy, " 'Behold, your king is coming to you, humble, and mounted on an ass' " (Matt. 21:1-11).

Gentlemen in the sixteenth century did not ride mules. This was a definite social disgrace in *Il libro del cortegiano*, although Castiglione's dislike of the beast may have derived from his only experience of the wounds of war. A mule once fell on his foot, he reported, and "made me see stars by daylight."[5] The ascendancy of the mule over the horse in the sixteenth century was strongly opposed by governments to save the breeding of the horse as a military weapon. Mules were agricultural animals used for ploughing and transport. Although they were numerous in Spain, about 100,000 strong,[6] especially in those kingdoms gentlemen did not ride mules. Alfonso X forbid the Order of the Knights of the Band, or Scarf, to ride a mule at the fine of a silver mark, as preserved in the historical romance of Antonio de Guevara, *Libro aureo de Marco aurelio*. Even later in the sixteenth century Montaigne would repeat these items, adding that the exceptions to the rule were the Abyssinians. The nobler they were, the more proudly they rode mules in imitation of their master Prester John.[7] And so Loyola begins his pilgrimage, a little like Jesus the Savior, a little like Prester John the adventurer, and a lot like the mule on which he rides. As Erasmus explained the simile, "The mule, sprung from horse and ass, is neither one nor the other, like some people who try to be both courtiers and churchmen and are neither."[8]

Loyola is accompanied by his other brother, a prototype of the virtuous companions he will seek on the road of pilgrimage as the Society of Jesus. En route they keep a chivalric vigil at the shrine of Our Lady of Arançuz (Aránzazu), where he prays for fresh energies for the journey.[9] In the sixteenth century shrines were essential institutions of local religion, establishing the sacred in the Spanish landscape. They commemorated the supernatural signs of the saints, especially Mary, whose images supplanted the popularity of the bodies or relics of martyrs and hermits as healing sites. She became protectress of a community. She was notably "Our Lady of *this* place," whether of this tree or this spring. There were annual feasts and processions organized around shrines, guardians of the sites, registers of their history and miracles, and even shrines on geographical maps. Since Marian shrines in sixteenth-century Spain were most renowned for the cure of cripples,[10] Loyola's visit is unlikely a disinterested piety. The shrine at Aránzazu commemorated a shepherd's discovery of a resplendent image of the Madonna with a large cowbell at her side in a verdant hawthorn in the remote mountains. The history compared the shepherd to Moses on Horeb before the burning bush. The site was named etiologically from the Cantabrian Basque *aranza*, or "thorn," and the diction *çu*, or "wonderment,"[11] to express pious amazement that an image of the Madonna should appear in such a wild place. The location of the statue in a hawthorn (*espino*) derived from Mount Sinai, which medieval guidebooks for pilgrims interpreted as meaning "bramble."[12]

This local devotion replicated a common anthropological pattern. That was the discovery of images, either statues or paintings, by a male herder in a wild locale. Herders, as the wildest of men, who ventured into uncultivated places, were the intermediaries between society and nature. The image was typically located at apertures to the numinous:

caves and springs as openings to the underworld, or trees and mountaintops to the sky as at Aránzazu in a shrub in the mountains. Such findings, which were popularly considered miraculous, mediated through the images between the local populace and the forces of nature, particularly the weather. It was consistent that the inaugural miracle through the intercession of Our Lady of Aránzazu was to bring rain to the region. An image of the Madonna, the mother with child, symbolized natural creativity.[13] It was also religiously consistent that shepherds should be its discoverers, for they had first sought and adored that living image at the Nativity (Luke 2:8–20).[14]

The archetype of this site was announced in the preface by the dating of the conversation in the garden between Gonçalves da Câmara and Loyola as "the fourth of August, the vigil of the feast of Our Lady of the Snows."[15] This time is a rhetorical place. Our Lady of the Snows was not venerated explicitly in the universal liturgical calendar. The medieval feast was and still is celebrated among Spaniards in a mountainous locale at Espinosa de los Monteros, about 100 kilometers north of Burgos[16] and the same distance from Loyola's native seat near Azpeitia in Guizpúcoa. The celebration seems to have been in the sixteenth century more rowdy than religious. The diocesan synod of Burgos in 1511 denounced parochial pilgrimages to such shrines, for they produced pitched battles between the local people and the mass procession. Pilgrims were forbidden to move with arms, hurdy-gurdies, or drums.[17]

That local feast of Our Lady of the Snows is a celebration by shepherds in the roles of the principal performers. They praise the Madonna of nature, who sends rain miraculously to melt the snows on Monte Esquilino (Sheep-shearing) and to cause grasses to grow in the pasturages to the content of the highlanders. The municipality of Espinosa de los Monteros, because of the pure-blooded nobility of its populace, had a claim as the home of its eponymous *monteros*. Those were originally the medieval masters of the royal hunt; later under Alonso VII, the guards of the king's private chambers. Of anthropological interest are the regional highlanders, who were granted by the Crown extensive grazing privileges and whose major permanently settled center is at the convergence of four rivers, Las Machorras.[18] It was legendarily to such a shepherd that there appeared in the summer pasturages, or variously in a hawthorn, a large image of the Madonna.[19] On the eve of the feast, the date of the seminal conversation in the garden between Gonçalves da Câmara and Loyola, the performers hold a general rehearsal, and the village youths plant in the plaza before the church the maypole, a tall tree trunk festooned with a banner.[20] The feast is celebrated with a pilgrimage of about 6 kilometers to the hermitage of Nuestra Señora de las Nieves at Las Machorras. Its custom is the public recital of couplets, some improvised to entertain the natives, others traditional to honor the Madonna.[21]

These couplets define the boundaries of her cult as within the compass of a few miles from the site.[22] Puns on the grandeur of her apparition argue, however, that this is but a local version of a universal devotion. One couplet proclaims: "The best (*la mejor*) of your miracles was your holy apparition the fifth of August with a burning sun." Another: "Of all the miracles which cause wonder in the churches of the world, this is the greatest (*el mayor*)." Still another couplet betrays the Madonna's identity from her Roman provenance: "From the banks of the Tiber, crossing immense plains, you came to establish your throne in these grand heights."[23] She is the mother of God, in whose honor the basilica of S. Maria Maggiore in Rome was rebuilt by Pope Sixtus III as a "trophy" of her definition by the Council of Ephesus. That was the principal and perhaps most ancient church dedicated solemnly to the cult of the Virgin, one of the five patriarchal basilicas and seven principal churches of the city. Almost every historical discussion of it began with its legendary foundation, the miracle of the snow. On the night between the fourth and fifth of August, ca. 352 A.D., the Virgin appeared in a vision to Pope Liberius and instructed him to erect a church in her honor on the site where snow would cover the ground in the morning. The Virgin similarly appeared to a Roman patrician and his infertile wife to direct their investment of money in the church. In collaboration the pope marked at the snowy spot on the Esquiline the designated plan of the church. The Marian selection of the site and the miracle of the snow, depicted on an elaborate mosaic in the church, made it the focal point of the Western cult of the mother of God.[24]

Monte Esquilino, which she favors with sun rather than snow, is the local version of the Esquiline hill in Rome on which that church was erected. Spanish devotion translated her cult from the polluted snow of that city to the pristine snow of mountain peaks and rural solitudes, because the spotless snow of remote locales was deemed the most expressive symbol of the purity of the Virgin immaculate. Hundreds of appellations throughout Spain of church, chapel, altar, or statue are to Nuestra Señora de las Nieves, with five sites of her cult in Loyola's native Guizpúcoa.[25] St. Mary Major (Santa María la Mayor), feted at Las Machorras, is the patronal saint of the archdiocese of Burgos and of its cathedral, which displays centrally in the retable of the main altar her sumptuous, bejeweled silver statue.[26] The association of the Society of Jesus with the archdiocese was definite. The Jesuits settled in Burgos for apostolic activity in the autumn of 1550; and in 1553, the year of the conversation between Gonçalves da Câmara and Loyola, there arrived to inaugurate worship in that residence none other personage than the namer of the garden in Rome in which they spoke, Francis Borgia. The Society of Jesus had just been invited to settle in Burgos by the cardinal archbishop; its residence there was secured by a canon of the cathedral; and when Borgia inaugurated worship in that house the chapter of the cathedral lent its best ornaments for the solemnity.[27]

The iconography of this regional cult of the Virgin "with a burning sun," legendarily appearing in a hawthorn, specifies a privilege that was to secure its most effective promoters in the Jesuits.[28] Its types are the Virgin in the sun, developed from the apocalyptic woman (Rev. 12:1–6), and the Virgin in the burning bush, developed from the hierophany to Moses (Ex. 3:1–6). These types were appropriated as versions of the theologically controversial Virgin immaculate.[29] The Virgin in the sun was especially popular as a private image for devotion, owing to its indulgence of eleven thousand years instituted by Pope Sixtus IV, who established two offices for the new, much debated feast of the immaculate conception.[30] The modern commemorative statue of Our Lady of the Snows at Espinosa de los Monteros[31] is consistent with this iconography. It is of the type of the Virgin with playing child derived from a Byzantine icon,[32] which by late in the fifteenth century merged with the Virgin in the sun to become an image of the Virgin immaculate.[33] Her appellation in the local festal couplet as "white dove" is also consistently symbolic.[34] The conflation of Mary Major with the Virgin immaculate is coherent, since it was in anticipation of her role as mother of God that she was argued to have been created immaculate, singularly preserved from the effects of original sin.

The honor of the Virgin immaculate, conceived without original sin, is the epideictic antithesis to the blame of Gonçalves da Câmara as he confesses to Loyola in the garden on her vigil. The moral nature of the text is particularly revealed by the popular feature of that feast, the regional dancing. The festival is conducted by eleven dancers supervised by the principals, two gallant youths as chief shepherds and a boy fool. To the sound of flageolet and tamboril they perform during Mass before the Madonna's altar, in a nearby field, and in the processional to the hermitage. While their instrument in church is a large wooden sheepshears, the outstanding dances outdoors are all performed with sticks. As commonly performed in Spain at summer festivals, these rustic dances are defined in their movements as warlike. A simpler version of the sword dance, they are of primitive origin, perhaps in the diversion of soldiers during their brief periods of rest. Executed only at religious festivals, the dances with sticks are believed to symbolize the conflict between good and evil.[35]

When at the climax of the text Loyola will discern his alluring apparition as the devil in disguise, he will reject it with the *bordón* he usually carries.[36] This is no common stick picked off the ground but a pilgrim's staff. It also names the stick with which is performed this military dance during summer religious festivals in many parts of Spain, the *danza de bordones,* or in his Guizpúcoa, the *pordon-dantza.* This dance is still the activity of the males of the province on the feast of St. John the Baptist on 24 June to commemorate the victory of the Guizpúcoans over the Navarrese in the fourteenth-century battle of Beobíbar. Twenty-four youths perform, at their head four who carry halberds and a crier who bears an unsheathed sword covered with carnations and roses. The festival is not only in its solar, vegetal, and aquatic associations for preservation against evils, but also a bellicose recounting of armed force with a danced review of soldiers.[37] It is on this very feast that Loyola in the castle makes his confession on the verge of death.[38]

The movements of this stick dance as mimetic of war provide a cultural context for his ultimate moral struggle between good and evil. In medieval art the Virgin herself was frequently depicted as chasing the devil with a whip, scourge, sword, scepter, club, or stick (*Virgo,* "virgin," and *virga,* "rod"), an attribute adopted by the promoters of her cause as the immaculate.[39] Her association in this act with the dance is coherent. In sixteenth-century Spain national unification promoted a tremendous resurgence of robust and ebullient folk dancing, from a pride in customs that swept across social barriers. Popular dancing extraordinarily influenced all other forms, especially from its constant employment in religious plays, pageants, and processionals. In a contemporaneous *auto sacramentale* Mary and Jesus dance a duet in anger at the preference of the crowd at a fairground for the seven deadly sins, then drive them offstage with whips.[40] Loyola's motion toward the devil with the stick shares the military origin of the regional religious dances; yet it implies a certain grace, a bodily grace that intimates a spiritual grace, much like the issue of Gonçalves da Câmara's comportment of the eyes. As a renaissance treatise on dancing explained, "The virtue of dancing is as an action demonstrative of spiritual movement."⁴¹ Thus is intimated in the dating of the seminal conversation for this recital as "the fourth of August, the vigil of Our Lady of the Snows"⁴² a plot centered on the moral contest between good and evil, as if danced with a militant grace.

Pilgrims commonly made an itinerary of devotions by visiting the sanctuaries along the route to their final destination.⁴³ The initial place of Loyola's pilgrimage after his ascetic conversion, the mountainous shrine of Our Lady of Arançuz, reveals the primitive origins of his religious experience. Despite all the intellectual knowledge that a master of arts in philosophy from the University of Paris, or the cultural sophistication of an institution in renaissance Rome, may imply, Loyola's recital will conclude as it began: with a powerful image from nature. It was at that Marian shrine that Jesuit tradition has located his vow of chastity.⁴⁴ Although there is no evidence for this attribution, there is plausibility, for Marian shrines in cathedrals and monasteries, then in rural chapels, became centers of devotion based on vows.⁴⁵ The notoriety of Marian shrines in Spain for the cure of cripples suggests the rhetorical coherence of a vow of chastity against leggy lust.

Loyola parts at Oñate with his brother, who was to visit there the home of a sister.⁴⁶ This is a mnemonic marker, for the town is a place for the veneration of Our Lady of the Snows. In the cloister of the parish church in a vaulted niche is a statue with the Basque title of Our White Lady, while on the predella of the major retable and on a panel in relief is depicted the legendary apparition of St. Mary of the Snows.⁴⁷ Loyola's separation from familial affections is a choice of Hercules on the road. Proceeding to Navarrete, he collects some money owed him by the duke and disperses it between personal obligations and the adornment of a statue of the Virgin.⁴⁸ This transition from the Marian shrine to the ducal treasury, from piety to money, is also culturally coherent. Well-tended shrines with the promise of miracles meant to a region more business for its merchants, more construction for its laborers, Masses for its priests, and documents for its notaries. It was as if there were a contractual relationship of clientele and patronage between a social group and a sacred protector.⁴⁹ The Iberian economy depended on wool for the principal export of raw material from Castile and for the principal industry of textile weaving in Catalonia,⁵⁰ so that the supposed miraculous findings of shepherds were scarcely negligible. Manresa, the place of Loyola's supreme enlightenment, was one of the most important provincial centers of woolen manufacture. The Church benefitted from the expansion of the industry, since the demand for wool meant an increase in flocks, and the need for pasturage meant returns in ecclesiastical grazing land.⁵¹ A blessing of the Virgin on a shepherd in a pasturage portended for the populace material prosperity, not only spiritual blessing. It was thus coherent to invest money in return on the decoration of her image. Yet Loyola is still absorbed in appearances, in how the embellished image of the Virgin will reflect on his own reputation as a donor.⁵²

Here he relinquishes, however, the last vestiges of social status, as he bids farewell to his two servants and departs from Navarrete toward Montserrat "alone on the mule."⁵³ Since roads were uncertain and unsafe, pilgrims avoided traveling alone.⁵⁴ There were criminal codes and ecclesiastical censures against the molestation of travelers, and a papal bull *In coena Domini* anathematized the molestation of pilgrims. Yet pilgrims were fair game for the unscrupulous, and Basque villagers were notorious for robbing them on the road to Compostela.⁵⁵ Loyola's foolhardiness in solo adventure involves him in serious temptation. As he travels there overtakes him a Moor, a soldier also on a mule. Conversing they begin to speak of the Virgin.⁵⁶ The common greeting in Spanish streets was "Hail, Mary, most pure," with the response "Conceived without sin."⁵⁷ Their conversational subject develops into a complicated argument about her perpetual virginity, which the Moor disbelieves, while the Christian believes. Unpersuaded by Loyola's piety, the Moor spurs his beast to high speed until he is lost from sight. Reflecting on their argument, Loyola is visited by inclinations that make him discontent in soul, for it seems to him that in his tolerance of the Moor's speech he has failed to do his duty. These inclinations also cause him to feel indignant toward the Moor and obliged to restore the Virgin's "honor." Desires penetrate him to seek out the Moor and poniard him.⁵⁸

Dishonor to women, which ranged from insult to rape, always cast aspersions on sexual conduct or condition, for that was the singular basis of female honor in the Spanish kingdoms. Inaccessibility as chastity established their honor. Sexual slander demeaned women socially by blackening their name, compromising dignity and self-esteem, and destroying reputation. An ugly insult such as "whore" to a woman of repute legally required the payment of damages and the retraction of the affront.⁵⁹ A woman's sexual status also defined the social status of her male relations. She was part of their patrimony in her control of the lineage, as the bearer of the sons who made the family viable economically and politically.⁶⁰ An insult to her dishonored her protectors in the eyes of others by the ancient norm "what people will say." If sexual purity was the role of women of honor, the duty of its defense was the role of men. An unavenged affront to a woman—mother, wife, daughter, sister—desecrated male honor and was the equivalent of cowardice. Honor was susceptible to defilement or stain that required purification.[61] Although penalties were imposed for insults, and lawsuits were instigated, it was common among those who prided themselves on their worth to take justice into their own hands without recourse to law. This was frequently done with the assistance of lineage or kin. It was sufficient in tense situations for an insulted, outraged, or affronted man, especially in Basque territory, to holler for family—"Loyola! Loyola!"—so that they would rush to arm in defense.[62] The Moor's argument that the Madonna was defiled or stained sexually is culturally the archetypal affront to women and it requires Loyola's vengeance of his celestial mother's "honor."

Yet pursuit with intent to wound was also an "outrage," legally an action dishonoring a person without plausible reason.[63] The "natural reasons" the Moor presses in argumentation[64] are stereotypical of Islamic logic. The question of the perpetual virginity of Mary was not conciliarly defined, only theologically debated. It did not establish the Christian norm of orthodoxy nor provide a license for stabbing. Since the Qurān denies the divinity of Christ, it disallows Mary the title "mother of God." It does teach her virginity, however, although Muslims in the sixteenth century disagreed about whether that virginity was perpetual.[65]

The epithet with which Loyola dubs his antagonist is socially shameful. This "Moor" (*Moro*) is a Christian. Historically there were no Moors in Spain at this date. Ordinances beginning in 1501 enforced the baptism or expulsion of all Muslims from Spain following national reunification. The converts, usually termed *Moriscos*, were also known derogatorily as *Moros, Muhammadanes, Hagaranes* (after Hagar), and *Saracenos*, despite their baptism. Such appellations were applied scurrilously and indiscriminately throughout the sixteenth century, regardless of the sincerity of an individual's conversion. The terminology demeaned the converts by distinguishing them as "new" from the original or "old" Christians. Considered still aliens and heretics, they were marginalized or ostracized by legal edicts and by popular action, such as harassment by disorderly soldiers. Except for some romances about the frontier in which the converts were portrayed as chivalrous, they were ridiculed as an abomination to be eradicated,[66] precisely Loyola's intention.

The Moor symbolizes the infidel who must be convinced or killed, an attitude opposite to Loyola's maturer social justice, which will establish in Rome a house for Muslims seeking conversion to Christianity.[67] Here the encounter, or conflict, is potentially antagonistic, a mock imitation of the epic battles of the Cid and the romantic chivalric lists. In the medieval visionary allegory of pilgrimage such an opposition of believers was polemical. In Huon de Méri's poem, *Tournoiement Antichrist*, the hero as Everyman quit a war and entered a forest, where he encountered a Moor, Bras-de-fer (Iron Arms), a harbinger of Antichrist. The Moor only vanished after the hero witnessed a vision of the vices and virtues in processional and confessed his amorous sins.[68] The inclusion of the episode with the "Moor" reinforces Loyola's agonistic character introduced at the siege of Pamplona and it orients his pilgrimage within the chivalric traditions of epic and romance. It also serves an apologetic purpose to ensure Loyola's orthodoxy and loyalty to the papacy, for on 7 August 1555, during the recital of this very text, Pope Paul IV condemned those who disbelieved the perpetual virginity of Mary.[69]

It is not fortuitous that the subject of dissent is her "honor," for Loyola introduced himself as vaingloriously pursuing through combat "honor." Honor connoted in classical Latin respect, esteem, prestige. Two ideas developed in medieval society that distinguished its vernacular usage, however. Both restricted the ethical principle of classical antiquity that community was primarily citizenship. Those ideas were the barbarian sentiment of pride of blood and the Christian conviction that the righteous composed a community of faith. The lapse or even apostasy of the converted Muslims in Spain provoked an apologetic controversy and created a social class within the community of the faithful. That distinction between the "new" and the "old" Christians was allied with lineage and faction. The Inquisition, which was established to terminate the ensuing rivalries and riots—to prevent unjust persecution of the "new" Christians by the "old," while punishing severely any guilty apostates—condoned statutes of blood.

Those statues, which excluded the descendants of condemned apostates, and even without qualification any "new" Christians, penetrated tenantry and township, religious and military orders, cathedrals, professional guilds, and brotherhoods. Spain in the sixteenth century was socially dominated by a preoccupation with purity or cleanliness of blood (*limpieza de sangre*) and with impurity, stain, and blot. Purity of blood was equated with honor; impurity, with dishonor and disqualification from the very competition for honors. Muslim blood in the lineage of a Christian was a shame.[70] This was an extension to the ecclesiastical community of a pride of lineage that was tenacious among the Basques. In his history of the northern regions, *Las bienandanzas e fortunas*, Lope García de Salazar included the Loyola family. "The Lot (*solar*) of Loyola is an ancient lot and lineage." In his chronicle of the notorious atrocities of the Basques in the name of such honor he included the blood feud of Lope García de Loyola, which resulted in "many deaths and murders."[71] Vengeance for impurity of blood was in Loyola's bloodline.

The episode on the road with the "Moor" is a compelling profile of his native character. The Madonna must be avenged not merely because she is his sentimental Lady but also because the "Moor"'s disbelief in her perpetual virginity is the absolute affront to her honor. It is precisely her virginal womb that is the archetype of purity of blood: her blood conceived without stain of original sin and Jesus' blood conceived in hers, unmixed with any other human lineage. This purity exists not only for the Church but especially for the Society of Jesus. Loyola will found his company in the name of Jesus, who received his name at his circumcision, the ritual shedding of his blood in the temple that prefigured the redemptive shedding of his blood on the cross. That blood of the Savior was created in the womb of Mary, the immaculate one, ever virgin, the ultimate guarantor of purity in spiritual lineage. That social and religious complex of values, in which Gothic blood was better than Muslim blood, explains the "Moor"'s affront as the gravest possible. He who lacks purity of blood insults her who is the fountain of all purity of blood.

Although Loyola's mental agitation about the issue tenaciously persists, in the end he lapses into doubt about what he ought to do. The "Moor," who has ridden on, mentioned his destination as a place a little ahead on the same road, quite near to the highway but not intersecting it. Weary of examining what would be the good choice, and of not finding any definite resolution, Loyola decides on this: to let go of the reins of his mule until the crossroads. If the mule should take the road to town, he will seek out the "Moor" and poniard him; if it should choose the highway, he will let the "Moor" go free. Loyola acts upon his thoughts. And God wills that, although the village is only about thirty or forty paces on and the road toward it is very wide and very good, the mule takes to the highway and leaves behind the route to the village and the "Moor."[72] This is another choice of Hercules at the crossroads.

With it Loyola transcends the agonistic social values of honor and shame and initiates the missionary model for the Society of Jesus as acculturation. No important religious community suffered more in sixteenth-century Spain from the social obsession with purity of blood than the Jesuits. Loyola's intimates Diego Laínez and Juan de Polanco, who served the Society as second General and as personal secretary, were *conversos*, or converted Jews. Because of the inclusive policy of the Society, its initial attempts to establish in Spain were met from 1551–52 with the hostility of an interdict and with the further penalty of excommunication and fine for anyone assisting their infringement of it. The Jesuits lost many candidates among the Spanish nobility to orders like the Dominicans, who accepted only caballeros. To profess as a Jesuit was to commit "dishonor," to be stained as a "Jew." It was only in 1593 that the Society yielded to the social prejudice and adopted a statute of blood, its first deviation from the *Constitutiones* as composed by Loyola.[73] By its rule candidates are still to be questioned about whether they are established Christians or recent converts.[74]

The medieval *Disciplina clericalis*, a collection of oriental tales mediated to Christian piety by a converted Spanish Jew, reflected on such traveling as Loyola's in an alien society. "A philosopher said: 'Do not undertake a journey with anyone unless you know him already! If someone that you do not know joins you *en route*, and enquires after your proposed journey, tell him that you wish to go further than you have decided. If he draws a lance on you, turn to the right and if a sword, turn to the left.' " An Arab admonished, " 'My son, if on a journey with a fellow traveller, love him as yourself, and think not to deceive a person, lest you too be deceived.' " Its counsel not to leave the highway also proved prudent by experience. As the Arab continued, " 'Follow the main roads even if they are a longer way round than the footpaths.' "[75]

Loyola's dropped reins are also imitative. In sixteenth-century art Fortune at her wheel was depicted with a bridle around her neck, a bit her mouth, and her reins in God's hand extending from heaven. Or she was emblematized as fallen from a broken wheel attached to heaven by a cord and the motto "Fortune in the world is nothing; God governs all."[76] Adventure, the hub of chivalric activity in attempting to right wrong, involved the real danger of homicide, just as Loyola meditates. The episode with the "Moor" decisively imitates the judgment in Wolfram von Eschenbach's romance *Parzival*, in which its celebrated knight also dropped his reins. The action was another type of the choice of Hercules.[77] Parzival's horse, guided by no man's hand, took him through

The Ascetic 65

a wild, deserted region straight to Munsalvæsche, the castle of the Grail. Later after he failed the test there, his plea for "the highest hand" again to guide his horse led him providentially to the cell of Trevrizent the hermit. The poet celebrated the divine willingness to guide a knight who trusted in him by abandoning his reins. The divine control of Parzival's travels was marvelously revealed in his arrival at the right destination by the wrong paths.[78] He was guided by the God of the Pilgrims.[79] The reinless riding also graced him to avoid a tragic encounter in mortal combat with the knights of the Grail, who warded off all intruders to the territory. By his reinless riding Parzival preternaturally penetrated to the castle, while avoiding the enemy and the sin of homicide. God decided for Parzival without bloodshed,[80] as he does for Loyola.

Loyola thus arrives at a large town where he purchases for the costume he intends to wear to Jerusalem some sackcloth, a pilgrim's staff, and a small gourd. He places it all before the saddlebow of the mule and makes his way to the monastery of Montserrat, musing as usual on the deeds he must perform for the love of God. Since his mind is crammed with the affairs of *Amadís de Gaula* and similar romances, similar deeds occur to him. He determines to guard his weapons an entire night, neither sitting nor lying but either standing or kneeling, before the celebrated altar of Our Lady of Montserrat. There he intends to divest himself and put on the arms of Christ. Thinking on these proposals, he arrives at the monastery.[81] He may be imagined, like the noble in Bartolomé Bermejo's panel of the Madonna of Montserrat, utterly devoted.[82]

After prayer and arrangement with the confessor for pilgrims, he writes down for three days a general confession of sin.[83] Loyola's act of recollection comprising his recital becomes explicitly confessional as he labors to transfer his sins from the metaphorical tablet of memory to a literal piece of paper. Don Carnal (Lord Flesh) in *Libro de buen amor* ventured the same, only to be advised by a monk:

> "One cannot make confession in a letter or in writing,
> But only through the very lips of a sinner who's contrite.
> One cannot be absolved or freed of sin by written papers;
> Words said to holy confessor are essential to the rite."[84]

Yet the practice of bringing written notes to confession was recommended for those penitents who confessed infrequently, either by annual obligation or less often.[85] Its popularity was suggested by the entry in first place in *Libro de enxemplos* of the moral tale about the bishop who pardoned a sinner because there were tears on his written confession.[86] The practice led to abuse, as in the hagiography of the saint whose daily examination of conscience to jot down sins for a weekly confession ran wild. His habit became one of listing sins anywhere, anytime—before a hearth, in his oratory, during studies; even during travel one of his servants carried the discreetly folded scraps of paper detailing his offenses.[87] At his death a chest was discovered full of his lists of sins.[88] The practice establishes Loyola's scrupulosity.

Loyola also arranges with the confessor to shelter his mule and to have his sword and poniard hung in the church at the Madonna's altar, in the fashion of a votive offering. On the eve of the feast of Our Lady of March in the year 1522 he steals as secretly as possible to a pauper, before whom he strips and to whom he donates his clothing. Vested in sackcloth as planned, he returns to the Madonna's altar, where he keeps vigil, sometimes kneeling, sometimes standing, with his pilgrim's staff before the gold and polychromed but blackened statue.[89] Investiture with the arms of Christ was an elaborate topic derived from Ephesians 6:13–18 and developed in Prudentius's *Psychomachia*, since virtues protected the pilgrim, especially the type of the Christian soldier, from his spiritual enemies.[90] In *Pèlerinage de vie humaine* the guide invested the pilgrim not only with scrip and staff, but also with an array of armor: the gambeson of patience, the helmet of temperance, the gorget of sobriety, the gloves of continence, the sword of righteousness, the scabbard of humility, the girdle of perseverance, and the shield of prudence. Only his legs and feet remained unencumbered to facilitate flight from lust. The pilgrim was so burdened that in disgust at the weight of his armor he peevishly cast it all off, down to his drawers and stockings.[91]

This Marian vigil of Loyola was intimated in his conversation with Gonçalves da Câmara on the vigil of the feast of Our Lady of the Snows. The episode plots the reversal typical of medieval hagiography, in which the sinner became a penitent—as the merchant an almsgiver, or the lecher a eunuch, while the scholar pledged his pen to the Trinity and the knight his sword to Mary. There was the soldier who renounced his profession because of a dream about the pains of hell after he was almost killed in battle. There was the equestrian who exchanged his horse for a donkey and lived a penitential inversion of his worldly adventures. A knight who prayed to the Virgin before a tournament pledged himself to her service as a monk when she favored him in the jousting. A noble was converted from knightly pride to saintly humility; when summoned to a bishopric, he placed his sword upon the altar in dedication of his life to the Virgin.[92]

At dawn Loyola departs from the monastery stealthily on foot, traveling not by the road straight to Barcelona, where many would recognize and "honor" him, but detouring to the town of Manresa. There he intends to stay in a hospice for several days and to note some items in his copybook of consolations, which he carries very protectively. Only a league distant from Montserrat a man in hot pursuit overtakes him and questions him whether he has indeed given clothing to a pauper, as the pauper claims. As Loyola responds affirmatively, tears stream from his eyes in compassion for the pauper, for he realizes that his charity has involved the man in an accusation of theft.[93]

In lives of male saints the occasion of sin was an alien agent (in contrast to lives of female saints, where it was a domestic parasite). A knight's pride was a condition he could shed, like his armor.[94] Yet such external divestment proves ineffective for Loyola; it only exacerbates his temptation to vainglory. Loyola's social position, although as a soldier in active service he is at the least rank of nobility (*caballero*),[95] involves him in a dilemma. As Montaigne would shrewdly observe, "A man may be humble through vainglory."[96] The more assiduously Loyola shuns to be seen, the more others regard his asceticism. His tentative experiments in virtue—in keeping his plans secret except to the single confessor at Montserrat, in stealing about in charity to the pauper, or in keeping vigil in prayer to the Madonna under cover of dark—only betray him. And, as much as he flees esteem, he will regret that he is able to do little in Manresa without people remarking great things, as originating in the opinion formed at Montserrat. "Fame increased to declare more than what he was," that he had relinquished quite an income and other rumors.[97] Since the word "honor" was commonly employed as an equivalent of inheritance or patrimony,[98] Loyola in abandoning his family renounces not only property but also honor. The resolution of the dilemma about praise will prove to be his recommendation to Gonçalves da Câmara in the garden to "refer everything to God";[99] that is, not to hide good deeds from the public but to attribute them publicly to grace.

Loyola realizes from the accusation of theft against the pauper that he has only benefited him to his own benefit. His donation of clothing was a conventional token of piety.[100] It was also a temptation to vainglory. Medieval allegories of the virtues and vices contrasted vainglory with fear of the Lord, representing it artistically by examples reminiscent of the scriptural injunction to secret almsgiving (Matt. 6:1–4). The vainglorious man attempted to arouse admiration by showering gifts on a cripple; the God-fearing man, while engaged in conversation with a companion, secretly slipped alms into a beggar's hand.[101] Before Loyola, such saints of the nobility as Martin of Tours and Francis of Assisi had famously given away their cloaks.[102] St. Rayner at his conversion removed his clothing in full view of an astonished crowd, gave it to beggars, and had a priest invest him at the altar in a pilgrim's tunic.[103] The faithful reveled in such tales of the ascetic who shared his cloak or his crust with an even poorer soul,[104] so that Loyola's gesture was certain, if not calculated, to promote gossip. His charity was common, cheap enough, since cloth was the basic mercantile commodity of that province.[105] On this spot in the road commences his conversion, however. Its sign is still external but not sackcloth. It is tears. The tears that he had checked, unexpressed in physical pain during the operation on his legs or in spiritual compunction during his general confession, now spill.

Although for centuries it had been a commonplace that it was the monastic vocation to weep,[106] the devotion was universalized by late medieval piety. It promoted an affective meditation on the passion of Christ and an exorbitant vogue for penitence, as if to remedy the horrific historical calamities of pestilence and war. Although the religious phenomenon of tears was ancient, and even God was precedent (in scripture Jesus wept), the hagiography recorded a profuse and frequent weeping of intense fervor.[107] The depiction of tears became a contemporary phenomenon. Although weeping was literarily described as an ascetic practice and a spiritual gift, even in medieval manuscript illustrations of sadness other gestures were employed. Weeping was initially indicated by the gesture of a hand or scarf wiping or dabbing at the eyes. Only with the intensely affective devotion to Christ's passion did an artist like Rogier van der Weyden paint a tear rolling like a liquid pearl down a cheek. Yet the saintly faces that wept in paintings were never contorted by their crying, as in actual physiognomy; they remained ideally serene.[108]

With his tearful release of "compassion" for the innocent pauper, Loyola assumes the role of the hero, for if heroes were limpers, they were also weepers. Tears were not only the gift of saints but also the badge of heroes. There were shed many literary tears: tears of mourners in the consolatory genre, tears of lovers in a variety of poetry and prose, sentimental tears, and even intellectual tears.[109] Yet tears were particularly heroic. All of the great heroes of the *Iliad* wept as a sign of an active, energetic, viril suffering. The badge of tears was one of the elements that constituted their heroic nature. In the Homeric epics masculine tears were never a sign of weakness but a manifestation of force and vitality.[110] Roman men also wept in a public show of emotion. The nobility approved of an exaggerated and ostentatious display that was artificially induced. Weeping encompassed pleading, repenting, and longing, with the responsive audience also bursting into sympathetic tears.[111] In the medieval epic the weeping of heroes was commonplace: they wept in impatience and wrath, in discouragement and despair, in tenderness and compassion.[112] The pages of Loyola's favorite chivalric romance, *Amadís de Gaula*, are soaked in tears.

Here on the road from Montserrat to Manresa is Loyola's introduction to the complexity of conscientious emotion. In the castle he naively identified, by his responses to his religious fantasies, consolation with good—with the vision of the Madonna effecting in his soul "extreme consolation"—and desolation with evil.[113] In asceticism certain emotions were identified as moral indicators, as if symptomatic of the presence of good or evil spirits. A traditional criterion for a vision of a good spirit was initially fear, then pleasure and consolation. The test was current, practiced in the interrogations of the Inquisition.[114] Yet Loyola's conversion from confrontation to compassion disproves that simplistic equation. His emotional sadness, expressed in piteous and remorseful weeping for the pauper, becomes the very sign of his new moral felicity.

Loyola's next place—Manresa—is introduced by cataloguing his ascetic practices. The introduction of his daily begging for alms[115] follows immediately upon the report of rumors from Montserrat about his fame: how he relinquished a large inheritance.[116] His begging imitates the topic of vainglory in Augustine's *Confessions*, which observed that deeds known to men tempt from love of praise, "which gathers approving opinions as a beggar does alms, for the sake of a certain personal importance." The temptation remained active even when reproved by oneself, precisely because it was reproved. As Augustine explained, "Often, a man may become more vainglorious because of his very contempt for vainglory; thus, it is no longer because of contempt for glory that he glories, for when he glories, he does not contemn it."[117] Loyola's contest with vainglory at Manresa is disclosed during a fever to the point of death. There occurs to him the thought that he is just; he cannot repel it for all his might. When the fever slightly subsides, he implores his nurses, should he again approach death, to shout loudly to him, calling him a sinner and reminding him of his offenses before God.[118] He echoes the desert father who, even if the patriarchs should appear and declare to him, "You are just," would lack confidence.[119] The surfacing of vainglory in Loyola's crisis dramatizes his contest with the vice at the place Manresa.

Because, as was fashionable, Loyola has been quite fastidious in caring for his good head of hair, he decides to let it down "naturally," without grooming it, or cutting it, or covering it with anything by day or night. For the same reason he lets his toenails and fingernails grow, because he has also been neat in manicuring them.[120] Disdain for the body, signified by letting hair and nails grow freely, was since early medieval accounts a mark of the penitential pilgrim.[121] Just as Loyola disclosed his physical stature of lameness only in a moral context, however, so is this further detail about his good head of hair not flatly factual but also moral. The historiographic description of personal physique is absent from this text. In epideictic rhetoric the body is less physiological than moral, and its parts all display lessons. In appearance Loyola becomes something of a "wild man," that late medieval literary and artistic invention who differed from other men in the thick coat of hair, filthy and matted with dirt and debris, that covered his entire body. His universal attribute of a club is substituted here with the pilgrim's staff Loyola carries in hand. The wild man personified social outcasts. His iconographic convention of disheveled hair derived from ancient ancestors—in classical mythology from Hercules wearing the pelt of the Nemean lion, brandishing an enormous cudgel, and performing feats of superhuman strength. Hirsute appearance also symbolized a debased mental state, since melancholy was associated with shagginess. The wild man was commonly identified with eremitical saints like Anthony, Onuphrius, Mary Magdalene, and John Chrysostom in penitence.[122]

Loyola's mimicry of the appearance of the ancient ascetics betrays his puerile misjudgment of spirituality. He punishes external vanities about his body with external penances to it. Long hair and a long beard growing from a serious, pale face were indeed one of the external badges by which a pilgrim could be recognized.[123] Yet it was not the common decency. As Erasmus instructed in his manual on manners: "It is boorish to go about with one's hair uncombed: it should be neat, but not as elaborate as a girl's coiffure.... The hair should neither cover the brow nor flow down over the shoulders. To be constantly tossing the hair with the flick of the head is for frolicsome horses. It is not very elegant to brush back the hair from the forehead with the left hand; it is more discreet to part it with the hand." Hair was also to be clean, free of

The Ascetic

nits.[124] As for Loyola's lack of manicure, it was considered medically important to clean one's nails, for dirt under them was dangerous when scratching at vermin. The practice at table of taking food from a common dish with the hands (the fork as an eating utensil existed in the sixteenth century only among the upper classes as a luxury)[125] also suggests that Loyola's asceticism is not socially nice. His practices are so obviously countercultural that his appearance is certain to be noticed as vainglorious. In *Libro de buen amor* the fate of Nebuchadnezzar for his vainglory was to grow long fingernails.[126]

Loyola's decision not to cover his head involves the value that initiated the text: honor. To expose the head was an offense to honor. The ritualistic bestowal of honor in his culture centered on the head of the protagonist, as in the crowning of the king to whom all honor ascended and from whom all honor descended socially. The payment of honor in daily life was through the offering of precedence and through the demonstrations of respect associated with the head, as to whether it was bowed, touched, covered or uncovered. Dishonor was also a heady affair, as in the decapitation of criminals or in the practice Jesuit missionaries would witness: scalping.[127] Hats were so important in designating social status that even naked persons—in the tub or in hellfire—were artistically depicted with them still on.[128] Hats were doffed, exchanged, demanded, stolen, and knocked off.[129] There were laws and penalties in the Spanish kingdoms for the provocative tousling—even touching—of hair; for men violating the taboo of the wifely toque; for women grabbing the hair or beard of men; and for women uncovering a married woman's head and revealing her hair, so demeaning her to the status of a girl (*manceba en cabellos*). Such humiliations were affronts to honor.[130]

Loyola down the road will commit such an affront to honor and later correct one. En route from Ferrara to Genoa he is arrested as a suspected spy and taken for interrogation to the captain of the guards in a town. He determines not to show him any mark of respect, even to take his hat off to him. The result is that he is judged a "madman" and "brainless."[131] (He was not unique in his affront: Michelangelo used to keep his hat on in the presence of popes and was judged barbarous for it.)[132] The affront about the head that Loyola addresses concerns the common practice in his native region of mistresses of the clergy shamelessly covering their heads for public acceptance as wives. He persuades the governor to legislate the just punishment of such offenders, so that the abuse begins to be eliminated by his intervention.[133] It was the Spanish custom regarding an adulteress to tear off her headdress at the city gates.[134]

Loyola's decision not to cover his head with anything by day or by night is an election of social dishonor. The sentiment that regulated the laws governing fame and infamy, as yielding honor and dishonor, was the sense of shame. Shame as the basis for an honorable life included not only sexual modesty but also reverence for the law, respect for parents, courtesy in address, and personal neatness in dress.[135] Loyola is deliberately being shameless, courting personal dishonor and social infamy. Yet his self-humiliation, invested in external appearance, proves not necessarily to be humility. Moralists censured as vanity, even vainglory, the excessive attention of males to grooming and admiring the self in a mirror. As Petrarch reminisced with his brother, "What should I say about the curling irons and the care we took of our hair? . . . What fear we felt that a single hair might fall out of place or that a light breeze might spoil our elaborate coiffures." Torture by pirates was preferable to the cruel pain inflicted by hairdressing. It was better to have hair neatly combed and gathered out of eyes and ears. Primping was the vanity of youths eager to be pleasing in the eyes of others, to be conspicuously pointed out by people saying, in the words of Seneca, " 'There he goes.' "[136]

Yet Seneca also argued the opposite. The subject of hair, which Loyola lets down "naturally," introduces a famous moral, the tonsorial topic. Among the ancient Stoics an index of a rigorist orientation was attitude toward matters tonsorial, with policy on hair indicating a general stance on the spectrum from asceticism to moderation. Epictetus and Musonius asserted that cosmetic practices such as cutting the hair and shaving the beard were unnatural and thus should be avoided. Seneca, who adopted a more moderate ethical position, criticized such unwillingness to resort to a barber and any other bizarre example of personal appearance. A man should be clean-shaven with neatly trimmed hair on his head and depilated armpits. As he argued with wit and acuity, the slob may be just as much a poseur as the fop. An unconventional appearance might mask a perverted desire for self-display. Such behavior, moreover, was unreasonable for the philosopher since it might alienate his audience. Deliberate lack of grooming by a sage was a sign neither of virtue nor of common sense. Christian theologians decisively shifted the original focus of this doctrine by applying it primarily to the censure of women and their vanities. Augustine, however, baptized it by immersion, rinsing every Stoic stain. In a handbook for some unruly monks in his diocese he criticized them for wearing their hair long. He accused them of masking their vices hypocritically by imitating the tonsorial practice of the

Judaic priesthood. He exhorted them to examine their souls, reform their lives, and cut their hair as a sign of humility.[137] It was classical morality that excessive carelessness was as reprehensible as excessive care.[138] With experience, Loyola matures toward such moderation. After he begins to be consoled by God and to see fruit in the souls for whom he is caring, he abandons his ascetic "extremes." He cuts his hair and nails.[139] Loyola's moral reform is exemplified in the *Constitutiones*. Jesuits are to maintain a good appearance, the better to edify others. Ugly men are constitutionally excluded from the Society,[140] in an application of the convention that ugliness was wickedness.[141]

Later, after Loyola's recovery from a violent illness that left him weak and subject to stomachaches, the ladies who have nursed him to health insist that he dress properly against the severity of the winter: clothing, hat, and shoes. They make him accept two brown doublets of bulky cloth and a matching cap.[142] Clothing was the body of the body and from it could be inferred a person's character, as instructed in Erasmus's manual on civility.[143] The function of a garment was traditionally to contribute to the making of a self-conscious, individual image, associated with all the other imaginative and idealized visualizations of the human body. Clothing derived its visual authenticity and importance from figurative art, so that a garment was more like a painting than like other household objects such as a chair. Personal preoccupation with the details of one's clothing indicated among the moralists a shallow heart and dull mind. Yet clothes were metaphors and illustrations. Clothes did not make the man but they were the image of the man. Clothes were like the conventions of literature whose canon had been assimilated by the public. They were a form of visual fiction.[144]

The early Christian artists borrowed from the clothes and attitudes of Roman statesmen and seers. They depicted Christ and the apostles in classical drapery, a convention that persisted in medieval practice and became codified as the suitable dress for holy persons. Renaissance artists developed this convention with an even more faithful imitation of antiquity, so that the long loose tunic with wide sleeves and a cloak slung over it was considered the correct dress for Jesus, the angels, and the saints. The adaptation associated draped cloth and lofty ideals. That idealization concealed the human body as wretched and silly, while conferring an ennobling and decorative dimension to it. Artists used cloth in such emphatic and expressive ways—for which there was a vogue in Spain—that the very presence of drapery, even in a portrait, inferred the solemnity of religion or allegory.[145]

When Loyola purchases cloth and has it made for his pilgrimage to Jerusalem into a long loose garment, in which he vests for the vigil at Montserrat,[146] he is in this idealized tradition of drapery. His was not the proper outfit for pilgrims to Jerusalem, who wore a tunic called a *sclavina*, a red cross, a cincture, and sandals.[147] The other usual attire of pilgrimage was a scrip, a soft pouch, usually of leather, for belongings; a staff; and, by then, a great broadbrim turned up at front.[148] Loyola is projecting the image of a holy man, although his garment to the feet is only covering up the scarred legs on which he spiritually, as well as physically, limps. He eschews the basic item in the renaissance male wardrobe, the shirt. It was a simple rectangle, which could be of fine white cloth or of coarse heavy material like linen or hemp. Since it was worn next to the skin, hygiene depended on this garment, which could be washed frequently, unlike lined overgarments of wool or silk. Pilgrims to Jerusalem from Venice were advised to take three or four dozen shirts to provide them with a fresh garment for each day of the journey.[149]

Castiglione noted that sobriety was characteristic of the Spaniards in clothing.[150] Personal neatness and proper dress were part of the national sentiment of shame as allied with honor.[151] Yet Loyola's purchase of cloth sufficient for only one garment, necessarily worn daily, is austere. Even the basic monastic rule provided for a nightly change of clothing.[152] Loyola's singular robe is certain to be smelled as well as seen. Erasmus wrote on manners that clothing should not be conspicuous by its shabbiness.[153] There was parallel to the tonsorial topic the sartorial topic, in which disarrayed clothing, like disheveled hair, signified not wisdom but vainglory. In the Spanish kingdoms social distinctions were apparent in dress to display rank, so that since medieval times there were sumptuary laws against excessive personal expenditure on appearance.[154] Dressing finely was considered among moralists a sign of vainglory.[155] Yet so could dressing shabbily.

Although Loyola's vestment in sackcloth divests him of the social status of the soldier, it invests him in the superior status of the ascetic. He spends less money on sackcloth than on silk but gains in stature by his apparent imitation of the saints. With the acceptance of the doublets Loyola acquires some sense about religiosity, if only on the authoritative orders of confessors and nurses. He is still concerned about self-image, as betrayed by his recital of the details of the color and texture of the cloth, and even the fashion of the coordinated doublet and cap. Spanish confessional manuals declared that if a male sought, or even spoke about, novel fashions, so as to appear more excellent than others or so

The Ascetic 75

that others should notice him, it was a sin.[156] His cap, especially a knitted beret, was merely fashionable. The doublet was condemned by moralists, because as a short, tight garment that did not cover the buttocks and genitals, it necessitated the wearing of hosiery—and worse, the codpiece. Males in doublets seemed to the imagination nearly naked.[157]

The women who so invest him are identified as "important ladies" (*señoras principales*). This identification is a guard and a guarantee of his chastity, for they must nurse him during the night at his bedside. After his ordination upon entry into Rome, Loyola will counsel his companions, " 'We must always be on our guard and hold no conversations with women, unless they be noble matrons' " (*donne illustri*). The misogynist topic is extended by examples of how two Jesuit advisors to women were deceived. One woman became pregnant, although the confessor was absolved from suspicion when the father was discovered; another woman was caught in fornication.[158] The assault of the lewd woman on the celibate male was a standard topic of medieval hagiography. Chastity under trial was a form of spiritual heroism the hagiographers relished, dwelling on the length and persistence of the temptations, the voluptuousness of the women, and the difficulty of resisting their advances. The stories were often shallow and even prurient but could never be repeated often enough. Celibate males were typified as delectable prizes, not only for lewd prostitutes but even for respectable matrons. Women were portrayed as inflamed by their innocence and so as schemers of their seduction. In this drama of trial and victory the women were stock figures of conventional behavior, while the men were individual characters whose tension and torment were rendered so vividly as to emphasize the heroism of their resistance.[159]

Besides his austere dress, Loyola at Manresa also abstains from meat and wine, except for a little wine on Sundays, if offered.[160] Hagiography carefully noted a saint's rigorous observance of ritual abstinence and fasting, for a single lapse could reveal in the popular mind a failure or imposter.[161] In the Spanish kingdoms the man who drank wine was the definition of the bourgeois, although wine was often drunk mixed with water, or too frequently adulterated with lime, salt, or plaster. The common diet of the poor was chick peas, locust beans, asparagus, spinach, and lentils.[162] Once after Loyola fasts for a week without even a bite to eat, a confessor orders him to break the fast; he obeys, although he feels strong enough to maintain it. His firm perseverance in abstinence is interrupted one morning upon rising by an apparition of some meat to eat, just as if he had seen it with his bodily eyes. Although he has experienced no previous desire for it, a great assent of will comes to him from now on to eat meat, which he determines without a doubt to do. When a confessor instructs him to examine the matter, to determine whether the apparition was a temptation, Loyola's thorough deliberation convinces him that it was not.[163] His certainty is reminiscent of Dante's belief at the gate of purgatory that at dawn the mind is most unencumbered by flesh and becomes almost prophetic in its vision.[164]

On another issue Loyola also arrives at his own decision. Often when he retires to bed, great information comes to him, great consolation, so that he loses much of the slight time he has allotted for sleeping. He reflects that he has decided on so much time for relating to God in the seven hours of the daily office, then the remainder of the day for thinking about those divine subjects he has meditated upon or read. He doubts whether these nocturnal notices come from a good spirit and he arrives at the conclusion that it would be better to forsake them and to get the appointed sleep. He does this.[165] This is a conscious rejection of traditional ascetic vigilance against the devil on the prowl. In their vigilance, or in their vanity, some ascetics hardly slept, while others slept on stones or thorns.[166]

Yet Loyola's bedevilment is his "many troubles with scruples" concerning sacramental confession. Although he made at Montserrat a general confession in writing with sufficient diligence, still it sometimes seems to him that he has not confessed certain sins. This concern greatly afflicts him, because, although he confesses them, he remains unsatisfied. Loyola begins to search for some spiritual guides who might remedy these scruples, but nothing helps him. A very spiritual doctor of the Seo, a preacher at the cathedral church, finally tells him one day in confession to write down everything he can remember. Loyola does this; but, after having confessed these sins, all the scruples return, splitting hairs, so that he is very upset. Although he recognizes that these scruples are harming him greatly, and that it would be good to free himself from them, he is unable to get rid of them himself. He sometimes thinks that the remedy would be for his confessor to order him in the name of Jesus Christ never to confess to him anything of past matters. He wishes that the confessor would indeed so order him but he does not have the audacity to tell that to the confessor.[167] In his immaturity of conscience Loyola has a problem with external authorities, notably confessors as judges, which will afflict him until he summons "audacity": not to speak his desire to them so that they might order his conscience, but to speak his will to himself so that he might order it for himself.

Yet his confessor does order him to not confess anything of past matters, unless it is something very clear. Since Loyola considers everything very clear, this command is of no avail, and he remains continually troubled. At this time he is located in a small room the Dominicans have granted him in their "monastery." There he perseveres kneeling for the seven hours of the divine office, rising continually in the middle of the night, and in the rest of his exercises. In all of these practices he finds no remedy for his scruples, which have tormented him for many months now. Once in great tribulation from them he places himself in prayer with such fervor that he begins to cry aloud to God saying, "Lord, help me, who finds no remedy among men or in any creature. If I should think it findable, no trouble would be great to me. Show me yourself, Lord, where I might find it; and, even if it should be necessary to follow a puppy for the remedy, I shall do it."[168] Animals in folklore befriended the saints, as in the example of the jackal who led lost holy men out of the wilderness.[169] Loyola's bargain to trot even after a puppy for the remedy is, however, an irony about the Dominicans with whom he lodges. They were popularly called "the dogs of the Lord" (*Dominicanes*). The mother of their founder, Dominic, had dreamed in pregnancy that she bore a small dog with a lighted torch in his mouth, with which at birth he set the world on fire.[170] Loyola's quip participates in a broad tradition of antifraternal satire provoked by their privileges and practices, including the contentious usurpation of confession from the pastoral care of the parish priests, and especially of cases reserved for episcopal absolution.[171] He expresses disdain for the Dominican "dogs" who fail to guide him by his bargain with God to follow even a "puppy."

Disturbed by scrupulosity, Loyola is frequently visited by very impulsive temptations "to cast himself from a lofty pinnacle that his room had and that was near to the place where he used to pray."[172] This Dominican "monastery" (*monasterio*) is a curious place, since those friars have never lived in monasteries but rather in convents (*convento*; in Catalan, *convent*).[173] The specification that the Dominicans allowed the cell to Loyola renders intelligible his critical prayer there about the "puppy." Although in modern Spanish the text translates that Loyola is tempted to throw himself "from a large hole" (*de un agujero grande*) that his little room had, this rendition is illogical. He could only throw himself "into" (*en, dentro*) such a hole.

Loyola's "little room" (*camarilla*) imitates the place of the meditation in Augustine's *Confessions* that disclosed his fascination with the phantasm of vanity. Augustine discovered there that the search for external joy led to vanities rather than to enlightenment. That conversion took place, he said, "in the interior of my private little room" (*cubili*); that is, in his heart.[174] The place of Loyola's perilous temptation in his imitative "little room" is not "a large hole," as in the extant text, but "a lofty pinnacle." The modern philological difference is slight—from *agujero* to *aguja*—but the significant difference is substantial. An *agujero* is, besides a "hole" or "dugout," a maker or seller of the *aguja*. This item (*aguja*) is a "needle." The meaning of the two words was conflated in sixteenth-century discourse, as is evident from the other occurrence of *agujero* in the text. When after his pilgrimage Loyola resumes the ascetic practices of Manresa, he makes in the soles of his shoes a "pinpoint" (*agujero*), which gradually widens until only the uppers remain.[175] The term *agujero* meant originally not just any hole, such as a human body might hurl itself into, but the particular hole made by a needle when sewing. It is this connotation that resolves the puzzle, for an *aguja*, or "needle," was also a "spire" or "steeple," such as that of a church.

The notion of a pinnacle in Loyola's cell, or near the place where he prays, may seem physically odd but it is rhetorically coherent. The epideictic genre is not invented from the factuality of geographical places but from the propriety of topical places. Loyola's allusion by his temptation is to those hermitic heroes of the desert whom he mimics in his religious practices, the stylites. Those anchorites, a phenomenon of Eastern asceticism in the early medieval age, lived on top of lofty pillars or columns. It is precisely Loyola's vainglorious ambition to ascend to perfection, as symbolized by such a height of sanctity as a pinnacle, that involves him in scrupulosity. He is a perfectionist at religiosity. In his self-righteousness he cannot accept sacramental absolution for sin but must justify himself remorselessly in his conscience by its own moral work: relentless examination and confession of every imagined fault.

Asceticism was traditionally motivated not only by expiation or devotion but also by competition. The athletic model of the stylites evidenced this agonistic spirit in recording austerities, contending in mortifications, and boasting in achievements.[176] Anthropologically asceticism might be explained as seeking social status:[177] favor from God as "grace" and so honor among people. The eremitical literature was populated with vainglorious sinners. The originator of the scheme of the seven vices, Evagrius, was himself blamed in the Lausiac history as "intoxicated with vainglory." In another tale a virgin in sackcloth was immured for six years, denying all pleasures. Yet she succumbed to lust "because of her overweening pride . . . because she had practiced asceticism for the sake of human applause rather than for religious purposes and out of the love of God." As the author concluded, "Vainglory and evil intentions are the cause of that." Then there was an anchorite living in a cave "deluded in dreams by the madness of vainglory." Although he chastised his body, "his thinking powers were utterly deranged by the great evil of vainglory."[178]

In yet another tale the devil deceived a vainglorious monk into believing that he was angelic, too good to partake of the Eucharist. By this sign the other ascetics recognized his delusion. They fettered him for a year in chains and converted him through prayer and the prescription of ordinary occupation. The incident was included as a caution against inflation in virtue, for even virtue, when not perfected with the right intention, might occasion a fall. As the summary moralized, "We have commemorated men and women who aimed at the highest virtue, but who in many cases were pulled down toward the deep pit of hell by vainglory, the so-called mother of pride. The perfection of asceticism which they had desired, and for which they had struggled and worked so hard for so long a time, was lost in one minute by pride and self-esteem."[179]

Loyola's temptation to hurl himself down from the pinnacle is not generated by despondency, although he sometimes experiences desolation. Anxiety was integral to the formation of early modern culture, as society struggled to cope with the dissolution of medieval boundaries.[180] The case of Luther's scrupulosity was historic. He universalized in medieval fashion his fault as Everyman's fault and his remedy of justification by faith as Everyman's remedy. Yet Loyola's experience was different, as expressed in this epideictic rhetoric. Despondency was itself differently understood: it was the capital sin of sloth (*acedia*). Independent of external circumstances, independent of will, sloth was a phenomenon of estrangement from a world void of significance. It was experienced as the spiritual vacuity of a soul deprived of interest in action, life, and the world, whether this world or the next. The immediate consequence of the encounter with nothingness, it had as its immediate effect a disaffection with reality. A sudden incursion, it was sometimes identified as a disease, sometimes as a vice. As the malady of the monasteries it was a syndrome of four principal symptoms: the predominance of melancholy, restlessness of place, loathing, and vague sorrow. Other symptoms were obsession with death, lack of involvement, monotony, immobility, and distorted perception of time and space. Although originating in the soul, it produced a paralysis of both soul and body, thought and action. Spiritually there was indifference to duties and obligations; mentally, a lack of emotion leading to boredom, rancor, apathy, inertia, or sluggish thought. Physically there was cessation of motion and indifference to work, yielding the laziness, idleness, and indolence that defined sloth.[181]

In this withdrawal from society and service there was an aimless drifting of the mind, a restlessness of spirit, nagging anxiety, and spiritual despondency. The vacuity of a nameless woe promoted an indifference that led to a disgust for the spiritual and an abhorrence of its good. Morose joylessness promoted despair and suggested suicide in the movement by which vague disinterest led to total abnegation. The psychological concatenation in which one vice generated another yielded in scholasticism to a profound analysis of moral acts in which the vices gnawed at the roots of the appetitive faculty. With Thomas Aquinas's definition of sloth as the theological vice—the aversion to spiritual good—it lost its attachment to the monastic class. Sloth became secularized from the spiritual inappetence of the monk to the ordinary laziness of the laity. It became a popular image of external idleness in religious observance, with the sleeping apostles as its iconography. The vice that had entered eremitical literature to tempt the monk with disgust of the cell now prowled the whole world in search of lay victims.[182]

Loyola on the pinnacle is not the victim of that nameless woe. He is, like the moral limper, enlightened in his intellect although disordered in his will. He states that his demon is scrupulosity and he knows that its remedy is not to confess again any past sins. The remedies for sloth were different. Its physical phenomena of idleness and somnolence were to be cured by manual labor; its spiritual phenomena of intellectual sluggishness, lack of fervor, and tedium were to be cured by practicing fortitude and nourishing hope.[183] Loyola is active, even eager, in seeking the remedy for his scruples.

He is not tempted to leap from the pinnacle by sloth as despair. The prostration of the self on the ground, especially in sackcloth such as Loyola wears, was a scriptural gesture of penitence. Yet hurling oneself to the ground, or merely falling to it, was not in medieval or renaissance cultures an act of suicide. Violence to the self in despair, or in fear, was a motif that emerged early in fourteenth-century art in scenes of the judgment of the damned and later was expressed in those of the expulsion from paradise and the lamentation for the crucified Christ. The gestures of despair involved not the feet but the hands: the biting of the back of the hand, the pulling open of the mouth with the fingers, and the laceration of the cheeks with the fingernails.[184] It was a classical declamatory exercise in the schools to develop the topic of the father who poisoned a son so mad that he bit and rent his own flesh.[185] Margery Kempe, in the initial English "autobiography," was tormented during puerperal fever with visions of devils with flaming mouths. "She would have destroyed herself many a time at their stirrings and have been damned with them in Hell, and in witness thereof, she bit her own hand so violently, that the mark was seen all her life after." Quite "out of her senses" she tore at her breast with her fingernails.[186] Loyola conformed to that convention of manual expression for the emotion of grief when during the surgery on his legs he tightly clenched his fists.[187]

Suicide was considered since Prudentius's *Psychomachia* the work of wrath (*ira*), not despair (*acedia*).[188] Its iconographic type, derived from the stabbing in that text, was the sword plunged through the body.[189] The popular exemplar in renaissance art was Lucretia's suicide following her rape.[190] Although male suicide was rarely depicted,[191] it was also a stabbing.[192] As Leonardo da Vinci recorded in his notebooks, "How to Represent a Man in Despair: You must show a man in despair with a knife, having already torn open his garments, and with one hand tearing open the wound."[193] Its iconography was definitely not the human body plunging through space into a hole on the ground.

Falling from a height was rather the archetypal act of pride. The inversion of a person in space headfirst was a powerful semiotic strategy of the medieval artist to negate that figure. Inversion related to the original fall of the angels and of humans; it was also applied to the toppling of tyrants, the subjugation of idols, and the overcoming of vices.[194] In the medieval equation of stability with order and instability with chaos artists portrayed evildoers in such disequilibrium. A treatise on virtue and vice, Friar Laurent's *Somme le roi*, juxtaposed a falling Orguel Ocozias (2 Kings 1:2) with humility. The initial for that verse in other biblical manuscripts perpetuated the motif. The fall of Saul from his horse on the road to Damascus was also blamed on pride, and he was depicted in the ridiculous posture of an inverse body, headfirst.[195] Falling represented the essential dehumanization of the upright stance.[196] Defamatory paintings of civic enemies on the walls of Florentine public buildings portrayed them hanging upside down. It was a denigrating pose, a standard form for depicting culprits. The figure upside down as a symbol of infamy dated to antiquity, and the damned in hell were so painted in Giotto's Last Judgment.[197]

Loyola had practiced the upright stance in his initial prayer of stargazing. Now at prayer he is tempted to fall down. The inventor of the scheme of the capital vices wrote that pride conducted to the gravest fall, by inciting the soul not to recognize the grace of God but to believe itself the cause of its good actions.[198] Proverbially, "Pride goes before a fall." Loyola's temptation to fall belongs to the topic of pride, not despair. The generation of his scrupulosity from the vice of vainglory is patent from the place of the pinnacle in the paradigmatic temptation. That was not the temptation of the stylites but of Jesus himself. After his baptism Jesus was led by the Spirit into the wilderness, where he fasted and was tempted in recapitulation of the experiences of the Israelites in the desert. In the second temptation the devil took him to Jerusalem and placed him on the pinnacle of its temple. He commanded Jesus to throw himself down, for if he was indeed the Son of God the angels would bear him up before he dashed his foot against the ground. Jesus rebuked him with the saying against tempting the Lord (Matt. 4:1–7).

In medieval theology the temptation of Jesus was paralleled with the temptation of Adam and interpreted according to the tripartite division of evil as "the lust of the flesh and the lust of the eyes and the pride of life" (1 John 2:16). In an association of sins with the process of sinning the lust of the flesh was gluttony and suggestion, the lust of the eyes was avarice and delectation, and the pride of life was vainglory and consent. The devil had tempted Adam with vainglory when he promised him that he would be like God. The temptation of Jesus to cast himself down from the pinnacle of the temple was also to vainglory. The pride of life was equated in Augustine's *Confessions* with concupiscence of the eyes, thus with being noticed as vainglory. The exegetical tradition was established by Gregory the Great in his homilies and endorsed by Peter Lombard in his *Sententiae* and Thomas Aquinas in his *Summa theologiae*.[199] Bernard of Clairvaux in a sermon on conversion cautioned vigilance for "any of you who have climbed up to the pinnacle of the temple," especially the clergy. "How ungrateful, indeed how harmful, to the great mystery of ungodliness you are, if you consider godliness a means to gain. How unfaithful to him who consecrated this ministry by his own blood, if in it you seek your own glory, which is nothing; if you look after your own interests and not those of Jesus Christ." Throwing oneself down to earthly things was an unworthy response to the divine condescension that made humans sublime by the dispensation of his humility. "All those who cast themselves down from the heights of virtue to the void of vainglory and seek their own satisfaction, offend the Lord of hosts instead of thanking him when he bore among us so very much in order to impress on us the likeness of holiness."[200] The comparison was taught in such popular manuals for the laity as *Specchio di croce*, available in Catalan as *Mirall de la creu*, by the Dominican known as "the hospitaler," Domenico Cavalca. He stated that the temptation for Jesus to throw himself from the pinnacle of the temple was to vainglory and that its moral was not to perform miracles but to pursue the good life.[201]

The rhetoric of place clarifies the coherence of the exegesis, since a pinnacle and vainglory are both lofty positions. The traditional exegesis also clarifies Loyola's rebuke to Gonçalves da Câmara in the tower about the comportment of his eyes: " 'Obey the rule!' " The three temptations were paralleled by the three vows. In monastic renunciation of "the world" the lust of the flesh was countered by chastity, the lust of the eyes by poverty, and the pride of life or vainglory by obedience.[202] Obedience to the rule of the Society of Jesus is the essential juridical remedy to Gonçalves da Câmara's vainglory; that explains Loyola's insistence on the issue. Medieval institutions also offered ideologies to reckon with the tripartite pleasure, property, and fame for those who could, or would, not resolve the temptations of the world with vows. Those were courtly love for the lust of the flesh, feudalism for the lust of the eyes, and chivalry for the pride of life or vainglory.[203] Loyola's chivalry at religion, epitomized in his vigil before the Madonna of Montserrat, is a secularized renunciation of vainglory.

Loyola is often tempted impulsively to throw himself down from its great pinnacle. Recognizing that it is a mortal sin to get killed, he changes his mind and shouts, " 'Lord, I shall do nothing to offend you.' " He repeats these words frequently and also his bargain to follow a puppy for the remedy.[204] His cry imitates the rebuke of Jesus to the devil in the desert not to tempt him. The decision to fall or not to fall, as into a well or over a precipice, was also a philosophical example of moral decision. Aristotle illustrated with it the universal formation of unqualified judgments from this judgment that one course of action was better and the other worse,[205] a type of the choice of Hercules.

There occurs to Loyola the story of a saint who, to obtain from God something he greatly desired, fasted for many days until he succeeded. Loyola considers this for a long time and decides to imitate him, either until he obtains his desire or until the verge of death, at which extremity he would ask for bread and eat it. This is the fast his confessor orders him to break. Upon compliance, the following day he finds himself free of scruples. The next day at prayer they return, however, as he begins to remember his sins and lapses into musing from sin to sin of his past life. It again seems to him that he is obliged to confess them. At the conclusion of these thoughts there come upon him loathings for the life he has and impulses to quit it.[206] This is now the malady of the monasteries, the sin of the place, *acedia*, or sloth.

Loyola experiences its temptation second, during or a little before the suspicious consolation of a beautiful serpentine form hovering in midair. Sloth comes to him as a rigorous "thought" (*pensamiento*), replicating Evagrius Ponticus's term (*logismos*) for the seven capital vices. This thought bothers him by representing the difficulty of his vocation, by reproaching him within his soul, "And how will you be able to suffer this life the seventy years you have to live?" Sensing that the voice is the enemy, Loyola responds forcefully within, "O wretched one! Are you able to promise one hour of life?" He thus vanquishes the temptation and remains quiet and he experiences great consolation in daily high Mass and sung vespers. Yet later he begins to experience great variations of soul—sometimes so insipid that he finds no enjoyment in any prayer, sometimes its sudden contrary—so that he seems to have lost the sadness and desolation as a cape drops from a man's shoulders. With such alternations Loyola considers that the Lord wishes to awaken him, as if from a dream. Loyola reverts to the experience he has already had of the diversity of spirits and its divine lessons. He begins to regard the means by which this spirit of sloth came to him and he determines to himself with great clarity no longer to confess anything of the past. That very day he remains free from scruples, certain that the Lord has willed to deliver him by his mercy.[207] Although this remedy for scrupulosity was ordered by his confessor, deliverance is only achieved by Loyola's examination of his own experience and formation of his own judgment to accept it—rather than acceptance of external authority as normative.

There are five particular "points" of experience, in conformity with the classical mnemonic practice of marking divisions at five,[208] which show Loyola how God is tutoring him as a schoolmaster does a child. They are pointers, like the apparition of the meat that convinced him to discontinue his ascetic practice of abstinence. Loyola explains that he does not know why God should have treated him so—whether because of his rough and homespun native wit, or because he had no one else to teach him, or because of the firm will that God himself had given him to serve him. Yet he clearly judged then, and still does judge, that God treated him in that manner. If he doubted it he used to think he was

The Ascetic

offending the divine majesty.²⁰⁹ All of the points are visual; the first is only apparently aural.

This initial point concerns the Trinity. Because Loyola is very devoted to the Trinity, he recites a daily prayer to each person, then one to the Trinity itself. The question occurs to him: Why four prayers to the Trinity? Yet it troubles him little, as of no importance. One day, as he is reciting on the monastery steps the Hours of Our Lady, his understanding begins to be elevated to see the most holy Trinity in the figure of three keys. He experiences this with such weeping and sobbing that he is unable to esteem himself. In this state he joins a procession issuing from the monastery and he is unable to check his tears until mealtime, after which he cannot stop talking about the Trinity with many and diverse comparisons and with much enjoyment and consolation. For his entire life there perdures this impression of feeling great devotion when praying to the Trinity.²¹⁰

The philology of the "keys" (*teclas*) connotes a musical instrument and suggests a theological interpretation such as the harmonization of the Trinitarian persons in one composition. The philology of Loyola's emotional reaction, however, which was traditionally itself the key to interpreting visionary experience, indicates the more common keys (*llaves*) that were tools to open locked barriers. Loyola's reaction is such weeping and sobbing that he is unable to value himself, to esteem himself, to consider himself of merit (*no se podía valer*). The context of that recital is Loyola's scrupulosity concerning the validity of sacramental confession.

There was a traditional relationship between spiritual visions and images meditated, especially in private piety.²¹¹ An example of art tutoring devotion that Loyola would have experienced was the retable of the Holy Spirit by the brothers Jaume and Pere Serra in Manresa's Seo, or cathedral church. Its titular patroness is the Virgen del Alba (Dawn), whose rosary is recited on the feast of Our Lady of the Snows, the date of the seminal conversation between Gonçalves da Câmara and Loyola.²¹² The retable was composed of twenty-four tables and thirty-six small figures painted on the uprights. Its scenes devolved in perfect order, like an open book that the congregation could read in exposition of the mysteries of salvation.²¹³

Images of the Trinity in art and theology did not involve keys. The usual Spanish mode in that period for symbolizing the Trinity was God the Son as crucified in the arms of the Father with the Spirit hovering as a dove.²¹⁴ The Trinity in the Seo on which Loyola could have meditated was an altarpiece painted in 1501 by Gabriel Guardia, a native. It represents the Trinity in accordance with the specifications of the donor, as God the Father supporting the crucified Christ and the Holy Spirit proceeding from the Father and the Son together. The solid frontal arrangement of the group is exemplary of the Spanish artistic delight in the hieratic, iconic form, a tradition originating in the Pantokrator of the Romanesque basilica, continuing through Bermejo's retable at Santo Domingo de Silos, and concluding in this painting. Most distinguished of the figures is the bearded head of the Father with a halo in three points; he is enthroned holding the cross of the crucified Son in his extended palms.[215]

The persons of the deity in the painting all assume the posture of the letter Y. Its three branches are forked in the middle. The legs of Christ are smartly straight and his arms upstretched, with no sagging at the joints as in some scenes of crucifixion. Above his halo is the Spirit in the form of a dove, again with its erect body as the central form and its flanking wings upstretched as in the forks of a Y. This figure emerges from the breast of the Father as if by spiration. The Father forms an inverse Y, with his imposing body and arms outstretched downward to almost join with Christ's. The total effect of this juncture is a horizontal diamond. The Pythagoreans symbolized morality by the letter Y, the two branches of which represented virtue and vice, a figure adopted for the choice of Hercules.[216] It was frequently interpreted as a tree, as in the golden bough of Aeneas, and depicted as a bifurcated cross. The head of Christ typically inclined right toward the choice of virtue,[217] as in this retable.[218] Erasmus noted in a colloquy that the hanging of Christ's head to his right shoulder was a commonplace.[219]

It is such a moral, rather than intellectual, interpretation of the Trinity that informs Loyola's consolation by the keys. The ascetic who invented the concept of the seven vices stated that the contemplation of the Trinity was the first natural contemplation.[220] The philology (*teclas*) of the text suggests that Loyola's experience is a theological resolution to his speculation about why there are three prayers to the persons of the Trinity, then a fourth to its Unity. Yet his recital is episodic, not causal; it locates incidents under the Trinitarian topic. The inclusion of the remembrance about Trinitarian prayer is moral in import. Loyola does not praise himself as speculative, inquiring into a sublime mystery, but he does blame himself as scrupulous, reducing it to a juggle of numbers. He decides that the issue of how many prayers to say is unimportant and he dismisses it. The confessional context in which he relates this first point

The Ascetic

establishes its moral meaning. His emotional reaction, traditionally a key to evaluating visions, emphasizes this. He weeps and sobs and is unable to value himself. The historical context of his experience also indicates a moral meaning, for the theological talk of the continent in the early 1520s was not speculation on the Trinity but argumentation on merit. Another scrupulous soul, Luther, had pitched the question of the remission of sin to an international conflict, ecclesiastical and civic.

Keys were a scriptural metaphor for power (Is. 22:22; Rev. 3:7-8). They were not the property of the Trinity but they were the attribute of saints. The Madonna was the bearer of the key to open the gates of heaven.[221] St. Peter was entrusted keys, as famously reproduced in Perugino's fresco in the Sistine Chapel of the Vatican.[222] In a Catalan altar painting Peter holds in his left hand a key so large that it extends from his waist to the tip of his halo.[223] In another Peter with his right hand raised holds two keys, while with his left he grasps a soul uplifted to him by an angel. A small naked soul with hands folded in prayer looks up in yet another example to Peter, whose raised left hand holds two large keys extending from the bottom of his beard to the tip of his halo.[224] Jesus by tradition entrusted to Peter the keys to the kingdom of heaven, the power of loosing and binding, of forgiving or retaining sins (Matt. 16:19). These are the keys of Loyola's understanding about the Trinity. Peter has already intervened as the saint at whose intercession Loyola begins to recover at the point of death from the injuries and surgeries to his legs.[225] Now his presence is intimated to enlighten and console him in his penitential tribulations.

Authorities on that sacrament differed in the precise definition of penance. The contritionists in the tradition of Peter Lombard formulated forgiveness primarily as sorrow and amendment, as in the popular definition of Raymond of Peñaforte, "Penance is repenting past evils and not committing them again."[226] A Dominican and a Catalan, and the originator of the *summa* for confessors, he was the probable authority for Loyola's confessors at Manresa. Yet it is precisely the problem about whether Loyola has that virtue of penance, as repenting past evils, that involves him in scrupulosity. The alternative definition would aid him. It emphasized against personal penitence the sacramental power. As it was defined in the tradition of John Duns Scotus, "The sacrament of penance is that absolution of the priest having jurisdiction."[227] That was the "key of power" to absolve and it belonged to the ordained priest with jurisdiction over the penitent and his sins. To that key most authorities added the "key of knowledge," a certain native ability and spiritual learning of the confessor to understand and to judge. Yet there were conditions on the penitent as well as on the confessor, sixteen conditions whose achievement might have left a sinner more desolate than consoled about forgiveness. The principal condition was that a good confession must be complete. This condition created the premise for Loyola's doubts: had he confessed completely? To ease demands on the penitent, moralists generally tended toward the juridical, rather than the contritionist, definition by emphasizing sacramental efficacy as deriving from the work worked rather than the work of the worker. Its benefit came from the power of the keys expressed as the absolution by the priest. That mentality was fundamental to the function of consolation. There was a vague theory that the attrition of the penitent might be transformed into contrition by the power of the keys, which included even forgotten past sins.[228]

Yet the most convincing evidence for emphasis on sacramental grace independent of individual effort was the development of the words of absolution. The subjunctive formula "May God forgive you" changed in the thirteenth century to the indicative "I absolve you"—from the deprecatory to what in modern analytic philosophy is called the performative. There was considerable argument about whether that indicative formula should be simple or elaborate, but eventually there was appended to it the Trinitarian phrase. The prominent canonist Andreas de Escobar, early in the fifteenth century, concluded his wordy absolution with "in virtue of the passion of our Lord Jesus Christ and in the name of the Father, the Son, and the Holy Spirit." As stated by Johann Eck, a principal adversary of Luther, the proper formula for absolution was: "May Our Lord Jesus Christ mercifully deign to absolve you, and I, by His authority, which in His place I now enjoy, absolve you from the sentence of minor excommunication, and from all your sins, in the name of the Father, and of the Son, and of the Holy Spirit, Amen."[229] That was precisely the exercise of the power of the keys. And that is the form of Loyola's understanding of the Trinity as "keys."

Loyola experiences his understanding "on the steps of the monastery."[230] His place there is on the topical monastic steps of Bernard of Clairvaux's *De gradibus humilitatis et superbiae*. That manual was a practical guide on the monastic steps of humility in the Benedictine rule. Only Bernard, instead of describing their ascent, described their descent as the steps of pride. As he explained, he could only teach what he had learned and he knew more about falling down than climbing up. Yet careful examination would reveal the way up, he believed. "If you are going to Rome who can tell you the way better than one you meet coming from there? He will describe the towns, villages, cities, rivers and mountains he has passed and as you go along you will meet them in the reverse order. So, we have described the stages of the downward road and you will see them as you climb up and down them better from your own experience than from the description of our book." Those steps were curiosity, frivolity, foolish mirth, boastfulness, singularity, conceit, audacity, excusing sins, hypocritical confession, defiance, freedom to sin, and habitual sinning.[231] They are mnemonic places, not mathematical points. Loyola locates himself where his moral situation is: on these monastic steps. He typifies himself as proud. His own recital imitates Bernard's program. Like the man who has come from Rome, he is able to tell the traveler en route—the Society of Jesus as synecdochic in Gonçalves da Câmara—the landmarks, the villages, towns, and cities, the rivers and mountains of the spiritual geography. Loyola describes his own road to prescribe theirs, so that they may recognize the "places" of pride.

This rhetoric of place is established by the book Loyola is reading when his trinitarian understanding occurs. The topic is again the conversional opening of the book, as during his convalescence in the familial castle. Loyola relates that he is praying the Hours of the Blessed Virgin. This is not a vague devotional reference but his specific indication of the enlightening book. It is very probably Raymond Lull's *Horas de nuestra Señora* in the prose version *Hores de sancta Maria*. Loyola indicates that he daily prayed it as a spiritual exercise, for when he says that he prayed for seven hours[232] he does not mean duration by the clock but the seven canonical hours from matins to compline. Lull's version began at matins with a meditation on the one God and then on each of the three Persons. That coincided with Loyola's statement about his own four prayers. The lesson at terce on "understanding" (*entendimiento*) explicated it not as intellectual comprehension but as moral judgment, in an appropriation of the definition more usually accorded the virtue of prudence. As Lull wrote and Loyola likely read, "The Holy Spirit gives the gift of understanding (*enteniment*) so that man might discern between good and evil." Understanding brought "contrition and weeping" so that faults and sins might be pardoned and the soul might be prevented from a bad death. At vespers there was a lesson "on penance," explicitly about "the keys." The prose version stated, "The priest absolves the sinner by satisfaction, our Lady by devotion. The priest locks shut the gate of paradise with the keys of St. Peter (*les claus de Sant Pere*) through his verdict of veto; the mother of God opens the gates of paradise with the keys of her Son through prayer." Penance required of the sinner "sighs and weeping" (*suspirs e plors*) that he had sinned; the Madonna required of the sinner the same sighs and weeping that he might have hope and love.[233] Loyola's understanding of the trinitarian keys—the sacramental formula of absolution—promotes the parallel affective response of weeping and sobbing (*lloras y sollozos*).

Absolution in the name of the Trinity is a counterpart to the "three" days he expended at Montserrat in writing down his general confession.[234] Although the sacramental formula may indeed have sounded like music to his ears, the trinitarian keys are juridical, not musical. It was Gonçalves da Câmara who did not understand his penitential reference and altered the sacramental keys (*llaves*) to musical keys (*teclas*). His rationale would have been the theological harmonization of three persons in one God. Numerology was the common denomination in the relation of particulars to universals in an epistemology of design that considered number the most certain path to wisdom.[235] Such an intellectual interpretation, as if Loyola's experience were contemplative of the Trinity, is alien to the moral, affective context of the episode, however.

It also misses the matter of "honor" and with that the foundation of the Society of Jesus. The text began with Loyola's confession that in character he was utterly vainglorious in his ambition for "honor" (*honra*).[236] As defined by *Las siete partidas*, a thirteenth-century Castilian legal code with even greater ethical importance, "*Honra* means an advanced station and the praise which a man obtains for the position he occupies, or for some eminent deed which he performs, or by reason of some excellence which he possesses." Honor was traditionally founded in the Spanish kingdoms by social position, individual action, or personal virtue. Honor was socially expressed in fame; dishonor, in infamy. Those ideas, based in the typical medieval code of law, were adjusted to Christian morality and classical ethics. Yet a new concept, another factor, intervened to exert an immense influence on generations to Loyola's and after. That was the concept of *valer*, or "worth," in which *valer mas* meant "prestige" or "esteem," and *valer menos* meant "disgrace" or "disesteem." The concepts introduced a type of action not strictly governed by virtue. Disgrace traditionally resulted from such an act as showing cowardice, which was at issue for Loyola concerning the "Moor"'s affront to the Madonna. It was a kind of infamy that could reduce persons of the most lofty lineage to social ruin. Prestige, however, was only won by force of arms, without much regard for the principle of moderation or of a courage that was serene and just.

In the late medieval period, according to its own historians, disputes over prestige and disgrace were the mainspring of human action. The historian of the lineages of the northern Spanish regions and of their "triumphs," García de Salazar, wrote of the bitter wars of Basque clans and families. He stated that they originated in the desire "for greater worth (*mas valer*), as it was in ancient times throughout the whole world, among all the generations to this day, and those that are to come while the world lasts." That new concept of honor revoked honor as established in classical ethics or Christian religion, since prestige was not attained through such ideals. The aspirational motive was not ideational but instinctual, not individual but collective. That collective honor was based on a system of patrilineal clans in which agnates and even more distant categories of relations were considered solidary. The prestige or disgrace of one member affected all. Each lineage thus nurtured pretensions to being worth more than the others, and those defeated in the competition were worth less. Such an agonistic social basis promoted an obsessive competition for the possession of public honors and offices, which then were hereditary within the lineage, accumulating on the senior kinsman or chief.[237]

When Loyola's understanding of the formula of absolution as trinitarian keys disallows him to "value" himself (*no se podía valer*), he is not merely confessing a spiritual state of unworthiness. He is also making a judgment about social values. He explicitly disassociates himself from the zeal for "honor" that had fueled his military exercises and fired Spanish society, particularly the Basques, with agonistic values. He allows himself to be integrated by the grace that heals the wounds of sin into another society, the Trinity. The honor as recognition that descended humanly from the king or the kinsman is displaced by the honor through forgiveness that condescends from the divine Society, with its radically different bond of charity. Worth is gratuitously conferred on Loyola, and he responds by weeping. This is a profound "understanding," yielding lifelong consolation, but one that requires for its comprehension not only spiritual sensitivity but social setting.

Loyola's experience also adumbrates the founding of the Society of Jesus. Honor, as conceived in the late medieval version, was associated with lineage, lineage competing in a social system of prestige and disgrace, offence and revenge. Honor was derived in long genealogies from purity of blood. That is the factor—purity of blood—the Christian convert on the road lacks to his very dishonor; and Loyola insults him for it with the epithet "Moor." In Loyola's repudiation of that social system by a trinitarian understanding, a repudiation already prophesied by divine election through Loyola's reinless riding, is implied a new source for purity of blood. This derives not from the lineage of the family Loyola but from the lineage of the covenantal Jesus. He, Jesus, derived his purity of blood from his mother, whose purest blood among mortals mingled with his in her womb. Fundamentally, according to current gynecology the contribution of the female in generation was precisely her menstrual blood (and not her fertile ovaries), so that Jesus was thought to be conceived from her blood.[238]

Loyola has a realistic understanding of this intimacy that displays the sensuality of his devotion. In his diary he records his imagination—with a copious, intense sobbing to loss of speech—of Mary propitious before the Father as a party or door of the grace he feels. At the consecration of the Mass she shows him "that her flesh is in that of her Son, with such intelligences that I would not be able to write."[239] The notion was not novel. In the medieval *De laudibus beatae Mariae virginis* Mary nourished her guests at banquet "in the sacrament in which is eaten the flesh of Christ, because the flesh of Christ and the flesh of Mary, just as the flesh of a mother and a child, are one flesh." It interpreted scripture on the sexual intercourse of the married as being "one flesh" (Gen. 2:24; 1 Cor. 6:16) to mean the blessed Mother and her son Jesus. "A most dainty dish to consume virginal flesh," it concluded on the Eucharist as Marian. That very popular work was misassigned to Albert the Great,[240] so that Loyola could well have been exposed to it during his lodging at Manresa with the Dominicans. There was even a liturgical use of the tabernacle and the pyx in the design of Mary's body, so that her halves opened to reveal the Eucharist.[241] Loyola's devotion to the Eucharist as both the body of Christ and the body of Mary typifies the physicality of his piety and that of his culture. Its theological implication—that Mary also died on the cross in Christ's body as the redemptive sacrifice—emphasizes, however, the naive realism of such theology.

Beyond popular devotion, Loyola's theology traced its anthropological roots in lineage. The maternal-filial bond explains why Loyola is so focused on Our Lady of the Snows, the mother of God, in her immaculate conception: not from abstract devotion but from interested fact. Her purity of blood, manifested in the defined Spanish honor for women as sexual chastity, in her singular privileges of immaculate conception and perpetual virginity, established Jesus' purity of blood. On that purity

Loyola established the Society of Jesus. It was in ritual circumcision that Jesus shed the first drops that prefigured his redemptive blood on the cross and received the name the Jesuits would adopt for their Society of Jesus. The *Exercitia spiritualia* includes in the meditation on the circumcision the unscriptural detail of mother Mary's "*compassion*" at her Son's bloodshed.[242] The principal painting in the Jesuit church in Rome, the Gesù, commemorates the circumcision, but not simply because of the act of naming. Nor are that church's many portrayals of early Christian martyrs simply prototypes of and models for the deaths of later Jesuit missionaries.[243] The rite of circumcision that legally incorporated Jesus into his society was the archetype for the incorporation of Loyola and his companions into the Society of Jesus. Theirs is a type of blood brotherhood. Its purity of blood is established and validated not in social lineage or prestige—not in the cry "Loyola! Loyola!"—but in the Incarnation and redemption—in the name "Jesus." The founding of this spiritual Society is implied in Loyola's understanding of the Trinity on the monastic steps to humility.

The other visual points of Loyola's memory, although less impressive, demonstrate his religious experience as imaginative. The second point concerns the Creation. There is represented once in his understanding with great spiritual joy the method by which God created the world. Loyola seems to see a white object with rays to which God has given firelight. He is unable to explain these matters or remember entirely the spiritual information God impressed in those times on his soul. The third point concerns the Eucharist. Once, while hearing Mass in the "monastery" church, at the elevation of the host he sees with inward eyes something like white rays from above. Although he still cannot explain this well, he nevertheless sees clearly with his understanding how the Lord Jesus Christ is in this most holy sacrament. The fourth point concerns the Incarnation. Frequently and extensively he sees during prayer with interior eyes the humanity of Christ. The figure seems to him like a white body, neither very large nor very small, but without the division of members. He sees this often in Manresa, thirty or forty times, and again in Jerusalem and once when walking to Padua. He also sees the Virgin in similar form. These visions confirm him in faith so that he often thinks to himself that, if there were no scripture to teach these matters of faith, he would still determine to die for them, only because of what he has seen.[244]

Loyola's visions are in his "understanding." The qualification of "interior" eyes emphasizes psychological, rather than sensory, visions. Yet they are vaguely described as undifferentiated white objects of light with rays. Their opacity to his understanding is connoted by their color of "white" as dull (*blanco*) rather than shiny (*cándido*). He can scarcely explain them, even decades later upon their recital. Augustine, who strained for contemplation of the light above the mind, who developed trinitarian doctrine in analogy with faculties of the soul, would have contemned such experiences as crude. He ridiculed such gropings in his own early experience, criticizing in his *Confessions* how as a Manichaean auditor he envisioned God materially. A floundering Augustine, immersed in matter yet struggling to emerge from it through comprehension, imagined creation as a great bounded mass and God as one of its components. "It was like a sea, everywhere and in all directions spreading through an immense space, simply an infinite sea. And it had in it a great sponge, which was finite, however, and this sponge was filled, of course, in every part with the immense sea." It was from that watery abyss in which he was blindly drowning that Augustine strove to elevate the gaze of his mind, only to be bogged down in carnal sensation, until he discovered in Neoplatonist intellection the method of spiritual ascent.[245]

Loyola's envisioning of spiritual realities as white lights with rays is indebted to Augustine's intellection, which established the medieval tradition of theology as contemplative. Light was the standard metaphor for contemplation in Christian theology, as in Neoplatonist philosophy; and a light was considered a better metaphor for the spiritual, even for God, than was a sponge. Yet Loyola's visions are material, crude, less primitive than the finding of statues in brambles, but exceedingly less sophisticated than even the ordinary theological exercise he will essay at university. They parallel the religious development of Augustine's experience from the phenomenal to the contemplative.

Loyola has been petitioned by the Society of Jesus to relate how God dealt with his soul from the time of his conversion[246] and he does so. His introduction to the five points—on his inchoate understandings of the Trinity, Creation, Eucharist, Incarnation, and finally the great illumination—is self-deprecatory. He does not term them gifts or favors. He terms them lessons, on the model of God as "schoolmaster" and himself as a "child." He explicates with rhetorical hesitation[247] that he does not know why God should have so treated him. He wonders whether it is because of his "coarseness and dense native ability" (*rudeza y grueso ingenio*) or, attributing nothing to his homespun talent, that perhaps it is because of the firm will that God himself had given him to serve Him.²⁴⁸ This confusion about the origin and purpose of a vision or dream applies the rhetorical topic of uncertainty, as in the proem of Chaucer's *House of Fame*.²⁴⁹ Loyola's points are rhetorical, not theological, and they are epideictic: to praise God, however crude the understanding.

Loyola characterizes himself at Manresa not as visionary but as blind. "His soul was still blind (*ciega*), although with grand desires to serve him in everything he could understand, and thus he determined to do great penances, not having yet sufficient eye (*ojo*) to satisfy for his sins but to please and placate God." When he resolves to perform some penance in imitation of the saints, he proposes to do "the same and even better." In these thoughts is his "entire consolation," without considering "a single interior matter," such as humility, or charity, or patience, or the prudence to regulate and moderate these virtues. "His entire intention was to perform these grand external feats, because thus had the saints done them for the glory of God." Loyola does not notice (*non mirar*) this circumstance, just as he has indicted himself for his lack of perception in the defense of the fortress, the performance of "courtly" love, and the sally to Jerusalem. He perseveres in a state of joy, he confesses, "without having any knowledge of interior spiritual matters." It is only when he experiences great variations in his soul that he wonders, "What new life is this we now begin?"²⁵⁰ Loyola strives to imitate the saints but limps into other roles. To cite some *P*s: Parzival, Polyphemus, Prester John, Pyrgopolinices.

Loyola establishes his blame of his spiritual formation at Manresa as vainglorious with a certain incident. Loyola converses sometimes with spiritual persons, who esteem him as a person of reputation (*crédito*), because, "although he lacked knowledge of spiritual matters, in his speech he evidenced much fervor and much will to progress quickly in the service of God." There is in town at this time an old woman, very venerable as a servant of God and known as such in many areas of Spain, so much so that even the Catholic King (Ferdinand II) once summoned her to communicate some matters. This woman, in discussion once with Loyola, styled as "the new soldier of Christ," says to him, " 'Oh! May it please my Lord Jesus Christ that he will desire to appear to you one day.' " Loyola in astonishment takes the remark "crudely" (*a la grosa*): " 'How would Jesus Christ appear to me?' "²⁵¹

A stock character of the romance was the old woman feigning sanctity who was actually a procuress, such as Trotaconventos, abettor of seduction and love.²⁵² In hagiography women other than mothers or sisters were similarly sexual in import. They served no function but to enhance the stature of the saint by an attempted seduction. Tales for a celibate clergy perpetuated a stereotype of woman as sinful Eve. There was a telling increase during the Catholic Reformation in the literary assault on holy men by lewd women, as the new emphasis on clerical, male leadership promoted misogyny over the familial values of the two preceding centuries.[253] An amorous role is implied for Loyola's old woman: to act as an intermediary in his conflict of loves. She is not a sexual but a spiritual figure, however, in the tradition of wise female discoursers reverting classically to Diotima or scripturally to Anna. Loyola's venerable woman acts as a go-between to God for him, but by astutely indicting him of vainglory.

With the eclipse early in sixteenth-century Spain of lay and public visionary experience, such as the common discovery of Marian statues, other means of ascertaining the divine will survived. Visionaries continued to be believed, but privately among women—not by men as the officials concerned with the town or the parish. Nuns as professed religious and other pious females were consulted by individuals, sometimes by bishops and even kings. The issues were no longer public calamities such as plague or famine, however, but private concerns such as one's personal state of grace, or the destination of particular souls after death, or inquiries about a prospective spouse or child. Some of the *beatas*, as they were called, were famous and influential like Loyola's example, while others were discreet and simple. Most reputedly had visions in trances. Although some were repressed by the Inquisition, the cultural type persisted throughout the early modern period. As subjected to some ecclesiastical discipline, they were more tolerable to the authorities than ordinary lay seers like shepherds.[254]

The celebrity among the *beatas* was María de santo Domingo, a Dominican tertiary whom Ferdinand II indeed consulted, revered, and protected. Since the text states that "at that time" the woman in question was in Manresa, there is possibility of María's visit there, perhaps to the Dominicans, for she lived until 1524. Yet she was supposedly confined to the convent in Aldeanueva, under orders that no one could speak to her without ecclesiastical permission, at the directive of Tommaso de Vio (Cajetan), the Dominican superior general. The woman was the oracle of the rigorist movement in that order but controversial for her bleedings and bracelets and for her practice of having confessors on her bed at night to ward off diabolical assaults. Her utterances published in 1518[255] suggest by their banality and pathology that she lacked the wit or the wisdom to have formulated the response to Loyola. Since the text states *mujer*, not *sor* or *beata* or even *mujer de orden*, a type seems indicated. Most of the female characters in the text are merely *mujer*, in disregard of the Castilian social distinctions; his nurses, for example, are *señoras principales*, not *señoras de casa* or a proper equivalent.[256]

The role of such charismatics as María de santo Domingo in communicating the divine will differed from that of the occasional lay seers. They were not consulted about, nor did they advise about, specific prospective disasters to the public. Their activity was a habitual communication manifested in reported trances. Some moralists thought women were tempted to have visions as a means of acquiring the attention and power they lacked socially. Jean Gerson warned typically about the character and comportment of all female visionaries. "All the more it is true if these women itching with curiosity are the kind whom the Apostle describes: 'Silly women who are sin-laden and led astray by various lusts: ever learning yet never attaining the knowledge of the truth' (2 Tim. 3:7). For where truth is absent, it follows that vanity and deception are present."[257] As he formulated the misogynist rule, "Every teaching of women, especially that expressed in solemn word or writing, is to be held suspect, unless it has been diligently examined, and much more than the teaching of men." He so explained: "Why? The reason is clear; because not only ordinary but divine law forbids such things. Why? Because women are too easily seduced, because they are too obstinately seducers, because it is not fitting that they should be knowers of divine wisdom."[258] Even in hagiography females sought out the poor and the sick with unsolicited advice and if they preached at all it was to the few who would listen. That was in contrast to the hagiography of males to whom the faithful flocked and around whom they swarmed. A woman whose religious impulses directed her into the streets was considered fair prey for ridicule and even for violence.[259]

Loyola's encounter with the prophetess of Manresa is free of this misogyny; it even reverses its judgment. This woman is not vainglorious as in the suspicious stereotype. It is she, rather, who convicts Loyola of vainglory. And it is she alone of all the spiritual persons—including the male confessors, whom he habitually seeks for counsel in Manresa, beyond in Barcelona, and even in hermitages remote from there—who detects his vice. As he emphatically concludes his recital up to the point of departure by ship on pilgrimage to Jerusalem, neither in Barcelona nor in Manresa, for the entire time he was there was he able to find persons who could help him as much as he wanted. There was only "that woman" who told him that she would pray to God for Jesus Christ to appear to him. She alone seems to him to have penetrated more into spiritual matters. And so, after the departure from Barcelona, he entirely loses his eagerness to seek out spiritual persons.[260]

Loyola initially interprets her comment, as he admits, "crudely." He takes it literally to mean that this venerable spiritual woman, consulted even by the king, hopes that he will experience a divine vision. He misinterprets it precisely because he is vainglorious. Since he wishes to appear holy to the approval of other holy persons, such a sanction as the apparition of Christ to him would be marvelous. Yet the prophetess hopes that there will appear to him *her* (*mí*) Lord Jesus Christ, not his version of him. Her comment is irony, a medieval trope of allegory whose striking feature was often associated with the practice of praising someone when criticism was intended. As Isidore of Seville explained, "It is irony when, through pretence, it is desired that something different from what is said be understood. This is the case when we praise what we want to vituperate." Most rhetoricians employed this formula of criticism through feigned praise. Of the many sources, the authority of Quintilian best displayed the fault of Loyola that the prophetess discerns. "That class of oratory in which the meaning is contrary to that suggested by the words, involve an element of irony, or, as our rhetoricians call it, *illusio*." This was evidenced to the understanding by the delivery of the speech, the character of the speaker, or the nature of the subject. If something was out of sorts in the words, the intention of the speaker, rather than what he said, should be examined. In most tropes it was important to consider not merely what was said but also about whom it was said, since what was said might in another context be literally true. It was permissible, taught Quintilian, to censure with counterfeited praise and to praise under a pretense of blame.[261]

Irony implies two audiences, the initiated and the uninitiated. The initiated understand the subtlety and complexity of the situation, while the uninitiated stupidly and unsuspectingly misinterpret the remark. The effect of irony depends on the possibility that someone—here Loyola—will misunderstand the comment and take it literally. It was considered, however, that there was hardly anyone so foolish that he did not understand if he was being praised for what he was not, as the Abyssinian for his whiteness, the lame man for his agility, or the blind for his sight.[262] Loyola is such a limper playing, and played for, the fool. He is ironically mocked as a blind man expecting a vision of Jesus. The woman is legally giving him an "infamy" of the type that arose from fact, as defined in *Siete partidas*: that a person of repute spoke ill of one.[263] He fails to recognize the infamy because he is focused on fame. Yet the ironic practice of denigration, which could be cruel, is mitigated, for the prophetess couches her criticism as a blessing. It was the rhetorician Quintilian who defined irony as "illusion" (*illusio*), sanctioning the venerable woman's usage of the trope to address Loyola's problem prophetically, like with like. Loyola is in illusion. It will be another term of Quintilian's that he will remarkably adopt to define his conversion from illusion to reality. This is *illustratio*, the famous fifth point of memory about the place Manresa.

THREE

The Flying Serpent

The thing appears to Loyola initially in the hospice, an appropriate place for a pseudosacred vision. Although the physical site is unnamed, it was the Hospital de santa Llúcia.¹ A *hospital* in sixteenth-century vocabulary was a hospice for wayfarers, such as Loyola, or for dying paupers.² The endowment and maintenance of such places was a common form of lay piety,³ a charity that might have attracted a former soldier, since the hospitalers were elite military orders.⁴ This particular hospice of Manresa is the perfect place for Loyola: St. Lucy is the patroness of eyes. An early virgin-martyr commemorated in the canon of the Mass, Lucy signifies "light."⁵ Her attribute is the lamp and, especially from the fourteenth century on, a pair of eyes held in her hands or on a plate. The ocular attribute developed from her legendary response to denunciation by her pagan betrothed: to pluck out her own eyes and deliver them to him on a plate. The Virgin rewarded her with more beautiful, luminous eyes, from which derived her name.⁶ In Spanish folklore St. Lucy was the tracer of order before the reform of the Gregorian calendar, as in the proverb "Saint Lucy makes the night wane and the day grow."⁷ As the miraculous healer of ophthalmia and even blindness, she was attributed in its sixteenth-century cult with the cure of eyes by water from a spring.⁸ Loyola will experience the highlight of his life when his eyes encounter certain local waters. In another allegory of pilgrimage Lucy was situated in the mystical rose opposite Adam. It was she who urged Beatrice to rescue Dante, "when you were bending your brows downward to your ruin," from the midst of the dark wood of error.⁹

At the hospice Loyola frequently sees in broad daylight in the air beside him a thing that affords him much consolation, because it is very beautiful in grand style. He does not descry well its species, but somehow it seems to him that it has the form of a serpent and that it has many objects that glisten like eyes, although they are not. He delights and consoles himself greatly in its vision; when it disappears from sight, he is displeased. One day he goes to a church a little more than a mile from Manresa along the road following the river. In his devotions he sits down for a while with his face toward the river, which runs deep there. The eyes of understanding begin to be opened to him: not that he sees any vision but he understands and knows many things—as much about spiritual matters as of those of faith and letters, with an *illustración* so great that everything seems to him new. Loyola is unable to state to Gonçalves da Câmara the particulars he understood then, although there were many, only that he received a great clarification in his understanding. In the entire passage of his life up to the past sixty-two years the collection and summation of all the many assistances he has received from God and all the many subjects he has known do not seem to him to have accomplished as much as that singular time.

After this experience, which lasts a good while, Loyola goes to kneel down at a nearby cross to give thanks to God. There appears to him the vision that often appeared to him without his ever recognizing it, the thing that seemed to him very beautiful with many eyes. But he sees well before the cross that it does not have such a beautiful color as usual and he has very clear recognition, with great assent of will, that it is the devil. After these frequent apparitions the thing persists for a long time, appearing to him habitually. In a gesture of disdain Loyola rejects it with the pilgrim's staff he carries.[10]

The episode is traditionally named after its site as the Cardoner experience. Through Manresa flows the river Cardoner, on whose bank Loyola locates himself. This is appropriate spiritual geography, for fresh waters running clear in rivers and springs were symbolic since antiquity of inspiration and revelation. Because they originated underground, waters were privy to the secrets of the chthonian spirits.[11] The Castalian font, source of the Muses' inspiration and the Pythia's utterance, flowed under the most celebrated of all oracular sites, the temple of Apollo at Delphi.[12] As Seneca attested of the classical spirit, "We worship the sources of mighty rivers; we erect altars at places where great streams burst forth suddenly from hidden sources; we adore springs of hot water as divine, and consecrate certain pools because of their dark waters or their immeasurable depth."[13] The belief in waves as gifted with prophecy, so that visions in the coursing of a river evoked the notion of glory, was contemporary with poetry such as Joachim du Bellay's *Odes* and Pierre de Ronsard's "A Monsieur le Dauphin" and "A Diane de Poitiers."[14]

In the rushing of the Cardoner there echoes in its initial and final letters—hard *C* and *r*—the river whose site afforded a paradigm for visionary experience in the Judeo-Christian tradition.[15] "In the thirtieth year, in the fourth month, on the fifth day of the month, as I was among the exiles by the river Chebar, the heavens were opened, and I saw visions of God" (Ezek. 1:1). That was the testimony of the prophet Ezekiel of his inaugural vision while hostage during the Babylonian captivity of Israel. It was from such rivers, the irrigation canals that webbed Babylon, that originated a belief in the god of fresh running water on the surface of the earth and in the underground abyss. As personified wisdom, Ea symbolized the privilege of secrets, the knowledge of conjuration, the power of magic, the ability to understand, and therefore, supremacy in sapience, counsel, and skill.[16]

Loyola distances himself from Ezekiel in specifying that there was "no vision" for his understanding.[17] Yet like that ancient prophet by the river, also in about his thirtieth year, he is impressionable. A vision does appear. Loyola retains a crucial detail from Ezekiel's visionary vocation: multiple eyes on an aerial creature. In the vision at the Chebar the prophet beheld a north wind propelling a massive cloud ringed with brightness and flashing a fire whose intense center was gleaming bronze. From the center emerged the image of four living creatures elaborately described. Those cherubim who bore the flaming throne of God across the sky were the tetramorphs. Animal in form, each had four faces arranged in opposing pairs, with the visages of man, eagle, lion, and bull. Their four wings were a pair folded and a pair extended, with which they darted forward like lightning by a spiritual impetus. Each creature was accompanied by a whirring wheel, sparkling like chrysolite and constructed as a wheel within a wheel. Those concentric wheels were capable of moving in any of four directions without turning. The rims and spokes of the wheels and the wheels themselves were "full of eyes." Wherever the cherubim traveled, the wheels accompanied them as inhabited by their spirit (Ezek. 1:4–21; 10:9–17).

The cherubim have been related to the monstrous winged quadrupeds of Mesopotamian or Syro-Palestinian art and to the tetramorph Baal.[18] They have been compared formally with the Egyptian type of the Bes called Pantheos or Hamerti. In that example the body is studded with eyes, and the frontal face is profiled by animal faces on either side, while the feet are bestial like the calves' hooves of Ezekiel's cherubim.[19] Whatever their provenance, the creatures winged into Christian imagination. The Byzantine exemplar symbolized Ezekiel's vision as a winged circle or wheel covered with eyes. The wheel and wings represented constant mobility; the eyes, vigilant intelligence. An angel might be depicted as two fiery interlocking circles with eyes around the rims and ocellated wings, as in the mural painting from a thirteenth-century Athenian church. The angels on Byzantine monuments typically had this rotary form as the bearers of the divine chariot upon which God the Father or Son stood. From that Eastern exemplar the eyes were transferred to angels depicted in human form. Such was the usual iconography in the Latin Church. An angel with ocellated wings sculptured at the cathedral of Chartres in the thirteenth century stands on the symbolic wheel as if on a footrest.[20]

Many cherubim and tetramorphs in Western art retained nothing of the ocular imagery of Ezekiel's visions.[21] Some versions suggested vision on angelic wings by short strokes or dots within semicircles.[22] Large stylized dots arched with feathery strokes suggest pupils with eyelids and eyelashes in the paintings of Bartolomé Bermejo, the medieval Spanish master of the Flemish style.[23] Yet sufficient depictions from various periods, regions, and styles represent the eyes realistically: sculptured on an altar, painted in a sacramentary or bible, or designed in a mosaic.[24] As no longer the exclusive vision of Ezekiel, the cherubim surrounded the throne of Christ triumphant. They also adopted the six wings that were the proper attribute of the seraphim. Often the cherubim were transformed into symbols of the four evangelists.

Striking examples of the multiple ocular motif appear in depictions of the apocalyptic vision of the Lamb with the four living creatures of Ezekiel (Rev. 4:6–8). In a ninth-century illumination in the so-called Alcuin Bible from Tours eyes stud wings of the beasts, who surround the sacrificial Lamb with the instruments of the passion and a chalice for the drops of his blood.[25] In the Trier Apocalypse, a Carolingian manuscript based on an Italian early Christian model, the tetramorph surrounding the triumphant Lamb has eyes on all its wings. The Lamb has six additional eyes covering its head.[26]

With illuminations of Spanish provenance the ocular motif assumes importance. In a manuscript of Gregory the Great's *Moralia in Iob* the seraphim flanking Christ in a mandorla are covered with eyes on their wings.²⁷ The celebrated Catalan bibles of Roda and Ripoll portray Christ in majesty accompanied by angels with both stylistic and realistic eyes.²⁸ For the vision of Isaiah another manuscript has cherubim and seraphim with realistic eyes on wings.²⁹ The Beato from San Millan of about the millennium portrays the Lamb with seven eyes on its profiled head. It holds a book locked with seven seals, with probable ocular motifs of a circled dot. Three of the tetramorphs have dotted feathers.³⁰ Less dramatically but more typically, in the Beato of Fernando I y Sancha the creatures enclosed within a wheel have eyes on their wings, as does the inner wheel that encloses the victorious Lamb.³¹ In the celebrated Beato known as the Apocalypse of Saint-Sever, in the depiction of the second glorification, the encircled tetramorph has, except for its human figure, definite eyes on the bodies. The angel who reaches down from a cloud in the vision of the four horsemen extends to the evangelist a hand with an eye on it. There are three more eyes on the angel's garment and two on its neck.³² A major work of Spanish illumination and Romanesque art, the *Liber testamentorum regium*, portrays Alfonso II with his armor-bearer at prayer. The angels who bear Christ in a mandorla have eyes on their wings, notably the two golden eyes on the blue wings of the seraphim who embrace its top and bottom.³³

The most awesome, perhaps, of all artistic angels adorn the polychrome murals of a group of Romanesque churches Loyola could readily have visited. All are located in the northeast triangle of the Hispanic peninsula where it joins with France, east of Pamplona near the border and northwest of Manresa and Montserrat. These seraphim with wings full of eyes and eyes on their hands and feet appear at Sant Quirze de Pedret, at Esterrí de Cardós incensing the Eternal One, at Santa Eulàlia d'Estaon, at Sant Clement de Taüll, where the Lamb has eight eyes, and at Esterri d'Àneu. In the fresco for the central apse of this last example are two seraphim with eyes on the four folded wings and an eye on the extended palm of each hand. Beside each is a prophet, Isaiah, whose lips a seraph cleanses with glowing coals, and Elijah. In the center are two flaming intertwined wheels of a chariot.³⁴

The multiple ocular motif symbolized omniscience. That quality was not necessarily virtuous, as in Greek culture, where knowledge defined virtue, so that its presence need not signify good. Had not Satan fatally promised Adam and Eve the knowledge of good and evil that they might be like gods? In the Apocalypse of Saint-Sever, in the very scene of the angel with the eyes on its garment and neck who assists the evangelist, coexist evil winged animals. Two have eyes covering their bodies, while the third has two extra eyes on the top of its head.³⁵ The motif cannot be naively identified with good or with evil. The devil had multiple eyes. Jewish legends reported Sammael (Satan) as full of eyes.³⁶ Azrael, the angel of death in both Judaic and Islamic lore, had as many eyes as there are humans; as each person died, an eye closed.³⁷ In Spanish manuscript illuminations of the Apocalypse there were evil beasts with many eyes, such as the one in the Beato of Madrid who stalks the earth with defined red eyes spangling his purple body.³⁸ In Christian art and literature the devil is sometimes represented with three faces or three heads in antithesis to the Trinity, as in Dante's description. It may also have a head on its stomach or rump or eyes for kneecaps.³⁹ In a Catalan example by the Mestre de Glorieta the archangel Michael lances a devil who has miniature heads on his shoulders and knees and a huge head from the waist to the genitals.⁴⁰ Although multicephalism can be merely monstrous—demoniacal and not divine—it is a variant of the omniscience of celestial beings as symbolized by their many eyes.⁴¹

An ocular motif may also decorate the wings of devils (as if anticherubim), although rarely. An Anglo-Saxon manuscript of the early eleventh century typically depicts a human devil with bristling hair and protruding claws, but with the deviant detail of realistic eyes on its wings.⁴² Diabolical humans, dragons, and monsters emerged in the thirteenth century, with the sinister wings of nocturnal bats transferred to Satan, prince of darkness.⁴³ Although these wings are usually undecorated, eyes can appear between their membranes, as in the Triumph of Death attributed to Orcagna in the Campo Santo of Pisa.⁴⁴ The dominant devil in the Last Judgment who seizes and devours souls is covered with the ocular motif of a circle within a circle.⁴⁵ In a retable of Michael the archangel by Jaume Ferrer II the same motif appears on the breast and between the membranous bat's wings of a devil with heads on its knees and shoulders. The archangel in counterpoint has the multiple ocular motif of peacock's wings.⁴⁶ Bestial and anthropomorphic demons similarly appear in the upper scene of the Breaking Out of the Imprisonment of Hell by the most important of medieval Spanish painters, Bermejo. Satan as the central figure in the background has a head like a cock, while on his body and arms shine oval jewels, as if knowing eyes. The demon on his left has the same ovals on the outer part of his batlike wings, while a demon meditative with chin in hands is dotted on his wings and legs.⁴⁷ In a more notable example by Miguel Jiménez the devil whom the archangel Michael lances has a cock's crest, a feathered body, and the claws of a bird. In rows between the membranes of its bat's wings are realistic eyes of the same type traditionally depicted on the cherubim.[48] The motif of multiple eyes is ambivalent. It signifies omniscience—but not necessarily as a good, in symbolic contradiction to the Greek culture of wisdom.

Ezekiel envisioned the cherubim with "the whole body full of eyes in their four wheels." Indeed, "the whole body, and the necks, and the hands, and the wings were full of eyes in the circle of the four wheels" (Ezek. 1:18; 10:12 Vulg.).[49] Philo and Origen concurred that their name meant "full of science." John Chrysostom thought that it denoted "full perception," and that their eyes symbolized "clairvoyance."[50] As Augustine defined, "Cherubim is the seat of the glory of God, and is interpreted as the fullness of knowledge."[51] The treatise that established the nine choirs of angels and their attributes for theology and art, Pseudo-Dionysius the Areopagite's *Celestial Hierarchies*, specified the cherubim and the seraphim as the "many-eyed and many-winged ones." Together with the lesser thrones they comprised the first celestial order, as most intensely illumined by the divine light. From their Hebrew denotation of "an abundance of knowledge or an outflowing of wisdom," the text elaborated that "the name cherubim denotes their power of knowing and beholding God, their receptivity to the highest gift of light, their contemplation of the beauty of the Godhead in its first manifestation, and that they are filled by participation in divine wisdom, and bounteously outpour to those below them from their own fount of wisdom." It interpreted the ocular symbolism as "the power of sight as an image of their most transparent upliftment to the divine light, their single, free, unresisting reception of that light, their responsiveness, and pure receptivity without passion to the divine illuminations." The details of "eyelids and eyebrows represent the guarding of intellectual conceptions in divine contemplations."[52] Although this was the speculation of an anonymous monk writing in about the fifth century, the text enjoyed a quasicanonical status until discredited in the sixteenth century. But by then its angelic ideas had worked their influence.[53] Multiple eyes had become a symbol of contemplation. Hildegard of Bingen illustrated the inaugural vision of her *Scivias* with a figure covered with eyes, symbolizing fear of the Lord as the beginning of wisdom.[54]

Knowledge was not originally an implicit attribute of the deity or his angels, however. It was a defined ideological complex as a specific attribute of celestial gods, astral gods, and gods associated with that realm of light. The concept of omniscience was detached from any particular environment such as monotheism or polytheism. It developed in pastoral societies, which regarded the sky for survival, rather than in agricultural societies, which focused on the earth. The omniscience of the divine beings who inhabited the heavens was visual. Knowing was seeing. In literature and art those bright gods were equipped with eyes that were the very stars or the sun and moon. In contrast, the omniscience of earth was of a magical or oracular kind, as in the waters flowing in the depths of the Chebar or the Cardoner where Ezekiel and Loyola had each stood. That universal sight was ascribed concretely in many cultures to the eyes of those gods. They were uncommon organs of intense luminosity, as in the testimony that "the eyes of the Lord are ten thousand times brighter than the sun" (Eccl. 23:19).

The abnormality of divine omniscience was more commonly a matter of quantity, however. Transcendence was symbolized anthropomorphically by a multiplicity of form: many eyes. The eyes of the deity were more numerous than usual, either as divided among many heads, or as scattered all over the body, like the Egyptian figure of Bes pantheos. Similar patterns prevailed since antiquity in Hittite, Phoenician, and Babylonian cultures. A Babylonian captive envisioning celestial creatures with multiple eyes was the prophet Ezekiel. The cherubim appeared to him as the typical instrument for omniscient retribution, a meteorological event. They were a thunderstorm, flashing with lightning, whirring with the wheels of the winds, and having the four faces of zodiacal design. Their many eyes were the attributes of the celestial deity as omniscient. They symbolized the power to initiate the prophet into revelations about human deeds and divine retribution, since the divine omniscience did not survey the universal range of knowledge but focused on man and his activities. It penetrated not only human deeds and words but also, as another prophet told, inmost thoughts and secret intentions (Jer. 11:20). That visual omniscience was one of vigilant benevolence and just retribution. Corresponding to that equity was a religious experience of the incertitude of the human condition and the disquiet of moral conscience. In the spontaneity, originality, and simplicity of the ideological complex was mythical thought.[55]

Loyola's visionary aerial thing with multiple eyes is consistent with this celestial mythology. The Basques as shepherds were pastoral people who observed the sky. The earliest recorded name, dating to the twelfth century, for God among the Basques was *Urcia*, or "sky," in relation to *ortz* as "thunder," or in his native Guipúzcoa, *ostegun*.[56] Loyola's vision is also literarily imitative of the masterful allegory of pilgrimage. The tetramorphs with multiple wings full of eyes appeared to Dante in purgatory as guardians of the triumphal chariot of the Griffon as Christ. The poet compared their ocular motif to Argos and he advised the reader to consult Ezekiel's vision for their description.[57] Loyola's experience proves not so simply religious, however; ultimately he descries the creature as the devil. Angels appeared in the heavens, but so did demons.[58]

Stock stories portrayed ascetics as subject to incessant attacks from the forces of evil, whether interpreted as external creatures or internal creations.[59] The demons could assume visible form, changing shape at will into an aerial giant or a black boy, a natural beast or a monstrous centaur. They attacked with the din of robbers, furiously whipping and clubbing their victims. The event was horribly documented in the seminal *Vita Antonii*.[60] The cult of that saint flourished in the fifteenth and early sixteenth centuries, with the most popular of all ascetic scenes being that of his temptation. Although it inspired painters from all schools,[61] it was most inspired (and repulsive) in Matthias Grünewald's masterpiece, the Isenheim altarpiece, where the prostrate saint is assaulted by a swarming chaos of hybrid men and beasts. The extravagant organisms attack with the infernal violence of nightmares as the beleaguered hermit grips only a rosary and a stick.[62] There was a retable of Anthony in the Seo at Manresa[63] for Loyola to consider. At his next destination, Barcelona, was the most remarkable, perhaps, of the many legendary cycles, a retable painted by the Catalan primitive Jaume Huguet for the church of San Antonio Abad attached to the hospice of the canons.[64] Loyola's vision of the flying serpent compares poorly with these brutal confrontations of the desert father. One amusing monster, quite pretty, too, tamely appears and is dismissed with a staff.

Yet the devil had two methods: when violence failed, he resorted to trickery. He could appear alluringly in a nocturnal vision as a woman. Or he could be a seemingly pious monk plying a sinner with false counsel. The most insidious deception of the devil was to transfigure himself into an angel of light, playing the harp, singing psalms, reciting scriptures. The apparition goaded the ascetic to excessive devotions, then disgusted him with the futility of asceticism and its grievous burdens.[65] The episode of Loyola and the flying serpent has the appeal of folk tales in which the cunning of the devil was symbolized by animal tricksters outwitted by ingenious humans.[66] Monasticism perpetuated the ascetic image of a vivid, ferocious, and ubiquitous devil. Homilists exploited those notions to terrify the faithful into good behavior. In folklore, where the devil was even more colorful and immediate, a popular tendency prevailed to make the devil ridiculous or impotent. The devil thus oscillated between the roles of master and fool. With the decline of medieval culture, the furious devil also diminished through the influences of scholasticism, nominalism, mysticism, and humanism. The Neoplatonist theory of evil as privation especially rendered the devil vacuous and contemptible.[67]

Yet even the ancient ascetics had believed that. *Vita Antonii* insisted that the demons, as already vanquished by Christ, were powerless except to threaten. The tempted soul should venerate the cross. The most important defense against diabolical stratagems was to practice the discernment of spirits, whether an impulse was from God or the devil.[68] Such discernment was not easy. The devil did not always appear true to the iconographic type. Although in the East it was a monstrosity of animal forms—fabulous, gigantic, and incoherent—in the West its figure was more restrained. The hideous depictions only began in about the eleventh century but they achieved their ultimate horridness in the sixteenth. Before then the devil was a cruel man with bristling hair or a little black imp. In medieval art the primary characteristic of demons was the nakedness of the damned with the innuendo of animality and sexuality. The body was hairy, furry, or leathery. Its color was usually black like hell, but it could be an infernal red, serpentine green, or pallid gray. Particular characteristics were spiky hair standing on end like flames, glowing eyes, a mouth spread to oxlike ears, a hooked nose, the horns of a faun, the feet of a he-goat, claws protruding from hands and feet, the membranous wings of a bat, and a monkey's tail. The demon was armed with a trident, hook, or pitchfork as an instrument of capture and torture.[69]

The devil could also appear treacherously as an angel of light, as scripture warned and anchorites attested. In its primary Christian portrait the evil angel on a Ravenna mosaic is only distinguishable from the good angel by color.[70] Satan is portrayed in other examples as indistinguishable from a graceful philosopher, celestial angel, or Christ himself, except perhaps by a mauve tint or protruding claws.[71] The devil could assume a human form, young or old, in a variety of secular occupations. More frequently and more ironically he appeared in the sacral guise of a holy man—priest, monk, or pilgrim. As skilled in rhetoric and logic he could also be a theologian. He dared to mimic Mary and even Christ.[72] In renaissance art the iconography reverted to its origins, and the devil again assumed human tendencies. He was frequently clothed in a monastic habit with only claws, horns, or bat's wings betraying his identity. In the performance of the mystery plays a professorial Satan even wore spectacles as a sign of his knowledge.[73] Although less developed a character in Spanish drama than in the French mysteries, the devil usually appeared there in black but sometimes costumed as a dragon, a serpent, or a maiden.[74] Agents of the devil or of the seven capital vices in disguise provided entertaining relief from its moral didacticism. Their very delight tempted their victims to sin.[75] This is the dramatic experience of Loyola with the flying serpent.

The devil was often identified with animals, an iconography originating in the fantasies of anchorites and exploited in folklore. Fifty-eight species, from adder to worm, have been catalogued as diabolical guises. The most popular were the serpent or dragon, the goat, the dog, and the ape.[76] Augustine scoffed at flying serpents in detailing the calamities that befell Rome before the Christian era. "I say nothing of manifestations which were more remarkable than harmful; talking oxen, unborn infants shouting from the womb, flying serpents, women turning into men, hens into cocks and so on, which are recounted not in books of fables but in historical works, and which, whether true or false, produce astonishment rather than ruin among men."[77] The crowd was credulous, however. The generic flying serpent was the dragon, a monstrous hybrid of reptilian and avian features that had terrorized the populace for centuries.

In the year 1551, just prior to Loyola's recital, the distinguished naturalist Ulisse Aldrovandi claimed to have received an actual specimen of a true Abyssinian dragon, just as reported in the classics. In his history of dragons and serpents he illustrated it as a biped armed with claws. Its body ornamented with green dusky scales had five prominent tubercles on its back, wings for flight, and a long flexible tail with yellowish scales like those that shone on its belly and throat. The head had eyes with black pupils and tawny irises, a mouth full of sharp teeth, two ears, and two open nostrils. Aldrovandi reported from men esteemed worthy of confidence a recent sighting of a great scaly dragon near Pistoia and a published account of one near Styria. That natural history he reinforced with the authority of such experts as the encyclopedist Isidore of Seville and the classicist Julius Caesar Scaliger.[78] Extant at Manresa itself are two decorated ceramics whose juxtaposed scenes portray in popular imagination a vision of a flying serpent. The basin depicts a young man in a pleasance into which the tail of a serpent writhes. On the server is a flying serpent, having the body and legs of a cock but the smooth neck and head of a serpent crested with a feathered diadem.[79] The dragon as a winged serpent also appeared in Basque tales, as in the myth related

The Flying Serpent

by fishermen to children in the ports of Guizpúcoa about Erensugue, an enormous monster lurking in the hollows of the stepped seabed, or in the legends of illustrious knights in the image of St. George, who slew such creatures.[80]

The flying serpent who allures then annoys Loyola is no such generic dragon, however. It is a peacock. Although in modern zoology a peacock is a bird, in the medieval aviary it was a hybrid[81] of a bird and a serpent. The peacock appeared with the serpent in ancient India as a mythological motif of hostility against a small or dwarfed race, although it was not outstanding as an eater of serpents or as a flier. The motif on pottery of a man swallowed in a peacock's belly comments on the subjugation of an ophiolatrous society.[82] Among the Spaniards the great encyclopedist Isidore of Seville described the peacock's head as serpentine.[83] That description was confirmed by an even greater philosopher and scientist, Albert the Great, in his *Liber animalium*.[84] It was frequently repeated by both moralists and naturalists in such diverse sources as Brunetto Latini's *Li livres dou tresor*[85] and Aldrovandi's *Orinthologiae*.[86]

The physical appearance of a peacock coincides exactly with Loyola's flying serpent. He says it is very beautiful and colorful, with many objects glistening like eyes that are not eyes. This feature is the ocellation of the tail feathers of the male of the species, whose brilliant plumage earned its reputation since antiquity as the most beautiful of all birds. In classical legend the ocellation derived from Argos panoptes, the Graeco-Roman version of the multicultural creatures with many eyes, such as Bes pantheos and the cherubim.[87] In Ovid's *Metamorphoses* Argos was a monster of a hundred eyes appointed by Juno to guard with celestial vigilance her rival Io, who had been changed into a cow. Mercury lulled Argos to sleep with his pipes, then hacked off his unnatural head. An enraged Juno plucked out its multiple eyes and set them with jeweler's art in the tail feathers of the peacock.[88] The scene would be most famously depicted by Peter Paul Rubens,[89] who was incidentally the most celebrated painter of Loyola.[90] There was also a medieval moralization of the myth, in which the Christian was to be Argus, and his soul, the cow Io, which he guarded with vigilance. The hundred eyes were the good deeds and pious services by which that was to be secured. The thief was the devil, who lulled Argus to sleep by vices and so captured Io, the soul.[91]

From its Indian provenance the peacock became associated in classical culture with the celestial queen. It was an attribute of the principal goddess Juno, her sacred pet. As a symbol of the apotheosis of Roman empresses, the peacock was portrayed at their thrones and carved into their tombs and on their funereal lamps. From pagan monuments the peacock became transferred to Christian sepulchres as a sign of the ascent of the sanctified soul to God.[92] Since its tough flesh resisted putrefaction, as an experiment by Augustine confirmed, it was believed incorruptible.[93] The peacock became an emblem of the resurrection of the corruptible body; its splendid plumage, of the glories of heaven. As a symbol of paradisiacal joys, it adorned frescoes in catacombs[94] then mosaics in churches.[95] Peacocks appeared on an episcopal cathedra, on choir gates, stone reliefs, a gate plate, an ornamental plaque, sarcophagi, and more mosaics.[96] The bird frequently appeared in renaissance art, such as perching on the windowsill in Domenico Ghirlandaio's painting of the Last Supper.[97]

Its particular place of delight was the garden. Among the birds of the park and gardens of Charlemagne were peacocks. In a painting for Queen Isabella of Spain by a follower of Hans Memling the Madonna is portrayed in a summer house with a prospect of the garden in which peacocks have freedom of the lawns. In Jan van Eyck's rendering of the Madonna in a garden overlooking a Gothic city a walk-wall behind the battlements is enlivened by peacocks. A peacock perches on the garden wall in a painting of St. Catherine's spiritual marriage. In a miniature in the Hennessy Book of Hours SS. Cosmas and Damian share an open book as they sit on a bench of turf in the daisied lawn of a large mansion, with specimen trees, pinnacled Gothic fountain, trellised herbier and tunneled arbor, and a peacock. Yet the peacock did not only grace holy gardens. A scene at the Court of Burgundy has a peacock perched on the trellised railing of an enclosed herbier and on the trellised fence of the most famous of pleasure gardens, in the Flemish illustrations to *Roman de la rose*.[98]

This popular symbol of immortality appealed also to the Spanish imagination. A full-page illustration of a peacock decorates a tenth-century *Moralia in Iob*. The bird appears in Spanish manuscripts as part of the repertory of celestial or paradisiacal symbols in the arcades of canon tables. It also plays an important role in peninsular Islamic depictions of celestial or royal settings.[99] Extant from medieval Navarre are several other examples, most impressively the royal peacocks in Byzantine style on the capitals of the cathedral of Pamplona,[100] the city in whose defense Loyola was wounded.

The peacock would have presented an attractive image to the ascetic Loyola, a vision of the immortality for which he labored. A hymn of

Ephraeum Syrus compared the spiritual beauty of the ascetic with the physical beauty of the peacock.[101] The medieval revelations of Mechthilde of Magdeburg attested that among the ornaments of the spiritual bride "she has a hat of peacock's feathers; that denotes holiness on earth and high honour in Heaven."[102] The peacock was the special attribute of a saint whom Loyola would have known well, St. Barbara. The bird was her earliest attribute, portrayed on an eighth-century pillar in the church of S. Maria Antiqua in Rome. It was not only a symbol of immortality but also probably an allusion to the legend in which the cane with which Barbara's father beat her was transformed into a peacock's feather. She held it erect in her iconography in substitution of the standard palm of victory and also in allusion to her patronage against sudden death. St. Barbara became in the fifteenth century the patroness of artillery men, who were exposed to sudden death from accidental explosions. She guarded artilleries, forts, and arsenals. Her patronage of soldiers was also attributed to the legend in which her father was struck by thunderous lightning for having decapitated her. She was thus patroness against death by lightning, and in Basque territories against thunderstorms, since the fiery booming of artillery echoed that celestial phenomenon.[103]

As a soldier Loyola may well have invoked St. Barbara's protection against death. It was a wound by artillery, the cannon shot blasting his legs, that terminated his military career. As the pacifist Erasmus mocked her invocation by the limping soldier of his colloquy "Militia":

HANNO:	Weren't you worried about the destination of your soul if you fell in battle?
THRASYMACHUS:	Oh, no, I was confident, because I had commended myself once for all to St. Barbara.
HANNO:	Did she undertake to protect you?
THRASYMACHUS:	Yes, she seemed to nod her head a little.[104]

There is another acute association between them. Because Barbara began to study the mysteries of the Christian faith so young she became, together with the more illustrious yet elusive Catherine of Alexandria, the patroness of scholars and students. A famous fortress of learning under her protection was the Collège de Sainte-Barbe at the University of Paris. That was the very place where Loyola would arrive by October 1529 for three and a half years of study toward the baccalaureate examination, finally gaining a licentiate and a master of arts in philosophy in March 1533. Loyola attests difficulty in applying himself to his lessons.¹⁰⁵ He may well have invoked the St. Barbara in whose college he toiled as earnestly as he may have prayed to her in the fortress at Pamplona. It is her attribute, the peacock's feather, that invests with meaning his great learning at the Cardoner.

The peacock also conveyed a significance that would have stirred his chivalric spirit. It commonly adorned medieval courts, both royal and ducal, where it was esteemed for its beauty, for its plumes as adornments in helmets, and as a delicacy at table.¹⁰⁶ The pope in state, while processing into St. Peter's basilica in Rome, carried the flabellum, a fan of ostrich feathers onto which were sewn the ocellations of peacock's feathers.¹⁰⁷ In *Parzival* the paragon of castles for Gawain, the Schastel Marveile, had a roof with the appearance of peacock's feathers; while kings Anfortas and Gramoflanz sported the plumage in their bonnets.¹⁰⁸ An early sixteenth-century colored wood carving by Hans Burgkmair the Elder portrayed Kaiser Maximillian I with the order of the golden fleece and with peacock's feathers as plumage on his helmet.¹⁰⁹

The peacock was the image of a very voguish cycle of poems that amplified and glossed the adventurous and moralizing *Roman d'Alexandre*, the most important text in the medieval Spanish kingdoms for the idea of fame. Jacques de Longuyon's *Voeux du paon* was one of the most popular of late medieval romances and the most popular of the immense literature on Alexander the Great.¹¹⁰ In its chivalric plot a captive during a truce slew a peacock flaunting in a courtyard. The assembling lords and ladies pardoned him and dispatched the bird to the kitchen. At a sumptuous feast each vowed to the peacock a feat of valor. The peacock was presented to the bravest swearer, and the vows were fulfilled in battle and in marriage.¹¹¹ Its sequel, Jean Brisebarre's *Li restor du paon*, developed the oath to restore the peacock wrought in gold and set with gems symbolizing the courtly virtues of a lover. A panegyric to the peacock was declaimed at a banquet, and the members of the company each genuflected before the image, offering it a gift. After the ceremony Alexander proposed that each deliver an opinion on how well the original oaths to the peacock had been performed; a prize was awarded to the best debater. The conclusion of the cycle, Jean de la Mote's *Le parfait du paon*, displayed the restored peacock, to which vows were again sworn, although few of Alexander's men would survive the battle. The peacock was not unique among birds to whom chivalric vows were made¹¹² but it was the most splendid and celebrated.

Loyola's lady is the Madonna, the woman of his conversional vision during convalescence in the castle. He has pledged himself her knight in vigil before her altar at Montserrat and perhaps vowed chastity at her shrine in Arançuz. Since the peacock had a definite Marian association it would have especially appealed to his chivalric imagination. The classical theme of Juno in her celestial chariot drawn by peacocks was transferred in renaissance art to Mary as the new queen of heaven. Paintings portray the peacock at her house in Nazareth and in scenes of the annunciation in the garden near her chamber or on its windowsills and balustrades. In an altar painting by Carlo Crivelli of Mary as Juno caelestis a peacock perches above her chamber. Its tail points at her head and intersects with the inspirational ray of the descendant dove of the Spirit that touches her forehead. The archangel Gabriel remains outdoors in conversation with a bishop.[113] The peacock has become the celestial messenger, the substitute for the announcing archangel. Chaucer poetized the inversion in *Parlement of Foules* as "the pecok, with his aungels fethers bright."[114]

The ethereal matter of angelic wings was feathers. Alain de Lille in his treatise on the six wings of the cherubim ascribed definite forms of virtuous behavior to their plumage, with the first wing designating confession.[115] Feathers acquired theological symbolism when artists plucked the tail feathers of the peacock. In a seventh-century mosaic from Cyprus the archangel Gabriel has peacock's wings.[116] In the Annunciation by the Siennese master Simone Martini the angel Gabriel saluting Mary has blue and gold peacock's feathers for its wings.[117] Gabriel also has peacock's wings in the Annunciation by Filippo Lippi.[118] The motif was a favorite of Giovanni da Fiesole, who, for his exquisite paintings of angels, earned the title Fra Angelico.[119] A Florentine fresco by Benozzo Gozzoli depicts chorusing angels with peacock's wings, while another angel feeds a peacock perched on a fence.[120] In Tobias and the Three Archangels by Giovanni Botticini the central figure of Raphael, who guides Tobias on his journey, has peacock's wings.[121]

The motif was not an Italian monopoly. In the Last Judgment by Jan van Eyck the archangel Michael, who straddles the skeleton of death above a gaping hell, has peacock's wings.[122] In Rogier van der Weyden's version Michael weighing souls in the scales of judgment also has peacock's wings.[123] In Hugo van der Goes's Adoration of the Shepherds the angel in white before a vase has the unusual coloration of white peacock's feathers at the tips of its white wings.[124] In Catalan examples the angel Gabriel on the retable of Cardona has peacock's wings[125] as he does in the Annunciation in Bernat Martorell's *Llibre d'hores*.[126] An archangel Michael trampling Satan has peacock's wings.[127] Combining such iconography with the original image of the cherubim is the illustration in the fifteenth-century Bamberg Apocalypse, where a peacock angel upholds a mandorla of Christ enthroned with a book and surrounded by the tetramorph.[128] In Hieronymus Bosch's painting of John of Patmos a heraldic angel with peacock-feathered wings reveals in a celestial sphere the Madonna crowned with peacock's eyes.[129]

Animals, biological and legendary, were especially examined in the bestiaries, popular manuals that exploited natural history for moral doctrine. The beasts became a repertory of metaphors applicable to the meaning of the universe and of man. Symbolic interpretations of animals could and did conflict, however. A single image evoked a multiplicity of significant associations. While that confusion of meaning caused the symbolic approach to nature to be rejected in the seventeenth century by the scientific revolution, polysemy was embraced by medieval and renaissance thinkers seeking the hidden connections in creation. Symbolic thought tended to be obsessed with a single theme; in animal imagery, most importantly with the perils that beset the soul in quest of salvation and the aids it might obtain from divine powers. It approached nature with its manifold phenomena as a lesson designed by God to impress that theme on human minds. Within that major theme of salvation any single image might assume a generous range of different, and often contradictory, meanings. Although each animal specimen could not be docketed according to class and species in the moral order, such variance was no embarrassment to the symbolic mind. It decided the relevance of a particular meaning in a given context.[130] That is the very task of Loyola toward the flying serpent: the discernment of spirits.

The peacock was no exception to the ambivalence of animal imagery. Its presence could victoriously symbolize immortality, even daring to adorn the throne of Christ in glory.[131] Antithetically it could symbolize the vice that most threatened salvation, pride as vainglory. Despite all the divine, angelic, and saintly associations of the peacock, Christian moralists, in condemning sensual beauty as diabolical in origin and influence, emphasized the imperfection and ugliness concealed in its showy display. The peacock, they decried, had the voice of a devil and the gait of a thief in angelic garb. The peacock was commonly said to weep at the sight of its incongruously ugly feet. The brilliant hues of its fanned tail contrasted with a cry so strident that the name "peacock" (*pavo*) was derived from "fear" (*pavor*), since its voice terrified its hearers. Its raucous nocturnal screaming for fear that its beauty might be lost symbolized the human soul imperiled of losing grace.

The moral was not only Christian. The peacock had its chorus of critics since pagan antiquity. Aristotle typified it: "jealous and self-conceited." Ovid symbolized it as pride; Pliny catalogued it as ostentatious, spiteful, salacious, alien, and proud. *Physiologus*, the primary source for medieval bestiaries, named the peacock, among all birds, "the boaster." Its habit of strutting and of displaying its exotic plumage suggested to Boethius pride and vanity. Although it was the male of the species that displayed its tail, the peacock incongruously symbolized female vanity.[132] As Stefano Guazzo observed in *La civil conversazione*, it was as common for women to display themselves as vain as for peacocks to fan their tails.[133] In Hieronymus Bosch's Garden of Delights a peacock graces the edge of the pool where women bathe.[134] In the engraving of Superbia in Pieter Breughel the Elder's series of the seven vices a peacock accompanies a woman looking into her mirror.[135] This is the usual iconography of pride;[136] it so appears on the choir stall of the cathedral of Barcelona.[137]

The peacock also had pride of place in contemporary natural history, occupying the initial three chapters of Aldrovandi's *Orinthologiae*. The naturalist subjected the creature to exquisite scrutiny: *ordinis ratio, aequivoca, synonyma, genus et differentiae, pavonis nostratis, locus, coitus et partus, incubatus et educatio, vox et aetas, volatus, mores et ingenium, sympathia et antipathia, corporis affectus, cognominata, denominata, praesagia, mystica, moralia, hieroglyphica symbola, proverbia, usus in sacris iconis: numismata, usus in externis, usus in medicina, usus in cibis, apologi, fabulosa, historia*. Nor did he neglect the white peacock or the Japanese peacock. As he recorded, the bird owed its fame to the extension of its colorful tail to the sun, enacting a pomp of its beauty. That was attested not only by the ancients Lucian and Oppian but also by the moderns Tasso, Cardano, and Scaliger. Aldrovandi's own description of the peacock began, citing Albert the Great's authority, with its serpentine head. Its tail feathers were distinguished by "small orbs" (*orbiculi*) as a metaphor for eyes; or, as Pliny and Theophrastus had literally written, "eyes" (*pennarum oculi, opsthalmoi tou ptirou*). Its feathers were green like sparkling chrysolite, gold, and sapphire. The colors of its eyes, which varied the splendor of sunlight, were gold, then chestnut, green, and azure or sapphire. Aldrovandi reported that a Jesuit named Julius Mancinellus once obtained for his examination a specimen of the pavonine gem, so called because its partly green, partly amethyst color emulated the peacock's tail.

Aldrovandi discoursed gravely on its moral. The peacock could be an elegant image of the Savior, as Anthony of Padua had allegorized. The saint preached that the peacock fanned its feathers like the primal tree of Eden shooting forth its foliage; and, after those feathers were ejected, like the tree, it became foliated and fructified. The primal tree was Christ planted in the garden of delight, the womb of the Virgin Mary. The foliage of the tree was his speech. When the sinner acknowledged the word of God thrust forth by the preacher in his sermon, he cast off his feathers, his costly ornaments. At the general resurrection, when all trees—all saints—would begin to flourish, the peacock who cast off the feathers of mortality would receive those of immortality. Anthony also designated by the bird a disdain for temporal glory and he repeated the moral about its ugly feet as the repentance that rejected mundane glory. Truly, decided Aldrovandi, the entire composition of the peacock's body seemed to have a mystical sense.

Its small crested head was, again, as Albert the Great had reported, serpentine; its tail was decorated with various colors, its gait concealed, its voice terrible and raucous. It was popularly said to be vested like an angel, to have the voice of the devil, and the gait of a thief. Its serpentine head, concealed tail, and gait suggested it was a crafty creature, a type of fallacious people. Such deceivers displayed their beautiful feathers in a feint of neighborly love but soon insinuated themselves as thieves. Aldrovandi extended the lore of the peacock to the devil. His fraudulent impulses were initially trivial and easily repelled; but, persisting with blandishments, the devil proposed vain promises, until he exercised his tyranny. The hidden gait of the peacock meant his secret temptations; its hidden tail, his transitory powers and delights. Its terrible voice meant his tyranny. The twelve eggs it was said to lay were the mortal sins of adultery, fornication, homicide, theft, deception, immodesty, lust, blasphemy, pride, and folly. (Aldrovandi also reported the contrary interpretation that the peacock was said to chase away poisonous beings with its voice. Such beings were the devils, and all heretics, sycophants, decliners, and good-for-nothing men of that sort who not only did not hear the voice of the peacock—the salutary warnings, confessions, and sermons of just men—but also avoided the places where it was proclaimed.)

The peacock was detailed as an emblem of vice. Its popular association as Juno's pet with her envy made it a representative of the professional jealousy of the learned. The male peacock's ambush of the female's eggs was a type of the powerful person who preyed on the poor. Its exultation in the extraordinary beauty of its body was a symbol of pride. The very verb "to peacock" (*pavoneggiare*) meant to admire oneself vainly or to parade haughtily. Yet the peacock's retraction of its feathers on seeing the deformity of its feet allegorized persons who proclaimed their beauty or published their fortunes only to reconsider their affairs in meditating on death. The display of the peacock and its tough flesh also compared with the avaricious. They pompously delighted in the cultivation of an ornate body, while their spirit was vile, scurrilous, and imbued with every vanity.[138]

The peacock most emblematized the capital vice of pride, as in the slogan "as proud as a peacock." An elaborate moral and encyclopedic treatise by Matthias Farinator extended the conventional association of the capital vices with animals into a complicated zoological symbolism. In his *Lumen animae* the virtues and vices each rode in procession on an animal and bore a symbol on a helmet, a shield in hand, and a mantle over the shoulder, with sometimes an object in hand. More than sixty animals were introduced in this incomparable treatment of the symbolism of sin with its vast zoological lore. Superbia (pride) headed the procession with a peacock on her helmet.[139] In an Italian engraving of the seven vices from the late fifteenth century Queen Pride is flanked by her horned attendants; on her immediate right is vainglory, who holds a staff flourishing with her sins and a shield depicting the head of a peacock.[140] In a woodcut in a contemporaneous Bavarian manuscript St. Benedict with a cross opposes an allegorical figure of the world as a woman. "Get behind me, Satan," commands the monk. "Never recommend to me what is vain. Evil is what you offer; drink the poison yourself." The silent World, personifying the seven capital vices, wears a diadem of peacock's feathers labeled "superbia."[141] In *Pèlerinage de vie humaine* the vice of Pride has a peacock's tail.[142] William Langland's allegorical *Vision of Piers Plowman* compared a peacock and a lark. Pride could not fly high because its tail trailed on the ground, and so it was easily caught. With its loathsome feet and flesh and its unlovely voice, the peacock symbolized pride.[143] The illustrated prow of the famous ship of fools had a streamer with a peacock as its emblem,[144] and in Edmund Spenser's *Faerie Queene* the coach of Lucifera, or Pride, was drawn by peacocks.[145] In the first illustrated edition of Loyola's *Exercitia spiritualia* there is an engraving of a man in a landscape, blindfolded and naked, crawling in fetters on all fours. His back is straddled by two baskets filled with animals and by a devil with dotted bat's wings, who reins and flogs him toward the pit of hell. On the man's rump, behind the devil's rear, perches a peacock with a fanned tail.[146]

The capital vices were originally associated with devils or demons. Despite medieval personifications of the sins as humans, the diabolical association was perpetuated by the belief that demons infested the air to attack souls. The earliest listing of the cardinal vices was in the pseudepigraphic *Testament of the Twelve Patriarchs* as "seven spirits of deceit." The ascetic who popularized the tradition, Evagrius, extended it to eight: *gula, luxuria, avaritia, tristitia, ira, acedia, vanagloria, superbia*. It was the desert fathers who personified those sins as diabolically possessed animals. Their unsystematic linking appropriated animal lore for moral instruction. The list of John Cassian, who mediated Eastern to Western monastic spirituality, had: *gula, luxuria, avaritia, ira, tristitia, acedia, inanis* or *vana gloria*, and *superbia*. Gregory the Great reduced that list to seven in a devotion no longer monastic but popular: *vana gloria, ira, invidia, tristitia, avaritia, gula, luxuria*. Later *acedia* replaced *tristitia* and *vana gloria* merged with *superbia*. Of the two basic lists, the Cassianic and the Gregorian, the papal one was more influential in the West, with most medieval authors employing it or a variant. Peter Lombard in his *Sententiae*, required for commentary by all medieval aspirant bachelors of theology, listed *inanis gloria* first; so did Thomas Aquinas and Bonaventure. This remained the order in modern catechisms, rendered widely popular by the Jesuits through their mnemonic *saligia*.[147] The *Exercitia spiritualia* includes in its first method of prayer a meditation on the seven capital vices, which Loyola in a very common error identifies as "the seven deadly sins."[148] By the thirteenth century *superbia* usually substituted for *vana* or *inanis gloria* as the chief of the capital vices. The principal authority in penitential literature, Raymond of Peñaforte, in his *Summa casuum poenitentialis* established *superbia* as the root of all vices but in his list of the seven capital ones he included *inanis gloria*.[149] It was with such lists that Loyola expended three days at Montserrat writing a general confession of sins.

Not only were there professional manuals for the clergy there were also popular formulas for the laity, such as Pedro López de Ayala's rhymed confession.[150] Although the concept of the seven capital vices developed in Spain somewhat later than in the rest of Europe, it was integrated with its culture.[151] *El libro de Alixandre*, perhaps by the father of Castilian literature, Gonzalo de Berceo, digressed on hell extensively. Pride as the sin of its protagonist Alexander the Great was typically the queen of the deadly sins. The seventh of those was *orgullo*, or *vana gloria*, which desired human blessing and praise.[152] Although that elaborate personification of the sins was unrivaled for two centuries, the tradition continued in sermons, mirrors for princes, tracts on good conduct, and vernacular bibles.[153] Juan Ruiz's *Libro de buen amor*, a fourteenth-century entertainment and edification on the complexities of love, decried the capital sins with exemplars from animal fables. The illustration of envy was the crow jealous of the peacock's fanned tail, as symbolizing a vain woman. The crow plucked off her black feathers and decked herself out in the borrowed plumes of the peacock, delirious with joy in her colorful fancy as now the fairest bird. The peacock discerned the hoax, snatched the feathers, and flung them into a bag. The moral was one of surpassing friends from an envy so inflated that it almost split the body.[154] Although that Aesopic tale of the unmasking of the jay in peacock's feathers illustrated envy, it equally illustrated vanity or vainglory.[155]

In Juan de Mena's important *Coplas de los siete pecados mortales* the faculties of Reason and Will debated. The appetitive faculty was a deformed female monster with seven heads, representing the capital vices on the model of the apocalyptic beast. Pride (Soberuja) spoke first as the most vicious evil. She recounted her five origins in knowledge, beauty, wealth, lineage, and poverty. As she confessed that final source,

> "poverty with religion
> touched with vainglory
> makes me show without gain
> great desire for affection."

Reason castigated pride for the religious presumption that inflated the soul with vainglory, so as to publish its virtue, its disdain for crime, and its contempt for the world, while prizing only to be accounted holy. The vainglorious person desired to be perceived as good without being so. That was denounced as vile hypocrisy, which tricked observers with a simulation of virtue.[156]

Loyola in his asceticism is vulnerable to the temptation of the flying serpent: the peacock as vainglory. Although vainglory was commonly conflated with pride, it was subtly distinguished from it. Evagrius best explained its nature and psychology. Vainglory was clever in obscuring the virtues because it always pursued human glory, and thus expelled faith from the soul. He cited Jesus' question to the Pharisees, " 'How can you believe, who receive glory from one another and do not seek the glory that comes from the only God?' " (John 5:44). The good was to be chosen for itself, not for something else, the realization of the good that is God, not the drive toward the good that was lesser. "The thought of vainglory is a very subtle thought that dissimulates itself easily among the virtuous, desiring to publish its combats and pursuing the glory that comes from men. It makes the monk imagine demons shrilly protesting, frail women cured, a crowd touching his mantle." It predicted his ordination to the priesthood, with people flocking to his door. As he continued its evils, "it also makes him exalt himself with vacuous hopes; it takes flight and abandons him to temptations, whether pride or sadness, which in turn introduce other thoughts contrary to these hopes." It was difficult, he reflected, to escape vainglory, because whatever effort was taken might occasion further vainglory. Manifestations of humility might become sources of vainglory by exposing to the monk and the crowd the grandeur of his virtue. Yet whoever attained to spiritual contemplation and cultivated its pleasure would not be convinced by the demon of vainglory proposing to him all the pleasures of this world. What could vainglory promise greater than spiritual contemplation, he posed?[157]

Augustine taught that pride contended with charity in external works. Both impulses might perform deeds of mercy, even suffer martyrdom, but with different intentions. Scripture summoned the believer from external display before people to internal examination of conscience with God as witness. If the heart did not accuse, all was well; but one should fear doing good for praise. Vainglory practiced a "crafty semblance of holiness." As he argued, "We must particularly point out that vainglory can find a place, not only in the splendor and pomp of worldly wealth, but even in the sordid garment of sackcloth as well, and it is then all the more dangerous because it is a deception under the pretence of service to God."[158] In classical morality the love of glory was an incitement to virtue. Glory was a present or posthumous reputation or renown, either praise by others or esteem by self for virtues and possessions, especially the prestige of knowledge and wisdom. Yet medieval authors adopted the contrary judgment of Augustine and often cited him on vainglory. Thomas Aquinas decided vainglory a capital vice against charity because it denied what was owed to the Creator in its immoderate craving for human excellence.

Jean Gerson condemned it severely. In examining the spectacle of the contemporary Church he decried the love of human honor as the source of schism. Vainglory also caused doctrinal errors, for theologians advanced contestable theses in hope of personal promotion. Preachers prized reputation more than truth. Vainglory was a dangerous passion that precipitated an individual toward corrupt goods. The religious person who coveted reputation did not shrink even from lying but fabricated extraordinary experiences such as visions. The desire to shine originated superstitious beliefs and bizarre practices. Yet no deed performed for mundane glory accrued any moral value. The appetite for glory was deranged, like the folly of Satan who desired to be master of the universe, equal to God. To God alone belonged honor and glory; the creature only participated by imitation in the divine praise. The remedy for the vice was again contemplation, which by the love of God would rout worldly care, especially such love of honor and dignity.[159]

The immorality and iconography of vainglory were popularly exemplified by the anonymous *Fiore di virtù*, a successful compendium on the virtues and vices. Knowledge as the first cause of love was explained as entering a person through the senses, especially the eyes, then proceeding to the intelligence, which resided in the imagination of the intellect. There was a movement from memory to pleasure to desire. Everything under the sun was vanity, however, except for the love of God. Because the love of the world filled a person with this vanity, it saddened him. The treatise then described each virtue or vice, followed by an example from the animal kingdom and one from human history. Vainglory was the vice opposed to magnanimity. It might be of three kinds. The first was vainglory proper, the popular desire to show off greatness and to be praised beyond measure. The second was bragging about and praising oneself. The third consisted in praising oneself falsely or of displaying more to others than there really was. That was hypocrisy.

The animal embodying the vice of vainglory was the peacock. "We may compare the vice of vainglory to the peacock who is full of vainglory and who knows no greater pleasure than to admire his own feathers and spread out his tail to be praised by everybody." Vainglory was the most tenacious of vices, persisting even when all others had been overcome. Advisory quotations followed from Solomon, Cato, Plato, Isidore of Seville, Seneca, Cicero, and Augustine. The historical example of vainglory was a tale from the lives of the fathers, in which an angel disguised in human form traveled with a hermit. Upon passing the stinking carcass of a dead horse, the hermit covered his nose, while the angel seemed unbothered by the smell. Later when they passed a groomed and well-dressed young man, the angel covered his nose. When the hermit expressed surprise, the angel explained, "Vainglory smells worse to God than all the carrion in the world." The importance of that vice was emphasized by the titular woodcuts of some of its sixty-six editions, which display the peacock on the crest of the entrance to a monastery garden.[160]

Loyola's contemporary John Calvin scathingly identified monks as peacocks: "They are all completely unlearned asses, though because of their long robes they have a reputation for learning. If one of them has even tasted fine literature, he spreads out his feathers, proud as a peacock, his fame spreads wonderfully and he is worshipped by his fellows. The old proverb holds that ignorance is bold, but the extraordinarily insolent pride of monks arises from the fact that they measure themselves only by themselves."[161] Calvin's cameo of asinine monks decked out with peacock's feathers replicated the essential elements of vainglory: the presumption of knowledge or virtue and the cupidity to display its grandeur to the applause of others. Vainglory was not the proper desire for good but the perverse desire to be acknowledged as good. The peacock flaunting to Loyola's imagination with its ocellated feathers promises him what the devil had originally promised Adam and Eve, the knowledge of good and evil, which would make humans like God.

Loyola's association of the serpent of his vision with broad daylight, with the sky, and with its multiple orbs of omniscience, identifies it as the noonday devil. This demon was invented by a false translation of scripture. Although modern versions render the text correctly as "the destruction that wastes at noonday" (Ps. 90:6), the Vulgate ignorantly collapsed five Hebrew words into two Latin ones, *daemonio meridiano*. Thus was created another devil to tempt humans.[162] In Loyola's experience it is not the noonday demon commonly interpreted as persecution or sloth. His is the noonday demon as false illumination. That demon's temptation resonated with vainglory. Augustine, interpreting it as persecution, identified the reason for succumbing to its temptation as a lack of humility. A Christian, he preached, must possess an implicit and absolute trust in God, without presumptuous pride in his own strengths and merits. It was those who presumed upon themselves who apostatized. In Jerome's alternative exegesis the noonday devil was the heresiarch in the guise of an angel of light. It corrupted with the promise of an abundance of knowledge and virtue, as symbolized by noon, the hour when light and heat are most intense. The phrase "at noon" meant "in perfect knowledge, in good works, in clear light." As Jerome moralized, "When the heretics give some mysteriously sounding promises concerning the kingdom of heaven, concerning chastity and fasts and holiness and renunciation of the world, they are promising the [light of] noonday. Yet, because it is not the light of Christ, it is not the [true light] of noonday, but the devil of noonday."[163]

Richard of St. Victor also warned of the midday devil as the deceptive source from which sprang all heresies and errors. Transfigured into an angel of light through its revelations, it promoted the misinterpretation of false visions.[164] But it was Bernard of Clairvaux who in his commentary on the Song of Songs interpreted the noonday devil as the wiles of invisible powers, which lie in ambush to deceive men through simulated good. He counseled that those who had attained to the grace of devotion must be on guard and he quoted the scriptural warning about the angel of Satan transformed into an angel of light. In discharging duties with sensible devotion, a person might be so attracted to asceticism as to injure his health with indiscreet austerities—to great spiritual loss. The ascetic must be enlightened by the day of discretion, the mother of virtues and the crown of perfection. Prudence taught the avoidance of excess in everything.[165]

The detection of the midday fiend as false illumination was popular in late medieval spirituality.[166] Walter Hilton, in *The Scale of Perfection*, spied it as a deception through the manifestation of a false light under the color of a true light. This demon who feigned light but was darkness affected souls who had abandoned the world outwardly but not inwardly. Its victims imagined themselves to be holy in virtue and learned in scripture. Because they fulfilled the commandments literally they imagined that they loved God perfectly. So they posed as capable of preaching and teaching all other men, as if they had received the grace of understanding and the perfection of charity from some special gift of the Spirit. That light and heat, he analyzed, derived not from the sun of righteousness as Christ but from its mimic, the noonday devil. Its operation could be detected by the presence of two black rainy clouds: the upper one presumptuous pride, the lower one deprecation of fellow Christians. In Hilton's exposition of psalm ninety the noonday devil was the last temptation, the most private and perilous one, which quietly assailed chosen and elevated souls at the state of perfection. Like the spirit of darkness as an angel of light, it manifested to a soul its loftiness with wonderful knowledge and spiritual conceits. It thus persuaded someone that he was at the summit of contemplation and the perfection of love, beyond the common living of other good men. He might live as he liked, for he would not and could not sin. Those were false lights from which emanated errors and heresies. The remedy was meekness and trust in God.[167]

In treatises on the discernment of spirits, attributed to the author of *The Cloud of Unknowing*, the devil appeared as a good spirit to cause damage under the guise of virtue. He inspired souls to affect an extraordinary holiness beyond their capacity. He goaded them to external observances such as fasting and hair shirts as signs of a great devotion simulating charity. The worst trap of the noonday devil was to persuade a soul to a special vow binding it to unusual practices. That was a veneer of holiness in contradiction to Christian freedom. The devil's motive in such deceptions was love of the dissention and slander arising from inappropriate displays of holiness.[168] Richard Rolle's *Incendium amoris* warned of that "false and feigned devotion into which those who are ignorant of contemplative life are beguiled by the devil at midday, because they think themselves to be very high, whereas they are very low." Resistance was to fix the mind on God and to be busy with love, forgetful of vanity.[169] Gerson also identified as the noonday devil the danger of committing sin through the aspiration of achieving something lofty. "So that you may understand how nothing is safe even in the very love of God, while we pilgrimage to the Lord, ponder with profound reflection that among those practiced in the love of God and proceeding in other virtues there can be a terrible deception. What kind of deception?" he asked. "Such a kind that these devout, by the just but hidden permission of God, for instruction or for perdition, are deluded by the noonday devil of pride, transfigured into an angel of light under the appearance of a great good."[170] That great good was symbolized by the peacock in Marcus of Orvieto's *Liber de moralitatibus*, one of the most elaborate medieval handbooks for preaching. The beautiful blue feathers on the bird's breast were moralized as deceptive vanities of the devil transforming himself into an angel of light.[171]

The peacock shared with the cherubim the omniscience of aerial creatures and celestial gods, whose extraordinary vision was symbolized by multiple eyes. It was such omniscience, the divine knowledge of good and evil, that the serpent had promised the primordial pair in the garden of Eden. Early in sixteenth-century art the tempter, coiled about the tree offering its fruit to Eve, acquires on its head the crest of a peacock. The serpent is so depicted in Albrecht Dürer's engraving of the Fall of Man and his woodcut for the Small Passion, and also in Hans Baldung Grien's woodcut of the Fall of Man. In a Netherlandish painting of the Fall attributed to Michael Coxie the serpent acquires a more realistic peacock's crest and even the bird's beak. The peacock's crest appears most alarmingly on the lurid, feathered angel who lurks in the shadows of the Isenheim altarpiece playing a viol for the Madonna.[172] It is the discernment of such spirits that Loyola practices at the Cardoner. He relates as his fifth tutorial and memorial point how he once went to that river and, with his face toward its deeply flowing surface, experienced a great learning.[173]

The virtually universal metaphor for understanding was vision, and vision was symbolized artistically as a mirror.[174] Water was the natural mirror, both feared as a reflector of the soul and exploited for divination. Since antiquity peoples believed their reflection to be their soul. A dread maxim warned against regarding it, lest spirits dragged the reflection underwater, leaving a person soulless—to perish.[175] It was also contrarily believed that the potential divinatory disposition of the soul became effective under the influence of a spirit that approached through running water. Plutarch wrote, "The prophetic current and breath is most divine and holy, whether it issue by itself through the air or come in the company of running waters." That created an "unaccustomed and unusual temperament, the peculiarity of which is hard to describe with exactness." Among its analogies he proposed that it was like dipping steel into cold water to make it tense and keen. The prophetic power of the soul was especially like an eye.[176]

The most famous male ever to gaze into the reflecting surface of water was the fair Narcissus. In mythology he was prophesied longevity if he did not "know himself." Although pursued by youths and maidens, he proudly spurned their love; but they prayed to the gods for revenge on his disdain. Once when fatigued from the hunt Narcissus reclined by a clear, deep pool for refreshment. His physical thirst increased into an amorous desire for the image reflected in its water. Fixed speechless, he gazed at its starry eyes and divine form, enchanted by his own charms. Narcissus bent to kiss and embrace the elusive image in the silver well, until he died wasted by his efforts at its grassy edge.[177] The classical motif of Narcissus was illusion unto death. His error was not a deliberate and arrogant self-love but deception by a beautiful illusion that victimized him. Narcissus's love was for his reflection, for his image, not for himself, whom he initially failed even to recognize. His was a foolish infatuation for the imitative and elusive. The choice of an object for his passion was mistaken. Narcissus was a sympathetic dupe, regarding an image as real. Its very unreality, incapable of requiting his love for it, sealed his fate. Narcissus was perpetually fixed before his image with no release from entrapment by illusory beauty. His classical myth was not about perilous love, as the courtly tradition would so convert it, but about reliance on sensory perception without any comprehension of its propensity for error. As a symbol of the transitory beauty of the material, the myth introduced the theme of vanity.

In medieval literature the myth was adapted to the perils of ordinary human experience in moralizations, romances, narrative and epic poetry, and handbooks. The mythological elements were suppressed as Narcissus was translated to medieval dress and feudal society. He was exploited in moralizations on Ovid's *Metamorphoses* about the deceptions of love and in courtly lyrics about the perils of drowning in the pools of a lady's eyes. The revenge of Amor, whose power mocked reason and moderation, was dramatic. The most notorious of the lovers was Amant, the protagonist of Guillaume de Lorris's and Jean de Meun's *Roman de la rose*, the most important and influential medieval composition in the vernacular. In a dream Amant chanced into a pleasance upon a river in whose clear water he washed his face for refreshment. Following the course of the river, he entered into the garden of mirth to its source in a shady fountain. An inscription warned, "Here perished the fair Narcissus." After hesitation, Amant dared to peer within the fountain and there he beheld reflected prismatically in twin crystals at its bottom the myriad pleasures of the garden. From those enticements he chose a rosebush laden with blossoms and from those beauties, one perfect bud. The rape of the rose became his quest, as he related obscenely his penetration of the pudendal emblem with his pilgrim's staff.[178]

Since Narcissus was hardened against his lovers by pride, treatises philosophical, moral, and natural introduced allegorical explanations of the myth. In John of Salisbury's *Policraticus* the figure of Narcissus strove for power, glory, and praise. People who yielded to such ambitions pursued the fantasies of their own confused imaginations. Like Narcissus they were captivated "imprudently," for their desired object was a vacuity created by the self in muddled judgment. Those vainglorious persons despised others in comparison with themselves and sought to attain the impossible. They gloried in deceptive images, for power was nothing in itself—only a false concept. Arnulf d'Orleans moralized on Ovid about the conceited person whose excellence was illusory and who ended in ruin like an ephemeral flower. Alexander of Neckham in *De natura rerum* specified that "by Narcissus is meant the vainglory which is tricked by its own vanity, since it admires and praises itself too much." John of Garland also moralized about Narcissus as greedily deceived by the splendor of objects. Pierre de Beauvais in his *Reductorium morale* wrote that Narcissus set store by the beauty of the soul concerning knowledge. Spiritual persons who reflected upon their own virtue and despised others would turn into flowers and end in hell.[179]

The peacock was the animal symbol of the illusion of vainglory; Narcissus, its human counterpart. In both lores figured vainglory and illusion; or, as the moralizers conflated those, vainglory was illusory. Water as the place of retribution for Narcissus's pride in spurning lovers becomes the place of redemption for Loyola's pride in coveting lovers. Although Loyola's desires are not erotic but vainglorious, they are still cupidinous. The frigid, sunless landscape in which Narcissus was metamorphosed in death becomes penetrated in Loyola's experience by light from a crucifix. The violent death of Jesus substitutes for the tragic fate of the sinner. From the sensual image of his own face reflected in the river Loyola proceeds methodically from vision to contemplation. He begins to understand "as much about faith as about learning." This understanding is about his cupidity for the knowledge of good and evil, with which the serpent had seduced the primal parents in Eden and now allures him in the guise of the peacock. The tempter promised immortality through omniscience, the attribute of the many-eyed astral beings. Yet the misuse of vision in the regard of self and others was the characteristic of Vice in the choice of Hercules: "Now she eyed herself; anon looked whether any noticed her; and often stole a glance at her own shadow."[180] Loyola will perceive in the light of the cross the vainglorious peacock as a projection of himself, like the reflection of his face in the water of the Cardoner river.

Loyola *is* the peacock. He struts about ascetically like the gay, brave, young lover of *Libro de buen amor* who walks erect as a peacock.[181] While Erasmus warned in his manual on civility that preening before others in elegant, opulent clothing was for peacocks,[182] by the moral of the sartorial topic so was displaying oneself to them in poor, shabby garb. Loyola decks himself out in such peacock's feathers when he dons the sackcloth at Montserrat. There he appears before the Madonna's statue, posturing in the scene that peacock angels most frequently visited in renaissance art, the annunciation. It is the very feast of the annunciation (25 March) for which he keeps vigil. The angel saluting Mary is none other than Loyola the peacock, embodying asceticism as "the angelic life." In his diary, composed about twenty years later, he still has the thought or judgment in prayer that he should behave or be like an angel, and his eyes suavely mist over.[183] This is why at Manresa the peacock appears aerially "next" (*junto*) to him: it is his double. Loyola is playing autofascination.[184] He gazes at the peacock with his two eyes; its multiple iridescent eyes reflect him. He sees in them himself gloriously multiplied—an infinity, an immortality of Loyolas. This is the motif of the pupillary soul.[185] As Leonardo da Vinci stated the phenomenon, "If you look into the eye of another person you will see your own image."[186] Loyola's vision also related to the amatory motif of lovers gazing mutually into each other's eyes, a variant on the commonplace of the unilateral glance as an arrow that penetrated the eyes of the lover and wounded the heart.[187] Looking into the beloved's eyes as a mirror implied self-love.[188] The peacock's eyes spy Loyola out in judgment, just as the river Cardoner in which his image is reflected divines his soul. The peacock cogently appears at this climactic understanding and judgment about goods. Loyola is able to dismiss the thing for what it is: a creature, an attractive but lesser good than God.

Splendor, especially false glitter, was related since Christian antiquity to the pomps of the devil. Those pomps were not grave sins such as murder but rather vain praise, glory, proud insolence. As the diabolical vanities were denounced in a medieval treatise on baptism, "His pomps are ambition, arrogance, vainglory and others of this type that are discerned as flowing from the fountain of pride."[189] Loyola recognizes the identity of the peacock "in the light of the cross." A cross is not a light; its only beams are of dense, opaque wood. Yet it is for Loyola the source of his great enlightenment. This understanding identifies in his conscience all other lights—from the spangled sheen of the peacock's tail to the shining surface of the river Cardoner—as merely reflective surfaces, imitations of reality. The supreme good is the source of those lights, their Creator. The imagery is Platonist, as mediated through Augustine's Neoplatonist theory of illumination. Loyola moves in place from the river to the crucifix. Although the major Catalan shrines like Montserrat were dedicated to images of the Madonna, the miraculous signs of the sixteenth century became almost exclusively dedicated to crucifixes or other images of the passion.[190] Loyola wounded with self-love considers before the crucifix the wounds of selfless love.

In medieval lyrics on the crucifixion the wounds of Christ were appealed to for protection against the seven capital vices.[191] There was also an ancient and general convention that Christ was a mirror. On ivory cases for mirrors the crucifix was prominent among religious motifs as a shining exemplar.[192] Another artistic practice was to set the wounds on crucifixes with five carbuncles, whose deep red color symbolized blood.[193] The carbuncle was esteemed as the most luminous of all gems because it was self-luminous.[194] Petrarch associated it with the sun and by allusion with Apollo, the solar god.[195] As a reflector of eternal light it was allegorically a natural mirror of God. In *Roman de la rose* a carbuncle in the park of the Good Shepherd countered the crystals in the garden of delight. Those gems in the perilous pool of Narcissus could reveal nothing without the penetration of sunlight. They were mere imitations, fake gems.[196] In Piero della Francesca's predella of the stigmatization of St. Francis an aerial crucified seraph is a sharp source of light, artistically novel in throwing the surroundings into deep neutral obscurity.[197]

The crucifix is especially illuminative for Loyola by the same rhetorical topic that had already afforded him light toward conversion, the opening of the book. Although a crucifix may seem no more a book than a light, it was revered as such. Since the art of the catacombs the sacrifice of Christ was symbolized by the pastoral motif of the mystical lamb,[198] whose attribute was a book. In manuscript illuminations of the biblical book of Revelation (Apocalypse) the slain but victorious Lamb was depicted standing on a scroll or on the very book of revelation with the seven seals, or even opening it.[199]

Augustine wrote of the cross as a school in which the master Christ taught the thief; the wood on which he hung became his professorial chair.[200] He also compared the stretched skin of Christ crucified to the leather on a timbrel, the gut on a psalter, or a woolen garment.[201] Mendicant authors developed the analogue into a book. The Franciscan spiritual observant Jacopone da Todi poetically announced of Christ crucified:

> I am the book of life, sealed with the seven seals;
> When I am opened you will find five signs,
> The color of red, red blood. Ponder them.[202]

Angela of Foligno advised that for "superillumination" in prayer the faithful should read the book of life that is Christ.[203] A devotional poem of the Beguines spoke of going to school in the glorious book of Christ's side[204] rent with a lance at the crucifixion. Some medieval charters of Christ specified the deed of redemption as his crucified body. That deed was written on the parchment of his skin with pens that were the scourges of the Jews; the letters were his wounds; the sealing wax, his blood.[205] The meditations on the crucified by a hermit of Farne elaborated the five principal wounds as vowels, the remainder as consonants.

He enjoined the believer not merely to read the book but to "eat" it, as sweet in the mouth and understanding but bitter in the belly and memory. There were many, he wrote, who knew all manner of things, such as the movements of the stars, but because they were ignorant of the crucified Christ, their knowledge would profit them nothing toward salvation.[206]

Among the Dominicans Henry Suso wrote a book on wisdom only less popular than the writings of Bernard of Clairvaux and the *Imitatio Christi*. In it Christ recommended asceticism as "the beginning of the school of wisdom, which is to be read in the open and wounded book of my crucified body.... See, the diligent contemplation of my loving passion makes of a simple man a high learned master. It is indeed a living book, in which one finds all things; how truly blessed is the man who has it at all times before his eyes and studies it." The servant replied, "Alas, Lord, if I could but write thee upon my heart, if I could but engrave thee in the very depths of my heart and soul in golden letters, so that Thou would never be erased in me!"[207] Cavalca advised the vainglorious to glory in nothing save the cross. The medicine for their pride was the humility of Jesus. Of vainglorious scholars he pronounced: better a holy man who is illiterate than a savant sinner. In his mirror of the cross he taught Christ crucified as the book of perfect and useful knowledge in which Everyman, learned or unlearned, might read in abridgment the entire law and scripture. A book, he elaborated, was nothing more than a well-shorn sheepskin stretched between two poles, on which there was writing in black letters with red for the principal initials in majuscule. In this guise was Jesus on the cross like a book. His skin and flesh were that of an immaculate, sinless lamb; his naked body stretched out and nailed on the cross between two beams. He was blackened with beatings, and his bloody wounds were the capitals of illumination. On his body was cancelled the writ of sin (Col. 2:14). Cavalca's mirror was written expressly for the use of simple laity, who did not read the Latin of theological treatises. A translation into Catalan, *Mirall de la creu*, was made in the fifteenth century from a manuscript by a monk of Montserrat.[208]

Catherine of Siena lauded the cross as the professorial chair of Christ. "Christ has written His doctrine on His body; He made a book of Himself, with initials so large and so red that even the dullest and most unlearned can see them and read them plainly." On his body he wrote in great initial capitals the eternal truth of the ineffable love by which man was created to share in the supreme Good. As master Christ was elevated on the professorial chair of the cross so that people might better study the suffering that honored the Father and restored beauty to the soul. The devil propped up before their eyes the contrary book of sensuality, in which was written all the vices and evil inclinations that come from self-love. She exhorted, "Let us then choose the heart-felt love, founded on truth, shown us in this book of life." Its charity had destroyed on the cross the charter Adam had underwritten to the devil. The parchment became the immaculate Lamb who wrote the human race upon his own body, cancelling the original debt.[209]

Unless, she warned, a person attended the school of the Word, the Lamb slain and abandoned on the cross, he would not lead a good life. One must behold him to see oneself, for humans were created in the divine image and Christ was incarnated in the human image. In his sweet school people learned the doctrine of humiliation. When the soul saw itself not for its own sake, but self for God and God for God, it found in the supreme Good the image of the creature and in itself as an image, him. Contemplating the divine love for himself, the creature was compelled to love his neighbor. Then he was moved "to love self in God and God in self, like a man who, on looking into the water, sees his image there and seeing himself, loves and delights in himself." That watery mirror was the "wellspring of the sea of the divine Essence." Catherine advised that the wise person would be moved to love the water rather than himself, for the water provided the primary essence in which he might perceive his image to love it, and it also revealed to him a smudge on his face.[210] That spiritualization of the perilous pool of Narcissus occurred in a letter to Raymond of Capua, her Dominican confessor. Catherine was illiterate and used to dictate her communications, although the friar claimed that she had been miraculously taught to read with the skill of a scholar.[211] Except for her personal obsessions with the purgatives of blood, food, and fire, her dictations were ascetic commonplaces. Her proposal that a human as Narcissus saw Christ crucified in his own reflected image was plausibly a popular oral tradition rather than a personal literary invention.

It was a dictum that the images and pictures of the saints, but especially the cross of Christ, were the books of the laity.[212] The cross is the book that Loyola opens for self-knowledge toward conversion. He may be imagined in the landscape like the most bookish of all ascetics, that saint whose admiration and imitation was so much in vogue, Jerome. In reading the lives of the saints during convalescence, Loyola proposed to himself the medieval models Dominic and Francis; yet the paradigms of this text are the ancient archetypes Peter and Jerome. Its relation about his enlightenment at the Cardoner was that he understood there matters of "faith and learning." Faith and learning was a topic. In his humanist manifesto *Antibarbari* Erasmus instructed the way to the finest praise as the emulation of the finest persons. The truly attentive imitator not only chose unerringly the right example but also the noblest qualities in that example. "Take Peter and Jerome, the one first among the apostles, the other first among the doctors. In Peter there was the ardor of faith at its highest; in Jerome there was learning at its best. It is for you to imitate the spirit of the one and the scholarship of the other."[213] Peter and Jerome were humanist archetypes of faith and learning. The Petrine motif of the text is plain, yet the Hieronymite motif is also prominent. Loyola in his precepts for holding an opinion with the Church mentions Jerome first among the positive doctors.[214]

The cult of Jerome exploded in the fourteenth century with the discovery of some apocryphal writings proclaiming him the virtuoso ascetic, prodigious in miracles. Devotion especially imitated his austerities. Colombini, the irascible husband converted by the opening of the book of the saints, organized his lay congregation in imitation of Jerome. It was in Spain that the cult of Jerome especially flourished with the Hieronymites, who maintained among their magnificent monasteries the Escorial, the royal repository of the largest collection of his relics beyond Bethlehem. Jerome had compelling associations for Loyola in excess even of his legendary asceticism, for which he was portrayed as bloodying his breast with a stone. Jerome was devoted to the Madonna, and his treatise in defense of her perpetual virginity—the subject of Loyola's altercation on the highway with the "Moor"—was the foundation of Western Marian theology. Under the pseudonym of Jerome, her assumption and her immaculate conception were taught by Paschasius Radbertus, whose text on her dazzling snowy whiteness was retained in the Roman breviary for the office of the immaculatist feast.[215]

Jerome's presence to Loyola's recital is whispered in the opening phrase of the preface, which dates the conversation in the garden to the vigil of the feast of Our Lady of the Snows. Jerome was buried precisely in its archetypal site, S. Maria Maggiore in Rome. The translation of his remains there from Bethlehem was arranged, evidently by the Dominicans, so that he might be with its Presepio, the huge reliquary containing the ancient oratory of the holy manger.[216] Loyola's devotion to the Presepio is salient. He will on Christmas eve of 1538 celebrate his first Mass as a priest at its altar.[217] The relics of Jerome were housed in a freestanding altar-chapel erected in the aisle in front of the Presepio, so that the men were very close indeed. The Gesù, in which church Loyola would himself be entombed, acquired the relic of Jerome's arm,[218] and Jerome was painted there with the other Western fathers.[219] S. Maria Maggiore also housed art about Jerome. An important altarpiece, generally attributed to Masolino and Masaccio, was executed for one of the small chapels near the high altar. It depicted the Miracle of the Snow flanked by the ascetics SS. Jerome and John the Baptist. Iconography of the saint was added in the sixteenth century. The altar of a chapel to the Madonna had a pair of reliefs of her with SS. Jerome and Bernard.[220]

Jerome was frequently painted in the posture of Loyola in this episode, kneeling in penitence in the wilderness (often an attractive landscape) before the cross. He was portrayed there with his attributes, the lion and the cardinal's hat, and in almost fifty examples[221] with the book. An instructive exemplar for situating Loyola's experience in a Catalan landscape is a painting by the Master of the Seo of Urgel.[222] It depicts Jerome alone in penitence on the ledge of a crag above a verdant landscape, through which winds a shining ribbon of river. He kneels attentively before a crucifix praying. Scattered about him are five locked books and one open book with a fluttering page, directly beneath the crucifix in the line of sight. The topic of the book of the cross as conversional illumination informs this and similar scenes, the most overt statement of which is a painting by Paolo Veronese. There the crucifix is spread out on the open pages of the book Jerome reads.[223] Books are not only scattered in these landscapes but also juxtaposed. The book of the cross is the archetypal text; the texts of Jerome's scholarship are imitations. The scene ripples back to the manuscript illuminations of the Apocalypse in which the slain but triumphant Lamb stands upon the book with the seven seals, its body covered with seven eyes, surrounded by Ezekiel's whirring, peering tetramorphs. The peacock, their artistic ally, appears in several paintings of Jerome,[224] but facing in the direction opposite the saint. Jerome's sight is fixed on the cross; he has renounced the vision of vainglory.

This is the symbolic book of conversion Loyola opens: the crucifix. It is "in the light of the cross" that he recognizes the peacock as the devil. The illuminating crucifix, the enlightening book, is *luz* rather than *lumbre*, that matchlight struck in the dark when during convalescence he read the lives of the saints.[225] Now he reads the ultimate exemplar, the death of the crucified. The difference between *luce* and *lume* was current in renaissance artistic theory, as in da Vinci's distinction. There was the luminary, not simply light or brightness but the very source of light, the pure, undimmed brightness inherent in the nature of the illuminating body (*luce*). Then there was the light that emanated from it, derivative light as less intense and mixed with shadow (*lume*). Although the distinction was common in medieval theology and philosophy,[226] it is its primary source that illuminates Loyola's experience. His metaphorical allusion of light (*luz* vs. *lumbre*) is to the myth of Plato's cave. In his *Republic* there was another epideictic composition, the "hymn of dialectic." The faculty of sight imitated the effort of the intellect, for it beheld the real animals and stars, and finally the sun. In dialectic a person began the discovery of the absolute by the light of reason only, without any sensory assistance, and he persevered until by pure intelligence he arrived at the perception of the absolute good. That was the goal of the intellectual realm as sight was that of the visible.

This philosophy was illustrated by the myth of the cave. There eyes unaccustomed to looking at forms in daylight looked instead with weak eyes at shadows and at "likenesses and reflections in water." Liberated eyes would gradually adjust to sunlight and look at the sun itself—and not merely at reflections or phantasms of the sun on earth like the shadows cast by firelight. The myth illustrated how the mind turned from the sensible to the intelligible. In the ascent from their underground den to the sunlight prisoners were released from their chains and transferred from shadows, to images, to light. Even with feeble eyes they were able to perceive the images in the water, which were divine shadows of true existence. Those were unlike the shadows cast by firelight (*lumbre*), which was only an image of the sun.[227]

The myth illustrates Loyola's spiritual pilgrimage, which will culminate not fortuitously in visions of Christ as the luminary sun. Until now he has only been admiring shadows of the Good: imitative knights and saints, and his own amiably illusory reflection in the likeness of the peacock and the water of the Cardoner. The meaning of Loyola's *grande illustración* becomes luminous. The noun *illustratio* occurred but once in classical literature. Quintilian wrote that from impressions arose the vividness (*enargeia*) that Cicero had termed *illustratio*. It was the quality that promoted the exhibition, rather than narration, of a scene and stirred the emotions as actively as if the reader were actually present at the event.[228] The Castilian *illustración* means just such an "illustration" and also "learning, erudition; elucidation, explanation; enlightenment; learning; illustrated or pictorial publication." Loyola employs it as a direct translation of "the grand learning" (*megiston mathēma*) of Plato's *Republic*, which was repeated and glossed by Plotinus's *Enneads* as "the huge illumination."[229] A *mathēma* in classical philosophy was an insight to be learned, and the most important (*megiston*) of those was the subject of the good.[230] It is precisely the ancient question of the supreme good that involves Loyola at the Cardoner.

Water served the sun as a mirror. The sun, which could not be perceived directly, could be seen through its reflection on the surface of a river, a phenomenon since Plato for expressing an indirect apprehension of the inapprehensible sublime.[231] The sources of water for a Spanish town—springs, fountains, streams—were womanly places for drawing the drinking and cooking water for households. The laundry was frequently taken just outside a town to the banks of a river, where the women would scrub the linen and wash their hair.[232] As a female place of meeting riverbanks acquired a certain connotation. When Loyola confesses going to the river for his great learning he is not just narrating a geographical itinerary. The phrases "to go to the river" and "to come to the river" were medieval Spanish expressions, or euphemisms, for a lovers' tryst. The river and the fountain were dramatic places of encounter, for the heroine went there to meet her lover and bathe with him. Numerous love poems commenced with "riverbanks" as the key to this motif.

> "I went to bathe
> at the banks of the river. There I met, mother,
> my fine beau."

The banks were frequented in poetry by maidens singing amorously, and the blossoming of flowers there was no natural development but an allegory for the bower of love.

> "The riverbanks, mother,
> grow flowers of love,"

and,

> "I have come, mother,
> from the banks of a river: There my loves
> in a rosebush flowered."

The maiden invited her beau:

> "To the river carry me, friend
> and carry me to the river."

The ultimate euphemism was falling into the river.[233]

There was also in medieval Spanish literature a legend of a noonday apparition of a god or goddess, as in Juan de Mena's vision in a pleasance by a river of a procession of loyal lovers.[234] Or the apparition might be the demon Empusa.[235] There was the visionary Melosina, the enchanting woman who was a serpent from the waist down, with aerial and aquatic features from the folklore of fairies metamorphosed.[236] And in Micer Francisco Imperial's *Dezir a las syete virtudes* seven flying basilisks as heresies appeared by a brook springing from a clear fountain.[237]

Loyola's experience at the river converts the erotic encounter into a charitable one; yet the event remains amorous. With the detail of his face to the river he betrays what sort of lover he is: a Narcissus, an Amant. He also in his meditation imitates the hero of the chivalric romance *Amadís de Gaula*, with whose adventures he confessed himself heady as he began his pilgrimage. Its knights were spurred by a zest for fame and by a concern to maintain and increase it. They engaged in danger so that they might participate in glory, pursuing praise for great deeds to perpetual memory.[238] Amadís, having lain down his arms, retired penitentially under the assumed name of Beltenebros to a hermitage at sea in renunciation of worldly honor. He became involved in a dangerous confrontation, however, which accorded him unexcelled honor and prowess, especially the favor of his lady Oriana. Setting out to meet her at Miraflores, he entered the densest thick of a forest, where he discovered a river beneath large groves. Dismounting for his horse to graze, he washed his hands and face and drank of the water.

"And he sat down thinking of the changeable things in the world, recalling the great despair in which he had been, and how of his own free will he had asked for death, not expecting any relief for his great distress and grief, and that God, more through his compassion than through his own merits, had so restored everything, not only in leaving him as he was before, but also with much more glory and fame than ever." He mused especially on possessing his beloved Oriana, whose absence caused him great sadness and tribulation. That amorous thought "led him to recognize how little confidence men in this world ought to have in those things in the pursuit of which they suffer and toil, devoting to them so much zeal, so much love, not remembering how quickly they are won and lost, forgetting to serve that all-powerful Lord, who gives them and can confirm them." Secure worldly prizes were taken from men to great anguish of heart; yet the losses were sometimes returned to them by God, as he had done to Amadís concerning his lady's favor. Amadís's understanding was that "neither in things acquired nor things lost should one have faith, but that, doing what people are obliged to do, they leave them to That One who commands and rules them without any contradiction, as one without whose hand nothing can be done." From that meditation he proceeded with apparent divine blessing to an erotic encounter with his beloved.[239]

Amadís as Beltenbros was "meditating beside that stream voluntarily restraining the great pleasure and pride that came to him from those very great adventures" he had just performed.[240] Loyola's "understanding" while he is similarly seated at the river is "as much about faith as about letters."[241] Whether or not it exactly mimics the meditation of Amadís on created goods as transitory, compared with the Lord who disposes them, it concerns the same problem of the good. Loyola is engaged not only in the Herculean task of choosing between good and evil but also in choosing in an Augustinian scheme among goods, in a hierarchy from created goods to the supreme good.

What Loyola sees reflected in the surface of the Cardoner is his image, much as his contemporaries viewed themselves in the moral mirror both realistically and correctively. Mirrors in literature could be factual, exemplary, prognostic, or fantastic. Exemplary mirrors, in analogy with their use for toiletry, were held up to the self for interior discernment and moral beautification. Virtues and vices were portrayed as exemplary and admonitory mirrors in numerous manuals, either as cataloguing behavioral rules or as compiled from the deeds and fate of individuals. Some admonitory mirrors, like Loyola's *Acta*, deterred vice by an image of blatant evil depicted with force and exaggeration.[242] As Shakespeare will portray the conversion of King Richard II from conceit to humility, the protagonist sends for a mirror:

> I'll read enough
> When I do see the very book indeed
> Where all my sins are writ, and that's myself.

He looks into the flattering glass only to discover that "a brittle glory shineth in this face."[243]

Concluding his catalogue of the moral disposition of animals with the peacock as "ostentatious," Aristotle climaxed it with the judgment that "the only animal that is deliberative is man."[244] It is such deliberation that Loyola requires to understand and judge his fantasy of vainglory. As Augustine taught, the soul was deceived through its own erroneous opinion, through a lack of understanding that confused different objects because of their similarity.[245] Loyola is bedeviled by the ambiguity of his vision. The virtue in classical and Christian morality that distinguished between good and evil was prudence, the correlative of the charism of the discernment of spirits Loyola applies in recognizing the peacock as vainglory. Although prudence as foresight could be symbolized by the peacock's feathers,[246] the attribute of prudence, as the science of scriptures, was established since Carolingian times as the book.[247] It is the book of the cross, in which Loyola reads the lesson of divine glory humiliated for love, that allows him to discern as evil human glory exulting in self-love. As the stock of attributes for the cardinal virtues increased, prudence acquired the serpent and the dove (Matt. 10:16).[248] It also acquired the mirror.[249] Yet mirrors were tricky. There were innumerable artistic examples of pride with a mirror.[250] Who looks in the mirror—prudence or pride—when Loyola turns his face to the Cardoner river? Pride, as discerned by prudence.

The peacock had the nature of a mirror. The Catalan bestiary in its translation of a Tuscan original varied significantly the attribute of eyes. "The peacock is a beautiful bird with a grand tail that is entirely fashioned in the semblance of mirrors" (*mirals*, for *occhi*). It committed vainglory when it fanned its tail into a wheel and gloried in its beauty, although when it regarded its ugly feet it retracted the tail. Its many mirrors (*espills*, for *occhelli*) signified that a person had wisdom, or providence, of all past matters, whether or not his life was pleasing to God.[251] That is the moral Loyola descries in the mirror, although the peacock has previously appeared to him as angelic, an emblem of his asceticism. Angels were since the writings of Pseudo-Dionysius the Areopagite revered as mirrors and they appeared in Dante's pilgrimage as mirrors in which the divine ray was divided.[252] The peacock is in Loyola's pilgrimage the angel of darkness in the guise of the angel of light, the trick mirror.[253] The ambiguity of that beast mirrors the perplexity of humans, who must discern between good and evil as not always clearly black or white. The peacock was classically an unlucky bird. As the attribute of the most envious of all the deities, Juno, it was a mischiefmaker. The bird was associated with the envious glance, the "evil eye"; and its feathers were used in eye-spells and in magical craft.[254] The glance of the peacock at Loyola is spiritually lethal.

Loyola's habitual failure to descry the peacock as vainglory is due to its ambiguous and illusory nature. His inaugural impression, that of the Madonna during convalescence, functioned narratively to eliminate one possibility, the peacock as a symbol of lust. There remained other attractions, however. The peacock was the Madonna's pet bird. Its feathers adorned angels, saints, and knights as a prize of immortality. Loyola sees a peacock only fabulously; he elects it as a symbol of the vice of vainglory, for which his recital is to serve as a mirror. This artistic choice involves dramatic irony, for the initiated reader recognizes the devil in disguise while the protagonist Loyola does not. It was a device of the allegory of pilgrimage that the audience viewed the visionary world as simultaneously seen by the stumbling narrator and in its universal significance. The detachment of irony was involved in the discrepancy between amusement at or sympathy for the protagonist.[255] The plot of Loyola's pilgrimage is to involve readers in this act of the recognition and rejection of vainglory.

The reader is birdlimed, as is Loyola, by curiosity. The peacock as a hybrid of bird and serpent implied that fault, for Augustine's exegesis of the dominion of humans in the divine image over other creatures (Gen. 1:26) was that birds symbolized pride, while serpents symbolized curiosity.[256] In his interpretation of the three temptations "the lust of the eyes" was curiosity. That was the first among the insidious and deceitful suggestions by which the devil held sway over the body, since the eyes lusted for curiosity. The scope of curiosity was broad: in spectacles, in theaters, in diabolical sacraments and magical arts, in all dealings with darkness.[257] Curiosity darting from the eyes toward displays wounded the soul.[258] The association of the peacock with curiosity was especially colorful. "The lust of the eyes cannot but be lying; it has a colour, it has no truth. . . . For is not the lust of the eyes that which transforms him to an angel of light?"[259] It was vainglory, Augustine taught, that prompted people to desire equality with the angels by desiring the angels to descend to their level. They should rather seek the humility that Jesus manifested.[260] In his analysis of the two societies issuing from the love of self and the love of God Augustine cogently cited scripture. Humans glorying in their own wisdom became fools and "exchanged the glory of the immortal God for images resembling mortal man or birds or animals or reptiles (Rom. 1:22-23)."[261]

This is the vice pestering Loyola. The peacock appears to him in the guise of good. It is a beautiful object by the classical definition of form and color. Even its serpentine form does not necessarily insinuate the devil that tempted the primordial pair in the garden of Eden. In renaissance art the serpentine form popularly reclaimed classical *contrapposto*, or antithesis. As Aristotle taught, "This kind of style is pleasing, because contraries are easily understood and even more so when placed side by side." There was da Vinci's maxim, "Opposites always appear to intensify one another," so that the painter ought to juxtapose the ugly and the beautiful. *Contrapposto* in serpentine form conveyed an important notion of grace and beauty of line.[262]

The blue coloration of the peacock suggests ultramarine, whose unique vividness accorded it the dominant position in painting. It was commonly used for the sky and for the Virgin's robe, to distinguish her excellence from other figures. As ground from lapis lazuli it was a costly color, and its usage stipulated in contracts between donor and artist signified a liberal piety.[263] When Loyola kneeling before the cross has yet another vision of the flying serpent, he notices that it lacks its usual beautiful color.[264] Color, as observed theoretically by Alberti and taught definitively by da Vinci, was the quality of reflected light.[265] The peacock as "colorful" contrasts as reflected light with Loyola's impressions of Jesus and Mary as "white." They are pure light, illuminative sources rather than illuminated bodies.[266] In the light of the cross as an illuminative source the peacock as an illuminated body loses before Loyola's very eyes its colorful appearance.

The plumage of birds was since classical antiquity an important indicator of color in artistic theory. The pseudo-Aristotelian treatise *De coloribus* taught that the plumage of feathers, when blended with sunlight, produced a great variety of chromatic effects. The necks of pigeons looked lustrous when light was reflected from them because there was continuity and density. Variety of hue was characteristic of the plumage of birds because feathers were smooth objects, with a variety of blends into which the impinging rays of light entered to show various colors.[267] Lucretius in *De rerum natura* wrote specifically about peacock's feathers. "A color is changed by the light itself," he instructed, "according as the brightness responds to a direct or oblique impact of light." An example was a dove's plumage in the sun, about the nape and encircling the neck. Sometimes it was as red as the blazing carbuncle, while from another perspective it appeared to fuse emerald green with blue. "And the peacock's tail, when it is suffused with plenteous light, in like manner changes the colours as it turns; and since these colours are caused by a certain impact of light, assuredly you must not think that it can be produced without it."[268] A peacock since antiquity designated not just a brilliant blue but the quality of iridescence,[269] as da Vinci noted.[270] There was a fashionable color in dress called "peacock" (*pavonazzo*),[271] which may have meant such variegation. A phenomenon similar to peacock's feathers in renaissance textiles was shot silks, in the contemporary term, "changing." They were a taffeta woven with the warp and the woof in different colors; the fabric obtained its effect from the reflection of changing lights from different perspectives. The paler color predominated in the light, the darker in the shadow.[272] Changing colors were frequently painted as draperies for angels to denote exotic, expensive silks.[273] Changeables in color were also mentioned in manuals on courtesy.[274]

The color of the peacock's fanned tail reflects the light; it is not self-luminous. Blue was in optics and in art, from classical to renaissance theories, the final stage of color before black.[275] Blue and black were paired.[276] Lack of beautiful color in the peacock, as Loyola observes, is a failure of light in comparison with the elucidation reflected in the surface of the Cardoner and the light emanating from the cross. The fading of color was attributed by Lucretius to the pulling of an object into minute particles, as when purple wool was torn into bits.[277] In renaissance theory of art hues were mixed with white to pale them. This practice was like the effect of outdoor lighting in full sunlight when glare, reflection, and the adjustment of the eye to brightness lowers the perception of colors. In Alberti's *De pictura*, the initial primer on painting, the least illumined portion of the surface—the shadow—received the most intense or saturated colors. The well-illumined portions were lessened in intensity by the addition of white pigment. The most vibrant tones occurred in areas where, under normal conditions in the actual world, they appeared neutralized by the deprivation of light. The painted shadows thus attracted the eye and seemed to advance, while the lights, as neutralized, receded.[278] The changing color of birds' feathers was a traditional example of this illusion.[279] Loyola's initial admiration of the intense, saturated colors of the peacock is the attraction of the eye to the least illuminated part of his symbolic landscape. It is in reality the shadow. In full sunlight, radiating from the illuminative crucifix, he perceives the peacock's colors to fade and fail. He recognizes his vision as the ultimate dark thing, the devil, commonly painted black.

It was expounded in *De sublimitate* that in painting light is seen before shade, just as in rhetoric the brilliance of a figure may outshine and so conceal its artifice.[280] Sextus Empiricus argued the issue of illusion from positions, distances, and locations, according to which the same objects could produce great variety in sensory impressions. "The necks of doves, also, appear different in hue according to the differences in the angle of inclination."[281] It was a matter of perspective.[282] And that perspective was governed by movement. As da Vinci attested, "There are many birds in various regions of the world on whose feathers we see the most splendid colours produced as they move, as we see in our own country in the feathers of peacocks and on the necks of ducks or pigeons."[283] Loyola's perception of the peacock alters as he himself moves from place to place, beginning in the hospice of the patron saint of eyes, until he finally perceives it correctly in his posture of kneeling before the crucifix. A late medieval treatise that adapted a consideration of the eye to the knowledge of divine wisdom supplied yet another answer to Loyola's failure to discern his vice. In *De oculo morali et spirituali* Peter of Limoges moralized from the science of perspective. The deprivation of direct rays or lines of sight caused uncertainty about the quantity or size of an object of vision, while direct rays or lines of sight resolved the problem. That was evident from the case of objects viewed now through air, now through water. Similarly the recognition of sin and its relative enormity could only be known by an observer who looked straight at sin with the eye of reason. The sinner, however, did not recognize the exact degree of error or its enormity, because he did not view it directly but by an oblique and broken line of sight.[284]

The serpentine figure, such as the peacock, conveyed in renaissance art its important notion of grace and beauty of line precisely in comparison with the woodenness of sticks.[285] Loyola does dismiss the flying serpent with a wooden stick, his *bordón*. The pilgrim's staff was a long, sturdy stick cut to form a node in its middle, on which a hand could rest or a bag be hung. It had a crook at its end and a metal toe. The upper part unscrewed, for storage of relics or forbidden foreign items such as silkworms or saffron.[286] In *Pèlerinage de vie humaine* the pilgrim's staff was suggestively topped with a mirror, while a lower pommel was set with a carbuncle,[287] as if it saw and shone. Although neither an example nor an explanation is extant, entrepreneurs like Johannes Gutenberg, before his invention of movable type, manufactured glass mirrors for pilgrims. The badges commonly sold at shrines sometimes included small mirrors. Pilgrims may have used them to collect as souvenirs the rays emanating from the reliquaries during their solemn display.[288] The pilgrim's staff was a walking stick, a utilitarian object symbolic of the role. Its usage recalled Jesus' commissioning of the disciples, who were each to take a staff on his mission (Mark 6:8). That imitated the Exodus, in which the Israelites were to be ready with a staff in hand (Ex. 12:10), and it recalled the consolation offered by the divine shepherd in adversity (Ps. 23:4). The staff was blessed by the clergy as one of the rites of pilgrimage and it was a cherished item that many pilgrims had buried with them for their journey beyond the grave.[289] It was also the theme for most sermons delivered to congregations of pilgrims at their departure. The ritualistic presentation of the staff resembled the dubbing of the knight and the ordination of the priest,[290] so that Loyola's carrying of it in pilgrimage includes his past and future roles.

The staff could also be a defensive weapon. The promotional literature for the pilgrimage to Compostela, *Liber sancti Jacobi*, included a famous sermon "Veneranda dies" that expounded on the staff for driving off wolves and dogs as symbolic of diabolical snares. The staff was called the pilgrim's "third leg." It symbolized the conflict of the Trinity with the forces of evil.[291] In hagiography the saints were often described in recognition of the deceitful demon, the angel of darkness in the guise of light, as inflicting punishment on it,[292] as in that of St. Juliana, who beat it violently with a chain until it hollered its true name.[293] Loyola dismisses the flying serpent with a gesture. His use of his staff for rejection indicates that he is a pilgrim, one who has not yet arrived at the state worthy of the praise that vainglory perversely desires. His staff also replicates the stick with which was danced regionally the military imitation of the contest between good and evil, the *danza de bordones*, or *pordon-dantza*.

Quintilian instructed that the movements of the dance were frequently filled with meaning and appealed to the emotions without any assistance from words. The temper of the mind could be inferred from the gait.[294] The renaissance posture of the orator was the same as that of the dancer, and the dance was related to the epideictic genre both in praise and in virtuosity.[295] Loyola's gesture toward the peacock suggests "the peacock," a fashionable dance at parties and banquets in aristocratic homes, performed extensively in court masques and in entertainments. That dignified processional was the *pavane*, and the great continental favorite was the Spanish *pavana*.[296] The dance is also emblematic of the recital and the text, for as Quintilian wrote of memory, "As soon as the memory of the facts requires to be revived, all these places are visited in turn and the various deposits are demanded from their custodians, as the sight of each recalls the respective details. Consequently, however large the number of these which it is required to remember, all are linked one to the other like dancers hand in hand."[297]

The most famous, or notorious, pilgrim's staff in literature was the *burdón* with which Amant raped the reliquary shrine of the rosebud he had spied in the crystals in Narcissus's fountain. He even compared the difficulty of intercourse with a virgin to a Herculean task.[298] Loyola's dismissal of the peacock with his staff is its moral antithesis, as he rejects vainglory with its concupiscence for the love of others. Obscenity is replaced with spirituality. The problem of love is resolved with its proper ordering to God. Until now Loyola has not been a pilgrim but a *bordonero*, a spiritual vagabond. He has been acting at *bordonería*, or "wandering idly about on the pretense of a pilgrimage," gawking like any tourist at the sights. A blow with a stick was legal outrage,[299] and as Loyola takes the stick to the devil, literally he takes the matter of honor into his own hands. With this moral thrust of his *bordón* he chooses his direction.

FOUR

The Pilgrim

He calls himself "the pilgrim." Baptized Iñigo, titled Ignatius at university, at his destination Rome he will customarily adopt Ignazio. Yet in this text he is always simply "the pilgrim." The usage of the narrative third person was a method of establishing distance, the classical example of which was Caesar's commentaries. Classical literature vacillated between suppression and mention of the author's name. Although in medieval literature the citation of the name was much more common and a pride in authorship was relished, some writers still sought refuge in anonymity as a protestation of feeble talent. Loyola's distance reverts to Christian ascetic precepts that admonished the writer against the sin of vanity. The exemplar was Salvian's ascription of his *Ad ecclesiam* to Timothy, the Pauline disciple.[1] He resorted to a pseudonym lest the work perish as apocryphal from uncertainty about its author. Yet, he continued, in any volume it was more profitable to seek the instruction of the reading than the name of the author. The principal reason for his dissimulation he explained as the divine commandment that prescribed avoidance by all methods of "the vanity of earthly glory, lest while we seek the empty smoke of human praise we lose the heavenly reward." He likened the suppression of the author's name to secret almsgiving (cf. Matt. 6:3). "In suppressing his name the author wished to reserve to the knowledge of God alone what was done for the honor of his lord, and thus to render more commendable to God a deed that evaded public fame." The work proceeded not from a feigned humility but from the truth of simple judgment.[2] Sulpicius Severus concurred in the suppression of his name from the life of St. Martin. "It suffices that the subject speaks, not the author."[3] A device in monastic usage to suppress the name of the author was the pseudonym "Pilgrim" (*Peregrinus*).[4]

Medieval authors and scribes habitually falsified literature and documents. Their culture differed from modern psychological notions of the empirical, individual creator whose work is self-expressive. Their method was not originality but imitation, as invented from the commonplaces of an anonymous tradition. Citations could be manipulated, such as the ascription to Augustine's authority of the sayings of others or of oneself. Such play of substitutions in the attribution of the author's name supposed an indifference to any notion of a historico-biographical identity of the authorial subject or to literary propriety. The attribution of the name was largely an effect of structure, an element of its function, the choice dictated by the persuasiveness to be invented. Another method of dissimulation was forgetting. The author drew a mnemonic blank and failed to mention the authors whose works he was plundering. There were such ruses not only in fiction but in all sectors of learning, so that Alain de Lille could write in *De fide catholica* that "authority has a wax nose that can be molded into different meanings." Those resorts were common in exemplary rhetoric for the edification of the faithful,[5] the genre of Loyola's mirror of vainglory.

In medieval narrative and culture the individual subject, such as the hero or the protagonist, was more central and predominant than in modern versions. The subject was fundamentally decentered, however. He was represented as a void who was not the master of the discourse or of the will of the other characters, including God. The subjects in medieval narrative were related to other characters and objects intensely through desire. Desire was virtually the only principle of the description of character. The narrative always, and often only, disclosed what the character desired—intended, wanted, loved—not what he thought.[6] That affective, rather than intellectual, description is implied in Loyola's epithet "the pilgrim."

Dante explained in *Vita nuova* that "pilgrim" could be understood generally, referring in the classical sense to a foreigner, a person outside his country, or, specifically, to a traveler to the shrine of St. James in Compostela or another site. The term "pilgrim" especially applied to those people destined for that Spanish location, while those who pilgrimaged to Jerusalem or *oltramare* were "palmers," and those destined for Rome were "Romeos."[7] In the option of a name—the first personal topic of rhetoric—Loyola is quintessentially a type rather than an individual; he is a traveler at large while also bound for specific shrines. Although both Peregrinus and Viator were early Christian names,[8] Loyola is not "a" pilgrim but "the" pilgrim, or Everyman. There did exist third-person accounts of pilgrimage and impersonal guidebooks. An example of a pilgrim-author referring to the self in the third person was *The Book of Margery Kempe*, considered the first English autobiography, where the protagonist was "this creature." Even the usage of "I" and "we" by pilgrim-authors was little personalized in high medieval literature, until more personal touches were added in the thirteenth and fourteenth centuries. There were eyewitness accounts, anecdotes, apostrophes, exclamations, meditations and ruminations, and snatches of daily and domestic realism. As in the romance, the "I" developed into a person, so that the reader could experience the journey east though his eyes; and the exotic sights such as pyramids or bananas seemed more real because the author had actually witnessed them. Voice was articulated, whether in monologue or in soliloquy. Among journeyers to Jerusalem, the cheery Friar Felix, full of excitement, adventure, and sentiment, contrasted with the somber Friar Ricoldus, intellectual, objective, and stern. Yet neither writer presented himself as such for artistic effect. With some authors of pilgrimage the only bond with their readers was that of literate Christians, who were never addressed or invited into the scene but remained external to it and the page. The exception emerged with John Mandeville, who in his *Travels* seized the advantage of wearing a crude mask, that of the knight-errant of romance and of the almost faceless travelers whose accounts he knew. He addressed the reader frankly as "you." Chaucer in *The Canterbury Tales* capitalized on the possibilities of the narrative "I" as no previous writer had. He exploited the roles of the pilgrims as humorous exaggerations of his own experience and he assigned the reader an active role as listener and judge.[9]

Loyola refuses that prominent authorial role and reverts to the effacing allegorical type, "the pilgrim." The only nameless individuals in the world were the Atarantes, reported by Herodotus in that collective cognomen. Anonymity was synonymous with ciphers. Naming depended on social recognition and accord. In tragedy namelessness was a condition of being stripped of identity, like a ruler deposed of his title; in comedy the concealment of a name was often a ruse.[10] Loyola elects namelessness for himself to obviate the recognition and accord that vainglory craves and namelessness for others to enhance the celestial characters as the real actors in the plot. The text is populated with nameless characters until his initial arrival in Rome, where he receives the blessing for pilgrimage of Pope Hadrian IV, as acknowledged.[11] Persons previously named are celestial: the Virgin with the child Jesus, the persons of the Trinity, Jesus in his humanity, again Mary—all visionary beings; St. Peter, the healing intercessor; and St. Francis, St. Dominic, St. Paul, and Our Lady of Arançuz as places, either paginary or physical. Their naming distinguishes their reality from the mere shadows that are mortals.

Loyola reveals that he customarily addresses others, even distinguished personages such as a captain and an archbishop, as equals in the familiar form of *vos*. This practice he adopts in imitation of the address of Christ and the apostles,[12] again a literalism that is mimicry. It reverses the current social order with its hierarchical language and formal modes of address. The polite vocabulary of deference was inflated in the 1550s, perhaps by Spanish influence,[13] so that Loyola speaks contrary to the culture. Yet in the text many persons retain anonymity. The cast of characters comprises: the French, the commander, the caballeros, a comrade at arms as confessor, the physicians and surgeons, another confessor, a brother, the lady, the household, a servant, Carthusians, the duke of Nájara, another brother, a sister, a "Moor," another confessor, a pauper, a pursuer, the people, more confessors, Dominicans, a venerable woman, important ladies, another confessor, the captain, a mother and daughter, a young man, soldiers, a lady. The important ladies who nurse Loyola to health in Manresa are associated by the rhetoric of place with the only human name before his arrival in Rome. The town of Manresa places him for recovery "in the house of the father of a certain Ferrera, who later entered the service of Baltasar de Faria."[14] This singular naming is probably the work of Gonçalvez da Câmara and not original to Loyola's recital. Baltasar de Faria, as the agent in Rome from 1543–51 of the king of Portugal,[15] was likely known to Gonçalves da Câmara, who was not only Portuguese but was later appointed the royal tutor. The curative place of "a certain Ferrera," more typical of Loyola's own diction, bows to Our Lady of the Snows. As the titular mother of God she was invoked throughout Spain as the patroness of women in labor and all who suffered, as did Loyola acutely there, from stomachaches.[16]

The epithet belonged since Homer to the heroic popular tradition, as in describing the protagonist Rodrigo Diáz with the honorific title *el Cid* and the epithet *campeador*. It captured the essential quality of a figure and served, as in ballads, as a mnemonic device.[17] No ingenuity in onomastics is required to understand Loyola as "the pilgrim." The Christian archetype was established and developed in Augustine's *Confessions* from the Neoplatonist topic of departure and return. The soul was a wanderer from the One and a traveler to it for the restoration of its integrity. The route was not a physical journey by foot, coach, or ship, but an interior dialectic across the open sea of sensible matter to the homeland of intellectual vision. The mind, disciplined by an ascetic divestiture of the multiform, apprehended the One by a method of intellectual transcendence. The *Confessions* orated epideictically Augustine's own perilous voyage from the fluid womb, to the depths of the sea, to the beach of continence, and finally to the fields of faith, where he harvested his life as his very text.[18] "The entire Christian life is a holy desire to journey to the eternal fatherland," he preached. "On the day in which you say: now is enough, you are lost. Forward always, advance always, always walk. Do not rest on the road, do not turn back, do not leave it. He who does not advance, regresses; he who abandons faith, loses the route; more surely goes the lame man on the road than the runner off it."[19]

From the topic of human exile on earth in quest of heaven (Heb. 11:13–16) Christian authors projected an inner condition of estrangement or belonging onto an external geography of here and there. The traditional lexical units composing the pattern were pilgrim, exile, journey, heavenly fatherland, desire, and hardship. The universal journey commenced with Adam's fall and progressed with rejection of the wrong paths and election of the right ones. The metaphor of pilgrimage plotted human history, with Augustine's two cities as an exemplar of this tradition. Another tradition derived from Gregory the Great expressed the human internal condition of pilgrim as the tension between presence and absence and its correlates. The pilgrimage of desire was mapped in epistles of friendship. It was also prominent in dramas on the Emmaus pericope, which identified Christ himself as a "pilgrim" (Luke 24:18), with the earliest document from the monastery at Ripoll.[20] The earliest Western depictions of that scriptural scene were also Spanish, a miniature in the Ripoll bible and a sculpture in the cloister of Santo Domingo de Silos with Christ garbed like a pilgrim down to the emblematic detail of shells.[21]

Vernacular literature initiated in the thirteenth century the narrative quest of a pilgrim on a visionary journey toward an eschatological destination. Such works as Raoul de Houdence's *Songe d'enfer* and *Voie de paradis*, Huon de Méri's *Tournoiment Antichrist*, and Rutebeuf's *Voie de paradis* imagined visionary realms of common thematic and stylistic elements with the quest for salvation as the principal theme. Monastic historians and hagiographers had based their visionary accounts on the apocryphal Apocalypse of St. Paul for an imaginative meditation on the fear of hell to provoke conversion and repentance. Writers of romance began to represent events in time, causally linked by the action of the hero and bound to a particular landscape. They infused the history with moral or spiritual value. The most significant innovation was the personalization, rather than the instrumentality, of the narrator. In *Tournoiment Antichrist* the narrator became the hero of the romance as well as the wandering visionary, and his revelation of the apocalyptic conflict was filtered through personal and political history. Although the quest moved between the poles of sin and salvation, personal conversion through vision was treated as a historical event. Conventions of the genre were a sinning visionary, an otherworldly guide, revelations of a supernatural world, and education in guilt and grace. The earliest examples of the new spiritual quest were composed for Lenten use, particularly for Holy Week, as motivation toward sacramental confession.[22]

The proem to that religious visionary poetry, adapted from its secular version, *Roman de la rose*, revealed the symbolic structure and spiritual function of the entire composition in miniature. It introduced the pilgrim and it established themes predicting the narrative, often through a symbolic setting such as the garden.[23] Loyola's pilgrimage is similarly adumbrated in the garden of the preface—and not merely archetypally because Eden was the place from which Adam began his exilic wandering. Journeying was inherent in the design of the renaissance garden. Although the early plan was static and was viewed in its entirety from a fixed location, after the 1520s gardens became a series of visually isolated but successive spaces. They could only be experienced through movement through them. Their arrangement called for movement of spaces and levels, a planned itinerary by which a theme was revealed in a succession of episodes. The renaissance garden was a form of narrative, with its continuity provided by the spectator in confrontation with different experiences in spatial and temporal succession. In antiquity the garden or landscape had simply been a backdrop or setting, like an isolated description, for the action. In medieval design, as in Giovanni Boccaccio's *Decameron*, it was the place of assembly for listening to tales of action. By the second decade of the sixteenth century, however, even its natural elements were accorded a speaking role, like the talking myrtle of Ludovico Ariosto's *Orlando furioso*, which proved to be a metamorphosed knight.[24] The text of Loyola's recital encompasses the three natural types: the garden proper in the preface, the wild landscape that decorates the tale, and the pastoral vista of its ending.[25]

Loyola's desire for pilgrimage occurs during his convalescence in the familial castle, where he is conventionally the sinning visionary who has revelation of the supernatural realm in the visitation of the Madonna and is tutored through books about guilt and grace. The suggestion of pilgrimage is insinuated in his prayer of stargazing, since in mythology the Milky Way galaxy was the psychic road and its name in various languages was St. James Road, pointing to the shrine at Compostela.[26] In *Pèlerinage de vie humaine* the pilgrim had been reading *Roman de la rose* before he fell asleep and dreamed of pilgrimage.[27] Since Loyola's location while deciding on pilgrimage is also in bed, his chivalric fantasies, religious and secular, are waking dreams. His notion of the sally to Jerusalem imitates the experience of the protagonist of *Songe d'enfer*:

> "In dreams there must be fables;
> But dreams can come true,
> Whereof I know well that it happened to me
> That while in dreaming a dream there came to me
> The wish to be a pilgrim."[28]

Loyola's pilgrimage differs saliently from medieval allegory, however, in that he is the solo pilgrim, without a guide. Guides, patterned on Philosophia appearing at Boethius's very bedside, were stock characters of pilgrimage, as Natura to Alain de Lille, Vergil and Beatrice to Dante, Holichurch to William Langland, Grace-Dieu to Guillaume de Deguileville. The typical response to their wondrous appearance was stupefaction.[29] There is no such grace in Loyola's pilgrimage. He is Everyman but man on his own—a character cast from the individualism that is acknowledged to identify renaissance culture and society. In Barcelona, his destination from Manresa, he explicitly ends his hankering after guides and sets sail for Jerusalem alone.[30]

Here the landscape flattens. The text does not cover the territory of Loyola's life; it makes a point about it. Its climax has already been scaled on the banks of the Cardoner, so that the voyage on the Mediterranean and the further journeys ashore are anticlimactic. The entire pilgrimage is of particular interest to the companions he acquires on the road, the Jesuits. Yet even the papal approbation of the Society of Jesus is excluded from the text, which progresses only to 1538, Loyola's initial year in Rome. Bernard of Clairvaux before him proposed that the experienced traveler on the steps to humility was better prepared to map for successors the villages, towns, and cities, the rivers and the mountains of the ascent.[31] Erasmus in his treatise *Ratio verae theologiae* likened himself to a herm at the crossroads who pointed the way for the traveler with his index finger. Yet he argued that not stationary statues but shipwrecked sailors, who knew by experience the perils of the voyage, were the proper methodologists.[32] In his manual on courtesy Giovanni della Casa affirmed that "a man can well teach others to follow that road in which he took many wrong turns. In fact, those who lost their way perhaps remember better the misleading and dubious paths than the man who always kept to the right road."[33] In his recital Loyola assumes this authority from experience.

The ascetic who invented the concept of the seven capital vices asserted that the last one to be eradicated from the soul was vainglory.[34] Augustine had anguished in his *Confessions* about the problem of praise. He wondered whether the temptation to be feared and loved by others could ever cease, since it was necessary for certain social functions. The devil spread applause as a snare, so that people might rejoice in mortal fallacies rather than divine truth. So Augustine prayed, "Be Thou our glory." He prayed to be loved for the sake of the Lord and feared for his word. People should be praised for the interior divine gift, he believed. Yet a person could not easily judge himself in the daily temptation to vainglory, like other temptations, which could be investigated. In those he could interrogate himself: whether the privation of sexual pleasure or of idle curiosity was more or less troublesome. Praise disallowed such testing. Its deprivation, by living so wickedly as to be forsaken and detested by others, would be the ultimate insanity. Praise usually and properly accompanied a life of good works and should not be foregone any more than the virtue it incited. Yet the perception of disturbance or tranquillity in the absence of praise demanded the absence of praise. What to confess? he asked. "What, except that I am made joyful by praise? But, more by truth itself than by praise." Augustine preferred constancy in truth to the blame of all good men, rather than error to their praise. The dilemma of vainglory perplexed him, however. His resolutions were to perceive the advantage to one's neighbor when praise was directed to oneself, to be displeasing to oneself, and in secret groans to seek the divine mercy.[35]

The truism about the tenacity of vainglory was repeated in sources as diverse as *Fiore di virtù*[36] and Leonardo da Vinci's notebooks.[37] A colloquy by Erasmus reminded the character Glorylover that "after conquering so many monsters by his valor, Hercules had his final and most desperate struggle with the serpent."[38] Loyola confesses that, although he has dismissed the vainglorious peacock, it persists to tempt him. And, although he habitually thrusts at it with his pilgrim's staff,[39] the very project of pilgrimage ensures its persistence. He envisions the pilgrimage "to do penance"; yet the capital vice threatens to become his fellow traveler and even his final destination, as it had for other literary pilgrims. In *Voie de paradis* the Pilgrim met on his way Temptation and his companion Vainglory,[40] while in Jean de Courcy's *Chemin de vaillance* the Dreamer crossed the bridge of weakness only to be escorted by Flesh to the mountain of Vainglory.[41] Loyola fantasized during convalescence about a journey to Jerusalem as a "sally,"[42] and a sally indeed was pilgrimage in the judgment of moralists.

By the fourteenth century the devotional practice of pilgrimage was criticized in doctrinal pronouncements, royal decrees, homiletic warnings, popular adages, and satirical literature. Pilgrimage was discovered to mask a natural yearning to travel and explore, in which the journey, rather than the destination, was more the issue. It became a religiously sanctioned vacation. With its progressive secularization, a pilgrim to Jerusalem at the turn of the sixteenth century confessed to yearning after novelties as a thirsty man does for water.[43] Because of his "fear of vainglory" Loyola shuns telling the female almsgiver in Barcelona that he intends a pilgrimage to Jerusalem.[44] Pilgrims were traditionally respected persons, protected by ecclesiastical authority and admired as spiritual heroes by the settlers in the places through which they passed.[45] When Loyola tells the woman instead that he is on pilgrimage to Rome, her retort betrays the decline of even that tradition of honor. She contemptuously remarks that Rome will scarcely profit him spiritually,[46] echoing a moral topic that rebounded to an early epigram rebuking pilgrimage: "Coming to Rome, much labour and little profit! The King whom you seek here, unless you bring him with you you will not find him."[47]

Among the condemnations of pilgrimage was the suspicion of curiosity. That fault was condemned by such authorities as Augustine, Bernard of Clairvaux, and Thomas Aquinas, because curiosity about the universe could prevent concentration on eternity as the true human goal. Adam in the garden pursued knowledge under the impetus of curiosity to a disastrous fall. The instability, restlessness, even aimlessness of travel made it suspicious as succumbing to curiosity. Pilgrimage was criticized as merely a religiously sanctioned way of exploring the world. Eternity was stable, free of pilgrimages. Honorius of Autun condemned "rushing about the holy places either for curiosity or for the praise of men." Thomas à Kempis thought pilgrims were motivated by curiosity for the novelty, rather than by penitence for sin. The voyage should be undertaken solely for religious reasons, "not with the intention of seeing the world, or from ambition, to be able to boast 'I have been there' or 'I have seen that'—in order to be exalted by his fellow men, as perhaps some do, who in this case from now have received their reward." Even Friar Felix stated of his pilgrimage to Jerusalem "that many are prompted to it by sinful and idle curiosity cannot be doubted." With a change from curiosity as vicious to legitimate, the medieval pilgrim became displaced by the renaissance traveler.[48] The journals and letters of sixteenth-century travelers are dominated by the trait of curiosity.[49] A baroque moralist still castigates pilgrims with motives of curiosity and vainglory.[50]

Loyola's own voyage embarks with a strong wind filling the sails. The word *viento* also means "vanity, petty pride, airs." He determines, however, to evade vainglory by refusing a traveling companion. Since he desires to practice the theological virtues with God alone as his refuge, he fears that dependency on a companion will pervert those virtues to human trust and affection. With this disposition he even seeks to sail without provisions, but the captain refuses him the promised free passage without the required hardtack. Concerning the hardtack great scruples revive and persist to his considerable distress. In this ordeal Loyola fulfills the third of the temptations of Jesus in the wilderness. Having rejected those about the panorama of the kingdoms and about the leap from the pinnacle, he now confronts the temptation about the transformation of stones into bread. He fears that his provision of the hardtack will undermine his faith and hope in God alone as provider. In his indecision he relies on the judgment of a confessor, who determines that he should beg for the supply and take it with him. Even in begging Loyola rejects vainglory. He declines to divulge to an almsgiver his destination of Jerusalem for fear of vainglory; and the fear so plagues him that he refuses to divulge his origin, either country or family. With the acquisition of the hardtack he disposes of his remaining coins.[51] This also is a rejection of vainglory.

Loyola's pilgrimage involves a beggar's tale. At its outset he collects from his military employer, the duke of Nájera, some few ducats owed him, with which he pays his debts,[52] a condition of pilgrimage.[53] Daily he asks in Manresa the charity of alms, carrying a box and an image, amid rumors that he has relinquished quite an income. In Barcelona he arranges for free passage at sea but solicits at the gates for the hardtack. About to board ship, he discovers five or six *blancas* left over and discards them. His companions on the road to Rome are also beggars, although initially they collect no alms. Begging in a city Loyola finds many *quattrini*. In Rome everyone who speaks with him tries to dissuade him from the pilgrimage to Jerusalem, knowing that he carries no money and that free passage is impossible to arrange. Yet he receives six or seven ducats for the voyage, which he accepts as the only means for travel. The possession of the ducats—the important international medium of exchange—greatly bothers him as a sign of his lack of confidence in divine providence. He decides to spend them for the needy, usually the poor. In this fashion he arrives in Venice with only some *quattrini* left for provisions that night. He supports himself there by begging, making no special effort to search for passage, confident that God will provide; and a wealthy Spaniard does arrange passage for him through the doge.[54]

The return voyage proves more difficult in an episode about the distinction of classes by money. There were two types of Venetian ships available to pilgrims: a large oared galley that was safe and comfortable but expensive and a small ship for the poor, who were crowded on like the rats that trampled them.[55] The skipper of a rich and powerful vessel refuses Loyola for lack of money, quipping that if he were holy he could travel like Santiago, who was by medieval legend transported miraculously from Jerusalem to Compostela. At the request of some pilgrims, the skipper of a small ship agrees to take Loyola on board. Back in Venice a gentleman who previously aided him donates fifteen or sixteen *giulii*. When Loyola is himself asked by a pauper for alms, he gives him a *marchetto*, a coin worth five or six *quattrini*. To another beggar he gives another small coin worth more. To a third he gives one of his remaining *giulii*, and so on, until he dispenses his supply and must beg pardon of others.[56] This dispensation of alms by a pilgrim or pauper to an even needier soul was another charity in the stock of medieval hagiography.[57]

Passage to Spain is charitably arranged, and in Barcelona Loyola obtains free education and monetary support. In Alcalá de Henares he solicits alms to the laughter of a clergyman and his companions. They insult him (*decir injurias*) for begging while healthy. The administrator of a hospice offers him a bed and necessities, however; others also give him alms and lodging and goods to assist the poor. Toward further studies the archbishop of Valladolid offers him admission to his college in

Salamanca and four *escudos*. Later on arrival in Paris for studies a merchant gives him twenty-five *escudos* on draft, but another student spends the sum without repayment. Loyola is forced to find shelter in a hospice and to beg his way through university. He fantasizes himself as the servant of Christ and the apostles,[58] as in the hagiography of St. Catherine of Siena, who played such make-believe while doing housework.[59] Loyola fully endeavors to find employment from a master, but without success. He travels annually to Flanders, losing two months of study, to acquire sufficient funds for the year. Once, he goes to England, where he obtains more alms than usual. Back in Paris at the university he gives the Spiritual Exercises to three men, who themselves begin to beg. He questions taking the bachelor's degree because it costs an *escudo*, which some very poor students are unable to afford; but at the advice of his teacher he does so. For this decision he is detracted.[60]

The next monetary matter is the purchase by his companions of a small horse for a sickly Loyola to ride home, the place of convalescence. This horse is a sorry comparison with the winged steed Pegasus that traditionally symbolized fame,[61] although news of his arrival still precedes him. Refusing lodging in his brother's house, Loyola stays in a hospice from which he ventures to solicit alms in the region. He leaves without money, however, and declines donations in the native towns of his companions. Upon arrival back in Italy, the people of Bologna spare him not a single *quattrino*. The companions, however, are given in Rome drafts of two hundred or three hundred *escudos* as alms for their passage to Jerusalem, which donations they remit when the journey is cancelled. Dispersed in the Veneto, some live with Loyola in an abandoned dwelling in Vincenza. Twice daily they beg in the city but they receive such a pittance they can barely survive. With the return of the other companions, some seek alms in the surrounding villages. This is the itinerary of begging from place to place, until Loyola at the conclusion of his recital reads to Gonçalves da Câmara from his diary. He reports visions confirming something in the *Constitutiones*, and that matter is whether a church should have any income and whether the Society could assist itself from it.[62]

Not all moralists agreed with Loyola's decision of monetary abnegation as an imitation of Christ. Petrarch considered the love of poverty a magnificent act of virtue but did not define poverty as penury. An interior poverty that contemned wealth, while daily amid its circumstances, was no less meritorious than indigence, he argued. It was the mark of a more noble mind to scoff at the sight of gold than to shun its sight, just as victory over an enemy at hand was more glorious than the avoidance of one in approach.⁶³ That spiritual understanding of virtue contrasts with Loyola's physical deprivation. His begging deliberately extends to an entire life the moral condition of pilgrimage. Moralists execrated aristocratic pilgrims who traveled in comfort, even in luxury with splendid retinues. A famous sermon in *Liber s. Jacobi*, the promotional literature for the pilgrimage to Compostela, was severe. "The pilgrim may bring with him no money at all, except perhaps to distribute it to the poor on the road. . . . The pilgrim who dies on the road with money in his pocket is permanently excluded from the kingdom of heaven." The homiletic advice to observe and perpetuate the poverty of pilgrimage was scarcely observed, however; in the thirteenth century the statutes of Santiago's cathedral required an offering of cash or jewelry for the reception of the indulgence.⁶⁴ Loyola's poverty as a perpetual pilgrim is exceptional.

It is also a social problem. There was an increase in sixteenth-century Italy, where he begged, of a negative attitude toward the poor, arising from a polarization of rich and poor in a population pressing for subsistence. In the practice of relief there was serious discrimination between the foreign and the local poor, the genuine and the fake. The able-bodied were compelled to work, vagabonds were recommended for the galleys, and beggars were hunted down by officers of health.⁶⁵ Loyola's begging in his native Spain deliberately courts dishonor. The clergyman and his crowd who laugh at his begging "speak some injuries to him" (*decirle algunas injurias*).⁶⁶ This is a legal term concerning dishonor, just as the "Moor" on the road had spoken *injuria* of the Madonna. The incident is the first occurrence on Spanish soil of an "injury" inflicted upon Loyola by others; previously he has elected injury to himself, as in not covering his head. By rights he is obliged to address it. He accepts rather the charity of the administrator of a hospice. Although his *Exercitia spiritualia* advises indifference to created things, so as not to prefer honor to dishonor, Loyola defines that as imperfect humility. The ultimate degree of that virtue is that "I wish and choose poverty with Christ more than riches; opprobriums with Christ full of them more than honors; and desire to be esteemed inane and crazy for Christ, who was first held as such, more than wise and prudent in this world."⁶⁷

Money might seem the stuff of avarice, the vice that with the rise of the mercantile class supplanted vainglory in late medieval lists of sins.⁶⁸ Although pride of life was associated in the medieval conscience with concupiscence of the eyes, or vainglory, that concupiscence encompassed more than praise. Its objects were territory, households, power, honor, dignity, pomp, and riches. Riches meant money, either gold or silver, and gems. In his preaching Gregory the Great conflated the two vices. Avarice was not only for money but also for exalted social position, and that sort of avarice was pride.[69] Origen compared the spirit of vainglory with the love of riches and he contrasted the amassing of earthly wealth with the amassing of the heavenly treasury of the glory of God.[70] The ascetic Anthony was tempted by a vision of gold.[71] In the *Exercitia spiritualia* Loyola identifies the initial snare of Satan as the lust for riches; only then does he proceed to the snares of vain honor and pride.[72] His preoccupation with money throughout his pilgrimage is not only a material necessity but also a moral decision against vainglory.

The first leg of his journey is marked by an archetypal place. After a fearful voyage from Barcelona to Gaeta in a severe storm, Loyola lands to increased fear among the populace because of plague. Upon disembarkment he begins walking toward Rome, joined by several shipmates: a mother and her daughter dressed in boy's clothing and another youth—all begging their way. Arriving at a lodge, they find a large fire with many soldiers gathered around, who offer them some food and plentiful wine. The travelers separate, with the mother and child placed in an upstairs room, the pilgrim and the youth in a stable. In the middle of the night Loyola hears loud shouts from the upstairs and, rising to investigate, discovers the mother and child in the courtyard below, weeping and lamenting that the soldiers have attempted to rape them. With great emotion he hollers, "Do we have to suffer this?" and similar complaints. So effectively do they dumbfound the soldiers that no one touches him or them. Loyola and the women commence their journey in the middle of the night.[73]

Rape was considered a moral consequence of the traveler's vice of curiosity, typified by Dinah, the woman who traveled and was raped (Gen. 34:1-2). In the influential ascetic advice for women, Jerome's letter to Eustochium, he warned them to remain in the locked seclusion of their own room, for "Dinah went out and was seduced."[74] Bernard of Clairvaux chided Dinah, "You look about curiously, but more curiously you are looked at."[75] The sexual menacing of maidens by brigands or pirates was an element of medieval hagiography borrowed from travelogue and romance.[76] This episode is a matter of honor for Loyola, like the confrontation on the road with the "Moor" who disbelieved Mary's perpetual virginity. Rape was the severest shame to women in Loyola's culture, and he redresses the attempted affront, although now with recourse to speech, not a poniard. The lustful soldiers are the shadows of his former self, in their symbolic location around the firelight like the mob in Plato's cave. The mother and the daughter in boy's clothing are like the Madonna with child. In a humble inversion they lodge in the inn, while Loyola retires to the stable. The scene is an imitation of the *presepio*. Loyola as a figure of St. Joseph leads them away protectively in the middle of the night, as if on flight to Egypt and security (cf. Matt. 2:13–14). His charity in protection of the women is exceptional. The prosecution of cases of rape in renaissance Italy indicated a low evaluation of it as a crime. Rape was of little concern even to the nobility, unless the elderly or children were victimized.[77]

The significance of Loyola's first adventure on pilgrimage is emphasized by the rhetoric of place, for the inn (*stabulum*) was the essential site in its allegory. Augustine exhorted the human as the traveler, "Let him know that he walks a path, and in these riches enters as if into an inn. Let him take refreshment; he is a traveler. Let him refresh himself and pass on, for one does not take with him what he finds in an inn." About honor and other temporal goods he preached, "Let us place ourselves in the inn of this life as if pilgrims about to pass through, not as possessors about to remain." Against avarice he emphasized that such goods were like the inn of the traveler, not the mansion of the owner—merely for refreshment and passage. A person should use them as the pilgrim did the utensils at an inn. Gregory the Great concurred that the virtuous were cheered by temporal aids like a wayfarer enjoying a bed in an inn. He rested bodily but proceeded imaginatively to a further destination.[78]

Loyola's entry into Italy to establish a ministry is especially tested much later on the slippery slope of the pride that goes before a fall. The episode abridges the topic of the pilgrimage of life. On the road from Genoa to Bologna he loses the level path and begins to walk an elevated one by a deep river. It progressively narrows until he can neither go forward nor turn backward but is forced to all fours. By crawling he covers a good distance, but fearfully, for with every movement he believes he will fall into the river. This he reports as the greatest physical anxiety and labor of his life; but in the end he escapes it. Wishing to enter Bologna, as he tries to cross a small wooden bridge he falls off it. Loyola emerges from the river sodden with water and clay to the laughter of the many onlookers. In the city he collects not a single small coin, although he traverses it entirely.[79]

On pilgrimage there were dangerous paths, such as the ascent into the cave where Christ fasted in the wilderness. It edged a very deep valley so narrowly that pilgrims could only go sideways along the face of a sheer wall of rock to which they clung with both hands. They dared not glance down lest dizzily they plunged; they looked rather to their feet to see where to place the next step among the rifts.[80] Loyola's episode suggests the perilous path, too narrow and elevated for a man to walk erect on it, as the ascetic way. It reduces him to crawling fearfully like an animal, until fatigued he escapes the ordeal.[81] Life as an arched bridge crossed by a pilgrim was the simplest visualization of the theme of the ages of man. The journey up the incline and down the decline depicted the course of life in visual art and in morality plays.[82] The barrier of water, originating in oriental mythology, was a commonplace ordeal.[83]

Loyola on the bridge undergoes the trial from Gregory the Great's *Dialogi* concerning the otherworld, for which the bridge was a universal religious and cultural symbol of transition. A certain Roman soldier who had died of plague revived to narrate the supernatural scene of a river whose dark waters were misted over with malodorous vapors. Over the river was a bridge to a delightful pleasance. On the bridge, symbolic of the narrowness of the road to heaven, sinner and saint underwent a final test. The unjust persons slipped off and fell into the polluted river, the foul stream of carnal vices that flowed daily to the abyss. The just, unburdened by sin, crossed it freely and easily to the beautiful meadows beyond. Below the bridge the soldier reported seeing a former overseer of the Church lying prone in the river, fettered with iron chains. A foreign priest crossed the bridge confidently, for his life was sincere. Another man slipped and fell on it—the lower half of his body dangling over the edge of the bridge. Fiends from the river seized him and dragged him down, while nobles appeared on the bridge to rescue him. During that contest between good and evil spirits the visionary was summoned back to earth, so that the outcome was unknown. The explanation was the struggle of carnal evils with good works, precisely almsgiving. The uplifting spirits symbolized the man's zeal for almsgiving; the dragging spirits, his tendency to lust.[84]

The location at Bologna of Loyola's experience on the bridge is associated with the monetary topic, for this is the only place in the text whose citizens refuse him alms.[85] The visionary soldier had reported in *Dialogi* that in the celestial meadow were the shining dwellings of the just. Under construction from golden bricks was a handsome house of grand proportions. As he interpreted it, "Since the reward of eternal glory is won by generosity in almsgiving, it seems quite possible to build an eternal dwelling with gold." The bricks were furnished by the variety of people who benefited from the almsgiving of the just person soon to occupy the place.[86] By implication, in Loyola's judgment the citizens of Bologna, for their stinginess, are not going to heaven.

Loyola's own fall from the small wooden bridge confesses sin. Since he has successfully, if arduously and anxiously, completed the elevated path of asceticism without falling into the river, the fall from the bridge, as symbolic of the final trial of saints and sinners, is vainglory. That was traditionally the last vice to be overcome. The clay and water with which Loyola is caked and soaked upon his emergence from the river associates him with Adam, formed from clay and immersed since original sin in the sea of the world. Loyola's place in the river is an irony on the rhetorical topic of the waves of glory. Of classical origin, the wave was revived by Boccaccio and developed by numerous renaissance poets as an epideictic metaphor to acclaim sovereigns, pronounce their praise, and predict their exploits. In the poetry of Joachim du Bellay and others the Seine, the Marne, and the Yonne saluted their sovereigns and crowned them with roses. In Pierre de Ronsard's "Avantentré du roi" there was a sonorous wave when Henry II entered Paris.[87] The laughter of the onlookers at Loyola's sorry condition is the appropriate punishment for vainglory. The episode of his untriumphant entry into a city mocks his chivalric dreams of glory.

Another place on pilgrimage, the church of San Marco in Venice,[88] displays in its vestibule the mosaics of the creation, in which the patriarchal Noah holds a pair of peacocks as the animals privileged to enter the ark first.[89] Loyola boards the ship to Jerusalem on the topical sea of the world. The illustrations of *Le pèlerinage de vie humaine* depict its pilgrim surveying the sea awash with various pilgrims, one snared in seaweed, another topsy-turvy, one swimming bravely, another flying from it on wings—while Satan fishes for them all.[90] It was a practice to preach the maritime topic on board ships of pilgrims bound for Jerusalem.[91] Augustine established it in his *Confessions* from the Neoplatonist topic of departure and return and he elaborated it copiously. Immersed in evil yet struggling to emerge through comprehension, a floundering Augustine imagined creation visible and invisible as a great bounded mass. In the image he borrowed from Plotinus, "It was like a sea, everywhere and in all directions spreading through an immense space, simply an infinite sea."[92] The sea was the world that spurted, bitter and briny, from Adam's navel, across which the pilgrim journeyed to the haven of eternity. That watery abyss in which Augustine confessed himself awash in error was his principal metaphor for creation as corrupted by original sin.[93]

The single incident Loyola preserves from his voyage is typical of this topic. On board certain corrupt voyagers engage in some filthy practices and openly obscene behavior. Loyola condemns them severely. The other Spanish travelers caution him to silence because the crew deliberates marooning him on an island.[94] The incident blames his imprudence, for it was advisable that voyagers not stir up hatred toward themselves among the company. "It is a ruinous thing," wrote Friar Felix, "for a man to have enemies on board ship." He elaborated the despicable fate of a haughty pilgrim who had insulted and angered the crew.[95] Loyola's vessel speedily reaches the port of Cyprus, and after a trek overland to that of Las Salinas the pilgrims board another ship. Loyola takes no rations except confidence in God, whom he envisions frequently with strength and consolation. He seems to see a large round object, as if of gold, and this vision recurs frequently, from the departure from Cyprus to the arrival at Jaffa.

There the pilgrims mount small donkeys for the journey to Jerusalem.[96] This was the easier of the routes, from Jaffa to Jerusalem; the arduous pilgrimage debarked at the ports of the Nile and proceeded through the wilderness of Sinai in imitation of the Exodus, as replicated in Dante's *Commedia*.[97] A Spaniard, by appearance a noble, piously suggests that, since they will soon arrive at the spot where the holy city will become visible, they should proceed in recollected silence. Just before the place from which they will glimpse the city, they dismount when they notice friars awaiting them with a cross.[98] This place of initial sighting is *Mons Gaudii*, or "Mount Joy," two miles distant from the city by Mandeville's reckoning. Its name—"Mon Joie!"—was the battle cry of the crusaders and the penitential cry of pilgrims at Jerusalem, Rome, and Compostela, where Gothic crosses of stone were raised on its sites.[99] Loyola's response is typical. When the pilgrim eventually sights the city, he experiences great consolation; the others all affirm the same, saying that they all feel an unnatural "joy." Loyola feels this same devotion on all his visits to the holy places.[100]

And that, after the extensive determination and preparation for the sally to Jerusalem, is all Loyola relates about his destination, except for one detail of place. He definitely decides to remain in the city, continually visiting the holy sites. He presents his letters of recommendation,[101] which each pilgrim carried from his bishop as a kind of passport that allowed him under canon law to obtain fire, sanctuary, and water in the monasteries.[102] Yet the convent Loyola petitions is unable to support him financially; precedents are argued about the imprisonment and even murder of pilgrims who have elected to remain in the city. Loyola's insistence on staying in Jerusalem is terminated not by these arguments, however, but by the authority of the provincial to expel and to excommunicate pilgrims.

Since his departure is compelling, Loyola ardently desires to return to one place, to the Mount of Olives, on which there is a stone from which Christ legendarily ascended into heaven. He wants to see it and its visible footprints again. Secretly he steals away from the group and goes there alone, bribing the guards with a pen for admission to the site. After praying there with heartfelt consolation he has the urge to go to Bethpage. There he remembers that while on the Mount of Olives he did not fully notice the placement of the footprints, in which direction the right foot was pointing and in which the left.[103] Loyola is not unique in regretting pilgrimage as a brief rush about the holy sites without understanding and feeling their significance. Friar Felix complained about it, specifying that he was only allowed to walk over the Mount of Olives and its sites once and that he had a "burning desire to return."[104]

When Loyola ardently returns there, he bribes the guards again—this time with scissors, according Gonçalves da Câmara's intruding comment. When the friars learn that Loyola has departed without a guide, they seek him earnestly. Descending from the Mount of Olives, he meets a worker at the monastery who shakes a large staff at him with great annoyance, as if about to beat him. This servant grabs Loyola tightly by the arm and leads him along the road, much to his great consolation, until their arrival at the monastery, since he seems to see Christ above him the entire way,[105] as if under arrest during his passion.

From the trials of the long journey, pilgrims were vulnerable to sacred symbols; even those encountered daily at home assumed in these novel circumstances arresting importance.[106] Jerusalem was imaginatively full of impressionable rocks, waxen stones into which Jesus pressed his body, like the rock on the Mount of Olives that legendarily preserved his footprints at the ascension. The print of the right foot was reported plainer, although both were kissed; and one pilgrim poured into the impressions a flask of sweet wine that the crowd devoutly licked up.[107] The commonest, perhaps, of the commonplaces for aesthetic and moral imitation was the vestigial topic, the placement of one's footsteps firmly in those of another. The vestigial topic could express admiration for Vergil, for example, by asserting the inferiority of following in his footsteps reverentially from a distance. Emulation avoided plodding in his very tracks.[108]

Pilgrims journeyed to Jerusalem, as Friar Felix said, in devotion to Christ "to follow the holy footsteps of his shameful passion."[109] The practice was ancient. Even the Virgin on her legendary pilgrimage after the resurrection kissed the footprints on the Mount of Olives.[110] As Paulinus of Nola attested, "No other sentiment draws men to Jerusalem but the desire to see and touch the places where Christ was physically present, and to be able to say from their very own experience: 'We have gone into his tabernacle, and have adored in the places where his feet stood.' " He even approved as a blessing the practice of taking a pinch of dust from the site as a souvenir. Of all holy places none was more revered than the spot that attracts Loyola. This is the very place where his *Exercitia spiritualia* ends.[111] The site of the ascension on the Mount of Olives was singularly believed so hallowed by the divine footsteps that it rejected any cover of marble or pavement. Its soil threw off human adornment contemptuously. In the entire area of the basilica that was the sole spot that retained its natural turf. Its sand was visible and accessible to worshippers, preserving the revered imprint of Jesus' feet.[112]

Yet Loyola's preoccupation with the physical placement of Jesus' feet, as to the angle of each foot, left and right, is literal. A physical interpretation of vestigial imitation was criticized since patristic authors. Jerome, who was among the saints most associated with Palestine in sixteenth-century cult, allowed that it was Christian duty "to worship on the spot where the Lord's feet once stood." He spiritualized its significance, however. "I do not presume to limit God's omnipotence or to restrict to a narrow strip of earth him whom the heavens cannot contain. Each believer is judged not by his residence in this place or that but according to the deserts of his faith. . . . Not to have been in Jerusalem, but in Jerusalem to have lived well is praiseworthy."[113] Erasmus eloquently condemned the physicality that Loyola's piety exemplifies. As he upbraided the unspiritual soldier in his *Enchiridion militis christiani*, "What good is it to do it exteriorly if interiorly one's thoughts are quite the opposite? Is it any great feat to visit Jerusalem bodily when within you there is Sodom, Egypt, and Babylon? There is no great merit in treading where Christ trod with human footsteps, but it is a great thing to follow in the steps of Christ in the affections of the mind."[114]

There was a rhetorical and philosophical topic of the feet as base affection. In his oration on the dignity of man Giovanni Pico della Mirandola instructed, "Surely the foot of the soul is that most contemptible part by which the soul rests on matter as on the soil of the earth, I mean the nourishing and feeding power, the tinder of lust, and the teacher of pleasurable weakness."[115] The Jesuit lyricist and martyr Robert Southwell would exhort in *Mary Magdalens Funeral Teares* to the true, pure, and singular search for Christ. "Stand upon the earth, treading under this all earthly vanities, and touching them, with no more than the souls of thy feet, that is with the lowest and least part of thy affection."[116] It was considered the nearest imitation of Magdalen's kissing of the feet of Jesus (Luke 7:8) for a pilgrim to kiss his footprints in the basilica of the ascension.[117] Yet it is the interior disposition that is lacking in Loyola's confession of his absorption in the physical placement of those footprints. Nor has he any tears in this place where Christ had wept, where pilgrims like Jerome and Felix wept,[118] and exactly where practicers of his *Exercitia spiritualia* are to meditate upon the divine tears.[119]

Magdalene was a particular saint in the lachrymose legacy, but so was Peter, whose triple denial of Christ under arrest was a subject for artistic representation from the mosaics at Ravenna to the works of Rembrandt.[120] Although in the synoptic gospels his tears flowed inside or outside a courtyard (Matt. 26:69–75), on the pilgrims' route the place was beneath a rock.[121] In the climax of a contemporaneous poem by Luigi Tansillo, *Le lagrime di san Pietro*, Peter's tears pour passionately when he sees the footprints of Christ in the garden on the Mount of Olives.[122] That popular poem would be imitated by Malherbe in "Les larmes de saint Pierre"[123] and by Southwell in "Saint Peter's Complaint."[124] The example of Petrine tears had just been debated before Loyola's recital in the fourteenth session (1551) of the Council of Trent, concerning penance. In the later poem by the Jesuit Southwell, Peter will achieve contrition only by a solitary, tortuous self-examination in an emotional crisis that tempts him to despair. Yet the Council had pronounced his contrition "perfect through charity," with a certainty of pardon even without priestly absolution.[125] The tearful Petrine eulogies of Christ's footprints on the Mount of Olives contrast with Loyola's dry-eyed curiosity about their location. Loyola seeks to ground his meditation on the gospel in sensory impression conducive to volitional assent, as typical of the method of his *Exercitia spiritualia*. Yet the method was vulnerable to criticism, because the meditator could become so involved in the sensual experience, in curiosity about it, that he failed to progress to the volitional act. Loyola has succumbed to the pilgrim's vice, gawking at appearances rather than focusing on realities.

The other intention of Loyola, which he does not reveal to the provincial who refuses his request to remain in Jerusalem, is to help souls. For this task he returns to Barcelona for study. With his acquisition of literacy, names frequently appear in the text, so that it assumes a semblance of narrative history. Loyola begins learning grammar under a private tutor, with diligence but with difficulty because his efforts at the necessary memorization are interrupted and impeded by new understandings and enjoyments of spiritual matters. Only after discerning them as temptations does he progress at study, and after two years he is advised to advance to the liberal arts at the university of Alcalá de Henares. There he studies for a year and a half the texts of Domingo de Soto, Albert the Great, and Peter Lombard. These very names blame his judgment, for their dialectics, physics, and scholastic theology epitomized the reversal of the humanist ideal for which Xímenez Cardinal de Cisneros had established that university. Loyola's election of these courses is regressive, obsolete. Even the very conservative faculty of the University of Paris had discarded the medieval requirement for the bachelor in theology to comment on Lombard's *Sententiae*. Not only is Loyola unaware of the intellectual excellences of the university at Alcalá but he also chooses the subjects least likely to prepare him for pastoral practice: dialectics, physics, and scholasticism. Later when he advances to Paris he repeats his error by matriculating at the obscurantist Collège de Montaigu,[126] whose regimen Erasmus had ruthlessly satirized.[127] Loyola's intellectual project is vain, although there was a tendency in the later tradition to eliminate curiosity and knowledge from the topic of vainglory, perhaps because of the increasing stature of learning through the growth of universities.[128]

While studying in Alcalá, Loyola begins giving the Spiritual Exercises, which he explains to Gonçalves da Câmara toward the conclusion as composed incidentally from his own spiritual movements. He also explicates Christian doctrine to great crowds. Although many listeners acquire profound knowledge and enjoyment of spiritual matters, his ministry also attracts great talk. Here Loyola encounters the aerial creature with many eyes who will pursue him throughout the recital, not as the peacock but as Fame. "There hatched a great rumor through that entire region about the things that happened in Alcalá; and this person spoke in one way, that one in another." This is the topic of fame, derived from Vergil's *Aeneid*, where the protagonist is pursued through Libya's cities by its flight, "swift of foot and fleet of wing, a monster awful and huge, who for the many feathers in her body has as many watchful eyes below—wondrous to tell—as many tongues, as many sounding mouths, as many pricked up ears."[129]

The description was imitated in Ovid's house of fame and in Chaucer's *House of Fame*, which preserved the detail of the many spying eyes in explicit comparison with the apocalyptic tetramorphs.[130] Its iconography appeared from triumphs to tombs. Antique fame was rapid, as depicted by wings borrowed from Victory and from Glory, and it was also sonorous. Its status was ambiguous, sometimes a mere messenger, sometimes a goddess immortalizing humans; sometimes a liar, sometimes a verifier; sometimes a malefactor, sometimes a benefactor. As popularized by the illustrations for Petrarch's triumph of fame, the figure was awarded a trumpet, its usual renaissance attribute, as if it were a musical angel announcing the last judgment. Yet the initial illustrated edition of Boccaccio's genealogy of the gods retained from Vergil's description its many eyes; and Virgil Solis's engraving of Fame from about 1550 has its entire body covered with eyes, without tongues or ears. Fame's many eyes are still preserved toward the end of the century in Cesare Ripa's *Iconologia*: ten eyes exactly.[131]

This is the ocellated creature who spies Loyola everywhere. Since in renaissance art the figure of fame trumpeted news, many different tongues begin to wag about him. The topical sentence—some said one thing, while others said something else—summarizes the remainder of the text. It departs from the revelation of spiritual experience to the accounting of benefactors and opponents. The text becomes consumed with the issue of reputation. Although Loyola initiated the recital, from the place of Alcalá onward it is very probably elaborated and embellished by Gonçalves da Câmara from the collective memory of the companions whom Loyola began to acquire there. At this juncture there is a remarkable stylistic alteration in the mnemonic journey: from the dense, deep recital of Loyola's formation to the loose, superficial recital of the Society's formation. The cogent memory of Loyola's singular mind unravels in the tale. There are remarkable recollections, certain to be original, but there are frank intrusions by Gonçalves da Câmara.

Several of these are even indicated by his personal "I." There is the hagiography concerning Loyola's vision of the Madonna during convalescence. "Thus, from that hour until August of 53, when this is being written, never again did he have even minimal consent in matters of the flesh; and from this effect it can be judged that the matter was from God, although he did not dare to determine that or to say more than to affirm the aforementioned."[132] At Jerusalem two authorial conjectures intrude, concerning the provincial ("I believe he was the superior of the Order in that land") and concerning a bribe ("I believe that he gave scissors to the guards to allow him to enter").[133] Upon Loyola's return to Barcelona the pilgrim desires an apprenticeship in Manresa with a very spiritual friar ("a friar, I believe a Cistercian")—an erroneous conjecture since the Cistercians were not friars but monks. Gonçalves da Câmara also believes that the voyagers other than Loyola have the necessary medical certificate.[134]

In the preface Gonçalves da Câmara had avowed, "I have labored to set down not a single word other than those I have heard from the Father. Concerning the subjects I fear having failed, so as not to deviate from the words of the Father I have not been able to construe well the force of some of them."[135] As the author of the text from Loyola's recital, Gonçalves da Câmara necessarily plays the crow decked out in peacock's feathers, a metaphor in the theory of originality, imitation, and plagiarism.[136] Erasmus reprimanded the indiscriminate collection of phrases from other authors clumsily sewn on to one's own observations "exactly like a crow decking itself out in peacock's feathers."[137] Since the text is a moral for the formation of the Jesuits, of whom Loyola is himself a member, its authority is necessarily more collective than individual. Moreover, Gonçalves da Câmara did not memorize his recital verbatim but topically. What matters for the interpretation of an epideictic text is not its historical factuality—which its readers largely assume—but its moral effectiveness.

The typical style of a caballero, Loyola's social class, was to write in the vernacular, modeled on Seneca's pithy prose. The rhetorical ideal of the Spanish aristocracy was brevity,[138] as Loyola epitomizes in the point-form of his compositions. His personal presence emerges in this epideictic text especially in self-blame. The accusatory portrayal of himself as a wild man, although modified, continues in his increasing social encounters. Loyola's asceticism is egregious: to be observed and praised by others as heroic in valor. This is obvious from his very appearance. His face is so pallid that a man flees from him in fright.[139] His clothing is ridiculous. Against the standard advice to pilgrims of warm clothing,[140] on the return voyage from Jerusalem in the brunt of winter's bitter cold and snow Loyola is dressed in his only outfit. He wears some wide pleated breeches of coarse cloth to the knees, with bare legs, although he is shod; a jacket of black cloth in shreds at the back; and a threadbare short doublet. Later on land, upon his arrest as a spy, he is stripped, searched bodily, and taken bound, clad only in these breeches and jacket.

The interrogating captain returns Loyola his belongings with the remark that he is "brainless." During studies in Barcelona he decides to resume the penances he performed in Manresa before his abdominal illnesses forced him to wear shoes. He makes in the soles of his shoes a pinpoint, which widens little by little, until when winter arrives only the uppers remain.[141] Shoes so broken as to be soleless was a fact of pilgrimage, as Friar Felix learned from the ascent of Mount Sinai.[142] Loyola's incident evidences vainglory. The "pinpoint" in the soles of his shoes is an *agujero*, like the "pinnacle" from which he was tempted to leap with his feet in Manresa in the cubicle of his heart. The verb for the process of widening (*ensanchar*) the pinpoint in his shoes means not merely to enlarge or stretch spatially but also morally "to assume an air of importance."

A quasi habit donned by Loyola and his companions attracts the attention of the Inquisition. The judge orders them to distinguish their clothing from a religious habit by dying it; the pilgrim's and one other black, two others tawny, one as is. The pilgrim is not to go about discalced like some friar but to wear shoes. Although they all comply, sentence is then passed that they are to dress as students. The vicar provides them with gowns, collegiate caps, and the rest of a student's wardrobe. The companions are next questioned by the Dominicans about the appearance of one of them in a short smock, huge brimmed hat, buskins that only make him more hideous for his tall stature, and a pilgrim's staff. The explanation offered is that because of the heat the companion has given his long student's gown to a poor clergyman. The friar mutters classically between his teeth in displeasure, " 'Charity begins at home.' "[143] This sartorial topic again focuses on Loyola's vainglorious asceticism, the desire to appear religious by dress.

As alms the pilgrim is given further dress, a piece of cloth he laps over his stomach against the cold like a stomacher. Loyola fasts abstemiously, causing recurrent abdominal illness. In Paris as in Barcelona, when his stomachaches seem cured, he resumes penitential fasting—only to have them recur every fifteen days for at least an hour and cause a fever. Once, the pain persists for sixteen to seventeen hours without relief.[144] Loyola's dismissal of his bodily ailments as blameworthy is evident in retrospect from the solicitous examination of candidates for the Society, about whether they suffer from stomachaches.[145] The *Exercitia spiritualia* also includes rules about food as a means of discipline that caution against harm to health.[146] The moderated asceticism that Loyola later advocates is not evidenced in this text, because he is blaming the immoderation of his youthful asceticism.

At the threat of plague Loyola not only endangers his own health but jeopardizes that of others. He comforts a man dying of plague by touching his ulcerated hand. Then to overcome his fearful sensation he thrusts his contaminated hand into his own mouth, turning it about, so that he may become a carrier. As he chastises himself, "If you have the pest in your hand, you will have it also in your mouth." The episode is again reminiscent of the hagiography of Catherine of Siena, who entered the room of a leprous woman no one else would attend and clasped her hand. Loyola's one-upmanship in placing the infected hand in his mouth imitates her more famous deed, recounted even in Friar Felix's pilgrimage, in which she drank the bloody pus from an invalid's ulcer.[147] Loyola also neglects to obtain the medical documents necessary for passage at sea. For failure to be caught by the guards, either entering or leaving Venice, or by the inspector on board ship, he implicitly congratulates himself as providentially blessed. He departs for Jerusalem so debilitated from high fever that the physician predicts his demise there; but Loyola relates vomiting to his relief and recovery.[148] Although nausea was a fact of travel at sea,[149] the incident implies moral blame. Public vomiting was the prime rhetorical example of hyperbole, as a disgraceful and revolting circumstance. It was also an example of augmentation. "Vomiting," wrote Quintilian, "is an ugly thing in itself, even when there is no assembly to witness it; it is ugly when there is such an assembly," and so on.[150]

Loyola's fearlessness, or recklessness, betrays the individualistic bravado he displayed at the siege of Pamplona as simply transferred to another arena, that of spiritual combat. He is not dissuaded by war from journeying to France, where captured Spaniards are reputedly roasted on a spit. "Never did he have the slightest sort of fear." When confronted by war, in defiance of a military warning he boldly walks the highway between contending French and imperial armies—only to be arrested as a spy. He decides not to speak to the captain by seigniorage, or to give him reverence, or to doff his cap. For this lack of courtesy he is taken for "a madman" and dismissed as "brainless." On other occasions Loyola is the vainglorious prisoner. Under incarceration by the Inquisition he refuses multiple offers of free legal counsel. When there occurs a breakout from prison, he remains there—doors wide open—to be congratulated for his virtue. Rumors of the incident circulate to the edification of all citizens, and he is removed from the prison to a palace.[151]

The miraculous release of prisoners, especially crusaders, from chains was a stock episode in medieval tales. Penitential pilgrims were analogically pardoned by the miraculous sundering of their chains at the shrine.[152] Since St. Peter in the Acts of the Apostles (5:17–21) did not hesitate to accept release from chains, Loyola is vainglorious of being judged (in a Catholic maxim) as "holier than the pope."

Loyola even considers entering an unreformed and depraved religious order so that he can suffer all the more. He has great confidence that he will suffer well all the "affronts and injuries" (*afrentas e injurias*) its members might inflict upon him.[153] These are legal terms for the dishonor he courts. His asceticism, which he habitually ascribes to his trust in providence, displays a lack of prudence. Loyola portrays himself as something of a holy fool,[154] or plain fool. He seeks the third degree of humility, again as defined in the *Exercitia spiritualia*: "I wish and choose poverty with Christ the pauper more than riches; opprobriums with Christ full of them more than honors; and I desire more to be esteemed as inane and crazy for Christ, who was first held as such, than as wise and prudent in this world."[155]

The text of his recital is epideictic, for praise and for blame. Just as Loyola's activities attract fickle fame—some say one thing, others say another—so does his incipient ministry operate between moral antitheses. "We speak, says the pilgrim, sometimes of one virtue, sometimes of another, praising it; sometimes of one vice, sometimes of another, blaming it."[156] This method applies the syntactical force of antithesis, defined by Aristotle and sustained from classical rhetoric in a broad tradition climaxing in Petrarchan poetics. "This kind of style is pleasing," the philosopher wrote, "because contraries are easily understood and even more so when placed side by side, and also because antithesis resembles a syllogism, for refutation is a bringing together of contraries."[157] It was Leonardo da Vinci's artistic maxim that "opposites always appear to intensify one another," so that the painter ought to juxtapose the ugly and the beautiful, the large and the small, the old and the young, the strong and the weak.[158] This principle of antithesis was applied absolutely by Luther to invent an antagonistic theology of the divine and the human in willful confrontation.[159] Virtues and vices had habitually warred, as in Prudentius's medieval *Psychomachia*, but sixteenth-century culture especially relished their juxtaposition.

Moral choice is nowhere more compelling for Loyola than in his cases before the Inquisition. The rumors about him and his companions fly from Alcalá to Toledo, to the ears of the inquisitors, who arrive to investigate these "sackclothed" and (as Gonçalves da Câmara again intrudes) "I believe, *illuminati*." Although the inquisitors depart without summoning them, the vicar resumes the case only to acquit them. Four months later the investigation resumes, only to end without a summons. Four months later still Loyola is imprisoned for forty-two days, then freed. In Salamanca he is hounded by the Dominicans and imprisoned for twenty-two days, but released. In Paris a process is again initiated against him before the inquisitor, but dismissed. In Venice there is rumor that his effigy has been burned in those places, so that he is again brought to trial, but favorably sentenced. In Rome he is twice summoned before the governor and he ultimately appeals in person to the pope, who orders a favorable sentence. The trials by the Inquisition, although they acquit Loyola, are essential to the epideictic rhetoric. They are not mere hagiographic imitations of the tribulations of the just, as persecuted even by the religious establishment. They are integral to the ideology of vainglory—"what people will say"—by the topic of honor. Loyola begins in Pamplona zealous for acquiring honor and he ends in Rome zealous for its vindication. It does not satisfy him that the legate there imposes silence, a tacit acquittal. Loyola demands "the term of a sentence" and he appeals and obtains his demand personally from the pontiff.[160] This insistence is understandable not only from the history of his repeated trials and acquittals but also from the authority of the Inquisition to ruin him and his Society.

The Inquisition in Spain had condoned the statutes of blood to exclude new Christians—converted Muslims and Jews, like the "Moor" on the road—from social honors. All who sought entry to a renowned or honorable institution required evidence of purity of blood in all four genealogical lines. The effect was to demolish the patrilineal system. A powerful noble might be judged "stained" in lineage because one of his forebears had married a new Christian. His nobility or honor, as inherited directly from male to male, and his estates and titles could be jeopardized by his impurity in consideration of all four lines. Frequently the honor of a family was indeed jeopardized when its members sought honors the Inquisition denied it. Many denunciations, both signed and anonymous, circulated in the sixteenth century concerning the ineligibility of numerous families to receive such honors as the habits of military orders. These publications of libels were accompanied by the hanging in churches in each town and district of placards, the notorious *sambenitos*, which detailed the names of convicted penitents and their penances. These placards were notes of infamy, of disgrace, for they publicized that the Inquisition had pilloried a forebear. The stains and shames derived from Inquisitional decisions and sentences were recorded piteously from generation to generation. The ecclesiastical registers were copied over and over, although their possession was an offence because they were defamatory to so many noble families. Collective memory was regarded as a salutary means of preserving the faith.[161]

Loyola's individual memory in this recital must necessarily include his exoneration in collective memory. Not only are the personal consequences of an unfavorable sentence from the Inquisition final—he reports it as death by burning[162]—but also the social consequences are unremitting. The line of Loyola, every member of it from generation to generation, would have been stained with his shame, excluded from eligibility for honors. By analogy his spiritual line, regardless of the personal sanctity of its members (his companion Francis Xavier would be canonized with him), was also jeopardized. In the Spanish proverb, "Tell me with whom you travel, and I'll tell you who you are."[163]

The Inquisitional ordeals are a context for the importance of an experience Loyola relates about a place a few miles distant from his ultimate destination of Rome. Although ordained a priest, Loyola decides to delay the celebration of his first Mass for a year, preparing for it by praying to his Lady that she might desire to place him with her Son. En route, while praying in a church, he feels a considerable alteration in his soul and he so clearly sees God the Father place him with his Son that he has no mind to doubt it.[164] Pilgrims frequently reported approaching the holy site at the end of the way as "transformative." In proportion to their identification with the symbolic representation of the founder's experiences, they received the imprint of a paradigmatic structure that afforded coherence, direction, and meaning to their action. At the site the founder became a savior of the self as socially defined and personally experienced.[165] Loyola's petition to the Madonna for placement with her Son is not simply pious devotion but social necessity, for she is the guarantor of the purity of blood the Inquisition threatens to eliminate in him. The recital he has recollected from and plotted along the places of memory receives here its profound location. The placement of Loyola with the Son is the counterpart to his impression of the Madonna of the assumption during his convalescence, according to the hagiography that elevated his soul to the lustless state of the glorified body. The semantics of clarity and change emphasizes this complementarity. In the castle Loyola saw clearly (*vido claramente*) and experienced a change interiorly in his soul (*la mudança que se había hecho en su ánima interiormente*). In the church he experiences a change in his soul (*ha sentita tal muatione nell'anima sua*) and he sees clearly (*ha visto tanto chairamente*).

Although in this place he prays that Mary place him with her Son—in her arms—in his impression the Father places him with his Son—at his right hand. Scripture and creed proclaimed the right hand of the Father as the Son's triumphal place. The witness in the epistle to the Hebrews (8:1) is especially suggestive for Loyola's situation. It emphasizes Christ's intercession and mediation, a favorite method of prayer for Loyola in his diary; and it involves the priesthood, specifically the Mass for whose celebration he is prayerfully preparing. In the *Exercitia spiritualia* he states that the will of Christ is entry into the glory of the Father. The Christian who follows him in suffering will follow him into that glory.[166] The position at the right hand of the Father is that of triumpha glory, a victory Jesus traditionally gained by the cross. The just might aspire to share in this glory in their bodily glorification in heaven, especially the martyrs, then the virgins.[167] The chastity effected in Loyola by the impression of the Madonna, the Virgin with the child Jesus, during his convalescence is here made prophetic of his bodily glorification with Jesus in glory. That position of Christ throughout the Epistle to the Hebrews is achieved by the act of taking his blood into the sanctuary as a sacrifice. His blood was initially shed at the circumcision, when he received his name Jesus, the name the Society of Jesus adopts. As another verse interprets this glory, "Therefore God has highly exalted him and bestowed on him the name which is above every name, that at the *name of Jesus* every knee would bow, in heaven and on earth and under the earth, and every tongue confess that Jesus Christ is Lord, to the *glory* of God the Father" (Phil. 2:9-11).

Glory as a quality of God was scripturally a manifestation of his power and presence. Yahweh was originally a god of thunder, and his glory corresponded to its dreadful luminous and resonant manifestation as a revelation. The archetype was Ezekiel's inaugural vision of the tetramorph.[168] Loyola's placement with the Son at the right hand of the Father is a symbolic complex of glory, embracing the cherubim and the peacock—purity of body and purity of blood—in triumph. Where Loyola is determines who he is; place rhetorically defines his identity. Here he is glorious. His placement with triumphant Jesus by the archetypal Father simultaneously justifies the Society of Jesus he paternally bunds. It is not fortuitous that the artistic program of the Gesù, the Jesuit church in Rome, includes a painting on its ceiling of the Glory of the Cross as winged, like the classical goddess, and also includes multiple paintings of martyrs.[169] Martyrs were traditionally believed the supreme sharers in that glory.[170]

The papal approbation of the Society, which is not included in the text, is implied as a human recognition of a divine judgment. The papal order that favorable sentence be given against the persecutions of Loyola before the governor and legate in Rome allows the continuation of his ministry with his companions. With the mention of several works of piety initiated there, such as the house for Muslim and Jewish catechumens, the house for reformed prostitutes, and the society for orphans, the narrative closes. "The other things Master Nadal can narrate," Loyola says. Responding to the inquiry of Gonçalves da Câmara concerning the composition of the *Exercitia spiritualia* and the *Constitutiones*, he explains the former as composed incidentally and he promises to explain the latter that evening. Before supper Loyola summons him and solemnly avows that his intention has been to be sincere in his relation and that he is certain he has exaggerated nothing. Although he has often offended God, even in his service, he has never consented to mortal sin. His devotion is ever increasing, especially now, so that at whatever hour he wishes to find God, he does so.[171]

Loyola reportedly has frequent visions, especially of Christ as the sun, which occur as corroborations of important matters. During his celebration of Mass and during his composition of the *Constitutiones* he also has many visions. Their inclusion serves a patent epideictic purpose, to bless with supernatural approval Loyola's deliberations about the Society of Jesus. The matter of the visions is reported by Gonçalves da Câmara as easily provable from a very large bundle of writings from which Loyola has read to him a considerable portion. These papers mostly recorded visions confirming certain points in the *Constitutiones*, whether by visions of the God the Father, or of all three persons of the Trinity, or of the Madonna variously interceding for him or confirming him. Loyola especially speaks about certain issues under deliberation for which he has celebrated Mass daily for forty days, shedding many tears. That question is whether a church should have any income, and, if so, whether the Society could make use of it. Loyola explains his method in composing the *Constitutiones* as the daily celebration of Mass, the presentation of the point under consideration to God, and prayer over it—always with tears. Gonçalves da Câmara informs the reader, "I desired to see all those papers on the Constitutions and asked him to leave them with me for a while; he would not."¹⁷² So concludes the text in the form of a ringed composition, on a point of refusal.

Frequency of visionary experience is suggested by Loyola's habitual exercise of imagination from sensory impressions. The meditator of the *Exercitia spiritualia* is to visualize imaginatively a place, then apply all five senses to its experience.¹⁷³ Loyola established himself in the recital as early as his convalescence in the castle as *euphantasiōtos*, the person Quintilian defined as possessed of vivid imaginative power. What matters for interpreting Loyola's impressions is not their empirical reality but their epideictic function. Their effects are sometimes stated, as in the impression of the Madonna that erases carnal images or in the impression of the Father placing him with the Son that confirms him in confidence. The visions at Manresa are explained as tutorial; others are consolatory.¹⁷⁴ The prominent symbol in their concluding catalogue is Christ as the sun. The vision is mentioned as precedented, and that precedent is the round object, as if of gold, that Loyola frequently envisions during the leg of pilgrimage from Cyprus to Jaffa.¹⁷⁵ The journey from Cyprus on the thirty-fifth parallel south southeast to Jaffa above the thirtieth parallel is a descent toward the equator.¹⁷⁶ A solar allusion is appropriate. One of the most popular accounts of early pilgrimage to Jerusalem was Jerome's epistle on Paula's itinerary, praising how she had stood on the banks of the Jordan where Jesus was baptized and envisioned "the sun of righteousness."¹⁷⁷

That prophetic metaphor (Mal. 4:2) inspired and sustained a voluminous Christian literature. Among patristic authors Ambrose especially hymned Christ as the vivifying sun, universal source of all justice and knowledge and disperser of the darkness of sin.¹⁷⁸ Francis of Assisi composed his "Canticle to Brother Sun" in specific memory and honor of the prophetic title. As a memoir recorded, "And because he deemed and said that the sun is fairer than other created things, and is more oftened likened to our Lord, and that in scripture the Lord himself is called 'the Sun of Righteousness,' therefore giving that name to those Praises which he had made of the creatures of the Lord, what time the Lord did certify him of his kingdom, he called them 'The Song of Brother Sun.' "¹⁷⁹ Dante in paradise saw above the myriad lights their source in the sun, which revealed Christ's radiant substance as the intellect and power that opened the golden road from earth to heaven.¹⁸⁰ Among lyricists Petrarch exploited the prophetic verse to justify his poetic vocation as divinely enlightened to summon the papacy exiled at Avignon to Rome.¹⁸¹ Although the metaphor of Christ as the sun had contemplative association derived from the epistemology of illumination,[182] its political, papal association is also cogent in Loyola's recital. Renaissance poets were fascinated by splendor of the sun, which they appropriated for comparison with great personages, especially sovereigns. The apparition of the solar king, an epiphany in Pléiade poetry, was argued precisely in 1553, the year of Loyola's recital, for monarchy by divine right.[183]

The destination for the Society of Jesus was intended to be Jerusalem. Loyola's desires as a pilgrim to remain there for devotional visitation to its sites and for spiritual assistance to souls were thwarted—literally "bullied"—by the provincial who refused him permission. Now as a priest with status for ministry he expects to return there with his companions. He even delays the celebration of his first Mass in the hope of celebrating it at Bethlehem, the archetypal site of the Madonna. He is forced by circumstances to settle for the Presepio in S. Maria Maggiore,[184] a site late-sixteenth-century writers emphasized as papal, since its high altar was reserved wholly for the pope and for the archpriest to whom he entrusted the administration of the church.[185] After the ordination of Loyola and his companions in Venice, they disperse throughout the Veneto, since no ships are sailing to the East that year. The Venetians have ruptured relations with the Turks, and the possibility of a voyage seems remote. Loyola and his companions decide that, if they still secure no passage after a year, they will all go to Rome to offer their services to the pope.[186] Rome had already displaced Jerusalem historically as the favorable place for pilgrimage.[187]

Visions of Christ as the sun, now not appearing on the route to Jerusalem but hovering above Rome, are symbolic of Loyola's papal alliance. Jerusalem was revered as the center of the world, but Rome was at least median between Jerusalem and the Gates of Hercules (Gibraltar).[188] The sun could also be at its zenith there. Rome had associations with the sun that dated to its domestication of Apollo as a solar deity. The heroization of the Roman emperor was symbolized and sanctioned by a cult of the invincible sun, personified as Apollo.[189] The identification of Christ with that triumphal, solar deity developed from the evangelical metaphor of light (John 8:12; 9:5; etc.). The nocturnal course of the sun from west to east suggested to theologians Christ's burial and descent to hell and his ascent and resurrection to heaven. Especially significant was the ascription to him of the prophesied title "the sun of righteousness." "But for you who fear my name the sun of righteousness shall rise, with healing in its wings" (Mal. 4:2). That scriptural symbolism was prominent in the Easter liturgy and in the baptismal rite. As Jerome testified, "In the mysteries first of all we renounce him who is in the west [Satan], and we die to ourselves with our sins, and thus turned toward the east, we enter a covenant with the sun of righteousness [Christ], and we promise that we will serve him."[190]

An ageless Christ modeled on manly heroes began to appear on sarcophagi; then his prototype became the geniuses in the seasonal depictions on triumphal arches, the geniuses who as sons of the gods promised the Roman empire constant good fortune. From those pagan examples the beautiful style created a youthfully innocent Son of God who adorned sarcophagi and ivory carvings and was depicted in a famous statuette.[191] The impressive portrayal of Christ as Apollo was the mosaic forming the vault of a small burial chamber beside the Via Cornelia in Rome, now beneath the Vatican. At its splendid golden apex of intertwined vines is the figure of Christ with the Apolline attributes of a quadriga and horses. Seven equidistant rays emanate from his nimbused head, as beaming from the sun to the planets.[192] That solar personification was characteristic of Christian iconography in the era preceding and contemporaneous with the emperor Constantine.[193] The pope, as the vicar of Christ on earth, the spiritual Roman emperor, basked in solar rays. The victorious image of Apollo Belvedere at the Vatican was related to papal politics as the national liberator.[194]

Loyola cogently associates the headquartering of the Society of Jesus in Rome and its special vow to the papacy with solar visions of Christ. His epideictic rhetoric imitates Plato's hymn to dialectic, because the faculty of sight imitates the intellect, since sight was imagined "to behold the real animals and stars, and last of all the sun himself."[195] Loyola's vision of Christ as the sun was intimated in his gaze into the river Cardoner. Oracles, especially in Apolline prophecy, were classically summoned from water,[196] and water was the natural reflector of the sun.[197] Loyola's illumination of a solar Christ finally outshone the glitter of the peacock flaunting in the sunlight, whose glory it vainly strove to imitate. The *Exercitia spiritualia* defines humans fundamentally as "exiled among brute animals."[198] Like Job in his trials Loyola can confess, "I was the brother of dragons" (Job 30:29 Vulg.). The moral of his recital is the typical moral of the peacock, who sees his ugly feet and retracts his feathers. Loyola retracts his tail and closes his tale.

Loyola was never awarded his proper attribute, the peacock's feather, to wave in victory over vainglory. Instead he was dully handed the attribute of founders of religious orders, a rule book.[199] Something of his experience was obliquely caught, however, for a book was the traditional emblem of prudence,[200] the virtue that classically discriminated between good and evil. Prudence slew vainglory, as in the combat of virtue and vice in Herrad of Hohenbourg's *Hortus deliciarum*.[201] A minor attribute of Loyola was the abbreviation A.M.D.G. for *ad majorem Dei gloriam*, "to the greater glory of God." It is the motto, not by chance, of the Society of Jesus.[202]

The initial illustrated edition of Loyola's *Exercitia spiritualia* includes an engraving of a man in a landscape blindfolded and naked, crawling in fetters on all fours. His back is straddled by two baskets filled with animals and by a devil with dotted bat's wings, who reins and flogs him toward the pit of hell. On the man's rump, behind the devil's rear, perches a peacock with a fanned tail.[203] If Loyola's companions ever understood the meaning of his flying serpent, their successors distorted it. An engraving of 1587 illustrating Pedro de Ribadeneira's biography portrays Loyola seated on a rock by the Cardoner, pointing to it with an extended right hand while he holds in the left hand his pilgrim's staff. He is not looking into the river, however, as in the text; rather, celestial rays flood his face with light. In another scene he kneels in the distance on a promontory, supplicating before a life-size cross, while an irradiated snake with eyes marching down its body menaces him overhead. The inscriptions state: "On the riverbank he was divinely illumined" and "Before the cross, while prostrating and praying, he recognized the deceit of the devil."[204] In an illustration from the seventeenth century four intertwined snakes in midair menace Loyola's head, while he gazes at the cross above an open book in a grotto.[205] While the initial example depicts a realistically ocellated flying snake, in this example and others the crucial motif of the multiple eyes has altogether disappeared. The imagination of the Jesuits by then supposed the experience at the Cardoner to be the dictation to Loyola of the *Exercitia spiritualia*, or even of the *Constitutiones*, by the Virgin Mary. A tableau of that concept by Gerard Seghers was exemplary.[206]

Quintilian wrote well about the interpretation of rhetoric from a knowledge of the places from where its argument was drawn. "You will not succeed in finding a particular bird or beast, if you are ignorant of the localities where it has its usual haunts or birthplace . . . so not every kind of argument can be derived from every circumstance, and consequently our search requires discrimination. Otherwise we shall fall into serious error, and after wasting our labour through lack of method we shall fail to discover the argument which we desire. . . . But if we know the circumstances which give rise to each kind of argument, we shall easily see, when we come to a particular 'place,' what arguments it contains."[207]

The flying serpent was a denizen of public art. The Spanish conquerors of Mexico had just monumentally encountered it across the seas in the plumed snake Quetzalcoatl. The pioneering scholarly exponents of a historical design camouflaged in this myth were Jesuits, Francisco Calvigero, Manuel Orozco y Berra, and Alfredo Chavero. From the ancient premise of euhemerism all argued for Quetzalcoatl as an indigenous human, representing cultural values and articulating spiritual meanings. These first scientists of Mexican civilization perceived the mythical conflicts of Quetzalcoatl as accounts of the struggle between religious traditions and from that theory they composed the first reasonable biography of the Toltec king. Although the flying serpent may be as innumerable in appearances as the stars in the sky (Quetzalcoatl was the morning star),[208] a historian, like those early Jesuits, is obliged to discern and interpret the particular in the universal. Loyola's flying serpent, dazzling in its deceitful array of meanings, ultimately symbolizes vainglory.

The intriguing man is the self who walks off the pages of the text in 1537—the Loyola who by 1553 is able to review his experience critically, but with humor rather than the hatred he conceived against himself during convalescence. He has matured beyond simple disgust for sin, as in the *Exercitia spiritualia*, where the penitent is to meditate upon himself as just plain filthy.[209] Here Loyola presents himself as if dusty from the road of pilgrimage. The blame is lacking in the savage indignation of a Juvenal; classically, it is more like the detached benignancy of a Horace.[210] Although Loyola is a spectacle of vainglory, the reader is not his adversary but his intimate. The rhetoric does not provide a raw confrontation with that vice but rather invites a shared recognition of the human condition. The purpose of the text is not only reform but also relief: tears of consolation. That altered self is not the one whose development Loyola relates, however, because he exists beyond the purpose of confessing vainglory. His personal change cannot have been dramatic, for the climactic event was early indicated as the grand learning at the Cardoner in about 1522–23. The diary of 1544–45 betrays Loyola as still laboring in the ascetic syndrome of effort, with its emotions of shame and anxiety toward self, fear and anger toward God, and a craving for confirmation and consolation that interprets even tears as spiritual signs.

The change must have come with "facility," habit formed by practice, as mentioned in the conclusion. Loyola was "ever growing in devotion, that is, in facility (*facilità*) for finding God. And every time or hour he wished to find God, he found him."[211] Ease eased him. His spiritual journey, although not by straight lines, was from the ascetic to the charismatic to the habitual. That was an ability for which his *Exercitia spiritualia* trained his mental faculties. His finding God on the spot paralleled the ability of the skilled orator to find topics—as Cicero defined it, the location for searching and developing an argument.[212] The orator classically required the triadic resources of nature, learning, and zeal. The acquisition of eloquence was by personal exertion in the development of native genius. As Quintilian wrote, "He must form his own powers, his own experience, his own methods: he must not require to hunt for his weapons, but must have them ready for immediate use, as though they were born with him and not derived from the instruction of others. The road may be pointed out, but the speed must be our own." Art published the resources of eloquence; the individual should learn their usage. It was only by continual exercise that the orator developed the strength to use his acquisitions stored by study, "so that every word is ready at hand and lies under his very eyes." By following the instructions, he should find that the subjects would present themselves "spontaneously." If the powers of speech were carefully cultivated, language would readily serve, not only by appearing during searches but also by inhabiting the mind.[213]

Loyola's concept of facility also reflected renaissance theory of art. It was considered a difficult skill to paint figures as "prompt," the facility for diligence and quickness. As Leon Battista Alberti stated, "The intellect moved and warmed by exercise becomes very *pronto* and quick in its work, and the hand follows speedily where a sure intellectual method leads it."[214] Facility in artistic theory meant an ability that was not labored but talented. It was the grace to create a painting that did not harshly display the suffering involved in the work. It was spirited with a lightness, ease, agility. By facility the execution of the painting concealed its preparation.[215]

It has been said that the fool was the reigning person in the Renaissance, as was the pilgrim in the Middle Ages.[216] Loyola conflated the roles. In *Pèlerinage de vie humaine* the personification Hagiography introduced the pilgrim, brought to her by Lesson, to a mirror. This mirror of adulation into which the pilgrim curiously gazed pictured him to be fairer than he actually was, youthful and curly locked just like Hagiography. To his credit the pilgrim eschewed that mirror and elected the mirror of conscience. This glass reflected him as old and tonsured, paunchy and dissolute. As he cast it aside mournfully, Hagiography explained that conscience:

> schewith (by trewe experyence,
> With-out Eccho or fflateryre,
> Or eny other losengerye,)
> Vn-to a man, what ymage
> He bereth aboute, or what visage
> The portrature, ryght as it is,
> And in what thyng he dothe amys,
> And how he shal the bette entende
> Alle his ffylthes to amende.[217]

Yet in the artful moral of Augustine, whose confession was the epideictic paradigm, "As the beauty of a picture is not dimmed by the dark colors, in their proper place, so the beauty of the universe of creatures, if one has insight to discern it, is not marred by sins."[218]

If heroes are limpers, so are scholars. As in another author to her book:

> "I stretcht thy joynts to make thee even feet,
> Yet still thou run'st more hobling than is meet."[219]

Peacock. Konrad Gesner, *Historiae animalium*. Frankfurt, 1617–21. Courtesy of The Bancroft Library, University of California, Berkeley.

Notes

INTRODUCTION

1. The standard history is Georg Misch, *Die Geschichte der Autobiographie*, 6 vols. (Berne: A. Francke, 1949–62); but see Karl J. Weintraub, *The Value of the Individual: Self and Circumstance in Autobiography* (Chicago: University of Chicago Press, 1978). General theories are proposed by Marjorie O'Rourke Boyle, "A Likely Story: The Autobiographical as Epideictic," *Journal of the American Academy of Religion* 57 (1989):23–51; Geoffrey Galt Harpham, "Conversion and the Language of Autobiography," in *Studies in Autobiography*, ed. James Olney (Oxford: Oxford University Press, 1988), 42–50; Jürgen Lehmann, *Bekennen—Erzählen—Berichten: Studien zu Theorie und Geschichte der Autobiographie* (Tübingen: Max Niemeyer, 1988), 1–87; Antonio Gómez-Moriana, "Narration and Argumentation in Autobiographical Discourse," in *Autobiography in Early Modern Spain*, ed. Nicholas Spadaccini and Jenaro Talens, Hispanic Issues, 2 (Minneapolis, Minn.: Prisma Institute, 1988), 41–58; John Freccero, "Autobiography and Narrative," in *Reconstructing Individualism: Autonomy, Individuality, and the Self in Western Thought*, ed. Thomas C. Heller, Morton Sosna, and David E. Wellbery (Stanford, Calif.: Stanford University Press, 1986), 16–29; Susanna Egan, *Patterns of Experience in Autobiography* (Chapel Hill: University of North Carolina Press, 1984), 3–14, 196–202; Janet Varner Gunn, *Autobiography: Toward a Poetics of Experience* (Philadelphia: University of Pennsylvania Press, 1982); John Pilling, *Autobiography and Imagination: Essays in Self-Scrutiny* (London: Routledge & Kegan Paul, 1981), 1–7, 116–20; William C. Spengemann, *The Forms of Autobiography: Episodes in the History of a Literary Genre* (New Haven, Conn.: Yale University Press, 1980), xi-xvii; Olney, ed., *Autobiography: Essays Theoretical and Critical* (Princeton, N.J.: Princeton University Press, 1980); idem, *Metaphors of the Self:*

The Meaning of Autobiography (Princeton, N.J.: Princeton University Press, 1972), 3–50; Georges May, *L'autobiographie* (Paris: Presses universitaires de France, 1979); Louis A. Renza, "The Veto of the Imagination: A Theory of Autobiography," *New Literary History* 9 (1977):1–26; Elizabeth W. Bruss, *Autobiographical Acts: The Changing System of a Literary Genre* (Baltimore, Md.: Johns Hopkins University Press, 1976), 1–32; Georges Gusdorf, "De l'autobiographie initiatique à l'autobiographie genre littéraire," *Revue d'histoire littéraire de la France* 75 (1975):957–94; idem, "Conditions et limites de l'autobiographie," in *Formen der Selbstdarstellung: Analekten zu einer Geschichte des literarischen Selbstportraits*, ed. Günther Reichenkron and Erich Hasse (Berlin: Dunker and Humblot, 1956), 105–23; Philippe Lejeune, *La pacte autobiographique* (Paris: Seuil, 1975); idem, *On Autobiography*, ed. Paul John Eakin, trans. Katherine Leary, Theory and History of Literature, 52 (Minneapolis: University of Minnesota Press, 1989); idem, "Autobiographie et histoire littéraire," *Revue d'histoire littéraire de la France* 75 (1975):903–30; Randolph D. Pope, *La autobiografía española hasta Torres Villarroel*, Hispanistische Studien, 1 (Frankfurt: Peter Lang, 1974); John Claude Curtin, "Autobiography and the Dialectic of Consciousness," *International Philosophical Quarterly* 14 (1974):343–46; William Howarth, "Some Principles of Autobiography," *New Literary History* 5 (1974):363–81; Jean Starobinsky, "The Style of Autobiography," in *Literary Style: A Symposium* (London: Oxford University Press, 1971); Mary Sue Carlock, "Humpty Dumpty and the Autobiography," *Genre* 3 (1970):340–50; Francis R. Hart, "Notes for an Anatomy of Modern Autobiography," *New Literary History* 1 (1970):485–511; Bernd Neumann, *Identität und Rollenzwang: Zur Theorie der Autobiographie* (Frankfurt: Athenäum, 1970); Stephen A. Shapiro, "The Dark Continent of Literature: Autobiography," *Comparative Literature Studies* 5 (1968):421–54; Roy Pascal, *Design and Truth in Autobiography* (London: Routledge & Kegan Paul, 1960). Christian sacred biography illustrating the virtuous deed as a paradigm for social behavior is stated to be "a narrative which is epideictic because the goal of the text is not authentication, but persuasion" by Thomas J. Heffernan, *Sacred Biography: Saints and Their Biographers in the Middle Ages* (Oxford: Oxford University Press, 1988), 150. Since all three genres of rhetoric are for persuasion this designation does not explain "epideictic," however.

2. Boyle, "The Prudential Augustine: The Virtuous Structure and Sense of his *Confessions*," *Recherches augustiniennes* 22 (1987):129–50, citing Augustine, *Retractationes* 2.6.1.

3. See Erwin Panofsky, *Hercules am Scheideweg: Und andere antike Bildstoffe in der neueren Kunst*, Studien der Bibliothek Warburg, 18 (Leipzig: B. G. Teubner, 1930), 1–35 and Abb. 1–25.

4. Pierre Courcelle, *Recherches sur les "Confessions" de saint Augustin*, rev. ed. (Paris: E. de Boccard, 1968), 191–92.

5. Xenophon, *Memorabilia* 1.2.21–34. See also G. Karl Galinsky, *The Herakles Theme: The Adaptations of the Hero in Literature from Homer to the Twentieth Century* (Oxford: Basil Blackwell, 1971), 101–3; Marcel Simon, *Hercule et le christianisme*, Publications de la faculté des lettres de l'Université de Strasbourg, 19 (Paris: Belles lettres, 1955).

Notes to Introduction

6. Gusdorf, "Conditions et limites de l'autobiographie," 109.
7. Guillaume de Deguileville, *Pèlerinage de vie humaine* 81, 86–90. See also Ritamarie Bradley, "Backgrounds of the Title *Speculum* in Mediaeval Literature," *Speculum* 29 (1954):100–15.
8. "Autobiography," in *Powers of Imagining: Ignatius de Loyola*, trans. Antonio T. de Nicolas (Albany: State University of New York Press, 1986); *A Pilgrim's Journey: The Autobiography of Ignatius of Loyola*, trans. Joseph N. Tylenda (Wilmington, Del.: Michael Glazier, 1985); *The Autobiography of Saint Ignatius Loyola and Related Documents*, trans. Joseph O'Callaghan (New York: Harper & Row, 1974); *The Autobiography of St. Ignatius*, trans. J. F. X. O'Connor (New York: Benzinger Bros., 1900).
9. Fernando Zapico and de Dalmases, eds., *Acta*, p. 324.
10. W. W. Meissner, *Ignatius of Loyola: The Psychology of a Saint* (New Haven, Conn.: Yale University Press, 1992).
11. "Praefatio scriptoris" 1.
12. "Praefatio patris Natalis" 2.
13. *Exercitia spiritualia*, p. 164.
14. Theodore C. Burgess, *Epideictic Literature* (Chicago: University of Chicago Press, 1902).
15. Erasmus, *Epistolae* 396; *The Correspondence of Erasmus*, trans. R. A. B. Mynors and D. F. S. Thomson, in *The Collected Works of Erasmus* (Toronto: University of Toronto Press, 1976), 3:257.
16. Fernando Zapico and de Dalmases, eds., *Acta*, p. 328, and for the manuscripts, 331–37, 351–52.
17. See Roger Dragonetti, *Le mirage des sources: L'art du faux dans la roman médiévale* (Paris: Seuil, 1987), 38–40, 42.
18. Thomas M. Greene, *The Light in Troy: Imitation and Discovery in Renaissance Poetry* (New Haven, Conn.: Yale University Press, 1982), 1–2. See also George W. Pigman III, "Versions of Imitation in the Renaissance," *Renaissance Quarterly* 33 (1980):1–32; Jo Ann Della Neva, "Reflecting Lesser Lights: The Imitation of Minor Writers in the Renaissance," ibid. 42 (1989):449–79. For the issue of Ciceronian imitation among the Jesuits see Barbara Bauer, *Jesuitische "ars rhetorica" im Zeitalter der Glaubenskämpfe*, Mikrokosmos, 18 (Bern: Peter Lang, 1986).
19. Boyle, *Erasmus on Language and Method in Theology*, Erasmus Studies, 2 (Toronto: University of Toronto Press, 1977), 33–57.
20. Greene, *Light in Troy*, with bibliography on classical and renaissance theory and practice, 305–6 n. 1; 312–13 n. 34; 147.
21. Seneca, *Ad Lucilium* 7–8.
22. Petrarch, *Epistolae familiares* 23.19.11–12; *Letters on Familiar Matters: Rerum familiarum libri XVII-XXIV*, trans. Aldo Bernardo (Baltimore, Md.: Johns Hopkins University Press, 1985), 301.
23. "Praefatio scriptoris" 1 and passim.
24. "Praefatio scriptoris" 1.
25. "Praefatio patris Natalis" 2.
26. "Praefatio scriptoris" 1–2.
27. Ibid. 2, 3.

28. See G. Zanker, "*Enargeia* in the Ancient Criticism of Poetry," *Rheinisches Museum für Philologie* 124 (1981):297–311; Heinrich Lausberg, *Handbuch der literarischen Rhetorik: Eine Grundlegung der Literaturwissenschaft*, 2 vols. (Munich: Max Hueber, 1960), 1:paragraphs 810–19; Mary E. Hazard, "The Anatomy of 'Liveliness' as a Concept in Renaissance Aesthetics," *Journal of Aesthetics and Art Criticism* 33 (1975):407–18. For the comparison of writing and painting see Claire J. Farago, ed., *Leonardo da Vinci's "Paragone*,*"* 32–91; Michael Baxandall, *Giotto and the Orators: Humanist Observers of Painting in Italy and the Discovery of Pictorial Composition, 1350–1450* (Oxford: Clarendon, 1971), esp. 33–44; John R. Spencer, "*Ut rhetorica pictura*: A Study in Quattrocento Theory of Painting," *Journal of the Warburg and Courtauld Institutes* 20 (1957):26–44; Rensselaer W. Lee, "*Ut pictura poesis*: The Humanist Theory of Painting," *Art Bulletin* 22 (1940):197–269.

29. *Monumenta paedagogica societas Iesu*, cited by J. K. Sowards, introduction to *The Collected Works of Erasmus* (Toronto: University of Toronto Press, 1978), 25:li n. 150; 26:490.

30. Erasmus, *De duplici copia verborum ac rerum commentarii duo* 2, in *Opera omnia* (Amsterdam), 1-6:202; *Copia: Foundations of the Abundant Style*, trans. Betty I. Knott, in *The Collected Works of Erasmus* (Toronto: University of Toronto Press, 1974), 24:576.

31. Terence C. Cave, "*Copia* and Cornucopia," in *French Renaissance Studies, 1540–1570: Humanism and the Encyclopedia*, ed. Peter Sharratt (Edinburgh: Edinburgh University Press, 1976), 57, 66.

32. Zanker, "*Enargeia*"; Lausberg, *Handbuch*. Baxandall notes that *ekphrasis* was an epideictic device, without neutrality, in *Giotto and the Orators*, 87. See also my references in chapter two, n. 26.

33. Cave, "*Enargeia*: Erasmus and the Rhetoric of Presence in the Sixteenth Century," *L'Esprit créateur* 16 (1976):6.

34. For classical and renaissance precedents of Buffon's aphorism see Wolfgang C. Müller, "Der Topos 'Le style est l'homme même,'" *Neophilologus* 61 (1977):481–84.

35. See Baxandall, *Giotto and the Orators*, 19–20, referring to Cicero, *De partitione oratoriae* 6.20; Dante, *De vulgari eloquentia* 1.17.

36. See Walter J. Ong, *Orality and Literacy: The Technologizing of the Word* (London: Methuen, 1982), 10. For more recent background see Tony M. Lentz, *Orality and Literacy in Hellenic Greece* (Carbondale: Southern Illinois University Press 1989); Paul Zumthor, *La lettre et la voix: De la "littérature" médiévale* (Paris: Seuil, 1987).

37. See Zumthor, *La lettre et la voix*, 19, 57.

38. See Elisabeth Eisenstein, *The Printing Press as an Agent of Change: Communications and Cultural Transformations in Early Modern Europe*, 2 vols. (Cambridge: Cambridge University Press, 1979).

39. See Karl D. Uitti, "The Clerkly Narrator Figure in Old French Hagiography and Romance," *Medioevo romanzo* 2 (1975):394–408.

40. Acta 3.

41. See Ong, *Orality and Literacy*, 60.

42. Quintilian, *Institutiones oratoriae* 11.2.43.

43. Hesiod, *Theogonia* 53.
44. Cicero, *De oratore* 1.31.142; *Partitiones oratoriae* 3; *Rhetorica ad C. Herennium* 1.23; Quintilian, *Institutiones oratoriae* 3.3.1.
45. *Rhetorica ad C. Herennium* 3.16.28; *Ad C. Herennium*, trans. Harry Caplan (Cambridge, Mass.: Harvard University Press, 1968), 205.
46. *Institutiones oratoriae* 11.2.1; *The "Institutio oratoria" of Quintilian*, trans. H. E. Butler, 4 vols. (Cambridge, Mass.: Harvard University Press, 1933–36), 4:213. For this model see Carruthers, *The Book of Memory: A Study of Memory in Medieval Culture*, Cambridge Studies in Medieval Literature, 10 (Cambridge: Cambridge University Press, 1990), 33–45; Harry Caplan, "Memoria—Treasure House of Eloquence," in idem, *Of Eloquence: Studies of Ancient and Mediaeval Rhetoric*, ed. Anne King and Helen North (Ithaca, N.Y.: Cornell University Press, 1970), 196–246.
47. Frances A. Yates, *The Art of Memory* (Chicago: University of Chicago Press, 1966), 1–7. For the model of the tablet, the neuropsychology of memory, elementary design, and the arts of memory see in detail Carruthers, *Book of Memory*, 16–32, 46–155.
48. Yates, *Art of Memory*, 9, 18; Ong, *Orality and Literacy*, 57–68.
49. Quintilian, *Institutiones oratoriae* 11.2.48–49; trans. Butler, 4:241.
50. Yates, *Art of Memory*, 9–10.
51. Ibid., 20–21, 57–78, 82–104, 33–35. For practical application of the architectural model see Carruthers, "The Poet as Master Builder: Composition and Locational Memory in the Middle Ages," *New Literary History* 24 (1993):881–904; Bettina Bergmann, "The Roman House as a Memory Theater: The House of the Tragic Poet in Pompeii," *Art Bulletin* 76 (1994):225–56.
52. Quintilian, *Institutiones oratoriae* 11.2.21, 29; trans. Butler, 4:223.
53. Terry Comito, *The Idea of the Garden in the Renaissance* (New Brunswick, N.J.: Rutgers University Press, 1978), 70–71, referring to Cicero, *De oratore* 2.39.162; *Topica* 2.7; *De oratore* 2.34.146; *De inventione* 2.14.46. Comito's discussion distinguishes between memory and rhetoric. Since memory is a formal part of rhetoric, the correct distinction is between memory and invention; so I have adjusted the explanation.
54. *Exercitia spiritualia*, pp. 140, 160, 184–85 and passim, 234, 194, 188 and passim, 340. The influence of mnemonic art with places and images in Loyola's *Exercitia Spiritualia* was initially suggested by René Taylor, "Hermetism and Mystical Architecture in the Society of Jesus," in *Baroque Art: The Jesuit Contribution*, ed. Rudolf Wittkower and Irma B. Jaffe (New York: Fordham University Press, 1976), 65. The composition of place is also argued concerning religious poetry by Louis Martz, *The Poetry of Meditation: A Study in English Religious Literature of the Seventeenth Century* (New Haven, Conn.: Yale University Press, 1954), 25–32.
55. Marianne Wynn, "Geography of Fact and Fiction in Wolfram von Eschenbach's *Parzival*," *Modern Language Review* 56 (1961):28–43; idem, "Scenery and Chivalrous Journeys in Wolfram's *Parzival*," *Speculum* 36 (1961):393–423. For a Spanish example see Agustín Boyer, "Geography as a Linking-Device in the *Poema de mío Cid*," *Romanic Review* 84 (1993):463–74. See in general Charles Muscatine, "Locus of Action in Medieval Narrative," *Ro-*

mance Philology 17 (1963–64):115–22; and for an introduction to the conceptual importance of place through literature and art in modern cultural geography, Stephen Daniels, "Place and the Geographical Imagination," *Geography* 77 (1992):310–22.

56. *Acta* 1.7.

57. *Exercitia spiritualia*, p. 206.

58. Jerome, *Epistolae* 108.9–10. See also for geography in the literature of pilgrimage Blake Leyerle, "Landscape as Cartography in Early Christian Pilgrimage Narratives," *Journal of the American Academy of Religion* 64 (1996):119–43.

59. Felix Fabri, *Evagatorium*, 1:285–87; Francisco Guerrero, *El viaje de Hierusalem* 2. Cf. *Exercitia spiritualia*, p. 362. For a literary precedent see Pseudo-Bonaventure, *Meditationes vitae Christi* 88. See also Rogier van der Weyden, right wing of triptych, Christ appearing to his mother after the resurrection, Staatliche Museen, Berlin-Dahlem, and Metropolitan Museum of Art, New York. Reproduced in Martin Davies, *Rogier van der Weyden: An Essay with a Critical Catalogue of Paintings Assigned to Him and to Robert Campin* (London: Phaidon, 1972), pl. 15; Odile Delenda, *Rogier van der Weyden: Roger de la Pasture* (Paris: Cerf, 1987), between 32–33. The version now in the Berlin museum was called the Miraflores altarpiece from its location in the charterhouse of Burgos, but it was transferred in 1505 at the bequest of Queen Isabella to the Capella real in Granada.

60. Quintilian, *Institutiones oratoriae* 9.4.3–6; 9.4.9; trans. Butler, 3:511; 9.4.45; 9.4.147; 9.4.22.

61. Lee, "Ut rhetorica pictura," 264–65. See also Jack M. Greensten, "Alberti on *historia*: A Renaissance View of the Structure of Significance in Narrative Painting," *Viator* 21 (1990):286–87, 298–99.

62. For the meditations of Marcus Aurelius as based on tripartite philosophical topics see Pierre Hadot, *Exercices spirituels et philosophie antique*, 2d ed. rev. (Paris: Etudes augustiniennes, 1987), 135–53.

63. *Exercitia spiritualia*, passim, p. 322.

64. Plautus, *Miles gloriosus* 1292–95; *Plautus*, trans. Paul Nixon, 5 vols. (London: William Heinemann, 1924), 3:265–67.

65. See Marie-Madeleine Mactoux, *Pénélope: Légende et mythe*, Annales littéraires de l'Université de Besançon, 175, Centre de recherches d'histoire ancienne, 16 (Paris: Belles lettres, 1975), 23–25, 127, 169.

66. Augustine, *Confessiones* 7.17–18; *Confessions*, trans. Vernon J. Bourke (New York: Fathers of the Church, 1953), 213.

67. Cicero, *De oratore* 1.123–24; trans. E. W. Sutton and H. Rackham, 2 vols. (Cambridge, Mass.: Harvard University Press, 1967–68), 1:87; 1.:6.120; 1.27.122.

68. Lorne Campbell, *Renaissance Portraits: European Portrait-Painting in the Fourteenth, Fifteenth, and Sixteenth Centuries* (New Haven, Conn.: Yale University Press, 1990), 152.

69. "Praefatio scriptoris" 2.

70. Ibid. 2–3. For the sabbath see Jean Leclercq, *"Otia monastica": Etudes*

sur le vocabulaire de la contemplation au moyen âge, Studia anselmiana, philosophica, theologica, 51 (Rome: Herder, 1963), 50–59.
71. "Praefatio scriptoris" 3–4.
72. Ernst R. Curtius, *European Literature and the Latin Middle Ages,* trans. Willard R. Trask (London: Routledge & Kegan Paul, 1953), 87–88.
73. "Praefatio patris Natalis" 1–3, 3–4.
74. Ibid. 4.
75. *Constitutiones* 1.2.7; 1.3.13; 4.6.13.
76. Jonathan D. Spence, *The Memory Palace of Matteo Ricci* (New York: Viking, 1984).
77. See Carruthers, *Book of Memory,* 12–13, 20.
78. "Praefatio patris Natalis" 4.
79. See M.-D. Chenu, *La théologie au douzième siècle,* 2d ed. (Paris: Vrin, 1976), 353–57.
80. "Praefatio scriptoris" 4. For "Prester" see Francisco Alvares, *Verdadeira informação das terras do preste João das Indias.*
81. "Praefatio scriptoris" 5.
82. See Dragonetti, *Mirage des sources,* 38–40.
83. See A. Bartlett Giamatti, *The Earthly Paradise and the Renaissance Epic* (Princeton, N.J.: Princeton University Press, 1966), 123–24. To the examples cited may be added Petrarch's *Africa.*
84. Aristotle, *Rhetorica* 3.14.6; *The "Art" of Rhetoric,* trans. John Henry Freese (Cambridge, Mass.: Harvard University Press, 1975), 431.
85. Cicero, *De inventione* 1.15.20–1.16.21; *De oratore* 2.53.212–15.
86. Curtius, *European Literature,* 85–86.
87. "Praefatio scriptoris" 1.
88. "Praefatio patris Natalis" 4.
89. For the topic of modesty see Curtius, *European Literature,* 83–85.
90. See ibid., 84.
91. "Praefatio scriptoris" 3. See Quintilian, *Institutiones oratoriae* 9.3.88; Evelyn Birge Vitz, *Medieval Narrative and Modern Narratology: Subjects and Objects of Discourse* (New York: New York University Press, 1989), 54.
92. Curtius, *European Literature,* 85.
93. Cicero, *Orator* 1.1; *Brutus, Orator,* trans. H. M. Hubbell (London: William Heinemann, 1942), 307.
94. Baldassare Castiglione, *Libro del cortegiano; The Book of the Courtier,* trans. George Bull (Harmondsworth, England: Penguin, 1967), 39.
95. "Praefatio patris Natalis" 2.
96. Augustine, *Confessiones* 13.28.43; 13.32.47–13.33.48.
97. Boyle, "Prudential Augustine," 137–41.
98. Cicero, *De oratore* 2.45.189; trans. Sutton and Rackham, 1:333.
99. Johann Huizinga, *The Waning of the Middle Ages: A Study of the Forms of Life, Thought, and Art in France and the Netherlands in the Fourteenth and Fifteenth Centuries* (London: Edward Arnold, 1924), 4, 5.
100. Baxandall, *Painting and Experience in Fifteenth-Century Italy: A Primer in the Social History of Pictorial Style,* 2d ed. (Oxford: Oxford University Press, 1988), 65.

101. Quintilian, *Institutiones oratoriae* 11.3.75; trans. Butler, 4:285.
102. "Praefatio scriptoris" 5.
103. Heraclitus, *Fragmenta* 15; Quintilian, *Institutiones oratoriae* 11.2.34, cited in *Memory in Historical Perspective: The Literature before Ebbinghaus*, ed. Douglas J. Herrmann and Roger Chaffin (New York: Springer, 1988).
104. Cicero, *De oratore* 2.86-88.357; 3.59.221; trans. Sutton and Rackham, 1:177.
105. Quintilian, *Institutiones oratoriae* 11.3.72; trans. Butler, 4:283. For modern research confirming the mutual roles of listeners and speakers see Michael Argyle and Mark Cook, *Gaze and Mutual Gaze* (Cambridge: Cambridge University Press, 1976), 172.
106. Robert Sommer, *Personal Space: The Behavioral Basis of Design* (Englewood Cliffs, N.J.: Prentice Hall, 1969), 26-38.
107. Paul M. Insel and Henry Clay Lindgren, *Too Close for Comfort: The Psychology of Crowding* (Englewood Cliffs, N.J.: Prentice Hall, 1978), 144. E. H. Gombrich states that there is no systematic study of ocular contacts in art but he mentions the gaping onlooker in "Action and Expression in Western Art," in idem, *Non-Verbal Communication*, ed. R. A. Hinde (Cambridge: Cambridge University Press, 1972), 391, 375; rpt. in idem, *The Image and the Eye: Further Studies in the Psychology of Pictorial Representation* (Oxford: Phaidon, 1982), 78-104.
108. Argyle and Cook, *Gaze and Mutual Gaze*, 172, 29.
109. For an introduction see Jonathan Nicholls, *The Matter of Courtesy: Medieval Courtesy Books and the Gawain-Poet* (Woodbridge, Suffolk: D. S. Brewer, 1985), 1-74; Norbert Elias, *The Civilizing Process*, trans. Edmund Jephcott, 2 vols. (New York: Urizen, 1978), 1.
110. W. O. Evans, "Cortaysye in Middle English," *Mediaeval Studies* 29 (1967):151-57, referring at 152 to *Cursor mundi*, Trin. MS 1.2256.
111. Nicholls, *Matter of Courtesy*, 34.
112. Benedict, *Regula* 7; *The "Rule" of St. Benedict in Latin and English*, trans. Timothy Fry (Collegeville, Minn.: Liturgical Press, 1980), 201.
113. *Constitutiones* 3.1.4; *The Constitutions of the Society of Jesus*, trans. George E. Ganss, S. J. (St. Louis, Mo.: Institute of Jesuit Sources, 1970), 155. For Jesuit development of gesture see Alfred S. Golding, " 'Nature as Symbolic Behavior': Cresol's *Autumn Vacations* and Early Baroque Acting Technique," *Renaissance and Reformation* 10 (1986): 147-57.
114. *Exercitia spiritualia*, pp. 210, 208.
115. André Labhardt, "*Curiositas*: Notes sur l'histoire d'un mot et d'une notion," *Museum helveticum* 17 (1960):206-24; Heiko A. Oberman, *Contra vanam curiositatem: Ein Kapitel der Theologie zwischen Seelenwinkel und Weltall* (Zürich: Theologischer, 1974); *La curiosité a la Renaissance*, ed. Jean Céard (Paris: Société d'édition et d'enseignement supérieur, 1986); H. J. Mette, "*Curiositas*," in *Festschrift Bruno Snell* (Munich: C. H. Beck, 1956), 227-35; Hans Blumenberg, "Augustins Anteil an der Geschichte des Begriffs der theoretischen Neugierde," *Revue des études augustiniennes* 7 (1961):35-70.
116. Plutarch, "De curiositate" 515d, in *Moralia*, cited by Labhardt, "*Curiositas*," 206.

117. Bernard of Clairvaux, *Ad clericos de conversione* 14, cited by Leclercq, "*Otia monastica,*" 113-14.
118. Montaigne, *Essais* 1.27, cited by Françoise Charpentier, "Les *Essais* de Montaigne: Curiosité/incuriosité," in *Curiosité a la Renaissance*, ed. Céard, 111; *The Complete Works of Montaigne*, trans. Donald M. Frame (Stanford, Calif.: Stanford University Press, 1967), 135.
119. See Elias, *Civilizing Process*, 1:70-80, 102, 53-59.
120. Franz Bierlaire, "Erasmus at School: The *De civilitate morum puerilium libellus*," in *Essays on the Works of Erasmus*, ed. Richard L. DeMolen (New Haven, Conn.: Yale University Press, 1978), 239-51. See also Roger Chartier, "From Text to Manners, a Concept and Its Books: *Civilité* between Aristocratic Distinction and Popular Appropriation," in idem, *The Cultural Uses of Print*, trans. Lydia G. Cochrane (Princeton, N.J.: Princeton University Press, 1987), 71-79. The Jesuits sometimes used Erasmus's manuals, although they suppressed the name of the author, as noted by Bierlaire, 245, and see 242-43.
121. Erasmus, *De civilitate morum puerilium* 1, in *Opera omnia* (Leiden), 1:1033, 1041; "On Good Manners for Boys," trans. Brian McGregor, in *Collected Works of Erasmus*, 25:274, 286-87.
122. Aelian, *De natura animalium* 7.5.
123. Leonardo da Vinci, "Studies on the Life and Habits of Animals" 1255, in *Notebooks*.
124. Erasmus, *De civilitate morum puerilium* 1, in *Opera omnia* (Leiden), 1:1034; trans. McGregor, 274.
125. Quintilian, *Institutiones oratoriae* 11.3.66; trans. Butler, 4:279.

CHAPTER 1. THE KNIGHT ERRANT

1. *Acta* 1.1-2.
2. Fernando Zapico and de Dalmases, eds., *Acta*, pp. 14-24.
3. Bartolomé Bennassar, *The Spanish Character: Attitudes and Mentalities from the Sixteenth to the Nineteenth Century* (Berkeley and Los Angeles: University of California Press, 1979), 27-28.
4. Walter J. Ong, *Orality and Literacy: The Technologizing of the Word* (London: Methuen, 1982), 97-98.
5. See Harry Vredeveld, "The Ages of Erasmus and the Year of His Birth," *Renaissance Quarterly* 46 (1993):754-809; John B. Gleason, "The Birth Dates of John Colet and Erasmus of Rotterdam: Fresh Documentary Evidence," ibid. 32 (1979):73-76; Margaret Mann Phillips, "The Date of Erasmus' Birth," *Erasmus in English* 6 (1973):14-15; A. C. F. Koch, *The Year of Erasmus' Birth and Other Contributions to the Chronology of His Life* (Utrecht: H. Dekker & Gumbert, 1969).
6. "Praefatio scriptoris" 2.
7. Augustine, *Confessiones* 7.1.1. Brent D. Shaw, "The Family in Late Antiquity: The Experience of Augustine," *Past and Present* 115 (1987):3-51.
8. See Isidore of Seville, *Etymologiae* 11.2.16, cited by Charles W. Jones, *Saint Nicholas of Myra, Bari, and Manhattan: The Biography of a Legend*. See also in general Elizabeth Sears, *The Ages of Man: Medieval Interpretations of*

the Life Cycle (Princeton, N.J.: Princeton University Press, 1986); Phyllis Gaffney, "The Ages of Man in Old French Verse Epic and Romance," *Modern Language Review* 85 (1990):570–82; and for middle age, Mary Dove, *The Perfect Age of Man's Life* (Cambridge: Cambridge University Press, 1987).

9. Erich Köhler, "Sens et fonction du terme *jeunesse* dans la poesié des troubadours," in *Melanges offerts à René Crozet*, ed. Pierre Gallais and Yves-Jean Riou, 2 vols. (Poitiers: Société d'études médiévales, 1966), 1:569–83. For youth in comparative English literature see J. A. Burrow, *The Ages of Man: A Study in Medieval Writing and Thought* (Oxford: Clarendon, 1986), 166–77.

10. Georges Duby, "Youth in Aristocratic Society: Northwestern France in the Twelfth Century," in idem, *The Chivalrous Society*, trans. Cynthia Postan (London: Edward Arnold, 1977), 112–14, 116–17, 120.

11. *Acta* 3.21.

12. Andreas Wang, *Der "miles christianus" im 16. und 17. Jahrhundert und seine mittelalterliche Tradition: Ein Beitrag zum Verhaltnis von sprachlicher und graphische Bildlichkeit*, Mikrokosmos: Beiträge zur Literaturwissenschaft und Bedeutungs Forschung, 1 (Frankfurt: Peter Lang, 1975), 163–75.

13. For this type see Herbert Grabes, *The Mutable Glass: Mirror-Imagery in Titles and Texts of the Middle Ages and English Renaissance* (Cambridge: Cambridge University Press, 1982), 56–58.

14. Xenophon, *Memorabilia* 2.1.21, 30, 34.

15. Werner Jaeger, *"Paideia": The Ideals of Greek Culture*, trans. Gilbert Highet, 3 vols. (New York: Oxford University Press, 1939), 1:3.

16. For background see Beth Cohen, "From Bowman to Clubman: Herakles and Olympia," *Art Bulletin* 76 (1994):695–715.

17. *Acta* 1.1.

18. See Allardyce Nicoll, *Masks, Mimes, and Miracles: Studies in the Popular Theatre* (New York: Cooper Square, 1963), 246–52.

19. Plautus, *Miles gloriosus* 56–57, 89–90, 11, 17, 21–22, 42–46; *Plautus*, trans. Paul Nixon, 5 vols. (London: William Heinemann, 1924), 3:129, 133.

20. See David Coffin, *The Villa d'Este at Tivoli*, Princeton Monographs in Art and Archaeology, 34 (Princeton, N.J.: Princeton University Press, 1960), 55–56, 78–79, 85, 80–83, 3, 9; idem, *Gardens and Gardening in Papal Rome* (Princeton, N.J.: Princeton University Press, 1991), 19–20, 89–90; Hans Henrik Brummer, *The Statue Court in the Vatican Belvedere*, Stockholm Studies in the History of Art, 20 (Stockholm: Almqvist & Wiksell, 1970), 139–41, 142–52; Elizabeth B. MacDougall, "*Ars hortulorum*: Sixteenth-Century Garden Iconography and Literary Theory in Italy," in *The Italian Garden: First Dumbarton Oaks Colloquium on the History of Landscape Architecture*, ed. Coffin (Washington, D.C.: Dumbarton Oaks, Trustees for Harvard University, 1972), 53.

21. For war versus leisure see Livy, *Ab urbe condita* 3.32.4, cited by Jean Leclercq, *"Otia monastica": Etudes sur le vocabulaire de la contemplation au moyen âge*, Studia anselmiana philosophica theologica, 51 (Rome: Herder, 1963), 27; Horace, *Epodes* 2.1–8, cited by Michael O'Loughlin, *The Garlands of Repose: The Literary Celebration of Civic and Retired Leisure: The*

Traditions of Homer and Vergil, Horace and Montaigne (Chicago: University of Chicago Press, 1978), 53–55, 76.

22. *Acta* 1.2.

23. See Luis Vásquez de Parga et al., *Las peregrinaciones a Santiago de Compostela*, 3 vols. (Madrid: Consejo superior de investigaciones científicas, Escuela de estudios medievales, 1948–49), 1:210–20, 224, 226–27, 230, 235, 245; in general, Antonio López Ferreiro, *Historia de la santa a. m. iglesia de Santiago de Compostela*, 11 vols. (Santiago: Seminario conciliar central, 1898–1909).

24. Dante, *Inferno* 9.105.

25. Horace, *Ars poetica* 148–49.

26. Dante, *Inferno* 1.1–3; *The Divine Comedy*, trans. Charles S. Singleton, 6 vols., Bollingen Series, 80 (Princeton, N.J.: Princeton University Press, 1970–75), 1:3.

27. Erasmus, *De copia* 2, in *Opera omnia* (Amsterdam), 1-6:202. See also Andrew Sprague Becker, "The Shield of Achilles and the Poetics of Homeric Description," *American Journal of Philology* 111 (1990):139–53; Stephen W. Wheeler, "*Imago mundi*: Another View of the Creation in Ovid's *Metamorphoses*," ibid. 116 (1995):95–121; and for *ekphrasis* in renaissance poetics, Leonard Barkin, "Making Pictures Speak: Renaissance Art, Elizabethan Literature, Modern Scholarship," *Renaissance Quarterly* 48 (1995):326–51. For theoretical discussion see also D. P. Fowler, "Narrate and Describe: The Problem of *Ekphrasis*," *Journal of Roman Studies* 81 (1991):25–35; James A. W. Heffernan, "*Ekphrasis* and Representation," *New Literary History* 22 (1991):297–316.

28. Plautus, *Miles gloriosus* 1–4.

29. G. M. Paul, "*Urbs capta*: Sketch of an Ancient Literary Motif," *Phoenix* 36 (1982):144–55. Quintilian, *Institutiones oratoriae* 6.2.29–36.

30. See Raymond Klibansky, Erwin Panofsky, and Fritz Saxl, *Saturn and Melancholy: Studies in the History of Natural Philosophy, Religion, and Art* (Cambridge: Thomas Nelson & Sons, 1964), 295, 297. For an example see Cesare Ripa, *Iconologia*, p. 75.

31. *Acta* 1.2.

32. Ibid.

33. See Terry Jones, *Chaucer's Knight: The Portrait of a Medieval Mercenary* (London: Eyre Methuen, 1980), esp. 11, 145.

34. Baldassare Castiglione, *Libro del cortegiano* 1.43; *The Book of the Courtier*, trans. George Bull (Harmondsworth, England: Penguin, 1967), 89; 1.17; cf. 2.8. See in general Margherita Morreale de Castro, *Castiglione y Boscán: El ideal cortesano en el Renacimiento español* (Madrid: S. Aguirre Torre, 1959).

35. M. H. Keen, "Chivalry, Nobility, and the Man-at-Arms," in *War, Literature, and Politics in the Later Middle Ages: Essays in Honour of G. W. Coopland*, ed. C. T. Allman (Liverpool: Liverpool University Press, 1976), 32.

36. Ramon Lull, *Libre de contemplació* 112, cited by J. N. Hillgarth, *The Spanish Kingdoms*, 2 vols. (Oxford: Oxford University Press, 1976–78), 1:60.

37. Francesco Guicciardini, "Relazione di Spagna," 29–31, cited by Bennessar, *Spanish Character*, xi.

38. A. W. H. Adkins, *Moral Values and Political Behaviour in Ancient Greece: From Homer to the End of the Fifth Century* (London: Chatto & Windus, 1972), 14, 6, 60–61, 35–36; T. P. Wiseman, "Competition and Cooperation," in *Roman Political Life 90 B.C.–A.D. 69*, ed. idem, Exeter Studies in History, 7 (Exeter: University of Exeter Press, 1985), 3–19. For *aretē* see also Jaeger, "Paideia," 1:2–12.

39. See María Rosa Lida de Malkiel, *La idea de la fama en la edad media castellana* (Mexico: Fondo de cultura económica, 1952), 110; but for the reference see Lull, *Libre de meravelles* 8, proleg. The comparison with Adkin's analysis and with Loyola is mine.

40. Françoise Joukovsky, *La gloire dans la poesie française et neolatine du XVIe siècle (Des rhetoriqueurs a Agrippa d'Aubigne)*, Travaux d'humanisme et Renaissance, 102 (Geneva: Droz, 1969), 25–31, 33–52, referring at 25 to Cicero, *De inventione* 2.55.

41. Joukovsky, *Gloire dans la poesie*, 73–74.

42. Augustine, *De civitate Dei* 14.28; *The City of God*, trans. Gerald G. Walsh and Grace Monahan (New York: Fathers of the Church, 1952), 410.

43. Sophocles, *Trachiniae* 970. For Hercules as a comic figure see G. Karl Galinsky, *The Herakles Theme: The Adaptations of the Hero in Literature from Homer to the Twentieth Century* (Oxford: Basil Blackwell, 1971), xii, 81–100.

44. For surgery as butchery see Marie-Christine Pouchelle, *Corps et chirugie à l'apogée du moyen âge* (Paris: Flammarion, 1983), 125–29. For burlesque and satire of Spanish medical men see Yvonne David-Peyre, *Le personnage du médecin et la relation médicin-malade dans la littérature ibérique du XVIe et XVIIe siècle* (Paris: Hispano-americanas, 1971), 365–468.

45. *Acta* 1.2–3.

46. See Julio Caro Baroja, *Los Vascos*, 2 vols. (San Sebastian: Larrun, 1982), 2:403–4.

47. *Acta* 1.4–5.

48. Quintilian, *Institutiones oratoriae* 11.2.19.

49. *Rhetorica ad C. Herennium* 3.22.37; *Ad C. Herennium*, trans. Harry Caplan (Cambridge, Mass.: Harvard University Press, 1978), 221.

50. Quintilian, *Institutiones oratoriae* 6.1.30; *The "Institutio oratoria" of Quintilian*, trans. H. E. Butler, 4 vols. (New York: G. P. Putnam's Sons, 1921), 2:403; see also 2.15.6; 5.9.1.

51. See Nicole Loraux, "*Ponos*: Sur quelques difficultés de la peine comme nom du travail," *Aion: Annali del seminario di studi del mondo classico, Istituto universitario orientale* 4 (1982):171–92.

52. See Donald Weinstein and Rudolph M. Bell, *Saints and Society: The Two Worlds of Western Christendom, 100–1700* (Chicago: University of Chicago Pres, 1982), 156; and for patience in illness, Richard Kieckhefer, *Unquiet Souls: Fourteenth-Century Saints and Their Religious Milieu* (Chicago: University of Chicago Press, 1984), 57–58.

53. Augustine, *De civitate Dei* 14.9.6.

54. See Ralph A. Hanna III, "Some Commonplaces of Late Medieval Patience Discussions: An Introduction," in *The Triumph of Patience: Medieval and*

Renaissance Studies, ed. Gerald J. Schiffhorst (Orlando: University Presses of Florida, 1980), 70, citing Augustine, *Epistolae* 204.4.

55. Cicero, *De partitione oratoria* 23.81; *De partitione oratoria*, trans. H. Rackham (Cambridge, Mass.: Harvard University Press, 1918), 371.

56. See Hillgarth, *Spanish Kingdoms*, 2:62–63, citing Juan de Pineda, *Libro del passo honroso*; but see in my bibliography Pedro Rodriguez de Lena, *Lletres de batalla, cartells de deseiximents, i capitols de passos d'armes* 2.107–210; Martin de Riquer, *Caballeros andantes españoles* (Madrid: Espasa-Calpe, 1967), 52–99. Juan Ruiz, *Libro de buen amor* 1570–72.

57. See Kieckhefer, *Unquiet Souls*, 76. For this treatise in Spain see Dietrich Briesemeister, "The *Consolatio philosophiae* of Boethius in Medieval Spain," *Journal of the Warburg and Courtauld Institutes* 53 (1990):68.

58. Brunetto Latini, *Il tesoretto* 2608–10.

59. José Sanchez Herrero, "Los cuidados de la belleza corporal femenina en los confesionales y tratados de doctrina cristiana de los siglos XIII al XVI," in *Les soins de beauté: Moyen age, début des temps modernes*, Actes du IIIe colloque international Grasse (26–28 avril 1985), ed. Denis Menjot (Nice: Université de Nice, 1987), 279, 280.

60. Pouchelle, *The Body and Surgery in the Middle Ages*, trans. Rosemary Morris (London: Polity, 1990), 86.

61. Lorne Campbell, *Renaissance Portraits: European Portrait-Painting in the Fourteenth, Fifteenth, and Sixteenth Centuries* (New Haven, Conn.: Yale University Press, 1990), 197–98.

62. Quintilian, *Institutiones oratoriae* 11.3.66. For the orator's stances see also Elaine Fantham, "Quintilian on Performance: Traditional and Personal Elements in *Institutiones* 11.3," *Phoenix* 36 (1982):243–63.

63. Georges Vigarello, "The Upward Training of the Body from the Age of Chivalry to Courtly Civility," trans. Ughetta Lubin, in *Fragments for a History of the Human Body*, ed. Michel Feher with Ramona Nadaff and Nadia Tazi, 3 vols. (New York: Zone, 1989), 2:149–52. A book manuscript on the topic of erect bipedality is completed—Author.

64. Erasmus, *De civilitate* 1, in *Opera omnia* (Leiden), 1:1036.

65. Giovanni della Casa, *Galateo* 300–1.

66. Castiglione, *Libro del cortegiano* 1.20, trans. Bull, 61; 1.19; 1.17; cf. 2.8.

67. Transcript, Paris, Bibliothèque nationale, Fonds it. 972, cited by Mabel Dolmetsch, *Dances of Spain and Italy from 1400 to 1600* (London: Routledge & Kegan Paul, 1954), 3.

68. Guglielmo Ebreo da Pesaro, *De practica seu arte tripudii* 1; *De practica seu arte tripudii: On the Practice or Art of Dancing*, trans. Barbara Sparti (Oxford: Clarendon, 1993), p. 99.

69. Vigarello, "Upward Training of the Body," 149.

70. See Roberta D. Cornelius, *The Figurative Castle: A Study in the Mediaeval Allegory of the Edifice with Especial Reference to Religious Writings* (Bryn Mawr, Pa.: Bryn Mawr College, 1930), esp. 20–36, 68–72; Gaston Paris, "Les cours d'amour du moyen âge," in *Mélanges de littérature française du moyen*

âge (Paris: H. Champion, 1912), 473–97; Jill Mann, "Allegorical Buildngs in Medieval Literature," *Medium aevum* 63 (1994):198–201.

71. *Songe du castel* 46–48, 165–166, 145–154.
72. Wolfram von Eschenbach, *Parzival* 227.23–24; 229; 246; 248.
73. Joukovsky, *Gloire dans la poesie*, 517–42.
74. Ovid, *Metamorphoses* 12.
75. Horace, *Odes* 3.2.31–32; *The Odes and Epodes*, trans. C. E. Bennett (New York: G. P. Putnam's Sons, 1924), 177. For examples of punishnent or of a liar as wooden legged, dating to the turn of the seventeenth century, see Natalie Zemon Davis, *The Return of Martin Guerre* (Cambridge, Mass: Harvard University Press, 1983), 155 n. 11. See also Karl Friedrich Schlegel, ed., *Der Körperbehinderte in Mythologie und Kunst* (Stuttgart: Georg Thieme, 1983).
76. Horace, *Odes* 3.2.13, 17–18, 21–24; trans. Bennett, 175, 177.
77. *Acta* 1.5.
78. Sara T. Nalle, "Literacy and Culture in Early Modern Castile," *Past and Present* 125 (1988):67, 69, 70, 75, 76–77, 79, 80, 81, 86; Keith Whinnom, "The Problem of the Best Seller in Spanish Golden-Age Literature," *Buletin of Hispanic Studies* 57 (1980):184.
79. Brian Stock, "The Self and Literary Experience in Late Antiquity and the Middle Ages," *New Literary History* 25 (1994):839–52.
80. *Acta* 1.5–6.
81. Quintilian, *Institutiones oratoriae* 6.2.29–30.
82. See David Summers, *Michelangelo and the Language of Art* (Princeton, N.J.: Princeton University Press, 1983), 103–43.
83. Leonardo da Vinci, Paris, Bibliothèque nationale, MS 2038, fol. 26a, in *Literary Works*, 1:307.
84. Augustine, *Confessiones* 3.1. For courtly love as a pilgrimage see Juergen Hahn, *The Origins of the Baroque Concept of "peregrinatio"* (Chapel Hil: University of North Carolina Press, 1973), 64–113, with *amor de lonh*, 70.
85. *Acta* 1.6.
86. See Herbert Moller, "The Social Causation of the Courtly Love Complex," *Comparative Studies in Society and History* 1 (1959):137–63.
87. *Acta* 1.5.
88. Nalle, "Literacy and Culture," 80.
89. Edward Glasser, "Nuevos datos sobre la critica de los libros de caballerías en los siglos XVI y XVII," trans. Concepción Yañez, *Anuarios de etudios medievales* 3 (1966):393–410; D. W. Cruickshank, "Literature and the Book Trade in Golden-Age Spain," *Modern Language Review* 73 (1978):806.
90. Jerome, *Epistolae* 22.30. See Eugene F. Rice, Jr., *Saint Jerome in the Renaissance*, Johns Hopkins Symposia in Comparative History, 13 (Balimore, Md.: Johns Hopkins University Press, 1985), 13, 85.
91. Dante, *Inferno* 5.70–140.
92. *Acta* 1.7.
93. Augustine, *Enarrationes in psalmos* 120.5.
94. Régis Boyer, "An Attempt to Define the Typology of Medieval Hagiog-

raphy," in *Hagiography and Medieval Literature: A Symposium* (Odense: Odense University Press, 1981), 29–30.

95. See Weinstein and Bell, *Saints and Society*, 112–13, 247.
96. See ibid., 57, 102–3.
97. Celano, *Vita II s. Francisci* 2.90.127.
98. *Legend of Perugia* 43; *St. Francis of Assisi, Writings and Early Biographies: English Omnibus of the Sources for the Life of St. Francis*, trans. Marion A. Habig, 3d ed. rev. (Chicago: Franciscan Herald, 1973), 1021–22.
99. Augustine, *Confessiones* 8.6.13; 8.8.19; *Confessions*, trans. Vernon J. Bourke (New York: Fathers of the Church, 1953), 214.
100. See Kieckhefer, *Unquiet Souls*, 13.
101. *Acta* 1.7–9.
102. Augustine, *De civitate Dei* 9.5.
103. John of the Cross, *El subido del Monte Carmelo* 2.18.4; 2.19.11; and against knowledge by supernatural means, 2.21.4.
104. *Ephemeris*, p. 124.
105. *Yasna* 30, in *The Hymns of Zarathustra*; 1 QS III 13–4.26, in *The Dead Sea Scrolls in English*; *Der Hirt des Hermas* 36.3–5. See Marjorie O'Rourke Boyle, "Luther's Rider-Gods: From the Steppe to the Tower," *Journal of Religious History* 13 (1985):262–78; idem, "Angels Black and White: Loyola's Spiritual Discernment in Historical Perspective," *Theological Studies* 44 (1983):245–46.
106. *Vita Antonii* 35–36.
107. Erasmus, *Annotationes in Novum Testamentum* Matt. 3:2 ad loc., in *Opera omnia* (Leiden), 5.
108. *Acta* 1.9; 4.40; 5.52.
109. See Jonathan Sumption, *Pilgrimage: An Image of Mediaeval Religion* (London: Faber & Faber, 1975), 112–13.
110. *Acta* 1.9.
111. Ibid. 1.10.
112. Macrobius, *Commentariorum in somnium Scipionis* 3.2–11. For theory see Steven F. Kruger, *Dreaming in the Middle Ages*, Cambridge Studies in Medieval Literature, 14 (Cambridge: Cambridge University Press, 1992); Kathryn L. Lynch, *The High Medieval Dream Vision: Poetry, Philosophy, and Literary Form* (Stanford, Calif.: Stanford University Press, 1988); Lisa M. Bitel, "*In visu noctis*: Dreams in European Hagiography and Histories, 450–900," *History of Religions* 31 (1991):39–59.
113. Sixten Ringbom, "Devotional Images and Imaginative Devotions," *Gazette des beaux-arts* 6–73 (1969):159–70.
114. *Acta* 10.96; 2.14.
115. See Rona Goffen, "Icon and Vision: Giovanni Bellini's Half-Length Madonnas," *Art Bulletin* 57 (1975):511. The most complete study is Ronald G. Kecks, *Madonna und Kind: Das häusliche Andachtsbild im Florence des 15. Jahrhunderts*, Frankfurter Forschungen zur Kunst, 15 (Berlin: Gebr. Mann, 1988).
116. *Acta* 2.13; 1.1; 1.6; 2.15; 3.20; 3.21; 3.27; 3.32; 4.38.

117. See Carolly Erickson, *The Medieval Vision: Essays in History and Perception* (New York: Oxford University Press, 1976), 214.
118. William A. Christian, Jr., *Apparitions in Late Medieval and Renaissance Spain* (Princeton, N.J.: Princeton University Press, 1981), 8, 150–85, 203.
119. Petrarch, *Secretum* praef.
120. Boethius, *Philosophiae consolatio* 1.1.
121. Cornelius, *Figurative Castle*, 37–48, referring to Robert Grosseteste, *Château d'amour* 567–824. The sources for *castellum* as "castle" are dated much later, to the eleventh or twelfth century, by Mary Immaculate Creek, "The Sources and Influence of Robert Grosseteste's *Le chasteau d'amour*," Ph.D. diss., Yale University, 1941, 162–64.
122. Aline Rousselle, *"Porneia": On Desire and the Body in Antiquity*, trans. Felicia Pheasant (Oxford: Basil Blackwell, 1988), 157, 151, citing *Historia monachorum in Aegypto* 20; Palladius, *Lausiac History* 29; John Cassian, *Collationes* 7.1.
123. Victor Turner and Edith Turner, *Image and Pilgrimage in Christian Culture: Anthropological Perspectives* (New York: Columbia University Press, 1978), 154–55.
124. Augustine, *Confessiones* 8.11.26–27; trans. Bourke, 222, 223. Cf. *Pastor Hermae* 3.8.4.
125. Caesarius of Hiesterbach, *Dialogus miraculorum* 7.48; Frederick C. Tubach, *"Index exemplorum": A Handbook of Medieval Religious Tales* (Helsinki: Suomolainen Tiedeakatamia, 1969), no. 3009.
126. Hugues Farsit, *Libellus de miraculis Beatae Mariae Virginis in urbe Suessoniensi* 31, included in several other collections, notably Alfonso X el Sabio, *Cantigas*, and absorbed into immaculatist liturgical books, according to Mirella Levi d'Ancona, *The Iconography of the Immaculate Conception in the Middle Ages and the Early Renaissance*, Monographs on Archaeology and Fine Arts Sponsored by The Archaeological Institute of America and The College Art Association of America, 7 (New York: College Art Association of America with *Art Bulletin*, 1957), 61 and n. 143.
127. Peter L. Hays, *The Limping Hero: Grotesques in Literature* (New York: New York University Press, 1971), 17–27.
128. See Claus Westermann, *Genesis 12–36: A Commentary*, trans. John J. Scullion (Minneapolis, Minn.: Augsburg, 1985), 514–20, with bibliography, 512–13.
129. Homer, *Iliad* 5.303–317.
130. Hays, *Limping Hero*, 8, 65–66, 68–69.
131. Bernard of Clairvaux, *Sermones super Cantica canticorum* 80.2.4, in *Opera omnia*, 2; *On the Song of Songs*, trans. Irene Edmonds, Cistercian Fathers Series, 40 (Kalamazoo, Mich.: Cistercian, 1980), 4:149. Also cited in Anthony K. Cassell, "Failure, Pride, and Conversion in 'Inferno' I: A Reinterpretation," *Dante Studies* 74 (1976):19 n. 2.
132. John Donne, "The First Anniuersarie" 191–92.
133. John Freccero, "Dante's Firm Foot and the Pilgrim without a Guide," *Harvard Theological Review* 52 (1959):251–68; rpt. in idem, *Dante: The Po-*

etics of Conversion, ed. Rachel Jacoff (Cambridge, Mass.: Harvard University Press, 1986), 29–54.

134. Nancy H. Rosenberg, "Petrarch's Limping: The Foot Unequal to the Eye," *Modern Language Notes* 77 (1962):101–2.

135. *Acta* 1.2.

136. A book manuscript on this topic is completed—Author.

137. Gregory the Great, *Moralia in Job* 8.9.19.

138. *Vita Antonii* 5; Gregory the Great, *Dialogi* 1.2.4; Peter the Venerable, *De miraculis* 1.8; Teresa of Avila, *Vida* 31.4.

139. See Summers, *The Judgment of Sense: Renaissance Aesthetics and the Rise of Naturalism* (Cambridge: Cambridge University Press, 1987), 144–45. For vividness as a virtue of classical and renaissance art see also Leonardo da Vinci, *Paragone* 7, 14.

140. Augusine, *De trinitate* 11.2.5; *The Trinity*, trans. Stephen McKenna (Washington, D.C.: Catholic University of America Press, 1963), 321.

141. Brian Lawn, *The Salernitan Questions: An Introduction to the History of Medieval and Renaissance Problem Literature* (Oxford: Clarendon, 1963), appendix II, lines 82–83.

142. Laurent Joubert, *Traité du rire* 2 praef.

143. Albert the Great, *De animalibus* 22.5.10.

144. Augustine, *Quaestionum in heptateuchum libri VII* 1.93. The anecdote is not in the extant works of Hippocrates, according to Owsei Temkin, *Hippocrates in a World of Pagans and Christians* (Baltimore, Md.: Johns Hopkins University Press, 1991), 43.

145. Soranus, *Gynaecia* 1.39.

146. Paré, *De monstres* 9, 16; *On Monsters and Marvels*, trans. Janis L. Pallister (Chicago: University of Chicago Press, 1982), 54.

147. Leon Battista Alberti, *De re aedificatoria* 9. For examples of this belief in reformation texts see Hermann von Weinsberg, *Das Buch Weinsberg: Kölner Denkwürdigkeiten aus dem 16. Jahrhundert*, 1:96, cited by Steven E. Ozment, *When Fathers Ruled: Family Life in Reformation Europe* (Cambridge, Mass.: Harvard University Press, 1983), 113. Johann Coler, *Oeconomia ruralis et domestica* 2.4.5, cited by Ozment, *When Fathers Ruled*, 113.

148. Quintilian, *Institutiones oratoriae* 9.3.67; trans. Butler, 4:281.

149. Augustine, *Confessiones* 1.16.26; Terence, *Eunuchus* 584–91. Cf. for lust Augustine, *De trinitate* 11.4.7.

150. Michel de Montaigne, *Essais* 1.21, pp. 105, 91; *The Complete Works of Montaigne*, trans. Donald Frame (Stanford, Calif.: Stanford University Press, 1967), 97. He also cited animal examples such as Jacob's sheep. For the hairy child see also Marie-Hélène Huet, *Monstrous Imagination* (Cambridge, Mass.: Harvard University Press, 1993), 19–22. She also discusses some texts of Montaigne, Pietro Pomponazzi, and Paré, 13–19, 22. This book appeared after my research on this topic was completed.

151. *Acta* 1.10.

152. See Weinstein and Bell, *Saints and Society*, 244, 228, 76–79, 154, without reference to Loyola.

153. Hillgarth, *Spanish Kingdoms*, 1:111–14; 2:100.

154. Caro Baroja, *Vascos*, 2:363.
155. Erasmus, *Adagia* 2.9.49, in *Opera omnia* (Leiden), 2; Montaigne, *Essais* 3.11.
156. Hugh of St. Victor, *Diascalicon de studio legendi* 1.5; 6.14.
157. *Acta* 1.9.
158. For a contemporary argument see Erasmus, *Diatriba*.
159. See Weinstein and Bell, *Saints and Society*, 114–19.
160. Pierre Courcelle, *Recherches sur les "Confessions" de saint Augustin*, rev. ed. (Paris: E. de Boccard, 1968), 175–87.
161. Petrarch, *Epistolae familiares* 4.1. For bibliography see Boyle, *Petrarch's Genius: Pentimento and Prophecy* (Berkeley and Los Angeles: University of California Press, 1990), 166.
162. *Acta* 1.11.
163. See Mary Carruthers, *The Book of Memory: A Study of Memory in Medieval Culture*, Cambridge Studies in Medieval Literature, 10 (Cambridge: Cambridge University Press, 1990), 9.
164. Erasmus, "Cyclopes sive evangeliophorus," in *Colloquia*, in *Opera omnia* (Amsterdam), 3–3:603; *Epistolae* 135; *The Colloquies of Erasmus*, trans. Craig R. Thompson (Chicago: University of Chicago Press, 1965), 415; "Cyclops, or the Gospel Bearer," 417.
165. *Acta* 1.11.
166. Kieckhefer, *Unquiet Souls*, 11.
167. Plato, *Respublica* 7.532.
168. See Eugenio Garin, "La *dignitas hominis* et la letteratura patristica," *La rinascita* 1 (1938):102–46; and for some French renaissance authors, Lionello Sozzi, *La "dignité de l'homme" à la Renaissance* (Turin: Giappichelli, 1982), 12–21; and for a scholastic example, Thomas Aquinas, *Summa theologiae* 1.91.3 ad 3.
169. Seneca, *Naturales quaestiones* 1. praef. 10–13; *Naturales quaestiones*, trans. Thomas H. Corcoran, 2 vols. (Cambridge, Mass.: Harvard University Press, 1971–72), 2:11.
170. Plato, *Theatetus* 174a; Diogenes Laertius, *Vitae philosophorum* 1.34.
171. Chaucer, "The Miller's Tale," in *Canterbury Tales*; *The Canterbury Tales*, trans. David Wright (Oxford: Oxford University Press, 1986), 88.
172. Erasmus, *Moria*, in *Opera omnia* (Amsterdam), 4–3:144; *Praise of Folly and Letter to Martin Dorp 1515*, trans. Betty Radice (Harmondsworth, England: Penguin, 1971), 151. Boyle, "Fools and Schools: Scholastic Dialectic, Humanist Rhetoric: From Anselm to Erasmus," *Medievalia et humanistica* 13 (1985):175.
173. *Acta* 8.
174. Augustine, *De beata vita* 1.4; cf. Vergil, *Aeneid* 3.515.
175. Augustine, *Confessiones* 10.8.15; trans. Bourke, 276; Petrarch, *Epistolae familiares* 4.1.
176. Montaigne, *Essais* 3.13; trans. Frame, 857.
177. See Joukovsky, *Gloire dans la poesie*, 332–35.
178. *Acta* 1.12.
179. See Peter the Venerable, *De miraculis libri duo* 2.27.

180. Erasmus, "Militis et Cartusiani" in *Colloquia*, in *Opera omnia* (Amsterdam), 1–3:318; trans. Thompson, 132, 133.
181. Erasmus, "Militaria," in *Colloquia*, ibid., 154; trans. Thompson, 12.
182. Erasmus, "Militis et Cartusiani," in *Colloquia*, ibid., 315; trans. Thompson, 129.
183. Ibid.
184. *Acta* 2.12.
185. Weinstein and Bell, *Saints and Society*, 101, 18, 216, 196–98, 209.
186. Ibid., 18.
187. *Acta* 1.4, 10.

CHAPTER 2. THE ASCETIC

1. Donald Weinstein and Rudolph M. Bell, *Saints and Society: The Two Worlds of Western Christendom, 1000–1700* (Chicago: University of Chicago Press, 1982), 18.
2. *Acta* 2.1.
3. See Francis Rapp, "Les pèlerinages dans la vie religieuse de l'Occident medieval au XIVe et XVe siècles," in Freddy Raphaël et al., *Les pèlerinages de l'antiquité biblique et classique à l'occident médiévale* (Paris: Paul Geuthner, 1973), 130–31; Jonathan Sumption, *Pilgrimage: An Image of Mediaeval Religion* (London: Faber & Faber, 1975), 123–28.
4. Lull, *Libre de contemplació* 110–22, cited in J. N. Hillgarth, *The Spanish Kingdoms*, 2 vols. (Oxford: Oxford University Press, 1976–78), 1:46; Sumption, *Pilgrimage*, 122–25.
5. Baldassare Castiglione, *Lettere*, 1:7, cited by J. R. Hale, "Castiglione's Military Career," in *Castiglione: The Ideal and the Real in Renaissance Culture*, ed. Robert W. Hanning and David Rosand (New Haven, Conn.: Yale University Press, 1983), 148–49.
6. Fernand Braudel, *The Mediterranean and the Mediterranean World in the Age of Philip II*, trans. Siân Reynolds, 2 vols. (New York: Harper & Row, 1972), 1:284–85.
7. Montaigne, *Essais* 1.48. According to *Las siete partidas* of Alfonso X, knights were to ride only horses, not mules. Hillgarth, *Spanish Kingdoms*, 1:49. Disdain is also reflected in the conciliar decree that the concubines of the clergy were to be buried in the pits used for dead mules.
8. Erasmus, *Parabolae sive similia*, in *Opera omnia* (Amsterdam), 1–5:286; "Parallels," trans. R. A. B. Mynors, in *The Collected Works of Erasmus* (Toronto: University of Toronto Press, 1974), 23:252. For the ass as a symbol of sloth see Samuel Chew, *The Pilgrimage of Life* (New Haven, Conn.: Yale University Press, 1962), 100–2, 204.
9. *Acta* 2.1.
10. William A. Christian, *Local Religion in Sixteenth-Century Spain* (Princeton, N.J.: Princeton University Press, 1981), 124–25, 94–95; idem, *Apparitions in Late Medieval and Renaissance Spain* (Princeton, N.J.: Princeton University Press, 1981), 13–14.
11. *La más antigua historia de Aranzazu (1648)* 2.1.58; 2.5.76. The first

miracle through intercession of the image typically brought rain, 2.5.60. The discovery is dated at 2.1.58 as 1469 or 1470, coincident with the papal approval of the liturgy of the Virgin immaculate. There was a Franciscan convent on the site since 1514, 2.1.3-4. Since 1918 the Madonna of Aránzau has been patronness of the province of Guizpúcoa, with 9 September as her feast. Luis-Pedro Peña Santiago, *Las ermitas de Guizpúcoa* (San Sebastian: Txertoa, n.d.), 50; idem, *Fiestas tradicionales y romerías de Guipúzcoa* (ibid., 1973), 53-55.

12. See John Demaray, *The Invention of Dante's "Commedia"* (New Haven, Conn.: Yale University Press, 1974), 155. Anthropologists who have studied the cult have not made this association, but it is the probable reason why the statues are found in brambles (in Mexico, in cactuses).

13. See, without reference to Aránzazu, Christian, *Apparitions*, 16-20, 208-9. Since his data is confined to Castile and Catalonia, the application to Aránzazu is mine. For the medieval legends known as the shepherd's cycle see also Victor Turner and Edith Turner, *Image and Pilgrimage in Christian Culture: Anthropological Perspectives* (New York: Columbia University Press, 1978), 41-42.

14. Turner and Turner, *Image and Pilgrimage*.

15. "Praefatio scriptoris" 1. There is a statue of her at Uribarri in a roadside shrine on the route of ascent to the greater shrine at Aránzazu, although the documentation does not indicate its date. Gerardo López de Guereñu, *Devoción popular en España a la Virgen blanca y a nuestra Señora de las nieves* (Vitoria: Obra cultural de la caja de ahorros municipal de la ciudad de Vitoria, 1967), 201 with photograph.

16. For Espinosa de los Monteros in general see Jose Luis García Grinda, *Burgos edificado* (Madrid: Colegio oficial de arquitectos de Madrid, 1984), 217-21; Valentin de la Cruz, *Burgos: Guía completa de las tierras del Cid*, 2d ed. (Burgos: Diputación provincial, 1973), 156-59.

17. See Hillgarth, *Spanish Kingdoms*, 2:122.

18. Susan Tax Freeman, *The Pasiegos: Spaniards in No Man's Land* (Chicago: University of Chicago Press, 1979), 6, 10-11, 17.

19. Ignacio Ruiz Velez et al., *Leyendas y fiestas populares del norte de Burgos* (Villarcayo: Garcia, 1988), 13; Carlos Blanco, *Las fiestas de aquí* (Valladolid: Ambibo, 1983), 95-97.

20. Ruiz Velez et al., *Leyendas y fiestas populares*, 18; and for the maypole as a custom associated throughout Spain with various summer—usually August—festivals see Jose Luis Alonso Pongo, *Tradiciones y costumbres de Castilla y Leon*, Collection nueva Castilla, 3 (Valladolid: Castilla, 1982), 53-65; Julio Caro Baroja, *El estio festivo: Fiestas populares del verano*, Otra historia de España, 10 (Madrid: Taurus, 1984), 24-27.

21. Ruiz Velez et al., *Leyendas y fiestas populares*, 19; Blanco, *Fiestas de aquí*, 95-97.

22. "From Rioseco to Trueba, from La Sía to Lunada all call on you." Ruiz Velez et al., *Leyendas y fiestas populares*, 21. Rioseco and Trueba are two of the rivers that converge at Las Machorras; Lunada is about 6 kilometers north; but La Sía does not appear on the official map or in the gazetteer consulted. Rioseco is also a town between Burgos and Espinosa de los Monteros, and there

is also a town of Trueba near the site. Trueba, Lunada, and La Sía are also mountainous elevations, according to Valentin de la Cruz, *Burgos*, 159.

23. The couplets are cited in Ruiz Velez et al., *Leyendas y fiestas populares*, 20–22, but the interpretation of them is mine.

24. Stephen F. Ostrow, "The Sistine Chapel at S. Maria Maggiore: Sixtus V and the Art of the Counter Reformation," Ph.D. diss., Princeton University, 1987, 1–5, 27, 12; idem, *Art and Spirituality in Counter-Reformation Rome: The Sistine and Pauline Chapels in S. Maria Maggiore* (Cambridge: Cambridge University Press, 1996), 3; Mariano Armellini, *Le chiese di Roma del secolo IV al XIX*, 2 vols. (Rome: Nicola Ruffolo, 1942), 1:281–94.

25. López de Guereñu, *Devoción popular*, prologue by Placido Inchaurraga; and for sites in Guizpúcoa, 55, 86, 118, 130, and 201 (most with photographs).

26. Angel Dotor y Municio, *La catedral de Burgos: Guía histórico-descriptiva* (Burgos: Hijos de Santiago Rodríguez, 1928), 254–55. Main retable, Nuestra Señora la Mayor, silver statue, 15th century, cathedral, Burgos. Reproduced ibid., fig. 47, and Luciano Huidobro, *La catedral de Burgos*, Los monumentos cardinales de España, 8 (Madrid: Plus-Ultra, 1958), 138.

27. See Valentin de la Cruz, *Burgos: Remansos de historia y arte* (Burgos: Caja de ahorras municipal, 1987), 53, without reference to Loyola and Gonçalves dâ Camara.

28. See Levi d'Ancona, *Iconography of the Immaculate Conception*, 72; Edward Dennis O'Connor, *The Dogma of the Immaculate Conception: History and Significance* (Notre Dame, Ind.: University of Notre Dame Press, 1958), 242, noting that the Society of Jesus in its fifth general council of 1593 officially adopted this belief. See also Susanne L. Stratton, *The Immaculate Conception in Spanish Art* (Cambridge: Cambridge University Press, 1994), 1–66, with the Virgin with the sun at 46–58; Nancy Mayberry, "The Controversy over the Immaculate Conception in Medieval and Renaissance Art, Literature, and Society," *Journal of Medieval and Renaissance Studies* 21 (1991):207–24.

29. One of the most frequent representations of the Virgin immaculate with the child Jesus is in the guise of the apocalyptic woman, with the earliest examples dating from the fourteenth century. See Levi d'Ancona, *Iconography of the Immaculate Conception*, 56, 20–28, and for an example of the apocalyptic woman and the Madonna with playing child combined as the Virgin immaculate, see Virgin immaculate standing, German woodcut, after 1477, fig. 7. For the type of the Virgin in the burning bush, whose virginity burns without consumption, see 67–69; and for the Spanish oral tradition, Christian, *Apparitions*, 26–57 passim.

30. Sixten Ringbom, *Icon to Narrative: The Rise of the Dramatic Close-up in Fifteenth-Century Devotional Painting* (Åbo: Åbo Akademie, 1965), 165 and fig. 3. See also Francesco della Rovere (Pope Sixtus IV), *L'orazione della Immacolata*.

31. Photograph in Ruiz Velez et al., *Leyendas y fiestas populares*, 25, which notes that Isabella II donated for it a golden mantle, now lost, 13. The original statue was destroyed in 1936 during the Civil War. López de Guereñu, *Devoción popular*, 106.

32. Glykophilousia (Vzygranye), a variant of Eleousa, in which the infant

on arm reaches up toward the Virgin's face to touch her chin or cheek. The earliest example in the West is Madonna, Tuscan School, late 13th century, Gualino Collection (formerly), Turin. See Victor Lasareff, "Studies in the Iconography of the Virgin," *Art Bulletin* 20 (1938):42–46; 40, fig. 18. The fresco in S. Maria di Monserrato, Rome, is also of the type of the Virgin with playing child. Fresco, first half of 16th century, sacristy, S. Maria di Monserrato, Rome. Reproduced in Armellini, *Chiese di Roma*, 1:507.

33. d'Ancona, *Iconography of the Immaculate Conception*, 20–28, 56; and for the convergence of the images see also Stratton, *Immaculate Conception in Spanish Art*, 58.

34. Ruiz Velez et al., *Leyendas y fiestas populares*, 20–22.

35. These ancient dances are the *ahorcado*, the *pasacalle*, and the *caracol*, for which the authority is Justo del Río Velasco, *Danzas típicas burgalesas: Tradiciones y costumbres*, 2d ed. (Burgos: n.p., 1975). See also Caro Baroja, *Estio festivo*, 103, 110–15; Ruiz Velez et al., *Leyendas y fiestas populares*, 18–19, with illustration of the *ahorcado* at Espinosa de los Monteros, 19; Blanco, *Fiestas de aquí*, 95; *Canciones y danzas de España* (Madrid: Magerit, 1956), with an illustration of the *paleoteo*, n.p.; Valentin de la Cruz, *Burgos: Guía*, 160.

36. Acta 3.31.

37. See Juan Ignacio de Iztueta, *Viejas danzas de Guipúzcoa/ Gipuzkoa'ko dantza gogoangarriak*, 2d ed. (Bilbao: Gran eciclopedia vasca, 1968), 222–27. It is still conserved in Tolosa, the ancient capital, according to Caro Baroja, *Los Vascos*, 2 vols. (San Sebastian: Larrun, 1982), 2:405.

38. Acta 1.3.

39. d'Ancona, *Iconography of the Immaculate Conception*, 57, 60.

40. See Anna Ivanova, *The Dancing Spaniards* (London: John Baker, 1970), 65–71, 61.

41. Guglielmo Ebreo da Pesaro, *Trattato dell'arte del ballo*, ed. F. Zambrini (Bologna, 1873), p. 7, cited by Michael Baxandall, *Painting and Experience in Fifteenth-Century Italy: A Primer in the Social History of Pictorial Style*, 2d ed. (Oxford: Oxford University Press, 1988), 60.

42. "Praefatio scriptoris" 1.

43. Raphaël, "Pèlerinage: Approche sociologique," in idem, *Pèlerinages*, 14.

44. See Fernando Zapico and de Dalmases, eds., *Acta*, pp. 380–81 n. 2.

45. See Christian, *Apparitions*, 14, although his study is of public phenomena such as vows to spare the populace some disaster.

46. Acta 2.13.

47. López de Guereñu, *Devoción popular*, 130.

48. Acta 2.13.

49. See Christian, *Apparitions*, 203–24, 205.

50. For wool see J. H. Elliott, *Imperial Spain, 1469–1716* (New York: New American Library, 1977), 21–22, 108–10; and for sheep raising, Hillgarth, *Spanish Kingdoms*, 2:8. In particular see Manuel Riu, "Woolen Industry in Catalonia in the Later Middle Ages," trans. Roger M. Walker, in *Cloth and Clothing in Medieval Europe: Essays in Memory of Professor E. M. Carus-Wilson*, ed. N. B. Harte and K. G. Ponting, Passold Studies in Textile History,

Notes to Chapter 2

2 (London: Heinemann Educational Books, Passold Research Fund, 1983), 205–29.

51. David E. Vassberg, *Land and Society in Golden-Age Castile* (Cambridge: Cambridge University Press, 1984), 91–92; Riu, "Woolen Industry," 211–12; Carla Rahn Phillips, "Spanish Merchants and the Wool Trade in the Sixteenth Century," *Sixteenth Century Journal* 14 (1983):259–82.

52. The inclusion of this devotional detail in the recital of the 1550s also reinforces the Catholic cult of images against Protestant polemic. For this issue see Giuseppe Scavizzi, "La teologia cattolica e le immagini durante il XVI secolo," *Storia dell'arte* 21 (1974):171–213.

53. *Acta* 2.13.

54. Romain Roussel, *Les pèlerinages à travers les siècles* (Paris: Payot, 1954), 33; Rapp, "Pèlerinages dans la vie religieuse," 130–31.

55. Sumption, *Pilgrimage*, 177, 182.

56. *Acta* 2.14.

57. See Bartolomé Bennassar, *The Spanish Character: Attitudes and Mentalities from the Sixteenth to the Nineteenth Century* (Berkeley and Los Angeles: University of California Press, 1979), 77.

58. *Acta* 2.14–15.

59. Heath Dillard, *Daughters of the Reconquest: Women in Castilian Town Society, 1100–1300* (Cambridge: Cambridge University Press, 1984), 168–92. For the legal background see in general Rafael Serra Ruiz, *Honor, honra, e injuria en el derecho medieval español*, Anales de la Universidad de Murcia, derecho 23 (Murcia: Universidad de Murcia, 1969).

60. Jane Schneider, "Of Vigilance and Virgins: Honor, Shame, and Access to Resources in Mediterranean Societies," *Ethnology* 10 (1971):18, 21–22.

61. Julian Pitt-Rivers, "Honour and Social Status," in *Honour and Shame: The Values of Mediterranean Society*, ed. J. G. Peristiany (Chicago: University of Chicago Press, 1966), 25, 36, 42, 45.

62. Caro Baroja, "Honour and Shame: A Historical Account of Several Conflicts," in ibid., 91.

63. Ibid., 90–91.

64. *Acta* 2.15.

65. Louis Cardillac, *Morisques et chrétiens: Un affrontement polémique (1492–1640)* (Paris: Klincksieck, 1977), 268–79.

66. See Anwar G. Chejne, *Islam and the West: A Cultural and Social History* (Albany: State University of New York Press, 1983), vii, 2, 7, 8, 18, 180 n. 1. For Moriscos see also A. W. Lovett, *Early Habsburg Spain* (Oxford: Oxford University Press, 1986), 257–76; and for the expulsion, Norman Roth, "The Jews of Spain and the Expulsion of 1492," *Historian* 55 (1992):17–30.

67. *Acta* 9.100.

68. See Barbara Nolan, *The Gothic Visionary Perspective* (Princeton, N.J.: Princeton University Press, 1977), 129–31.

69. See Pope Paul IV, "Cum quorumdam hominum," in *Enchiridion*, ed. Denzinger, no. 1880.

70. See Caro Baroja, "Honour and Shame," 84, 100–1, 104.

71. Lope García de Salazar, *Las bienandanzas e fortunas* 4.20, 22. For the

system of lineage see Caro Baroja, "Linajes y bandos," in idem, *Vasconiana: (De historia y etnología)* (Madrid: Minotauro, 1957), 15–61.

72. *Acta* 2.15-16.

73. Albert A. Sicroff, *Los estatutos de limpieza de sangre: Controversias entre los siglos XV and XVII*, trans. Mauro Armiño, La otra historia de España, 5, rev. ed. (Madrid: Taurus, 1985), 315–36.

74. *Constitutiones* 2.3.44.

75. Petrus Alfonsi, *Disciplina clericalis* 17, 18; *The "Disciplina clericalis" of Petrus Alfonsi*, trans. P. R. Quarrie from Eberhard Hermes (Berkeley and Los Angeles: University of California Press, 1970), 135, 136. Cf. Climente Sanchez, *Libro de enxemplos* 362, 363, cited by John Esten Keller, *Motif-Index of Mediaeval Spanish Literature* (Knoxville: University of Tennessee Press, 1949), J21.5.

76. Chew, *Pilgrimage of Life*, 36. Fortune at her Wheel, George Pencz, woodcut, 16th century, reproduced, fig. 52; Hans Burgkmair in Petrarch, *De remediis utriusque fortunae*, Augsburg, 1532, fig. 53.

77. See, without reference to Loyola, Wolfgang Harms, *Homo viator in bivio: Studien zur Bildlichkeit des Weges*, Medium aevum, philologische Studien, 21 (Munich: Wilhelm Fink, 1970), 221–49.

78. Wolfram von Eschenbach, *Parzival* 224.19; 452.5-10. D. H. Green, *Irony in the Medieval Romance* (Cambridge: Cambridge University Press, 1979), 152–60.

79. Marion E. Gibbs, "Wrong Paths in *Parzival*," *Modern Language Review* 63 (1968):875.

80. Green, "Homicide and *Parzival*," in *Approaches to Wolfram von Eschenbach: Five Essays*, ed. idem and Leslie Peter Johnson, Mikrokosmos, Beiträge zur Literaturwissenschaft und Bedeutungsforschung, 5 (Bern: Peter Lang, 1978), 33–34.

81. *Acta* 2.16-17. For the site see Anselm M. Albareda, *Historia de Montserrat*, rev. ed. (Montserrat: Abadía de Montserrat, 1974).

82. Bartolomé Bermejo, Virgin and Child in a Landscape (Virgin of Montserrat), central panel, c. 1482–83, cathedral, sacristy, Acqui Terme. Reproduced in Eric Young, *Bartolomé Bermejo: The Great Hispano-Flemish Master* (London: Paul Elek, 1975), pl. 39, and detail, pl. 40; José Gudiol Ricart, *Pintura gótica*, vol. 9 of *"Ars hispaniae": Historia universal del arte hispánico*, 22 vols. (Madrid: Plus-Ultra, 1947–77), 270, fig. 230.

83. *Acta* 2.17.

84. Ruiz, *Libro de buen amor* 1128–1130; *The Book of True Love*, trans. Anthony N. Zahareas and Saralynn R. Daly (University Park: Pennsylvania State University Press, 1978), 291.

85. T. C. Price Zimmerman, "Confession and Autobiography in the Early Renaissance," in *Renaissance Studies in Honor of Hans Baron*, ed. Anthony Molho and John A. Tedeschi (Florence: G. C. Sansoni, 1971), 124, referring to Jacopo Passavanti, *Lo specchio di vera pentienza*, p. 128. Zimmerman's identification of the penitentials as the matrix of early renaissance autobiography at 126 is exceedingly restrictive.

86. Sanchez de Vercial, *Libro de los exenplos* 1, cited in Keller, *Motif-Index*, V21.6.

87. See Richard Kieckhefer, *Unquiet Souls: Fourteenth-Century Saints and Their Religious Milieu* (Chicago: University of Chicago Press, 1984), 125-26.

88. Johann Huizinga, *The Waning of the Middle Ages: A Study of the Forms of Life, Thought, and Art in France and the Netherlands in the Fourteenth and Fifteenth Centuries* (London: Edward Arnold, 1924), 168.

89. *Acta* 2.17-18.

90. See Andreas Wang, *Der "miles christianus" im 16. und 17. Jahrhundert und seine mittelalterliche Tradition: Ein Beitrag zum Verhaltnis von sprachlicher und graphischer Bildlichkeit*, Mikrokosmos: Beiträge zur Literaturwissenschaft und Bedeutungsforschung, 1 (Frankfurt: Peter Lang, 1975), 39-104; Chew, *Pilgrimage of Life*, 140-43; Françoise Joukovsky, *La gloire dans la poésie française et néolatine du XVIe siècle (Des rhétoriquers à Agrippa d'Aubigné)*, Travaux d'humanisme et Renaissance, 102 (Geneva: Droz, 1969), 386-87.

91. Guillaume de Deguileville, *Pèlerinage de vie humaine* 7253-8199, cited by Susan K. Hagen, *Allegorical Remembrance: A Study of the Pilgrimage of the Life of Man as a Medieval Treatise on Seeing and Remembering* (Athens: University of Georgia Press, 1990), 77-81. See also *Pelerinage de la vida humana*, pp. 140; 157, figs. 5, 6.

92. See Weinstein and Bell, *Saints and Society*, 100, 112, 111, 112, 109. For a knight placing his armor on Mary's altar and becoming a spiritual, rather than temporal, warrior see Caesarius of Heisterbach, *Dialogus miraculorum* 1.37.

93. *Acta* 2.18.

94. Weinstein and Bell, *Saints and Society*, 236.

95. For the term *caballero* see Hillgarth, *Spanish Kingdoms*, 1:63-65; Helen Nader, *The Mendoza Family in the Spanish Renaissance, 1350 to 1550* (New Brunswick, N.J.: Rutgers University Press, 1979), 36-37, 103.

96. Montaigne, *Essais* 2.17, p. 633; *The Complete Works of Montaigne*, trans. Donald M. Frame (Stanford, Calif.: Stanford University Press, 1967), 479.

97. *Acta* 2.18.

98. Caro Baroja, "Honour and Shame," 84.

99. "Praefatio scriptoris" 1.

100. Layman donating his garment to a poor man, Oxford, *Bible moralisée*, fol. 56. Reproduced in François Garnier, *Le language de l'image au moyen âge*, 2 vols. (Paris: Léopard d'or, 1982), 2:257, no. 360, and see p. 253.

101. See Adolf Katzenellenbogen, *Allegories of the Virtues and Vices in Mediaeval Art: From Early Christian Times to the Thirteenth Century* (London: Warburg Institute, 1939), 12-13.

102. E.g. Stefano di Giovanni, called Sassetta, St. Francis Giving His Cloak to a Poor Soldier, panel, 1437-38, National Gallery, London. Reproduced in Jill Dunkerton, Susan Foister, Dillian Gordon, and Nicholas Penny, *Giotto to Dürer: Early Renaissance Painting in the National Gallery* (New Haven, Conn.: Yale University Press with National Gallery Publications, London, 1991), pl. 19.

103. Sumption, *Pilgrimage*, 172-73.

104. Weinstein and Bell, *Saints and Society*, 157.
105. Hillgarth, *Spanish Kingdoms*, 2:8.
106. The locus classicus is Jerome, *Contra Vigilantium* 15. For a survey of the ascetic practice of weeping for sin see Sandra McEntire, "The Doctrine of Compunction from Bede to Margery Kempe," in *The Medieval Mystical Tradition in England*, Exeter Symposium 4, Papers Read at Dartington Hall, July 1987, ed. Marion Glasscoe (Cambridge: D. S. Brewer, 1987), 77–90.
107. Huizinga, *Waning of the Middle Ages*, 173–74; Kieckhefer, *Unquiet Souls*, 15, 182.
108. Moshe Barasch, "The Crying Face," *Artibus et historiae* 15 (1987):21–36; rpt. in idem, *"Imago hominis": Studies in the Language of Art* (Vienna: IRSA, 1991), 85–99.
109. For a survey see Sheila Page Bayne, *Tears and Weeping: An Aspect of Emotional Climate Reflected in Seventeenth-Century French Literature* (Tübingen: Gunter Narr, 1981), 22–76; Anne Vincent-Buffault, *Histoire des larmes* (Paris: Rivages, 1984). For emotion as a historical phenomenon see Lucien Febvre, "La sensibilité et l'histoire: Comment reconstituer la vie affective d'autrefois?" *Annales d'histoire sociale* 3 (1941):5–20.
110. Hélène Monsacre, *Les larmes d'Achille: Le héros, la femme, et la souffrance dans la poesié d'Homère* (Paris: Albin Michel, 1984).
111. Ramsay MacMullen, "Romans in Tears," *Classical Philology* 75 (1980): 254–55.
112. L. Beszard, "Les larmes dans l'épopée, particulièrement dans l'épopée française jusqu'à la fin du XIIe siècle," *Zeitschrift für romanische Philologie* 27 (1903):385–413, 513–49, 641–74; Heinz Gerd Wienand, *Tränen: Untersuchungen über das Weinen in der deutschen Sprache und Literatur des Mittelalters*, Abhandlungen zum Kunst-, Musik-, und Literaturwissenschaft, 5 (Bonn: Bouvier, 1958).
113. *Acta* 2.8, 10.
114. Christian, *Apparitions*, 199–201.
115. *Acta* 3.19.
116. *Acta* 2.18.
117. Augustine, *Confessiones* 10.38.63; *Confessions*, trans. Vernon J. Bourke (New York: Fathers of the Church, 1953), 319.
118. *Acta* 3.32.
119. *Vita Danieli*, p. 563, cited by Peter Brown, *The Cult of the Saints* (London: SCM, 1981), 68.
120. *Acta* 3.19.
121. Sumption, *Pilgrimage*, 101.
122. See Timothy Husband with Gloria Gilmore-House, *The Wild Man: Medieval Myth and Symbolism* (New York: Metropolitan Museum of Art, 1980), 1–3, 7, 8–10, 12, 94–109. For a Catalan example see Bermejo, Saint Onuphrius, from the predella of the Santa Engracia retable, c. 1474–77, Colegiata, Museo Parroquial, Daroca. Reproduced in Young, *Bartolomé Bermejo*, pl. 33. For the wild man in literature see Penelope B. R. Doob, *Nebuchadnezzar's Children: Conventions of Madness in Middle English Literature* (New Haven, Conn.: Yale University Press, 1974), 134–207; for Spanish examples, Oleh Ma-

zur, *The Wild Man in the Spanish Renaissance and Golden-Age Theater: A Comparative Study including the "Indio," the "Bárbaro," and Their Counterparts in European Lores* (Ann Arbor, Mich.: University Microfilms for Villanova University, 1980); Stanley L. Robe, "Wild Men and Spain's Brave New World," in *The Wild Man Within: An Image in Western Thought from the Renaissance to Romanticism*, ed. Edward Dudley and Maximillian E. Novak (Pittsburgh, Pa.: University of Pittsburgh Press, 1973), 39–53; Alan Deyermond, "El hombre salvaje en la novela sentimental," *Filología* 10 (1964):97–111. For Hercules' attribute see Beth Cohen, "From Bowman to Clubman: Herakles and Olympia," *Art Bulletin* 76 (1994):695–715.

123. Felix Fabri, *Evagatorium*, 1:65; Sumption, *Pilgrimage*, 172.

124. Erasmus, *De civilitate* 1, in *Opera omnia* (Leiden), 1:1035; "On Good Manners for Boys," trans. Brian McGregor in *The Collected Works of Erasmus* (Toronto: University of Toronto Press, 1978) 25:277.

125. Norbert Elias, *The Civilizing Process*, trans. Edmund Jephcott (New York: Urizen, 1978), 1:88, 69.

126. Ruiz, *Libro de buen amor* 306.

127. See Caro Baroja, "Honour and Social Status," in *Honour and Shame*, 25; and for crowns and hats in association with glory, Joukovsky, *Gloire dans la poésie*, 375–80. See also Paul-Henri Stahl, *Histoire de la décapitation* (Paris: Presses universitaires de France, 1986); Samuel Y. Edgerton, Jr., *Pictures and Punishment: Art and Criminal Prosecution during the Florentine Renaissance* (Ithaca, N.Y.: Cornell University Press, 1985), 128–29, 135, 65; Laurie Schneider, "Donatello and Caravaggio: The Iconography of Decapitation," *American Imago* 33 (1976):84–91.

128. For hats in the tub see A Bathing and Pleasure Palace, Valerius Maximus, Master of the Housebook, late 15th century, Galeria medievalia, London. Reproduced in Christine de Pizan, *A Medieval Woman's Mirror of Honor: The Treasury of the City of Ladies*, trans. Charity Cannon Willard (New York: Persea, 1989), 65, pl. 20. For hats in hell see Edgerton, *Pictures and Punishment*, 65 n. 23.

129. Natalie Zemon Davis, *Fiction in the Archives: Pardon Tales and Their Tellers in Sixteenth-Century France* (Stanford, Calif.: Stanford University Press, 1987), 38.

130. Dillard, *Daughters of the Reconquest*, 174–75. For the iconography of touching another person's hair see Garnier, *Langage de l'image au moyen âge*, 2:73–74.

131. *Acta* 5.51–53.

132. Robert J. Clements, *The Poetry of Michelangelo* (New York: New York University Press, 1965), 13.

133. *Acta* 9.89.

134. Jacques Roussiaud, *Medieval Prostitution*, trans. Lydia G. Cochrane (New York: Blackwell, 1988), 154.

135. See Caro Baroja, "Honour and Shame," 87.

136. Petrarch, *Epistolae familiares* 10.3; *Letters on Familiar Matters: Rerum familiarum libri IX-XVI*, trans. Aldo S. Bernardo (Baltimore, Md.: Johns Hopkins University Press, 1982), 60, 59, citing Seneca, *Ad Lucilium* 94.70. For the

clerical critique of the effeminacy of males at court wearing their hair long and curly see C. Stephen Jaeger, *The Origins of Courtliness: Civilizing Trends and the Formation of Courtly Ideals* (Philadelphia: University of Pennsylvania Press, 1985), 180. For the Spanish fashion see Ruth Matilda Anderson, *Hispanic Costume, 1480-1530* (New York: Hispanic Society of America, 1979), 33-34.

137. Marcia L. Colish, *The Stoic Tradition from Antiquity to the Early Middle Ages*, Studies in the History of Christian Thought, 24-25, 2 vols. (Leiden: E. J. Brill, 1985), 1:48; 2:211, citing Augustine, *De opere monchorum* 31.39-33.41; idem, "Cosmetic Theology: The Transformation of a Stoic Theme," *Assays: Critical Approaches to Medieval and Renaissance Texts* 1 (1981):5, 7-12. For Stoic cosmetology and hair see also Maud W. Gleason, "The Semiotics of Gender: Physiognomy and Self-Fashioning in the Second Century c.e.," in *Before Sexuality: The Construction of Erotic Experience in the Ancient Greek World*, ed. David M. Halperin, John J. Winkler, and Froma I. Zeitlin (Princeton, N.J.: Princeton University Press, 1990), 399-402. See also in general Gábor Klaniczay, "Fashionable Beards and Heretic Rags," in idem, *The Uses of Supernatural Power: The Transformation of Popular Religion in Medieval and Early-Modern Europe*, ed. Karen Margolis, trans. Susan Singerman (London: Polity, 1990), 51-78.

138. Quintilian, *Institutiones oratoriae* 11.3.137.

139. *Acta* 3.29.

140. *Constitutiones* 1.2.10; 1.3.15.

141. See Jan Zialkowski, "Avatars of Ugliness in Medieval Literature," *Modern Language Review* 79 (1984):1-20.

142. *Acta* 3.34. For male dress see Anderson, *Hispanic Costume*, 35-79.

143. Erasmus, *De civilitate* 1, in *Opera omnia* (Leiden), 1:1036.

144. Anne Hollander, *Seeing Through Clothes* (New York: Viking, 1978), xiv-xv. For an introduction to the period see Madeleine Lazard, "Le corps vêtu: Signification du costume à la Renaissance," in *Le corps à la renaissance*, Actes du XXXe colloque de Tours, 1987, ed. Jean Céard, Marie Madeleine Fontaine, and Jean-Claude Margolin (Paris: Aux amateurs de livres, 1990), 77-94.

145. Hollander, *Seeing Through Clothes*, 2-3, 15-16, 23, 51-52.

146. *Acta* 2.16, 18.

147. See Roussel, *Pèlerinages*, 30.

148. Sumption, *Pilgrimage*, 171-72.

149. Elizabeth Birbari, *Dress in Italian Painting, 1460-1500* (London: John Murray, 1975), 32-34, 30; and for the doublet, which was worn with hose, 43-47.

150. Castiglione, *Libro del cortegiano* 2.27.

151. Caro Baroja, "Honour and Shame," 87.

152. Georges Vigarello, *Concepts of Cleanliness: Changing Attitudes in France since the Middle Ages*, trans. Jean Birrell (Cambridge: Cambridge University Press, 1988), 52.

153. Erasmus, *De civilitate* 2, in *Opera omnia* (Leiden), 1:1037.

154. See Hillgarth, *Spanish Kingdoms*, 1:139; 2:48-49.

155. Domenico Cavalca, *Mirall de la creu* 19, reporting the opinion of Greg-

ory the Great; Brunetto Latini, *Il tesoretto* 2608–15. For the endurance of this topic in the 1550s see Joukovsky, *Gloire dans la poésie*, 69 n. 184.

156. José Sanchez Herrero, "Los cuidados de la belleza corporal femenina en los confesionales y tratados de doctrina cristiana de los siglos XIII al XVI," in *Les soins de beauté: Moyen age, début des temps modernes*, Actes du IIIe colloque international Grasse, 26–28 avril 1985, ed. Denis Menjot (Nice: Université de Nice, 1987), 286.

157. Aileen Ribeiro, *Dress and Morality* (London: Batsford, 1986), 45, 60, 62, 65, 69; Jacqueline Herald, *Renaissance Dress in Italy, 1400–1500*, History of Dress, 2 (New Jersey: Humanities, 1981), 53, 61, 211. For caps see ibid., 55; Irena Turneau, "The Diffusion of Knitting in Medieval Europe," trans. Maria Starowieyska in *Cloth and Clothing in Medieval Europe*, 389.

158. *Acta* 10.97.

159. Weinstein and Bell, *Saints and Society*, 81.

160. *Acta* 3.19.

161. Weinstein and Bell, *Saints and Society*, 154.

162. Hillgarth, *Spanish Kingdoms*, 1:35.

163. *Acta* 3.25, 27.

164. Dante, *Purgatorio* 9.13–18.

165. *Acta* 3.26

166. Palladius, *Lausiac History* 18.3; 2.2–3; 19.8; 38.11; 43.1; 48.2; 57.2. For the late medieval examples see Kieckhefer, *Unquiet Souls*, 26, 37, 144, 94, 95.

167. *Acta* 3.22.

168. *Acta* 3.23.

169. Sanchez, *Libro des los exenplos* 114, cited by Keller, *Motif-Index*, B563.4.1. For the friendship of holy men with animals see Clarence J. Glacken, *Traces on the Rhodian Shore: Nature and Culture in Western Thought from Ancient Times to the End of the Eighteenth Century* (Berkeley and Los Angeles: University of California Press, 1967), 310–11.

170. Jacob de Voragine, *Legenda aurea* 108. The iconography includes the vision by Dominic's pregnant mother of a dog with a torch and star. I. Frank, in *Ikonographie der cristlichen Kunst*, ed. Engelbert Kirschbaum, 8 vols. (Rome: Herder, 1968–76), 6:76; and see the reproduction of the detail of Francesco Triani, polyptych, Church of St. Catherine, Pisa, in Weinstein and Bell, *Saints and Society*, 22, fig. 2.

171. See Penn R. Szittya, *The Antifraternal Tradition in Medieval Literature* (Princeton, N.J.: Princeton University Press, 1986), esp. 60, 119.

172. *Acta* 3.23–24.

173. For the Dominican convent of St. Peter Martyr in Manresa see Cayetano Barraquer y Roviralta, *Las casas de religiosos en Cataluña durante el primer tercio del siglo XIX*, 2 vols. (Barcelona: Francisco J. Altés y Alabart, 1906), 2:59–62.

174. Augustine, *Confessiones* 9.4.9–10; trans. Bourke, 238. Cf. for the metaphor *Enarratio in psalmos* 4.6.

175. *Acta* 6.55. The philology is mine. The earliest occurence of *aguja* given in the historical Castilian dictionary is with reference to Pascual de Gayangos's

edition of *La gran conquista de ultramar*. The critical edition of Madrid, Biblioteca nacional, MS 1187, with a concordance, by Franklin M. Wallman and Louis Cooper has *monte agudo*, fol. 315r39 and *mont agudo*, fol. 322v13. The editors remark that Gayangos's edition is very corrupt with modernizations. The noun *agujero* does not appear in Antonio de Nebrija's *Vocabulario de romance en latín*.

176. Giles Constable, *Attitudes Toward Self-Inflicted Suffering in the Middle Ages*, Stephen J. Brademas, Sr., Lecture, 9 (Brookline, Mass.: Hellenic College, 1982), 8–10.

177. Kieckhefer, *Unquiet Souls*, 120.

178. Palladius, *Lausiac History* 38.8; 28; 58.5; *The Lausiac History*, trans. Robert T. Meyer, Ancient Christian Writers, 34 (Westminster, Md.: Newman, 1965), 112, 88, 140.

179. Ibid., 25; proem. 6; cf. praef. 14; trans. Meyer, 19. The proemium is only in some manuscripts and not in those of the best tradition, 167 n. 1.

180. See William J. Bouwsma, "Anxiety and the Formation of Early Modern Culture," in idem, *A Usable Past: Essays in European Cultural History* (Berkeley and Los Angeles: University of California Press, 1990), 157–89.

181. See Siegfried Wenzel, *The Sin of Sloth: Acedia in Medieval Thought and Literature* (Chapel Hill: University of North Carolina Press, 1960); Reinhard Kuhn, *The Demon of Noontide: Ennui in Western Literature* (Princeton, N.J.: Princeton University Press, 1976), 3–98, 373–76; Roger Caillois, "Les démons de midi," *Revue de l'histoire des religions* 115 (1937):142–73; 116 (1937):54–83, 143–86; Stanford M. Lyman, *The Seven Deadly Sins: Society and Evil* (New York: St. Martin's Press, 1978), 5–18. For its Spanish manifestation see Teresa Scott Soufas, *Melancholy and the Secular Mind in Spanish Golden-Age Literature* (Columbia: University of Missouri Press, 1990), 1–63.

182. Ibid.

183. See Wenzel, *Sin of Sloth*, 5, 21–22, 28, 32, 37, passim.

184. Barasch, *Gestures of Despair in Medieval and Early Renaissance Art* (New York: New York University Press, 1976), with my correction of his designation of prostration as a gesture of despair, 17. Although Barasch did not locate the source for the gesture of biting the hand, see the next note.

185. Elder Seneca, *Controversiae* 3.7. See Quintilian, *Institutiones oratoriae* 8.2.20; 8.5.23; cf. Ovid, *Metamorphoses* 8.877–78; Apuleius, *Metamorphoses* 8.27.

186. *Book of Margery Kempe* 1.1.

187. *Acta* 1.2.

188. Barasch, *Gestures of Despair*, 42, citing Prudentius, *Psychomachia* 145–54.

189. Garnier, *Langage de l'image au moyen âge*, 2:278–82.

190. See Ian Donaldson, *The Rapes of Lucretia: A Myth and Its Transformations* (Oxford: Clarendon, 1982); for artistic examples, H. Diane Russell with Bernadine Barnes, *Eva/Ave: Woman in Renaissance and Baroque Prints* (Washington, D.C.: National Gallery of Art with the Feminist Press at the City University of New York, 1990), 40–48. For recent studies of one artist's rendition see Patricia Emison, "The Singularity of Raphael's Lucretia," *Art History*

14 (1991):372–96; Julien Stock, "A Drawing by Raphael of Lucretia," *Burlington Magazine* 126 (1984):423–24.

191. Mary D. Garrard, *Artemisia Gentileschi: The Image of the Female Hero in Italian Baroque Art* (Princeton, N.J.: Princeton University Press, 1989), 212–14.

192. Albrecht Altdorfer, Pyramus and Thisbe, woodcut, 1513, National Gallery, Washington, D.C. Reproduced in Russell with Barnes, *Eva/Ave*, 188.

193. Leonardo da Vinci, Paris, Bibliothèque nationale, MS 2038, fol. 29b, in *Literary Works*, 1:342.

194. Michael Camille, *The Gothic Idol: Idolatry and Image-making in Medieval Art* (Cambridge: Cambridge University Press, 1989), 5–7.

195. Garnier, *Language de l'image au moyen âge*, 1:120–23. Orguel Ocozias face to humility in friar Laurent, *Somme le roi*, Bibliothèque Mazarine, 13th century, MS 870, fol. 89v. Reproduced 123, figs. A and B. Also, Fall of Ochozias, initial from Second Book of Kings, Bible de saint-Bénigne, 12th century, Dijon, Bibliothèque municipale, MS 2, fol. 135v; Initial from Second Book of Kings, Bible, 13th century, Laon, Bibliothèque municipale, MS 472. Fall of Paul on road to Damascus, reproduced figs. C and D.

196. Camille, *Gothic Idol*, 5–7.

197. Edgerton, *Pictures and Punishment*, 87–88.

198. Evagrius Ponticus, *Logos praktikos* 14.

199. Donald R. Howard, *The Three Temptations: Medieval Man in Search of the World* (Princeton, N.J.: Princeton University Press, 1966), 43–51, referring to Gregory the Great, *Homiliae in evangelia* 1.16; incorrectly to Peter Lombard, but see *Sententiae* 2.21.5; Thomas Aquinas, *Summa theologiae* 3.41.4; Augustine, *Confessiones* 10.36–40.

200. Bernard of Clairvaux, *Sermone de conversione* 14.5; "Lenten Sermons on the Psalm 'He Who Dwells,' " trans. Marie-Bernard Saïd, in *Sermons on Conversion*, Cistercian Fathers, 25 (Kalamazoo, Mich.: Cistercian Publications, 1981), 234.

201. Domenico Cavalca, *Mirall de la creu* 16.

202. See Howard, *Three Temptations*, 55–56, and 72 for a typical renaissance treatment in Coluccio Salutati, *De seculo et religione* 1.8; 21, 20; 2.3, 15.

203. See Howard, *Three Temptations*, 75.

204. *Acta* 2.24.

205. Aristotle, *Metaphysica* 1008b.

206. *Acta* 3.24–25.

207. Ibid. 3.20, 21, 25.

208. Frances A. Yates, *The Art of Memory* (Chicago: University of Chicago Press, 1966), 1–7.

209. *Acta* 3.27.

210. Ibid. 3.28.

211. See Ringbom, "Devotional Images and Imaginative Devotions: Notes on the Place of Art in Late Medieval Private Piety," *Gazette des beaux arts* 6–73 (1969):159–70.

212. Reproduced in Joseph M. Gasol, *Manresa: Panorama d'una ciutat*

(Manresa: Montañà, 1971), 102, fig. 101; José María Mas y Casa, *Ensayos-históricos sobre Manresa*, 2d ed. (Manresa, 1882), 335.

213. See M. Soler I March, "Les fréres Serra," in M. M. Duran I Sanpere et al., *La peinture catalane à la fin du moyen âge* (Université de Paris, Institut d'art et d'archéologie, bibliothèque d'art catalan, Fondation Cambró; Paris: Ernest Leroux, 1933), 33–36. For reproduction see Pere Serra, detail of retable, Seo, Manresa, *Art de la Catalagne*, pl. CLX, 248; Gasol, *Manresa*, 41; José Gudiol Ricart, *Ars hispaniae*, vol. 9, *Pintura gótica* (Madrid: Plus-Ultra, 1955), 76, fig. 50. For Catalan retables in general see Judith Berg Sobré, *Behind the Altar Table: The Development of the Painted Retable in Spain, 1350–1500* (Columbia: University of Missouri Press, 1989), 77–93.

214. Chandler Rafthon Post, *A History of Spanish Painting*, 14 vols. (Cambridge, Mass.: Harvard University Press, 1930–66), 8-1:79.

215. See Benjamin Rowland, Jr., "Gabriel Guardia: A Fifteenth-Century Painter of Manresa," *Art Bulletin* 14 (1932):242–57. Gabriel Guardia, retable of the Trinity (reconstruction), Colegiata, Manresa. Reproduced in ibid., fig. 1, 242. See also fig. 2, Moses and the Burning Bush and the Baptism of Christ; fig. 3, the Creation of Eve; fig. 4, detail of the Madonna; fig. 15, Abraham and the Three Angels. For his discovery of the retable see 243. Also reproduced in idem, *Jaume Huguet: A Study in Late Gothic Painting in Catalonia* (Cambridge, Mass.: Harvard University Press, 1932), fig. 60; and details, fig. 61. Reproduced in color in Gasol, *Manresa*, 41, and reported as still awaiting restoration and reinstallation, 43.

216. See G. Karl Galinsky, *The Herakles Theme: The Adaptations of the Hero in Literature from Homer to the Twentieth Century* (Oxford: Basil Blackwell, 1971), 64–68.

217. Wolfgang Harms, *Homo viator in bivio: Studien zur Bildlichkeit des Weges*, Medium aevum, philologischen Studien, 21 (Munich: Wilhelm Fink, 1970), 57–98. Y-Form Crucifix as vegetation, miniature, codex from southeast Germany, c. 1230, pl. 9.

218. Catalan crucifixes usually portrayed the head as frontal and erect, but when inclined, to the left. See Manuel Trens, *Les majestats catalanes*, Monumenta cataloniae, 13 (Barcelona: Alpha, 1966); and for the twelfth-century crucifix now in the museum of the Seo see Gasol, *Manresa*, 26, fig. 20; 101, fig. 100.

219. Erasmus, "Concio, sive Medardus," in *Colloquia*, in *Opera omnia* (Amsterdam), 1–3:655.

220. Evagrius Ponticus, *Six Centuries* 1.75; 3; passim.

221. Maurice Vloberg, *La Vierge notre médiatrice*, Art et paysages, 10 (Grenoble: B. Arthaud, 1936), 182–89.

222. Perugino, Donation of the Keys to St. Peter, fresco, Sistine Chapel, Vatican. Reproduced in Baxandall, *Painting and Experience*, 67, fig. 32.

223. Lateral face of an altar, episcopal museum, Vich. Reproduced in Duran I Sanpere et al., *Peinture catalane*, pl. II; and Josep Gudiol i Cunill, *La pintura mig-eval catalana*, vol. 2, *Els primitius segona part, La pintura sobre fusta* (Barcelona: S. Babra, 1929), fig. 94.

224. Tosses, detail of the frontal of the retable of St. Michael Weighing Souls,

lateral of an altar table, Suriguerola. Reproduced in Joaquim Folch i Torres, *La pintura romànica sobre fusta*, Monumenta cataloniae, 9 (Barcelona: Alpha, 1956), 56, pl. 89; Appendix, 50, pl. 81.

225. *Acta* 1.4.

226. Raymond of Peñaforte, *Summa de poenitentia et matrimonio* 3.34.1, cited by Thomas N. Tentler, *Sin and Confession on the Eve of the Reformation* (Princeton, N.J.: Princeton University Press, 1977), 105.

227. See ibid., citing a Scotist, Jacobus Lupi Rebello, *Fructus*, a. 23.

228. See, without reference to Loyola, Tentler, *Sin and Confession*, 96–97, 104–11, 263–73; and for the rigorist requirement of a complete confession, also Killian McDonald, "The *summae confessorum* on the Integrity of Confession as Prolegomena for Luther and Trent," *Theological Studies* 54 (1993):405–26.

229. Tentler, *Sin and Confession*, 281–94, citing Andreas de Escobar, *Modus confitendi*, B2b, 292; and Eck, 298, and see n. 68.

230. *Acta* 3.28.

231. Bernard of Clairvaux, *De gradibus humilitatis* 22.56; *The Steps of Humility and Pride*, trans. M. Basil Pennington, in *The Works of Bernard of Clairvaux*, Cistercian Fathers, 13 (Washington, D.C.: Cistercian Publications Consortium, 1974), 5:82; ibid. 1–21.

232. *Acta* 2.3.

233. Lull, *Horas de nuestra Señora* 1–4, 16; *Hores de sancta Maria* 41.3–4, 6.

234. *Acta* 2.17.

235. See Russell A. Peck, "Number as a Cosmic Language," in *Essays in Numerical Criticism in Medieval Literature*, ed. Caroline D. Eckhardt (Lewisburg, Pa.: Bucknell University Press, 1980), 15–64.

236. *Acta* 1.1.

237. See Caro Baroja, "Honour and Shame," 84–89; *Las siete partidas*, trans. Samuel Parsons Scott (Chicago: Commerce Clearing House for the Comparative Law Bureau of the American Bar Association, 1931), 353. For a review of anthropological interpretations of honor see John H. R. Davis, *People of the Mediterranean: An Essay in Comparative Social Anthropology* (London: Routledge & Kegan Paul, 1977), 89–101.

238. E.g. Thomas Aquinas, *Summa theologiae* 3a.32.4; *In 3 Sententiae* 3.5. For its basis in Aristotle see Prudence Allen, *The Concept of Woman: The Aristotelian Revolution, 750 B.C.-A.D. 1250* (Montreal: Eden, 1985), 83–126.

239. *Ephemeris*, p. 94.

240. Richard of St. Laurent, *De laudibus beatae Mariae Virginis* 12.1, 7.

241. Virgin as a tabernacle, Metropolitan Museum of Art, New York. Reproduced closed and open in Barbara G. Lane, *The Altar and the Altarpiece: Sacramental Themes in Early Netherlandish Painting* (New York: Harper & Row, 1984), 27 and 28, figs. 17–18.

242. *Exercitia spiritualia*, p. 330.

243. For the paintings of the circumcision and the martyrs, including Mary queen of martyrs, see Howard Hibbard, "*Ut picturae sermones*: The First Painted Decorations of the Gesù," in *Baroque Art: The Jesuit Contribution*, ed.

Rudolf Wittkower and Irma B. Jaffe (New York: Fordham University Press, 1976), 33, 35, and pls. 18a-21b. The interpretation is mine.

244. *Acta* 3.29.

245. Augustine, *Confessiones* 7.5.7; trans. Bourke, 168; cf. Plotinus, *Enneads* 4.3.9; 6.16.26; 7.3.5; 7.9.13-15.

246. "Praefatio scriptoris" 1.

247. See Quintilian, *Institutiones oratoriae* 9.3.88.

248. *Acta* 2.27

249. See Jesse M. Gellrich, *The Idea of the Book in the Middle Ages: Language Theory, Mythology, and Fiction* (Ithaca, N.Y.: Cornell University Press, 1985), 181, 189-90. For rhetorical hestitation see also Quintilian, *Institutiones oratoriae* 9.3.88.

250. *Acta* 2.14; 3.20; 3.21.

251. *Acta* 3.21.

252. See Michael J. Ruggiero, *The Evolution of the Go-Between in Spanish Literature through the Sixteenth Century*, University of California Publications in Modern Philology (Berkeley and Los Angeles: University of California Press, 1966); Jacques Bailbé, "Le thème de la vieille femme dans la poésie satirique du XVIe et du début du XVIIe siècle," *Bibliothèque d'humanisme et Renaissance* 26 (1964):98-119. For procuresses in Spanish society see Dillard, *Daughters of the Reconquest*, 199-201.

253. See Weinstein and Bell, *Saints and Society*, 98, 226.

254. See Christian, *Apparitions*, 185.

255. See sor María de santo Domingo, *Libro de la oración*; Mary E. Giles, *The Book of Prayer of sor María of santo Domingo* (Albany: State University of New York Press, 1990), 3, 19, 77, 112, and passim; Bernardino Llorca, *La Inquisición española y los alumbrados (1509-1667): Según las actas originales de Madrid y de otros archivos*, Biblioteca de teólogos españoles, 7 (Salamanca: Universidad pontificia, 1980), 37-64, 259-71; Hillgarth, *Spanish Kingdoms*, 2:606; Marcel Bataillon, *Erasmo y España: Estudios sobre la historia espiritual del siglo XVI*, rev. ed. (Mexico: Fondo de cultura económica, 1950), 69-70. See also Jodi Bilinkoff, "A Spanish Prophetess and Her Patrons: The Case of María de santo Domingo," *Sixteenth Century Journal* 23 (1992):21-34; idem, "Charisma and Controversy: The Case of María de sto. Domingo," *Archivo dominicano* 10 (1989):55-66.

256. For the titles see Dillard, *Daughters of the Reconquest*, 16-21.

257. Christian, *Apparitions*, 186, 197-198, citing indirectly Jean Gerson, *De examinatione doctrinarum* 2.2.

258. Gerson, *De examinatione doctrinarum* 2.2, cited by D. Catherine Brown, *Pastor and Laity in the Theology of Jean Gerson* (Cambridge: Cambridge University Press, 1987), 223, and see also 214-26.

259. See Weinstein and Bell, *Saints and Society*, 232.

260. *Acta* 3.37.

261. See Green, "On Damning with Faint Praise in Medieval Literature," *Viator* 6 (1975):117-69; idem, *Irony in the Medieval Romance*, 9, citing Isidore of Seville, *Etymologiae* 11.21.41, and Quintilian, *Institutiones oratoriae* 8.6.54-55; 9; trans. Butler, 3:333. See also Dilwyn Knox, *"Ironia": Medieval and Re-*

naissance Ideas on Irony, Columbia Studies in the Classical Tradition, 16 (Leiden: E. J. Brill, 1989), 15–16, 32, 43, passim; and for the difference between medieval and modern irony, Simon Gaunt, *The Troubadours and Irony*, Cambridge Studies in Medieval Literature, 3 (Cambridge: Cambridge University Press, 1989), 5–38.

262. Gaunt, *Troubadours and Irony*, 22, 10–15, citing at 10 Buoncompagno of Signa, *Rhetorica antiqua*, fol. 9v-10r, from "Appendix: Definition of Irony by Buoncompagno of Signa from His *Rhetorica antiqua*, fol. 9v-10r," 37, in John F. Benton, "Clio and Venus: An Historical View of Medieval Love," in *The Meaning of Courtly Love*, Papers of the First Annual Conference of the Center for Medieval and Early Renaissance Studies, State University of New York at Binghamton, March 17–18, 1967, ed. F. X. Newman (Albany: State University of New York Press, 1968), 19–42.

263. See Caro Baroja, "Honour and Shame," 86.

CHAPTER 3. THE FLYING SERPENT

1. José Maria de Mas y Casa, *Ensayos-históricos sobre Manresa*, 2d ed. (Manresa, 1882), 332.

2. William A. Christian, Jr., *Local Religion in Sixteenth-Century Spain* (Princeton, N.J.: Princeton University Press, 1981), 93.

3. J. N. Hillgarth, *The Spanish Kingdoms*, 2 vols. (Oxford: Oxford University Press, 1985–87), 2:149–50.

4. For an introduction with Spanish examples see *The Military Orders: Fighting for the Faith and Caring for the Sick*, ed. Malcolm Barber (Brookfield, Vt.: Variorum, 1994).

5. Jacob de Voragine, *Legenda aurea* 4.

6. Louis Réau, *Iconographie de l'art chrétien*, 6 vols. (Paris: Presses universitaires de France, 1955–59), 3-2:833–36 and pl. 54. Anonymous master of Estimariu (Catalan school), St. Lucy, Prado, Madrid. Cycle of St. Lucy, Catalan retable, An. Coll. Martin Le Roy, Paris. Maria Chaira Celletti, in *Bibliotheca sanctorum*, 12 vols. (Rome: Istituto Giovanni XXIII nella Pontificia università lateranense, 1961–68), 7:252–57; C. Squarr, in *Lexikon der christlichen Ikonographie*, ed. Engelbert Kirschbaum, 8 vols. (Rome: Herder, 1968–76), 7:415–20.

7. Julio Caro Baroja, *El estio festivo: Fiestas populares del verano*, Otra historia de España, 10 (Madrid: Taurus, 1984), 9.

8. Christian, *Local Religion*, 94.

9. Dante, *Paradiso* 32.136–38; "Paradiso" 1: *Italian Text and Translation*, trans. Charles Singelton, Bollingen Series, 80 (Princeton, N.J.: Princeton University Press, 1975), 367; *Inferno* 2.97–100.

10. *Acta* 3.19; 3.30.

11. See Martin Ninck, *Die Bedeutung des Wassers im Kult und Leben der Alten: Eine Symbolgeschichtliche Untersuchung*, 2d ed. (Darmstadt: Wissenschaftliche, 1960); Philippe Reymond, *L'Eau, sa vie, et sa signification dans l'ancient testament*, Vetus testamentum Supplements, 6 (1958), 208–22.

12. Pierre Amandry, *La mantique apollinienne à Delphes: Essai sur le fonc-*

tionnement de l'oracle (Paris: E. de Boccard, 1950), 134–39; and for the spring Cassotis, Georges Roux, *Delphes: Son oracle et ses dieux* (Paris: Belles lettres, 1976), 136–45. It was characteristic of the Apolline sanctuaries that all were important hydraulic installations. René Ginouves, *Balaneutikē: Recherches sur le bain dans l'antiquité grecque* (Paris: E. de Boccard, 1962), 327–44.

13. Seneca, *Epistolae* 41.3; *Ad Lucilium epistulae morales*, trans. Richard M. Gummere, 3 vols. (Cambridge, Mass.: Harvard University Press, 1961), 1:275.

14. Joachim du Bellay, *Odes* 2.6, and Pierre de Ronsard, cited by Françoise Joukovsky, *La gloire dans la poésie française et néolatine du XVIe siècle (Des rhétoriqueurs à Agrippa d'Aubigné)*, Travaux d'humanisme et Renaissance, 102 (Geneva: Droz, 1969), 344.

15. See Gershom G. Scholem, *Jewish Gnosticism, Merkabah Mysticism, and Talmudic Tradition*, 2d rev. ed. (New York: Jewish Theological Seminary, 1965); Wilhelm Neuss, *Das Buch Ezechiel in Theologie und Kunst bis zum Ende des XII. Jahrhunderts*, Beiträge zur Geschichte des alten Mönchtums und des Benediktinerordens, 1–2 (Münster: Aschendorff, 1912); and for an Ezekiel figure, Marjorie O'Rourke Boyle, *Petrarch's Genius: Pentimento and Prophecy* (Berkeley and Los Angeles: University of California Press, 1991), 92–112.

16. Raffaele Pettazoni, *The All-Knowing God: Researches into Early Religion and Culture* (London: Methuen, 1956), 78, cf. 145.

17. *Acta* 3.30.

18. Lorenz Dürr, *Ezekiels Vision von der Erscheinung Gottes (Ez. c. 1 u. 10) im Lichte der vorderasiatischen Altertumskunde* (Münster: Aschendorff, 1917), 54–60; W. F. Albright, "What Were the Cherubim?" *Biblical Archeologist* 1 (1938):1–2; Simon Landersdorfer, *Der Baal tetramorphos und die Kerube des Ezechiel*, Studien zur Geschichte und Kultur des Altertums, 9 (Paderborn: Ferdinand Schöningh, 1918).

19. Hugo Gressmann, *Die Lade Jahves*, Forschungsinstitut für Religionsgeschichte, Israelitisch-Jüdische Abteilung, 5 (Berlin: W. Kohlhammer, 1920), 49–51. The Demon Bes with Horus-eyes and the Holy of Holies of Solomon's Temple. Reproduced 51 and Abb. 10. Pettazoni, *All-Knowing God*, 59, 110, cf. Ezek. 1:7. Bes pantheos, Bronze statuette, Louvre, Paris, figs. la, b. Bes reproduced in Balaji Mundkur, *The Cult of the Serpent: An Interdisciplinary Survey of its Manifestations and Origins* (Albany: State University of New York Press, 1983), 66. See also the bibliography in Waldemar Deonna, *Le symbolisme de l'oeil*, École française d'Athènes, Travaux et mémoires des anciens membres étrangers de l'école et de divers savants, 15 (Paris: E. de Boccard, 1965), 130 n. 3.

20. Didron Ainé, "Iconographie des anges," *Annales archéologiques* 11 (1851):347–62; 12 (1852):168–76; 18 (1858):33–48; reproduced in 11: 355, fig. 2. See also Adolphe N. Didron, *Christian Iconography: The History of Christian Art in the Middle Ages*, trans. E. J. Millington, 2 vols. (New York: Frederick Ungar, 1965), 1:152, 355, fig. 3; 2:89, 91, fig. 152; 265. Paris, Bibliothèque nationale, biblia sacra, MS lat. 6.i, 12th century, 97, fig. 157. Rabula Codex, Laurentian Library, Florence, in Neuss, *Buch Ezechiel*, 154–58, fig. 10; Vatican Kosmas manuscript, 9th or 7th century, 159–62, fig. 11, and further

162-79; Coptic chapel in Bawît, 190-93, figs. 27, 28. Réau, *Iconographie de l'art chrétien*, 2-1:41. Reliquary of Saint Maurice, enamel, 12th century, Church of St. Pantaleon, Museum Schnutgen, Cologne. Reproduced in Aurelia Stappart, *L'ange roman: Dans la pensée et dans l'art* (Paris: Berg, 1975), pl. 10. For the enduring iconography see the cloister church of the Holy Name, 17th century, Ohridsee, Macedonia. Reproduced in Lothar Heiser, *Die Engel im Glauben der Orthodoxie* (Trier: Paulinus, 1976), Tafel XXXI.

21. See examples in Neuss, *Buch Ezechiel*, 162-276 passim; Jesús Domínguez Bordona, *Spanish Illumination*, 2 vols. (Florence: Pantheon, 1930), pls. 28, 44, 56, 106.

22. E.g. in the Catalan bible of Sant Pere de Roda. Paris, Bibliothèque nationale, Bible Cod. lat. 6. Rod. B III, fol. 45. Reproduced in Neuss, *Die Katalonische Bibelillustration um die Wende des ersten Jahrtausends und die altspanische Buchmalerei* (Bonn: Kurt Schroeder, 1922), table 30, fig. 95; cf. table 60, fig. 181. This stroked version is frequent, e.g. Apocalypse de Saint-Sever, Paris, Bibliothèque nationale, MS latin 8878, fol. 137v. The First Trumpet. Reproduced in Pedro de Palol and Max Hirmer, *Early Medieval Art in Spain* (London: Thames and Hudson, 1967), 70, fig. XVII. There is a Catalan cherub with two censers hanging from six wings with dotted semicircles in the upper arches in *Tractát dels Set Querubins*, Archive of the Crown of Aragon, MS n. 26, fol. 131. (Among the codices of Ripoll, a translation of Alain de Lille, *De septem querubim*). Reproduced in Josep Gudiol, *Els primitivs*, part 3, *Els llibres illuminats* (Barcelona: Caruda, 1955), fig. 219. The dotted circle appears on the wings and at the center of the wheels of the tetramorph in the Great Scene of Judgment in Herrad of Hohenbourg, *Hortus deliciarum*, fol. 253r, pl. 144.

23. Bartolomé Bermejo, Christ at the Tomb with Angels, Heirs of Miguel Mateu, Barcelona. Reproduced in Eric Young, *Bartolomé Bermejo: The Great Hispano-Flemish Master* (London: Paul Elek, 1975), pl. 9; Elias Tormo y Monzo, "Bartolomé Bermejo el más recio de los primitivos españoles: Resumen de su vida, de su obra, y de su estudio," *Archivo español de arte y arqueologia* 2 (1926):fig. 25. Entry into Paradise (Te Deum) and Ascension, retable, 15th century, Instituto Amatller de arte hispánico, Barcelona. Reproduced in Young, *Bartolomé Bermejo*, pls. 3 and 4; Tormo y Monzo, "Bartolomé Bermejo," fig. 29 and detail fig. 31, fig. 36, with details figs. 37, 39. Resurrection, Museo municipale del Parque, Barcelona. Reproduced in Tormo y Monzo, ibid., fig. 33; but not included in Young's catalogue.

24. Lombard artist, King Ratchis altar, 8th century, S. Martino, Cividale. Reproduced in Gunnar Berefelt, *A Study on the Winged Angel: The Origin of a Motif*, trans. Patrick Hort (Stockholm: Almquist & Wiksell, 1968), 52, fig. 35. Angels surrounding Christ in glory holding the Eucharistic host, Carolingian illumination, sacramentary of the cathedral of Limoges, 11th century, Paris, Bibliothèque nationale, MS latin 9438. Reproduced in Stappart, *Ange roman*, pl. 45. Miniature, Bible for Bishop Heinrich von Blois, Winchester Cathedral, mid-12th century. Reproduced in Neuss, *Buch Ezechiel*, 233-34, fig. 44. For other Romanesque figures see ibid., 234-48. Mosaics, domes of Monreale, Sicily, ibid., 254-55, fig. 61. Mosaic, cathedral, Cefalù. Reproduced in Peter Lamborn Wilson, *Angels* (New York: Pantheon, 1980), 128. La Pala d'Oro, detail,

12th century, S. Marco, Venice. Reproduced in Stappart, *Ange roman*, pl. 11. Miniature of Evangeliars, 13th century, Koniglich Bibliothek, Aschaffenburg. Reproduced in Neuss, *Buch Ezechiel*, 275–76, fig. 76.

25. So-called Alcuin Bible from Tours, written probably at Marmoutier between 834 and 843, Bamberg, Staatliche Bibliothek, MS 1, fol. 339v. Reproduced in Gertrude Schiller, *Iconography of Christian Art*, trans. Janet Seligman, 2 vols. (London: Lund Humphries, 1971), 2:fig. 397.

26. Trier Apocalypse, executed in northern France first quarter of 9th century, Trier, Stadtbibliothek, Cod. 31, fol. 18v. Reproduced in John Williams, *Early Spanish Manuscript Illumination* (London: Chatto & Windus, 1977), 26.

27. Moralia in Iob, 945 A.D., Madrid, Biblioteca nacional, Cod. 80, fol. 2v. Reproduced in Williams, *Early Spanish Manuscript Illumination*, pl. 8A. Cf. Moralia in Iob, 925 A.D., Madrid, Biblioteca Nacional, Vit. 14-2. Reproduced in Bordona, *Spanish Illumination*, 1:pl. 8; Francis Klingender, *Animals in Art and Thought to the End of the Middle Ages*, ed. Evelyn Antal and John Harthan (London: Routledge & Kegan Paul, 1971), 227, fig. 135. For the motif of the punctuated circle see Deonna, *Symbolisme de l'oeil*, 26–28.

28. Paris, Bibliothèque nationale, Bible Cod. lat. 6. Reproduced in Neuss, *Buch Ezechiel*, 203–17, figs. 35, 36. See also Rod. B, fol. 45, reproduced in idem, *Katalonische Bibelillustration*, table 30, fig. 95; cf. table 60, fig. 181. Cf. 2:fol. 129v. Reproduced in Walter Cohn, *Romanesque Bible Illumination* (Ithaca, N.Y.: Cornell University Press, 1982), 73; Gérard de Champeaux and Sébastien Sterckx, *Introduction au monde des symboles*, 2d ed. (n.p.: Zodiaque, 1972), 25. Cf. II, fol. 109. Reproduced in Neuss, *Katalonische Bibelillustration*, table 25, fig. 83; Ainé, "Iconographie des anges," 11: 360, fig. 7; Gudiol, *Llibres illuminats*, fig. 21. Cod. Vat. lat. 5729. Neuss, *Buch Ezechiel*, 217–27; but incorrectly identified as the Farfa bible. Fol. 5v. Reproduced in Cohn, *Romanesque Bible Illumination*, 71. Cf. Fresco, S. Giovanni in Oleo, Rome. Reproduced in Stappart, *Ange roman*, 295, fig. 18.

29. Codex vigilianus seu albeldensis, A.D. 976, Escorial Library of the Royal Monastery, fol. 16v. Reproduced in Bordona, *Spanish Illumination*, 1:pl. 25; Champeaux and Sterckx, *Introduction au monde des symboles*, 109.

30. Beato de San Millán de la Cogolla, c. 1000, Madrid, Real academia de la historia, Cod. aemil. 33, fol. 92r. Reproduced in Williams, *Early Spanish Manuscript Illumination*, pl. 24; José Esteban Uranga Galdiano and Francisco Iñiguez Almech, *Arte medieval navarro*, 5 vols. (Pamplona: Aranzadi, 1971), 1:pl. 14; cf. fol. 209 in Bordona, *Spanish Illumination*, 1:pl. 19.

31. Beato de Fernando I y Sancha, Madrid, Biblioteca nacional, vit. 14-2, fol. 116v. Reproduced in *Beato de Liébana*, 91.

32. Paris, Bibliothèque nationale, MS latin 8878, fols. 121v-122r. Reproduced in *Apocalypse de Saint-Sever*; Xavier Barral i Altet, "Repercusión de la illustración de los Beatos en la iconografía del arte monumental románico," in *Actas del simposio para el estudio de los códices del "Comentario al Apocalypsis" de Beato de Liébana*, 3 vols. (Madrid: Joyas, 1980), 3:12, fig. 2; François Avril, "Quelques considerations sur l'execution materielle des enluminures de l'Apocalypse de Saint-Sever," ibid., 161, fig. 1. Paris, Bibliothèque nationale,

MS lat. 8878, fol. 108v-109r. Reproduced in *Apocalypse de Saint-Sever*; Klingender, *Animals in Art and Thought*, 235, fig. 146.

33. From the Liber testamentorum regium of Bishop Don Pelayo, 1126–29. Reproduced in Palol and Hirmer, *Early Medieval Art in Spain*, 96, fig. XXII.

34. See Josep Pijoan with Josep Gudiol i Ricart, *Les pintures murals romàniques de Catalunya*, Monumenta cataloniae, 4 (Barcelona: Alpha, 1948), 96–97. Reproduced as General view of apse, Seraphs with eyes on backs of hands, Sant Climent de Taüll, fig. 17; Lamb of the Apocalypse, fig 24; Decoration of the apse, St. Luke, Seraph with an eye above the wrist, St. John, Archangel, Santa Maria de Taüll, fig. 35; Esterrí de Cardós, Apse, Angels censing the eternal one, fig. 47; Estaon, Església de Santa Eulalia, Decoration of the apse, eyes on wings, hands, and feet, fig. 51. Església de Santa Maria, Decoration of main apse, Esterrí d'Àneu, fig. 57; detail, fig. 57. All are in the Museo de Arte de Cataluña, Barcelona. See also the detail of fresco of Santa María de Esterrí d'Àneu in Palol and Hirmer, *Early Medieval Art in Spain*, fig. XXIV, with bibliography; Sant Climent de Taüll, in *L'Art de la Catalogne de la second moitié du neuvième siècle à la fin du quinzième siècle* (Paris: Cahiers d'art, 1937), 122, pl. LXXX, design of a row of eyes marching down the center of uplifted wings, all over the downward wings, and on the back of the hands of the angel; Apse of Santa Eulàlia de Estaon, Seraphs with eyes on wings flanking Christ enthroned in a mandorla, Eduard Carbonell i Esteller and Jordi Gumí Cardona, *L'Art romànic a Cataluyna segle XII*, 2 vols. (Barcelona: Edicions 62, 1974–75), pl. 213, cf. detail of Santa María d'Esterrí d'Àneu, pl. 203; Seraph of Santa María d'Àneu in Stappart, *Ange roman*, 266–67, figs. c, e, f.

35. *Apocalypse de Saint-Sever*, fol. 108v-109r.

36. Louis Ginzberg, *The Legends of the Jews*, 7 vols. (Philadelphia: Jewish Publication Society of America, 1913–67), 2:308.

37. Adolf Jacoby, "Zur Erklärung der Kerube," *Archiv für Religionswissenschaft* 22 (1923–24); Uno Holmberg, "Der Todesengel," *Studia orientalia* 1 (1925):72–77; Pettazoni, *All-Knowing God*, 17, 111; Gustav Davidson, *A Dictionary of Angels Including the Fallen Angels* (New York: Free Press, 1967), 26, 64–65.

38. Beato de Fernando I y Sancha, Madrid, Biblioteca nacional, vit. 14-2, fol. 195. Reproduced in *Beato de Liébana*, 117. Consider also the beast before the temple with eyes on its body in Beato de Madrid, Madrid vit. 14-1, fol. 108v. Reproduced in P. K. Klein, "La tradición pictórica de los Beatos," in *Actas del simposio para el estudio de los Códices del "Comentario al Apocalypsis" de Beato de Liébana*, 3:64, fig. 16. See also the spots in Beato de Fernando I y Sancha, fol. 171v; the paisley eyes on the cavalry of beasts, fol. 171v; the spots on the adored beast, fol. 191v; the ocular scales on the dragon, fols. 186v, 187r, and on the frogs, fol. 220v. Scales like eyes may be a reminiscence of the legend of Leviathan with 365 eyes. Cf. stylized eyes on the head of the feathered and spangled serpent in Apocalypse de Saint-Sever, Paris, Bibliothèque nationale, MS latin 8878, fol. 13.

39. Réau, *Iconographie de l'art chrétien*, 2-1:61; Didron, *Christian Iconography*, 2:112–14. Dante, *Inferno* 34.37–54. See also Antonio Orbe, "La trinidad

maléfica (A propósito de "Excerpta ex Theodoto" 80, 3)," *Gregorianum* 49 (1968):726-61.

40. Mestre de Glorieta, Retable of Santa Anna, Sant Minquel, and Sant Sebastian, Table of St. Michael, second third of 15th century, private collection, Barcelona. Reproduced in Núria de Dalmases and Antoni José i Pitarch, *Història de l'art català*, 8 vols. (Barcelona: Edicions 62, 1983-85), 3:236.

41. Pettazoni, *All-Knowing God*, 19. For the multiplicity of organs see Claude Kappler, *Monstres, démons, et merveilles à la fin du moyen âge* (Paris: Payot, 1980), esp. 123-29; for the multicephalous see the grylle in Jurgis Baltrušaitis, *Le moyen âge fantastique: Antiquités et exotismes dans l'art gothique* (Paris: Armand Colin, 1955), 31-36; in general, John B. Friedman, *The Monstrous Races in Medieval Art and Thought* (Cambridge, Mass.: Harvard University Press, 1981); Gilbert Lascault, *Le monstre dans l'art occidental: Un problème esthétique* (Paris: Klincksieck, 1973); Heinz Mode, *Fabulous Beasts and Demons* (London: Phaidon, 1971); Centre de recherches sur la Renaissance, Université de Paris-Sorbonne, *Monstres et prodiges au temps de la Renaissance*, ed. M. T. Jones-Davies (Paris: Jean Touzot, 1980).

42. Paul Carus, *The History of the Devil and the Idea of Evil: From the Earliest Times to the Present Day* (1900 reprint; La Salle, Ill.: Open Court, 1974), 444; Thomas Wright, *A History of Caricature and Grotesque in Literature and Art* (London, 1865), 56.

43. Baltrušaitis, *Moyen âge fantastique*, 151-63, with examples of Chinese bat's wings with circles by Li Long-mein (A.D. 1081).

44. Orcagna, Detail of the Triumph of Death, Campo Santo, Pisa. In the second architectural division, the devil on the lower left beneath the inscription held by two angels. Reproduced in Raymond Régamy, *Anges* (Paris: P. Tisné, 1946), no. 20; *Métamorphoses du diable* (Paris: Hachette, 1968), 68.

45. The Last Judgment, fresco, Campo Santo, Pisa. Reproduced in Carus, *History of the Devil*, 485.

46. Jaume Ferrer II, Retable of St. Michael, c. 1444-47, Lleida, Paeria. Reproduced in Dalmases and José i Pitarch, *Història de l'art català*, 3:235. See also the ocular motif on bat's wings, 229. Bernat Martorell, Retable of Sant Jordi, central table, c. 1440, Art Institute, Chicago.

47. Bartolomé Bermejo, The Breaking of Hell, Museo Municipal del Parque, Barcelona. Reproduced in Tormo y Monzo, "Bartolomé Bermejo," 36-37, fig. 26.

48. Miguel Jiménez, Victory of St. Michael and Other Angels over the Devils, section of a retable, Gallery of Fine Arts, Yale University, New Haven, Conn. Reproduced in Chandler Rathfon Post, *A History of Spanish Painting*, 14 vols. (Cambridge, Mass.: Harvard University Press, 1930-66), 8-1:fig. 47. See also the Master of St. George, Retable of St. Michael, Cathedral of Tarragona, first half of 15th century. Reproduced in *Art de la Catalagne*, 287, pl. CXCI, and 289, pl. CXCII.

49. "Statura quoque erat rotis, et altitudo, et horribilis aspectus; et totum corpus oculis plenum in circuitu ipsarum quatuor. . . . Et omne corpus earum, et colla, et manus, et pennae, et circuli, plena erant oculis in circuitu quatuor rotarum."

50. Neuss, *Buch Ezechiel*, 30, 38, 78, 54.

51. Augustine, *Enarrationes in psalmos* 79.2; *Expositions on the Book of Psalms*, trans. H. M. Wilkins, 6 vols. (Oxford, 1853), 4:102; cf. 98.3.

52. Dionysius the Areopagite [pseud.], *Hierarchia caelestia* 6, 7, 15; *The Celestial Hierarchies*, trans. Editors of the Shrine of Wisdom (London: Shrine of Wisdom, 1935), 25, 26, 50 with alteration.

53. The order was accepted by Thomas Aquinas and Dante. For a comparative listing see Davidson, *Dictionary of Angels*, appendix: "The Orders of the Celestial Hierarchy," 336–38. See also C. A. Patrides, "Renaissance Thought on the Celestial Hierarchy: The Decline of a Tradition," *Journal of the History of Ideas* 20 (1959):155–66; idem, "Renaissance Views on the 'Unconfused Orders Angellick,' " ibid. 23 (1962):265–67.

54. Hildegard of Bingen, *Scivias*, between pp. 6–7. Reproduced also in Louis Baillet, "Les miniatures du *Scivias* de sainte Hildegarde conservé à la Bibliothèque de Wiesbaden," Fondation Eugène Piot, *Monuments et mémoires* (Paris: Ernest Leroux, 1911), 19:58, fig. 2; Hiltgart L. Keller, *Mittelrheinische Buchmalereizur in Handschriften aus dem Kreise der Hiltgart von Bingen* (Stuttgart: Ernst Surkamp, 1933), pl. 3; *Scivias by Hildegard of Bingen*, trans. Bruce Hozeski (Santa Fe, N.M.: Bear, 1986), 6.

55. Pettazoni, *All-Knowing God*, 5–10, 16–17, 19, 22, 24–25, 105–11, 145, 433–49. For multiple eyes see also Deonna, *Symbolisme de l'oeil*, 121–34.

56. See Caro Baroja, *Los Vascos*, 2 vols. (San Sebastien: Larrun, 1982), 2:376–77 without reference; but the source is *Guide du pèlerin de Saint-Jacques de Compostela* 7. For primitive Basque notions of the sky and sun and of rays as lightning see Caro Baroja, *Sobre la religion antigua y el calendario del pueblo vasco*, 3d ed., Estudios vascos, 1 (San Sebastian: Txertoa, 1973), 13–45.

57. Dante, *Purgatorio* 29.94–102.

58. See Jean Daniélou, "Les démons de l'air dans la *Vie d'Antoine*," *Studia anselmiana* 38 (1956):136–47.

59. See Jeffrey Burton Russell, *Satan: The Early Christian Tradition* (Ithaca, N.Y.: Cornell University Press, 1981), 165–88; idem, *Lucifer: The Devil in the Middle Ages* (Ithaca, N.Y.: Cornell University Press, 1984), 180–81, 174 n. 36.

60. *Vita Antonii* 22, 23, 31, 5, 6, 8, 9, 11, 24. The traditional ascription of this work to Athanasius has been challenged by T. D. Barnes, "Angel of Light or Mystic Initiate? The Problem of the Life of Antony," *Journal of Theological Studies* 37 (1986):353–63.

61. Réau, *Iconographie de l'art chrétien*, 3-1:101–15. Many plates are reproduced in Enrico Castelli, *Le démoniaque dans l'art: Sa signification philosophique*, trans. Enrichetta Valenziani (Paris: J. Vrin, 1958); Roland Villeneuve with Josselyne Chamarat, *La beauté du diable* (Paris: Berger-Levrault, 1983), 102–18.

62. Reproduced in Wilhelm Fraenger, *Matthias Grünewald* (Munich: C. H. Beck, 1963), pl. 16.

63. Josep M. Gasol, *Manresa: Panorama d'una ciutat* (Manresa: Montañà, 1971), 30, fig. 26; 41. Lluis Borrassà, Internment of Christ, fragment of retable of St. Anthony Abbot, 1410, Seo, Manresa.

64. See Benjamin Rowland, Jr., *Jaume Huguet: A Study in Late Gothic*

Painting in Catalonia (Cambridge, Mass.: Harvard University Press, 1932), 133–40 and fig. 36. The lost retable, housed in the Escolapios, was burned during the *semana tragica* of 1909 with no fragments remaining, only poor photographs and summary descriptions. See A. Duran I Sanpere, "El desaparecido retablo de San Antonio Abad," *Museum* 1 (1911):1–2. The central demon with upraised club has a bat's wings with oval motifs decorating the edges. For the contemporary cult of Anthony abbot in Spain see Caro Baroja, *Las formas complejas de la vida religiosa (Religión, sociedad y carácter en la España de los siglos XVI y XVII)* (Madrid: Akal, 1978), 96–99.

65. *Vita Antonii* 6, 23, 31–35, 39, 25–27.

66. For the cycle of the devil outwitted see August Wünsche, *Die Sagenkreis vom geprellten Teufel* (Leipzig: Akademischer, 1905).

67. Russell, *Lucifer*, 62–63, 67, 161, 225.

68. *Vita Antonii* 7 and passim, 5, 7, 13, 21–25, 35–41, 62–64, 75, and for discernment as most important, p. 175.

69. Russell, *Lucifer*, 129–33, 209–12; Réau, *Iconographie de l'art chrétien*, 1-1:61–62; and for a recent survey, Luther Link, *The Devil, a Mask without a Face* (London: Reaktion, 1995), 35–78. See the winged serpent, Paris, Bibliothèque nationale, MS coll. duc d'Anjou, c. 1200. Reproduced in Didron, *Christian Iconography*, 2:125, fig. 176.

70. Kirschbaum, "L'Angelo rosso e l'angelo turchino," *Rivista di archeologia cristiana* 17 (1940):209–27. Mosaic, c. 520, S. Appollinare Nuovo, Ravenna. Reproduced ibid., 211, fig. 1.

71. Paris, Bibliothèque nationale, MS graec 510, fol. 165. Reproduced in Henri Auguste Omont, *Les miniatures des plus anciens manuscrits grecs de la Bibliothèque nationale du 6e au 14e siècle* (Paris: H. Champion, 1929), pl. 35. Henri-Irenée Marrou, "The Fallen Angel," in *Satan*, ed. Bruno de Jesus-Marie (New York: Sheed & Ward, 1952), 78. See also Ivory plaque of the Metz school, c. 850; Ciborium of King Arnulf, c. 890; Vyšehrad Coronation Gospels of King Vratislav. Prague, National and University Library, MS XIV, fol. 24b. Reproduced in Schiller, *Iconography of Christian Art*, 1:144–45, figs. 391, 392, 393.

72. Russell, *Lucifer*, 67–91, 211; Carmelina Naselli, "Diavoli bianchi e diavoli neri nei leggendari medievali," *Volkstum und Kultur der Romanen* 15 (1942):233–54. For these guises of the devil in Spanish lore see John Esten Keller, *Motif-Index of Mediaeval Spanish Exempla* (Knoxville: University of Tennessee Press, 1949), G303.3.1.2-G303.3.3.18.4.

73. Didron, *Christian Iconography*, 2:127, 259–60; Schiller, *Iconography of Christian Art*, 1:144–45.

74. J. P. Wickersham Crawford, "The Devil as a Dramatic Figure in the Spanish Religious Drama before Lope de Vega," *Romanic Review* 1 (1910): 307–8, 311, 383.

75. Tempe E. Allison, "The *Vice* in Early Spanish Drama," *Speculum* 12 (1937):104–9.

76. Russell, *Lucifer*, 67, 211. See also Francis J. Carmody, "Le diable des bestiaires," *Cahiers de l'Association internationale des études françaises*, nos. 3–5 (July, 1953):79–85.

77. Augustine, *De civitate Dei* 3.31; *Concerning the City of God against the*

Pagans, trans. Henry Bettenson (Harmondsworth, England: Penguin, 1972), 133.

78. Ulysse Aldrovandi, *Serpentum, et draconum historiae*. See also Charles Gould, *Mythical Monsters* (London, 1886), 202-4, and for Aldrovandi's etchings, 233, figs. 51 and 52.

79. Alexandre Cirici with Ramon Manent, *Ceràmica catalana* (Barcelona: Destino, 1977), 76, cf. 80, reproduced 78-79, and in Marçal Olivar, *La ceràmica trescentista a Aragó, Catalunya i València*, Monumenta cataloniae, 8 (Barcelona: Alpha, 1952), figs. 168, 169; Dalmases and José i Pitarch, *Història de l'art català*, 3:280. This has been named plausibly the basilisk of Manresa but implausibly its harpy, since there was a Christian iconographical tradition of the diabolical serpent with a human face, such as this has. See Henry Ansgar Kelly, "The Metamorphoses of the Eden Serpent during the Middle Ages and the Renaissance," *Viator* 2 (1971):301-28; John K. Bonnell, "The Serpent with a Human Head in Art and in Mystery Play," *American Journal of Archaeology* 21 (1917):255-91.

80. Caro Baroja, *Vascos*, 2:384-85; idem, "Notas de folklore vasco," *Revista de dialectología y tradiciones populares* 2 (1946):372-75.

81. For hybrids see Sylvia Lefevre, "Polymorphisme et métamorphose: Les mythes de la naissance dans les bestiaires," in *Métamorphose et bestiaire fantastique au moyen âge*, ed. Laurence Harf-Lancner (Paris: École normale supérieure de jeunes filles, 1985), 215-46.

82. Mundkur, *Cult of the Serpent*, 99 and 100, fig. 47.

83. Florence McCulloch, *Mediaeval Latin and French Bestiaries*, Studies in the Romance Languages and Literatures, 33 (Chapel Hill: University of North Carolina Press, 1960), 153-54, citing Isidore of Seville, *Etymologiae* 12.7.48.

84. Albert the Great, *Liber animalium* 23.92.

85. Brunetto Latini, *Li livres du tresor* 1.168. Anonymous, *Volucraires* 251, 301-38.

86. Aldrovandi, *Orinthologiae* 1, pp. 8, 21-22. Konrad Gesner, *Historiae animalium* 3, 2-3:657.

87. See Pettazoni, *All-Knowing God*, 151-52.

88. Ovid, *Metamorphoses* 1.49-52.

89. Peter Paul Rubens, Juno places the eyes of decapitated Argos on the peacock, Wallraf-Richartz-Museum, Cologne. Reproduced in Ernst Thomas Reimbold, *Der Pfau: Mythologie und Symbolik* (Munich: Callwey, 1983), 129, Abb. 60; Gert von der Osten, *Wallraf Richartz Museum Köln*, 2 vols. (Cologne: M. DuMont Scauberg, 1966), 2:123.

90. Peter Paul Rubens, St. Ignatius Loyola as Worker of Miracles, Kunsthistorisches Museum, Vienna, and Dulwich College Picture Gallery, London. Reproduced in Julius S. Held, *The Oil Sketches of Peter Paul Rubens: A Critical Catalogue*, 2 vols. (Princeton, N.J.: Princeton University Press for the National Gallery of Art, 1980), pls. 398 and 400.

91. E. P. Evans, *Animal Symbolism in Ecclesiastical Architecture* (London, 1896), 313. Miniature, reproduced at 314 from Charles Cahier, *Mélanges d'archéologie*, 4 vols. (Paris, 1847-57), 2:xx.AB.

92. Helmut Lother, *Der Pfau in der altchristlichen Kunst: eine Studie über das Verhältnis von Ornament und Symbol* (Leipzig: Dieterich, 1929).
93. Augustine, *De civitate Dei* 21.4, cited by McCullough, *Medieval Latin and French Bestiaries*, 154.
94. Fresco, 3d century, Priscilla catacomb, Rome; Early catacomb, Vatican. Reproduced in Reimbold, *Pfau*, 94, Abb. 14, 15.
95. Mosaic of the Vineyard, S. Costanza, Rome. Reproduced in Klingender, *Animals in Art and Thought*, fig. 70. Mosaic in the Church of Beligna, 5th century, Museo paleocristiano aquileia. Reproduced in Reimbold, *Pfau*, Abb. 16.
96. Cathedra of Bishop Maximinianus of Ravenna, 546–556, Museo arcivescovile, Ravenna. Reproduced in Reimbold, *Pfau*, 97, Abb. 18. See also 98–103, 105, Abb. 19–29.
97. Ibid., 57–61. Domenico Ghirlandaio, Last Supper, refectory of the cloister of Ognissanti, Florence, Museo de san Marco, Florence. Reproduced as fig. 25.
98. Follower of Hans Memling, Virgin and Child with angels in a summer house, c. 1490, Capilla real, Granada. Jan van Eyck, Madonna with chancellor Rollin, c. 1425, Louvre, Paris. Master of the "Virgo inter Virgines," Mystical marriage of St. Catherine, c. 1490, Museu nacional de arte antigua, Lisbon. Simon Bening, SS. Cosmas and Damien, miniature, c. 1510, Hennessy Book of Hours. Illustration, Loyset Liédet, *Histoire de Charles Martel*, Brussels, Bibliothèque royale, MS 6, fol. 9. Illustration, *Roman de la rose*, Flemish, c. 1485, British Library, Harley MS 4425, fol. 14v. Reproduced in John Hooper Harvey, *Mediaeval Gardens* (London: B. T. Batsford, 1961), 90; 113, pls. 43 and VIIa; 100, pl. 48; 91, pl. 44; 89, pl. 42; 137, pl. 74; 108, pl. 60. Charlemagne's garden, 28.
99. Moralia in Iob, 945 A.D. Madrid, Biblioteca nacional, Cod. 80, fol. 3v. Reproduced in Williams, *Early Spanish Manuscript Illumination*, pl. 7. See also the twelfth-century Spanish silk weaving with a pair of peacocks in Byzantine style. Musée de Cluny, Paris. Reproduced in Reimbold, *Pfau*, 105, Abb. 30.
100. Ignacio Malaxecheverría, *El bestiario esculpido en Navarra* (Pamplona: Institución principe de Viana, 1982), 181.
101. Reimbold, *Pfau*, 44, citing Ephraeum Syrus's hymn 42.11, but without bibliography.
102. *Offenbarung der Schwester Mechthild von Magdeburg, oder das fliessende Licht der Gottheit* 1.46; *The Revelations of Mechthild of Magdeburg (1210–1297), or The Flowing Light of the Godhead*, trans. Lucy Menzies (London: Longmans, Green, 1953), 26.
103. Gian Domenico Gordini and Renato Aprile, in *Bibliotheca sanctorum*, 2:cols. 750–67; Leander Petzoldt, in *Lexikon der christlichen Ikonographie*, ed. Kirschbaum, 5:cols. 304–11; Hans Aurenhammer, ed., *Lexikon der christlichen Ikonographie* (Vienna: Brüder Hollinek, 1959), 280–91; Réau, *Iconographie de l'art chrétien*, 3-1:171–73. For the original of Barbara with a peacock see 8th century, S. Maria antiqua, Rome. Reproduced in *Bibliotheca sanctorum*, 2:col. 750. For other examples see Woodcarving, title page of Dionysius Carthusianus, *Summa fidei orthodoxi*, Cologne, 1535; Altar wing from the workshop of Stefan

Lochners or by a master of the Cologne school, second half of 15th century, Wallraf-Richartz Museum, Cologne. Reproduced in Reimbold, *Pfau*, 113, Abb. 39, 40. For her cult see also Caro Baroja, *Vascos*, 2:357; Hillgarth, *Spanish Kingdoms*, 1:23, 141. There was a Barbara altar by the Maestro de Mart de Torres, first half of 15th century, Museum del arte de Cataluña, Barcelona. Reproduced in *Lexikon der christlichten Ikonographie*, 5:col. 311.

104. Erasmus, "Confessio militis," in *Colloquia*, in *Opera omnia* (Amsterdam), 1–3:156; *The Colloquies of Erasmus*, trans. Craig R. Thompson (Chicago: University of Chicago Press, 1965), 14.

105. *Acta* 8.82; cf. 6.55.

106. See Stephen L. Wailes, "The Crane, the Peacock, and the Reading of Walther von der Vogelweide 19, 19," *Modern Language Notes* 88 (1973): 952.

107. *Dictionnaire d'archéologie chrétienne et de liturgie*, s. v. "flabellum."

108. Wolfram von Eschenbach, *Parzival* 11.565.7–12.; Joseph Campbell, *Creative Mythology* (New York: Viking, 1968), 501–3.

109. Reproduced in Reimbold, *Pfau*, 122–23, Abb. 51, 52.

110. George Cary, *The Medieval Alexander*, ed. D. J. A. Ross (Cambridge: Cambridge University Press, 1956), 32–33. The classical subjects most in vogue in medieval Spain were the life of Alexander the Great and the history of Troy. Ian Michael, *The Treatment of Classical Material in the "Libro de Alexandre"* (Manchester: Manchester University Press, 1970), 12–13. For the importance of the idea of fame in *Libro de Alexandre* see Maria Rosa Lida de Malkiel, *La idea de la fama en la edad media castellana* (Mexico: Fondo de cultura económica, 1952), 167–97. For the peacock see Néstor Alberto Lugones, "Los bestiarios en la literatura medieval española," Ph.D. diss., University of Texas at Austin, 1976, 187–95.

111. Jacques de Longuyon, *Voeux du paon* 12, 17, 21, 25. There are also more recent editions, although unpublished: Camillus Casey, "*Les voeux du paon* by Jacques de Longuyon: An Edition of the P Redaction," Ph.D. diss., Columbia University, 1956; Robert Alexander Magill, "Part I of the *Voeux du paon* by Jacques de Longuyon: An Edition of Manuscripts S, S1, S2, S3, S4, S5, S6," Ph.D. diss., Columbia University, 1964. Although the edition used does not indicate the association of Alexander with the peacock, the conqueror is said to have been so amazed in India by the beauty of these birds that he threatened the severest penalties for slaying one. See Aelian, *De natura animalium* 5.21.

112. See B. J. Whiting, "The Vows of the Heron," *Speculum* 20 (1945):261–78. For other birds and the military see Heinz Peters, "*Miles christianus* oder Falke und Taube: Eine ikonographische Skizze," in *Festschrift für Otto von Simson zu 65. Geburtstag*, ed. Lucius Grisebach and Konrad Renger (Berlin: Propyläen, 1977), 53–61.

113. Reimbold, *Pfau*, 57–61. Benvenuto di Giovanni, Annunciation, painted tableboard, c. 1470, Museo d'arte sacra della Val d'Arbia, Buonconvento. Carlo Crivelli, Annunciation, Maria as Juno Caelestis with Peacock, altar painting, 1486, National Gallery, London. Reproduced 116, Abb. 43; 119, Abb. 46; also in Jill Dunkerton, Susan Foister, Dillian Gordon, and Nicholas Penny, *Giotto to Dürer: Early Renaissance Painting in the National Gallery* (New Haven,

Conn.: Yale University Press with National Gallery Publications, London, 1991), 345, pl. 51.

114. Chaucer, *Parlement of Foules* 356.

115. Alain de Lille, *De sex alis cherubim*, cited in Adolf Katzenellenbogen, *Allegories of the Virtues and Vices in Medieval Art from Early Christian Times to the Thirteenth Century*, Studies of the Warburg Institute, 10 (Nendeln, Liechtenstein: Kraus Reprint, 1968), 62. See also French MS, second half 12th century, Stadtbibliothek, Frankfurt, fig. 63.

116. Archangel Gabriel, mosaic, 7th century, Church of St. Panagra Angeloktistos, Kiti, Cyprus. Reproduced in Wilson, *Angels*, 170.

117. Simone Martini, Annunciation, Uffizzi, Florence. Reproduced in Raymond Régamy, *Anges*, with analytic notes by Reneé Zeller (Paris: Pierre Tisné, 1946), no. 21, noting that Lippo Memmi probably painted the costume and wings. Although this and following examples are frequently reproduced, reference is given to Régamy's book for ease of comparison.

118. Filippo Lippi, Annunciation, 1435, cloister church of Suore Murate, Florence, Alte Pinkothek, Bayerischen Staatsgemäldesammlungen, Munich. Reproduced in Reimbold, *Pfau*, 117, Abb. 44, 45. See also the angel of the Annunciation with peacock's wings, painting by an unknown master, 1380–90, Wallraf-Richartz Museum, Cologne. Reproduced 114, Abb. 41.

119. Annunciation, Chapel of the Gesù, Cortona. Two Angel Musicians, detail of the Tabernacle of the Lenaioli, Museo de san Marco, Florence. Round of the Angels and the Elect, detail of the Last Judgment, Uffizzi, Florence. Coronation of the Virgin, Louvre, Paris. Angel of the sepulchre, Museo de san Marco, Florence. Supper of St. Dominic Served by the Angels, predella of the Coronation of the Virgin, Louvre, Paris. Reproduced in Régamy, *Anges*, nos. 28–29, 24, 25, 26–27, 30, 23, 33. Cf. the stylized eyes in Annunciation, fresco, Museo de san Marco, Florence, no. 24.

120. Angels Chanting the Gloria, fresco, chapel, Palazzo Riccardi, Florence. Reproduced ibid., nos. 65–66.

121. Tobias and the Three Archangels, Academie des beaux-arts, Florence. Reproduced ibid., no. 88.

122. Jan van Eyck, Last Judgment, Metropolitan Museum of Art, New York. Reproduced in Hans Belting and Dagmar Eichberger, *Jan van Eyck als Erzähler: Frühe Tafelbilder im Umkreis der New Yorker Doppeltafel* (Worms: Werner, 1983), frontispiece.

123. Roger van der Weyden, Detail of the Last Judgment, central part of polyptych, Hospice de Beaune. Reproduced Régamy, *Anges*, no. 54.

124. Hugo van der Goes, Adoration of the Shepherds, Portinari altar, Uffizi, Florence. Reproduced ibid., no. 56.

125. Angel Gabriel, detail of the retable of Gardona, 15th century, Museum of Ancient Art, Barcelona. Reproduced ibid., no. 130. See also Maestro de Rubió, Annunciation, Retable of Rubió. Reproduced in Gudiol Ricart, *Pintura gótica*, 69, fig. 44. Angels with peacock wings hold the cloth of honor in Ramón Destorrents, St. Anne, Retable of Almudaina, 1353, Museo das Janelas Verdes, Lisbon. Reproduced ibid., 58, fig. 40.

126. Annunciation, Bernat Martorell, *Llibre d'hores*, 1440–50, Institut mu-

nicipal d'història, Barcelona. Reproduced in Dalmases and José i Pitarch, *Història de l'art català*, 3:233.

127. Perhaps Jaume Huguet, St. Michael trampling Satan, Frau Kocherthaler, Berlin. Reproduced in Rowland, *Jaume Huguet*, fig. 45.

128. Reproduced in Wilson, *Angels*, pl. 44.

129. Hieronymus Bosch, John of Patmos, c. 1480–90, Preussische Kulturbesitz, Gëmaldegalerie, Staatliche Museum, Berlin. Reproduced in Reimbold, *Pfau*, 115, Abb. 42; but the detail is clearer in such reproductions as Günther Heinz, *Hieronymus Bosch* (Vienna: Anton Schroll, 1968), Abb. 82 and detail 83; Charles de Tolnay, *Hieronymus Bosch* (Baden-Baden: Holle, 1965), unnumbered.

130. Klingender, *Animals in Art and Thought*, 328–29. The theory that the bestiaries were mnemonic is proposed in Beryl Rowland, "The Art of Memory and the Bestiary," in *Beasts and Birds of the Middle Ages: The Bestiary and Its Legacy*, ed. Willene B. Clark and Meradith T. McMunn (Philadelphia: University of Pennsylvania Press, 1989), 12–25.

131. Schiller, *Iconography of Christian Art*, 3:177–78.

132. Aristotle, *Historia animalium* 1, cf. 8, 9, 9.1; Ovid, *Metamorphoses* 13.802; Pliny, *Naturalis historia* 10.22.43–44; *Physiologus* 12. For the peacock as a symbol of pride and vanity see Reimbold, *Pfau*, 51–54; Beryl Rowland, *Birds with Human Souls: A Guide to Bird Symbolism* (Knoxville: University of Tennessee Press, 1978), 127–30; Malaxecheverría, *Bestiario esculpido en Navarra*, 183; Klingender, *Animals in Art and Thought*, 88; Evans, *Animal Symbolism in Ecclesiastical Architecture*, 311–12; Morton W. Bloomfield, *The Seven Deadly Sins: An Introduction to the History of a Religious Concept, with Special Reference to Medieval English Literature* (n.p.: Michigan State University Press, 1952), appendix I: "The Association of Animals and Sins," 245; Réau, *Iconographie de l'art chrétien*, 1:130; George Ferguson, *Signs and Symbols in Christian Art* (New York: Oxford University Press, 1959), 9.

133. Stefano Guazzo, *Civil conversatione* 3.

134. Hieronymus Bosch, Garden of Delights, 1500?, Prado, Madrid. Reproduced in Reimbold, *Pfau*, 121, Abb. 49, 50.

135. Pieter Breughel the Elder, copper engraving of Superbia. Reproduced in ibid., 52, figs. 22, 23; Abb. 41. See also Superbia in the mirror in Bosch, Superbia from the painted tableboard with the seven deadly sins, Prado, Madrid. Reproduced in Benjamin Goldberg, *The Mirror and Man* (Charlottesville: University Press of Virginia, 1985), 123.

136. Herbert Grabes, *The Mutable Glass: Mirror-Imagery in Titles and Texts of the Middle Ages and English Renaissance* (Cambridge: Cambridge University Press, 1982), 153–58.

137. Isabel Mateo Gómez, *Temas profanas en la escultura gótica española: Las sillerías de coro* (Madrid: Consejo superior de investigaciones científicas, Instituto Diego Velásquez, 1979), 381–82. For the use of the peacock in the later emblem books see *Emblemata*, pp. 808–11.

138. Aldrovandi, *Orinthologiae* 1–3. See also such historical volumes as Jerome Cardano, *De subtilitate*, and Konrad Gesner, *Historia animalium* 3; and for a modern survey, Gould, *Mythical Monsters*, with classical references, 182–

92, classical and medieval dragons, 192–211, and references contemporary with Loyola, 202–4. Aldrovandi's etchings are reproduced, 233, figs. 51 and 52.

139. Bloomfield, *Seven Deadly Sins*, 138. For additional examples see Ruth Mellinkoff, *The Devil at Isenheim: Reflections of Popular Belief in Grünewald's Altarpiece*, California Studies in the History of Art, Discovery, 1 (Berkeley and Los Angeles: University of California Press, 1988), 26. The identification of the capital vices with animals became systematic in the twelfth and thirteenth centuries according to Bloomfield, *Seven Deadly Sins*, 150–51. See also Mireille Vincent-Cassy, "Les animaux et les péchés capitaux: De la symbolique à l'emblematique," in *Le monde animal et ses représentations au moyen-âge (XIe-XVe siècles)*, Actes du XVème congrès de la Société des historiens médiévistes de l'enseignement supérieur public, Toulouse, 25–26 mai 1984, Travaux de l'Université de Toulouse-le Mirail, 31 (Toulouse: Université de Toulouse-le Mirail, 1985), 121–32.

140. Reproduced in Arthur M. Hind, *Early Italian Engraving: A Critical Catalogue with Complete Reproduction of All the Prints Described*, 7 vols. (New York: M. Knoedler, 1938), 4:pl. 397. Cited by Bloomfield, *Seven Deadly Sins*, 245.

141. Manuscript, Metten (Bavaria), 1414, with illustrations of strong Bohemian influence. Munich, Clm. Cod. lat. 8201, fol. 95r. Fritz Saxl, "A Spiritual Encyclopedia of the Later Middle Ages," *Journal of the Warburg and Courtauld Institutes* 5 (1941):126–27. Reproduced fig. 31a, cf. pl. 31c; Angus Wilson et al., *The Seven Deadly Sins* (London: Sunday Times, 1962), title page.

142. Guillaume de Deguileville, *Pèlerinage de vie humaine* 14325–35.

143. Cited in Klingender, *Animals in Art and Thought*, 371. See also Alan J. Fletcher, "The Hideous Feet of Langland's Peacock," *Notes and Queries* 235 (1991):18–20.

144. Illustrations with woodcuts in Josse Bade's edition of *La nef des folles—Stultiferae naves*, cited by Carl Nordenfolk, "The Five Senses in Late Medieval and Renaissance Art," *Journal of the Warburg and Courtauld Institutes* 48 (1985):12.T.

145. Cited in Bloomfield, *Seven Deadly Sins*, 245.

146. Samuel Chew, *The Pilgrimage of Life* (New Haven, Conn.: Yale University Press, 1962), 251–52, citing its reproduction in René Fülöp-Miller, *The Power and Secret of the Jesuits*, trans. F. S. Flint and D. F. Tait (London: G. P. Putnam's Sons, 1930), pl. 8. The description of the engraving is mine, since the peacock has been overlooked. For peacocks and vainglory see also Chew, *Pilgrimage of Life*, 82–83, 93, 95–98.

147. Bloomfield, *Seven Deadly Sins*, 44–45, 59, 60–61, 69–72, 79, 85–87. He speculates that the Jesuit preference for the *saligia* formula is traceable to a Spanish predilection, perhaps from great interest in canon law, for the Ostiensic (after Henry of Ostia) rather than Gregorian sequence in the fifteenth and sixteenth centuries, 399 n. 142. See Arthur Watson, "Saligia," *Journal of the Warburg and Courtauld Institutes* 10 (1947):148–50. See also Wenzel, "The Seven Deadly Sins: Some Problems of Research," *Speculum* 43 (1968):122.

148. *Exercitia spiritualia*, pp. 312, 314–16.

149. Bloomfield, *Seven Deadly Sins*, 104, 124. The encyclopedist Vincent of Beauvais in his *Speculum naturale* listed *inanis gloria* first, 126.

150. See Pero López de Ayala, *Rimado de palacio*, stanzas 63–124; also E. B. Strong, "The *Rimado de palacio*: Lopez de Ayala's Rimed Confession," *Hispanic Review* 37 (1969):439–51.

151. Bloomfield, *Seven Deadly Sins*, 139–40; Eliezer Oyola, *Los pecados capitales en la literatura medieval española* (Barcelona: Puvill, 1979).

152. Gonzalo de Berceo, *Libro de Alixandre*, 2334–44, 2329–30, 2345–2411, with vainglory, whose exemplar is Zozimas, at 2395–2404.

153. Margherita Morreale, "Los catalogos de virtudes y vicios en las biblias romanceadas de la edad media," *Nueva revista de filología hispánica* 12 (1958):149–59.

154. Juan Ruiz, *Libro de buen amor* 217–387, with 276–85 for envy of the peacock and 304–10 for vainglory paired with wrath. See also Félix Lecoy, *Recherches sur le "Libro de buen amor" de Juan Ruiz, archiprêtre de Hita* (Paris: Droz, 1938), 172–86; Robert Ricard, "Les péchés capitaux dans le *Libro de buen amor*," *Les lettres romanes* 20 (1966):5–37; Ian Michael, "The Function of the Popular Tale in the *Libro de buen amor*," in *"Libro de buen amor" Studies*, ed. G. B. Gybbon-Monypenny (London: Tamesis, 1970), 177–218.

155. Michael, "Function of the Popular Tale," 198. For the type see Stith Thompson, *Motif Index of Folk-Literature*, rev. ed., 6 vols. (Bloomington: Indiana University Press, 1955–58), J951.2.

156. Juan de Mena, *Coplas de los siete pecados mortales* 19–20, 35, 51–58. See also for vainglory *Coplas fechas por Fernan Perez de Guzman de vicios e virtudes* 1299–1322, in *Cancionero de Juan Fernandez de Ixar*.

157. Evagrius Ponticus, *Logos praktikos* prol. 3, 13, 30–32.

158. Augustine, *In Epistolam Joannis ad Parthos tractatus* 8.9; *Homilies on the Gospel according to St. John, and His First Epistles*, trans. H. Browne, 2 vols. (Oxford, 1848), 2:1198. *De sermone Domini in monte* 2.12.41; *Commentary on the Lord's Sermon on the Mount with Seventeen Related Sermons*, trans. Denis J. Kavanagh (New York: Fathers of the Church, 1951), 149.

159. Françoise Joukovsky-Micha, "La notion de *vaine gloire* de Simund de Freine à Martin le Franc," *Romania* 89 (1968):1, 3, 4, 14–21.

160. *The Florentine Fior di Virtu of 1491* 1, 2, 30; trans. Nicholas Fersin (Washington, D.C.: Library of Congress, 1953), 81, 82; and see vii, xvi–xxviii. Woodcut, *Fiore di virtù*, 15th century, Venice. Reproduced also in Alessandro Tagliolini, *Storia del giardino italiano: Gli artisti, l'invenzione, le forme dall'antichità al XIX secolo* (Florence: Usher, 1988), 35, fig. 13. See also M. Casella, "La versione catalana del *Fiore di virtù*," *Revista delle biblioteche e degli archivi* 31 (1920):1–10.

161. William J. Bouwsma, *John Calvin* (Oxford: Oxford University Press, 1988), 61, citing Calvin, *Commentariorum* 2 Cor. 10:12.

162. Pierre de Labriolle, "Le 'démon de midi,'" *Bulletin Du Cange* 9 (1934):46–54.

163. Rudolph Arbesmann, "The *Daemonium meridianum* and Greek and Latin Patristic Exegesis," *Traditio* 14 (1958):20–23, 25–26, citing Augustine, *Enarrationes in psalmos* 90, and Jerome, *Tractatus sive homiliae in psalmos*.

164. Richard of St. Victor, *Benjamin minor* 81.
165. Bernard of Clairvaux, *Sermones super Cantica canticorum* 33.6.13; "In Circumcisione Domini, Sermo" 3.1. For the cultural dissemination of this exegesis see Kathleen M. Ashley, "The Specter of Bernard's Noonday Demon in Medieval Drama," *American Benedictine Review* 30 (1979):205-21.
166. Bloomfield, *Seven Deadly Sins*, 81, with references to Hilton, Rolle, and the author of the *Cloud*.
167. Walter Hilton, *The Scale of Perfection* 26; *Qui habitat* 6.
168. "A Treatise of Discrescyon of Spirites" and "A Pistle of Discrecioun of Stirrings," pp. 85-86, 70.
169. Richard Rolle, *Incendium amoris* 14; *The Fire of Love*, trans. G. C. Heseltine (London: Burns Oates & Washbourne, 1935), 60.
170. Jean Gerson, *De distinctione verarum revelationum a falsis*, p. 53.
171. Marcus of Orvieto, "De pavo" 6, *Liber de moralitatibus*. Transcribed in Friedman, "Peacocks and Preachers: Analytic Technique in Marcus of Orvieto's *Liber de moralitatibus*, Vatican lat. MS 5935," in *Beasts and Birds of the Middle Ages*, ed. Clark and McMunn, 192.
172. Mellinkoff, *Devil at Isenheim*, 27, 19-31, although the argument about omniscience, and not merely pride, is mine. Reproduced Albrecht Dürer, Fall of Man, engraving, 1504, and Fall of Man, woodcut, 1511, 39, figs. 14-17. Hans Baldung Grien, Fall of Man, woodcut, c. 1515, 40, figs. 18-19. Follower of Michael Coxie, Fall of Man, painting, 16th century, Wallraf-Richartz Museum, Cologne, 40-41, figs. 20-21. Many reproductions of Grünewald's peacock angel, passim. The identification of this angel as the devil was also made independently through the research for this chapter, "The Flying Serpent," several years before the publication of Mellinkoff's monograph.
173. *Acta* 3.30.
174. See Nordenfalk, "Five Senses," 1-22; and for the emblem of the sense of sight as a human head before a mirror, Chew, *Pilgrimage of Life*, 192-94.
175. James G. Frazer, *The Golden Bough*, part 2, *Taboo and the Perils of the Soul* (London: Macmillan, 1913), 92-96; Ninck, *Bedeutung des Wassers*, 50-51, 70-71.
176. Plutarch, *De defectu oraculorum* 432d, 433e; *Plutarch's Moralia*, trans. Frank Cole Babbitt (Cambridge, Mass.: Harvard University Press, 1959), 5:469, 471.
177. Ovid, *Metamorphoses* 3.339-510.
178. For Narcissus in Guillaume de Lorris, *Roman de la rose* see Larry C. Hillman, "Another Look into the Mirror Perilous: The Role of the Crystals in the *Roman de la rose*," *Romania* 101 (1980):225-38; Jean Rychner, "Le mythe de la fontaine de Narcisse dans le *Roman de la rose* de Guillaume de Lorris," in Y. Bonnefoy et al., *Le lieu et la formule: Hommage à Marc Eigeldinger* (Neuchâtel: Baconnière, 1978), 33-46; Patricia J. Eberle, "The Lovers' Glass: Nature's Discourse on Optics and the Optical Design of the *Romance of the Rose*," *University of Toronto Quarterly* 46 (1976-77):241-62; Thomas D. Hill, "Narcissus, Pygmalion, and the Castration of Saturn: Two Mythographical Themes in the *Roman de la rose*," *Studies in Philology* 71 (1974):404-26; Daniel Poirion, "Narcisse et Pygmalion dans le *Roman de la rose*," in *Essays in Honor of*

Louis Francis Solano, ed. Raymond J. Cormier and Urban T. Holmes, Studies in the Romance Languages and Literatures, 92 (Chapel Hill: University of North Carolina Press, 1970), 153–65; Erich Köhler, "Narcisse, la fontaine d'amour, et Guillaume de Lorris," in *L'Humanisme médiéval dans les littératures romanes du XIIe au XIVe siècles*, ed. A. Fourrier (Paris: C. Klincksieck, 1964), 147–66; Jean Frappier, "Variations sur le thème du miroir, de Bernard de Ventadour à Maurice Scève," *Cahiers de l'Association internationale des études françaises* 11 (1959):134–58; and see also Sarah Kay, "Love in a Mirror: An Aspect of the Imagery of Bernart de Ventadorn," *Medium aevum* 52 (1983):272–85.

179. Louise Vinge, *The Narcissus Theme in Western European Literature up to the Early Nineteenth Century*, trans. Robert Dewsnap et al. (Lund: Gleerups, 1967), 1–178; Frederick Goldin, *The Mirror of Narcissus in the Courtly Love Lyric* (Ithaca, N.Y.: Cornell University Press, 1967); Kenneth J. Knoespel, *Narcissus and the Invention of Personal History* (New York: Garland, 1985); and for Narcissus in Spain, José María de Cossío, *Fábulas mitológicas en España* (Madrid: Espasa-Calpe, 1952), 884–85, and in general, Rudolph Schevill, *Ovid and the Renasence in Spain*, University of California Publications in Modern Philology, 4 (Berkeley and Los Angeles: University of California Press, 1913).

180. Xenophon, *Memorabilia* 2.1.22; *Memorabilia*, trans. E. C. Marchant in *Xenophon*, 7 vols. (Cambridge, Mass.: Harvard University Press, 1968), 4:95.

181. Ruiz, *Libro de buen amor* 1486.

182. Erasmus, *De civilitate* 2, in *Opera omnia* (Leiden), 1:1037.

183. *Ephemeris*, p. 122.

184. For autofascination see S. Seligmann, *Der Böse Blick und Verwandtes: Ein Beitrag zur Geschichte des Aberglaubens aller Zeitenund Völker*, 2 vols. (Berlin: Hermann Boresdorf, 1910), 1:178–88.

185. For the double in the eye of the other see Eugène Monseur, "L'Ame pupilline," *Revue de l'histoire des religions* 51 (1905):1–23; and for the reflections of windows on eyeballs, Jan Bialostocki, "The Eye and the Window: Realism and Symbolism of Light-Reflections in the Art of Albrecht Dürer and His Predecessors," in *Festschrift für Gert von der Osten* (Cologne: DuMont Schauberg, 1970), 159–76. For Dürer's self-portraits in the mirror see John Pope Hennessy, *The Portrait in the Renaissance*, Bollingen Series, 35–12 (Princeton, N.J.: Princeton University Press, 1979), 126–29.

186. Leonardo da Vinci, Paris, Institut de France, MS A, fol. 37b, in *Literary Works*, 1:134.

187. For the motif see Robert Baldwin, " 'Gates Pure and Shining and Serene': Mutual Gazing as an Amatory Motif in Western Literature and Art," *Renaissance and Reformation* 10 (1986):23–48; for the eyes and love see also M. B. Ogle, "The Classical Origin and Tradition of Literary Conceits," *American Journal of Philology* 34 (1913):135–40.

188. Grabes, *Mutable Glass*, 119.

189. J. H. Waszink, "Pompa diaboli," *Vigiliae christianae* 1 (1947):13–41; Hugo Rahner, "*Pompa diaboli*: Ein Beitrag zur Bedeutungsgeschichte des Wortes *pompē-pompa* in der urchistlichen Taufliturgie," *Zeitschrift für Katholische Theologie* 55 (1931):239–73, citing at 272 Théodolphe d'Orleans, *De ordine baptismi* 1.

190. Christian, *Apparitions in Late Medieval and Renaissance Spain* (Princeton, N.J.: Princeton University Press, 1981), 221.
191. See Bloomfield, *Seven Deadly Sins*, 167–68, 189, 224.
192. Grabes, *Mutable Glass*, 75–76.
193. Ferguson, *Signs and Symbols*, 22.
194. *Les lapidaires français du moyen âge des XIIe, XIIIe, et XIVe siècles*, 52, 95–96, 134; *Le lapidaire du quatorzieme siècle*, 3–4; *Anglo-Norman Lapidaries*, 49, 175.
195. Petrarch, *Africa* 3.101–5.
196. *Roman de la rose* 19931–20026.
197. See J. S. Ackerman, "Early Renaissance Color Theory and Practice," in *Studies in Italian Art and Architecture*, ed. Henry A. Milton, Studies in Italian Art History, 1 (Cambridge, Mass.: MIT Press, 1980), 21. Piero della Francesca, Stigmatization of St. Francis, Predella from altarpiece, 1460s?, Gallery, Perugia, reproduced fig. 3. The seraph wears a loincloth of peacock's feathers.
198. Réau, *Iconographie de l'art chrétien*, 2-2:476.
199. Schiller, *Iconography of Christian Art*, 2:119, figs. 367, 397, 398, 406, 401, 400.
200. Augustine, *Sermo* 234; see also *In epistolam Iohannis ad Parthos* 119.2. For his professorial chair in heaven see ibid. 3.13; Bernard of Clairvaux, *Sermones super Cantica canticorum* 19.2.4. For the school of Christ see Adalbert de Vogüé, "L'École du Christ: Des disciples de Jésus au monastère du Maître et de Benoît," *Collectanea cisterciensia* 46 (1984):3–12. For Christ as the interior teacher in the school of the breast see Augustine, *De magistro* 12.40; cf. 14.46; *Confessiones* 9.9.21; cf. 11.3.5.
201. Augustine, *Ennarationes in psalmos* (1)33.9; cf. 33.7; (2)33.2; 149.8; 147.23.
202. Jacopone da Todi, *Laude* 27.42–44; *The Lauds*, trans. Serge and Elizabeth Hughes (New York: Paulist, 1982), 141.
203. Angela of Foligno, *Liber de vere fidelium experientia* 130, 174.
204. Patrick S. Diehl, *The Medieval European Religious Lyric: An "Ars poetica"* (Berkeley and Los Angeles: University of California Press, 1985), 216.
205. Mary Caroline Spalding, *The Middle English Charters of Christ*, Bryn Mawr College Monographs, 15 (Bryn Mawr. Pa.: Bryn Mawr College Press, 1914), xliiff.
206. John Whiterig, "Meditation Addressed to Christ Crucified" 53, cited by Richard Kieckhefer, *Unquiet Souls: Fourteenth-Century Saints and Their Religious Milieu* (Chicago: University of Chicago Press, 1984), 103. See also his reference to Richard Rolle's meditation on the body of the crucified as a book with red ink, 104.
207. Henry Suso, *Büchlein der ewigen Weisheit* 3, 14, 7; *Little Book of Eternal Wisdom and Little Book of Truth*, trans. James M. Clark (London: Faber & Faber, 1953), 56, 102, 76.
208. Domenico Cavalca, *Mirall de la creu* 8, 13, 16, 18, 25, 36; prol., pp. 11–12.
209. Catherine of Siena, *Lettere* 11, 25, 101, 177, 235, 242; 318 trans. in Johannes Jorgensen, *Saint Catherine of Siena*, trans. Ingebord Lund (London:

Longmans, Green, 1939), 165; *Lettere* 316 trans. in *I, Catherine, Selected Writings of St Catherine of Siena*, trans. Kenelm Foster and MaryJohn Ronayne (London: Collins, 1980), 203; *Lettere* 69. See also *Il Dialogo della divina Provvidenza, ovvero Libro della divina dottrina* 77, 145, 154. For continuation of the topic in the sixteenth century see Vittoria Colonna's poetic prayer that Christ's nails become her quills, his blood her ink, and his body her writing paper so that she might inscribe his suffering in herself interiorly, *Rime spirituali disperse* 1.

210. Catherine of Siena, *Lettere* 226; trans. Foster and Ronayne, 171.

211. *Legenda* 1.10.6–10, in *Acta sanctorum*, 3:862–967; *The Life of Catherine of Siena by Raymond of Capua*, trans. Conleth Kearns (Wilmington, Del.: Michael Glazier, 1980), 105. For the hagiographical topic of the illiterate woman who can miraculously read scripture by sight see *Vita Theclae* 45.8, cited by Peter R. L. Brown, *The Body and Society: Men, Women, and Sexual Renunciation in Early Christianity*, Lectures on the History of Religions, n.s. 13 (New York: Columbia University Press, 1988), 277.

212. The locus classicus is Gregory the Great, *Registrum epistularum* 9.209; 11.10.

213. Erasmus, *Antibarbari*, in *Opera omnia* (Amsterdam), 1–1:130; *The Antibarbari*, trans. Margaret Mann Phillips, in *The Collected Works of Erasmus* (Toronto: University of Toronto Press, 1978), 23:113.

214. *Exercitia spiritualia*, p. 410.

215. See Eugene F. Rice, Jr., *Saint Jerome in the Renaissance* (Baltimore, Md.: Johns Hopkins University Press, 1985), 49–83, 19, 46, 147. See since Rosemarie Muliahy, "Federico Zuccaro and Philip II: The Reliquary Altars for the Basilica of San Lorenzo de El Escorial," *Burlington Magazine* 129 (1987):502–9.

216. Rice, *Saint Jerome in the Renaissance*, 55–58, and now Stephen F. Ostrow, "The Sistine Chapel at S. Maria Maggiore: Sixtus V and the Art of the Counter Reformation," Ph.D. diss., Princeton University, 1987, 11, 13; and on the Presepio idem, *Art and Spirituality in Counter-Reformation Rome: The Sistine and Pauline Chapels in S. Maria Maggiore* (Cambridge: Cambridge University Press, 1996), 23–62.

217. *Epistolae* 19.

218. Rice, *Saint Jerome in the Renaissance*, 57.

219. Howard Hibbard, "*Ut picturae sermones*: The First Painted Decorations of the Gesù," in *Baroque Art: The Jesuit Contribution*, ed. Rudolf Wittkower and Irma B. Jaffe (New York: Fordham University Press, 1976), 35.

220. Rice, *St. Jerome in the Renaissance*, 14, 17.

221. For Jerome penitent in the wilderness before a crucifix see ibid., 75–83. For numerous examples of Jerome with the cross and the book see Herbert Friedmann, *A Bestiary for Saint Jerome: Animal Symbolism in European Religious Art* (Washington, D.C.: Smithsonian Institution, 1980), figs. 29, 30, 32, 35, 36, 37, 40, 42, 44, 45, 50, 59, 60, 64, 69, 70, 76, 77, 89, 102, 108, 131, 145, 158, 160, 167, 170, 172, 175, 176, 178, 185, 187, and for the cross and the book in his study, figs. 2, 17, 20, 83, 88, 91, 103, 104, 119, and 21 (pietà). See also School of Botticelli, St. Jerome in Penitence, Hermitage, Leningrad; and

a seventeenth-century example in which a manuscript is open directly behind the crucifix, Guercino, *St. Jerome Hearing the Trumpet of the Last Judgment*, S. Girolamo, Rimini. Reproduced in Bernhard Ridderbos, *Saint and Symbol: Images of Saint Jerome in Early Italian Art* (Groningen: Bouma, 1984), 80, fig. 37; 81, fig. 39; 72, fig. 33. Piero della Francesca, *St. Jerome and a Donor*, Galleria dell'accademia, Venice. Reproduced in Kenneth Clark, *Piero della Francesca: Complete Edition*, 2d rev. ed. (London: Phaidon, 1969), pl. 14.

222. Maestro of the Seo of Urgel, Saint Jerome praying before crucifix, Museo de Barcelona. Reproduced in Gudiol Ricart, *Pintura gótica*, 293, fig. 250.

223. See Paolo Veronese, Saint Jerome in the Wilderness, Samuel H. Kress Collection, National Gallery, Washington, D.C. Reproduced in Friedmann, *Bestiary for Saint Jerome*, 81, fig. 60.

224. Antonello da Messina, Saint Jerome in His Study, National Gallery, London; Gentile Bellini, Saint Jerome in Penitence, Toledo Museum of Art Toledo, Ohio; and Bartolomeo Montagna, Saint Jerome in Meditation, Accademia Carrara, Bergamo; Basaiti school, Saint Jerome in Penitence, Musée Hongrois des Beaux-Arts, Budapest. Reproduced in ibid., 158, fig. 119; 52, fig. 26, and detail of peacock fig. 27; 61, fig. 37; 206, fig. 145. Friedmann also mentions a peacock in a triptych by Jerome Patinir, Saint Jerome in the Wilderness, Metropolitan Museum of Art, New York, 284. For the painting by Messina see also Dunkerton et al., *Giotto to Dürer*, 319, pl. 41.

225. *Acta* 1.5.

226. Moshe Barasch, *Light and Color in the Italian Renaissance Theory of Art* (New York: New York University Press, 1978), 53, 55, 64.

227. Plato, *Respublica* 7.532b; *The Dialogues of Plato*, trans. Benjamin Jowett, 2 vols. (New York: Random House, 1937), 1:791, 792.

228. Quintilian, *Institutiones oratoriae* 6.2.32.

229. Plato, *Respublica* 505a; Plotinus, *Enneads* 6.36; 4.3.9.

230. Hans-Georg Gadamer, *The Idea of the Good in Platonic-Aristotelian Philosophy*, trans. P. Christopher Smith (New Haven, Conn.: Yale University Press, 1986), 20, 23, 35, 66, 121, 136.

231. See Plato, *Phaedo* 99d-100a, cited by Grabes, *Mutable Glass*, 72.

232. Heath Dillard, *Daughters of the Reconquest: Women in Castillian Town Society, 1100–1300* (Cambridge: Cambridge University Press, 1984), 150–51.

233. See Jeanne Battesti-Pelegrin, "Eaux douces, eaux amères dans la lyrique hispanique médiévale traditionelle," in *L'Eau au moyen âge* (Marseille: Jeanne Laffitte, 1985), 48–51, citing Jose María Alín, *El cancionero español de tipo tradicional* (Madrid: Taurus, 1968), 208, 226, 461.

234. Maria Rosa Lida de Malkiel, *Juan de Mena: Poeta del prerenacimiento español* (Mexico: Colegio de Mexico, 1950), 307–8; see also Alicia C. de Ferraresi, "*Locus amoenus* y vergel visionario en *Razón de amor*," *Hispanic Review* 42 (1974):173–83.

235. Joseph E. Gillet, "El mediodía y el demonio meridiano en España," *Nueva rivista di filologia hispanica* 7 (1953):307–15.

236. See *Historia de la linda Melosina* and Jean d'Arras, *Mélusine*. Cf. Walter Map, *De nugis curialium* 4.11.

Notes to Chapter 3 239

237. Micer Francisco Imperial, *El dezir a las syete virtudes* 17.51–52, 301–52. For their interpretation as heresies see Archer Woodford, "Edición crítica del *Dezir a las syete virtudes*," *Nueva revista de filología hispánica* 8 (1954):285–89nn.; idem, "Francisco Imperial's Dantesque *Dezir a las syete virtudes*: A Study of Certain Aspects of the Poem," *Italica* 27 (1950):88–100. See also Dorothy Clotelle Clark, "The Passage on Sins in the *Decir a las siete virtudes*," *Studies in Philology* 59 (1962):18–30. The identification of the flying serpents as basilisks, because they have crowns, is mine.

238. See Lida de Malkiel, *Idea de la fama*, 261–65.

239. Garci Rodríguez de Montalvo, *Amadís de Gaula* 2.56; cf. 2.48; *Amadis of Gaul: Books I and II*, trans. Edwin B. Place and Herbert C. Behm (Lexington: University Press of Kentucky, 1974), 544.

240. Ibid.

241. *Acta* 3.30.

242. Grabes, *Mutable Glass*, 39, 48–60, 137–39. Artists also employed mirrors in their workshops as aids. See Heinrich Schwarz, "The Mirror of the Artist and the Mirror of the Devout: Observations on Some Paintings, Drawings, and Prints of the Fifteenth Century," in *Studies in the History of Art Dedicated to William E. Suida on his Eightieth Birthday* (London: Phaidon for the Samuel H. Kress Foundation, 1959), 90–100; Bialostocki, "Man and Mirror in Painting: Reality and Transience," in *Studies in Late Medieval and Renaissance Painting in Honor of Millard Meiss*, ed. Irving Lavin and John Plummer, 2 vols. (New York: New York University Press, 1977), 1:61–72. For the iconography of mirrors see also François Garnier, *Le langage de l'image au moyen âge: Signification et symbolique*, 2 vols. (Paris: Léopard d'or, 1982–89), 2:223–28.

243. Shakespeare, *King Richard II*, act 4, scene 1, cited by Goldberg, *Mirror and Man*, 145; Grabes, *Mutable Glass*, 111, 214–16. See also Peter Ure, "The Looking-Glass of *Richard II*," *Philological Quarterly* 34 (1955):219–24.

244. Aristotle, *Historia animalium* 488b, cited by Klingender, *Animals in Art and Thought*, 88; *Historia animalium*, trans. A. L. Peck, 2 vols. (Cambridge, Mass.: Harvard University Press, 1965–70), 1:19.

245. Augustine, *De Genesi ad litteram* 12.15.52.

246. Richart de Fournival, *Li bestiaires d'amours*, p. 48. See also for amorous vigilance the tableau attributed to Jan Van Eyck, The Sorcery of Love, tableau, Museum of Leipzig. Reproduced in Villeneuve with Chamarat, *Beauté du diable*, 145.

247. Katzenellenbogen, *Allegories of the Virtues and Vices*, 55.

248. Ibid., 56.

249. Michel Colombe, Prudence at the mirror, Tombeau de Nantes. Hans Baldung Grien, Munich. Reproduced in Baltrušaitis, *Le miroir: Essai sur une légende scientifique* (Paris: Elmayan and le Seuil for Centre national des lettres, 1978), 8, fig. 2; 13, fig. 4. For prudence with the mirror see also Grabes, *Mutable Glass*, 158–60.

250. See Chew, *Pilgrimage of Life*, 97; Grabes, *Mutable Glass*, 153–58.

251. *Bestaris*, B 24. Cf. *Il bestiario toscano* 23. For background see Michel Salvat, "Notes sur les bestiaire catalans," in *Epopée animale, fable, fabliau*, Actes du IVe colloque de la Société internationale renardienne, Evreux, 7–11

septembre 1981, ed. Gabriel Bianciotto and Salvat, Publications de l'Université de Rouen, 83 (Paris: Presses universitaires de France, 1984), 499–508.

252. Grabes, *Mutable Glass*, 76, citing Dionysius the Areopagite [pseud.], *Hierarchia caelestia* 3.2; *De divinis nominibus* 4.2.2 (correction); and other medieval writings; Dante, *Purgatorio* 15.16–24; *Paradiso* 29.142–44.

253. For the eye of the peacock as a mirror having the ambivalence of viewer and viewed see Gaston Bachelard, *L'Eau et les rêves: Essai sur l'imagination de la matière* (Paris: José Corti, 1942), 42–44. This is in the context of the pool of Narcissus, 31–45. Although the sources Bachelard cites are later than Loyola, their affinity is significant. For mirrors as deceptive see Grabes, *Mutable Glass*, 131–32.

254. Reimbold, *Pfau*, 26–27, 45–47, 54–57. See also Campbell, *Creative Mythology*, 501–3. For the mythology see also Julius Schwabe, "Lebenswasser der Pfau, zwei Symbole der Wiedergeburt," *Symbolon: Jahrbuch für Symbolforschung* 1 (1959):138–72. For the evil eye see Tobin Siebers, *The Mirror of Medusa* (Berkeley and Los Angeles: University of California Press, 1983); Matthew W. Dickie, "Heliodorus and Plutarch on the Evil Eye," *Classical Philology* 86 (1991):17–29.

255. See Barbara Nolan, *The Gothic Visionary Perspective* (Princeton, N.J.: Princeton University Press, 1977), 141.

256. Augustine, *De genesi contra Manichaeos* 1.23.40.

257. Augustine, *In epistolam Iohannis ad Parthos* 2.13; *Enarrationes in psalmos* 9.8.

258. Augustine, *Confessiones* 1.10.16; 6.8.13.

259. Augustine, *Enarrationes in psalmos* 135.20; *Expositions on the Book of Psalms*, trans. Wilkins, 6:143.

260. Augustine, *De libero arbitrio* 3.9.28.

261. Augustine, *De civitate Dei* 14.28.

262. See David Summers, "*Maniera* and Movement: The *figura serpentinata*," *Art Quarterly* 35 (1972):269–301; idem, "*Contrapposto*: Style and Meaning in Renaissance Art," *Art Bulletin* 59 (1977):336–61, citing Aristotle, *Rhetorica* 1410a; *The "Art" of Rhetoric*, trans. John Henry Freese (New York: G. P. Putnam's Sons, 1926), 393; Leonardo da Vinci, *Trattato della pintura* 271; *Treatise on Painting (Codex urbinas latinus 1270)*, trans. Amos Philip McMahon (Princeton, N.J.: Princeton University Press, 1956), 348.

263. See Michael Baxandall, *Painting and Experience in Fifteenth-Century Italy: A Primer in the Social History of Pictorial Style*, 2d ed. (Oxford: Oxford University Press, 1988), 1–27. Blue for the Virgin's drapery was not a liturgical, but a humanist, convention. Barasch, "Renaissance Color Conventions: Liturgy, Humanism, Workshops," in idem, *"Imago hominis": Studies in the Language of Art* (Vienna: IRSA, 1991), 176–77; rpt. from *Color and Technique in Renaissance Painting: Italy and the North*, ed. Marcia B. Hall (New York: n.p., 1987), 135–50.

264. *Acta* 3.30.

265. Barasch, *Light and Color*, 20, citing Alberti, *Della pittura*, p. 64; Barasch, *Light and Color*, 64, citing in n. 86 from da Vinci many references. For color see also Martin Kemp, *The Science of Art: Optical Themes in Western Art*

from Brunelleschi to Seurat (New Haven, Conn.: Yale University Press, 1990), 264–74; and for technical discussion, Hall, *Color and Meaning: Practice and Theory in Renaissance Painting* (Cambridge: Cambridge University Press, 1992).

266. Acta 3.29. For white as a ritual color for light and splendor see Barasch, "Renaissance Color Conventions," 174.

267. *De coloribus* 2.792a28–30; 3.793a15–16; 3.793b8–12. See H. B. Gottschalk, "The *De coloribus* and Its Author," *Hermes* 92 (1964):59–85. References to *De coloribus* and *De rerum natura* are cited in David E. Hahm, "Early Hellenistic Theories of Vision and the Perception of Colour," in *Studies in Perception: Interrelations in the History of Philosophy and Science*, ed. Peter K. Maehammer and Robert G. Turnbull (Columbus: Ohio State University Press, 1978), 83. For the tradition about feathers see also H. Guerlac, "Can There Be Colors in the Dark? Physical Color Theory before Newton," *Journal of the History of Ideas* 47 (1986):3–20.

268. Lucretius, *De rerum natura* 2.799–809; *De rerum natura*, trans. W. H. D. Rouse, rev. Martin Ferguson Smith (Cambridge, Mass.: Harvard University Press, 1975), 159.

269. Mary Luella Trowbridge, *Philological Studies in Ancient Glass*, University of Illinois Studies in Language and Literature, 13 (Urbana: University of Illinois Press, 1928), 16–17.

270. Kemp, *Science of Art*, 269.

271. Stella Mary Newton, *The Dress of the Venetians, 1495–1525*, Pasold Studies in Textile History, 7 (Brookfield, Vt.: Scolar, 1988), 19–20, 178.

272. See Jacqueline Herald, *Renaissance Dress in Italy, 1400–1500*, History of Dress, 2 (New Jersey: Humanities, 1981), 73–75, without reference to peacocks. The comparison of shot fabrics to the peacock's feathers is mentioned by John Gage, *Colour and Culture: The Practice and Meaning from Antiquity to Abstraction* (London: Thames & Hudson, 1993), 140. He also discusses the peacock and alchemy, since its tail equaled all colors, 139–52.

273. Gage, "Color in Western Art: An Issue?" *Art Bulletin* 72 (1990):533.

274. Guazzo, *Civil conversatione* 2; Alessandro Piccolomini, *Dialogo de la bella creanza de le donne*, 20.

275. See Samuel Y. Edgerton, Jr., "Alberti's Colour Theory: A Medieval Bottle without Renaissance Wine," *Journal of the Warburg and Courtauld Institutes* 32 (1969):128–29.

276. Gage, "Color in Western Art," 533 n. 145.

277. Lucretius, *De rerum natura* 2.826–33.

278. Ackerman, "On Early Renaissance Color Theory and Practice," 13–14.

279. Summers, *The Judgment of Sense: Renaissance Naturalism and the Rise of Aesthetics* (Cambridge: Cambridge University Press, 1987), 46.

280. Pseudo-Longinus, *De sublimitate* 17.3.

281. Sextus Empiricus, *Outlines of Pyrrhonism* 1.91–92; *Outlines of Pyrrhonism*, trans. R. G. Bury (New York: G. P. Putnam's Sons, 1933), 120.

282. For perspective see Kemp, *Science of Art*, 9–98; Michael Kubovy, *The Psychology of Perspective and Renaissance Art* (Cambridge: Cambridge Uni-

versity Press, 1986); Edgerton, *The Renaissance Rediscovery of Linear Perspective* (New York: Basic Books, 1975); James Elkins, "Renaissance Perspectives," *Journal of the History of Ideas* 53 (1992):209–29.

283. Leonardo da Vinci, Windsor, Royal Library, MS W, fol. 19150a, in *Literary Works*, 1:288.

284. Peter of Limoges, *Liber de oculo morali*, fols. Aiiiv, Bvii, cited by Baxandall, *Painting and Experience*, 104–5, with text at 173.

285. Summers, "*Maniera* and Movement," 269–301.

286. Katherine Morris Lester and Bess Viola Oerke, *Accessories of Dress* (Peoria, Ill.: Chas. A. Bennett, 1954), 390–91.

287. Deguileville, *Pèlerinage de vie humaine* 6687–6723, cited by Susan K. Hagen, *Allegorical Remembrance: A Study of "The Pilgrimage of the Life of Man" as a Medieval Treatise on Seeing and Remembering* (Athens: University of Georgia Press, 1990), 70–71.

288. Schwarz, "Mirrors," 100–5, without the above example. His speculation about the use of mirrors by pilgrims seems plausible. Relics were compared with mirrors in Gregory of Nyssa's dream of his sister as precious relic that flashed in his eyes like a mirror reflecting sunlight, *Vita Macrinae* 15.12–22, cited by Brown, *Body and Society*, 300; and in Victricius of Rouen, *De laudes sanctorum*, on relics shining more brightly than the sun with a single invisible light to the universal faithful, cited by Eugene Vance, "Relics, Images, and the Mind of Guibert de Nogent," *Semiotica* 85 (1991):338.

289. Romain Roussel, *Les pèlerinages à travers les siècles* (Paris: Payot, 1954), 30; J. G. Davies, *Pilgrimage Yesterday and Today: Why? Where? How?* (London: SCM, 1988), 43; Freddy Raphaël, "Le pèlerinage: Approche sociologique," in idem et al., *Les pèlerinages de l'antiquité biblique et classique à l'occident médiévale* (Paris: Paul Geuthner, 1973), 17; Jonathan Sumption, *Pilgrimage: An Image of Mediaeval Religion* (London: Faber & Faber, 1975), 171.

290. Sumption, *Pilgrimage*, 172–73.

291. "Veneranda dies" in *Liber s. Jacobi* 1.17, cited by Sumption, *Pilgrimage*, 173.

292. Naselli, "Diavoli bianchi e neri," 243–44.

293. *Acta sanctorum*, February 16; Didron, *Christian Iconography*, 2:129–32.

294. Quintilian, *Institutiones oratoriae* 11.3.66.

295. Mark Franko, *The Dancing Body in Renaissance Choreography (c. 1416–1589)* (Birmingham, Ala.: Summa, 1986), 14–17.

296. See Anna Ivanova, *The Dancing Spaniards* (London: John Baker, 1970), 62–63; Reimbold, *Pfau*, 47–48.

297. Quintilian, *Institutiones oratoriae* 11.2.20–21; trans. Butler, 4:223.

298. Jean de Meun, *Roman de la rose* 21346–21780; with pilgrim at 21347, *bourdon* at 21605, Hercules at 21632.

299. See Caro Baroja, "Honour and Shame," 91.

CHAPTER 4. THE PILGRIM

1. See Ernst R. Curtius, *European Literature and the Latin Middle Ages*, trans. Willard R. Trask (New York: Pantheon, 1953), 515, 517. For an example

of medieval literary distance see Steven Shurtleff, "The Archpoet as Poet, Persona, and Self: The Problem of Individuality in the 'Confession,'" *Philological Quarterly* 73 (1994):373-84.

2. Salvian, *Epistolae* 9.3, 13-14.

3. Sulpicius Severus, *Vita s. Martinii* praef.

4. Gerhart B. Ladner, "Homo viator: Mediaeval Ideas of Alienation and Order," *Speculum* 42 (1967):237 n. 17.

5. Roger Dragonetti, *Le mirage des sources: L'Art du faux dans le roman médiévale* (Paris: Seuil, 1987), 17-55, esp. 45-48, citing Alain de Lille, *De fide catholica* 1.30. See also Paul Klopsch, "Anonymität und Selbstnennung mittellateinischer Autoren," *Mittellateinisches Jahrbuch* 4 (1967):9-25.

6. Evelyn Birge Vitz, *Medieval Narrative and Modern Narratology: Subjects and Objects of Desire* (New York: New York University Press, 1989), 2-3.

7. Dante, *Vita nuova* 40. For the semantics of *peregrinación* see Juergen Hahn, *The Origins of the Baroque Concept of "peregrinatio"* (Chapel Hill: University of North Carolina Press, 1973), 17-20, 28.

8. See Ladner, "Homo viator," 237.

9. Donald Roy Howard, *Writers and Pilgrims: Medieval Pilgrimage Narratives and Their Posterity* (Berkeley and Los Angeles: University of California Press, 1980), 85-87, 34. For recent study of Kempe as author see Diana R. Uhlman, "The Comfort of Voice: The Solace of Script: Orality and Literacy in *The Book of Margery Kempe*," *Studies in Philology* 91(1994):50-69; Lynn Staley, *Margery Kempe's Dissenting Fictions* (University Park: Pennsylvania State University Press, 1994). For the genre in general see Paul Zumthor, "The Medieval Travel Narrative," trans. Catherine Peebles, *New Literary History* 25 (1994):809-24.

10. Anne Barton, *The Names of Comedy* (Toronto: University of Toronto Press, 1990), 153-54, citing Herodotus, *Historiae* 4. For a renaissance example see Marvin Spevack, "Beyond Individualism: Names and Namelessness in Shakespeare," *Huntington Library Quarterly* 56 (1993):383-98.

11. *Acta* 4.40.

12. *Acta* 5.52; 6.63.

13. See Peter Burke, *The Historical Anthropology of Early Modern Italy: Essays on Perception and Communication* (Cambridge: Cambridge University Press, 1987), 88, 92.

14. *Acta* 1-4.39, with last reference at 3.34.

15. Identified by Ignacio Iparraguire, S.J., and Candido de Dalmases, S.J., eds., *Obras completas* (Madrid: Biblioteca de autores cristianos, 1963), 106 n. 20.

16. See Gerardo López de Guereñu, *Devoción popular en España a la Virgen blanca y a nuestra Señora de las nieves* (Vitoria: Obra cultural de la caja de ahorras municipal de la ciudad de Vitoria, 1967), passim.

17. Robert L. Hathaway, "The Art of the Epic Epithets in the *Cantar de mío Cid*," *Hispanic Review* 42 (1974):311-21; Thomas R. Hart, "The Rhetoric of (Epic) Fiction: Narrative Technique in the *Cantar de mío Cid*," *Philological Quarterly* 51 (1972):23-35; Rita Hamilton, "Epic Epithets in the *Poema de mío Cid*," *Revue de littérature comparée* 36 (1962):161-78; Edmund de Chasca, "El

epíteto," in *El arte juglaresco en el "Cantar de mío Cid,"* (Madrid: Gredos, 1967), 173-93.

18. Marjorie O'Rourke Boyle, "The Prudential Augustine: The Virtuous Structure and Sense of his *Confessions*," *Recherches augustiniennes* 22 (1987):137-49.

19. Augustine, *Sermo* 169.15, cited by Victorino Capágna, "Augustín, guía de peregrinos: Hacia una teología augustiniana de la peregrinación," *Helmantica* 26 (1975):73.

20. F. C. Gardiner, *The Pilgrimage of Desire: A Study of Theme and Genre in Medieval Literature* (Leiden: E. J. Brill, 1971), 11-14, 53-85, 86-156. For the plays about Emmaus see also Julia Bolton Holloway, *The Pilgrim and the Book: A Study of Dante, Langland, and Chaucer*, American University Studies, ser. 4, 42 (New York: Peter Lang, 1987), 19-43. For Christ as a pilgrim see also Hahn, *"Peregrinatio,"* 22, 29, 131-33.

21. Justo Pérez de Urbel, *El claustro de Silos* (Burgos: Aldecoa, 1930), 131-38, pls. at 133, 135, and reference to the Ripoll bible; Sixten Ringbom, "Some Pictorial Conventions for the Recounting of Thoughts and Experiences in Late Medieval Art," in *Medieval Iconography and Narrative: A Symposium* (Odense: Odense University Press, 1980), 50-51.

22. Barbara Nolan, *The Gothic Visionary Perspective* (Princeton, N.J.: Princeton University Press, 1977), 124-34.

23. Ibid., 136-39.

24. See Elisabeth MacDougall, "*Ars hortulorum*: Sixteenth-Century Garden Iconography and Literary Theory in Italy," in *The Italian Garden: First Dumbarton Oaks Colloquium on the History of Landscape Architecture*, ed. David R. Coffin (Washington, D.C.: Dumbarton Oaks, Trustees for Harvard University, 1972), 46, 50.

25. See A. Bartlett Giamatti, *The Earthly Paradise and the Renaissance Epic* (Princeton, N.J.: Princeton University Press, 1966), 39.

26. Dante, *Convivio* 2.14.

27. Guillaume de Deguileville, *Pèlerinage de vie humaine* 9-11, cited by Susan K. Hagen, *Allegorical Remembrance: A Study of "The Pilgrimage of the Life of Man" as a Medieval Treatise on Seeing and Remembering* (Athens: University of Georgia Press, 1990), 51. See also the illustration of the Pilgrim in Bed and his Vision of Jerusalem in the Spanish translation by Vincente de Maçuelo in *El pelerinage de la vida humana*, 65, fig. 2. See also Steven Wright, "Deguileville's *Pèlerinage de vie humaine* as "contrepartie edifiante" of the *Roman de la rose*," *Philological Quarterly* 68 (1987):399-422.

28. See Raoul de Houdenc, *Songe d'enfer* 1-7, cited by Nolan, *Gothic Visionary Perspective*, 153.

29. See Nolan, *Gothic Visionary Perspective*, 142-43.

30. *Acta* 3.35, 37.

31. Bernard of Clairvaux, *De gradibus humilitatis et superbiae* 22.56.

32. Erasmus, *Ratio verae theologiae*, pp. 178, 177, cited in Boyle, *Erasmus on Language and Method in Theology*, Erasmus Studies, 2 (Toronto: University of Toronto Press, 1977), 66, 60.

33. Giovanni della Casa, *Galateo* 267; *Galateo*, trans. Konrad Eisenbichler

and Kenneth R. Bartlett, Reformation and Renaissance Texts in Translation, 2 (Toronto: Centre for Reformation and Renaissance Studies, 1986), 49.

34. Evagrius Ponticus, *Logos praktikos* 13, 30–33.
35. Augustine, *Confessiones* 10.36.59; 10.37.60, 62; trans. Vernon J. Bourke, *Confessions* (New York: Fathers of the Church, 1953), 317.
36. *Fiore di virtù* 30.
37. Leonardo da Vinci, "Studies on the Life and Habits of Animals" 1230 in *Notebooks*.
38. Erasmus, *Colloquia*, in *Opera omnia* (Amsterdam), 1–3:668; *The Colloquies of Erasmus*, trans. Craig R. Thompson (Chicago: University of Chicago Press, 1965), 481.
39. *Acta* 3.30.
40. *Voie de paradis* 542.
41. Jean de Courcy, *Chemin de vaillance*, MS Royal 14.E.ii, cited by Siegfried Wenzel, "The Pilgrimage of Life as a Late Mediaeval Genre," *Mediaeval Studies* 35 (1973):375.
42. *Acta* 1.9; 4.40.
43. Christian Zacher, *Curiosity and Pilgrimage: The Literature of Discovery in Fourteenth-Century England* (Baltimore, Md.: Johns Hopkins University Press, 1976), 4–5, 6, 16, 53. See also Giles Constable, "The Opposition to Pilgrimage in the Middle Ages," *Studia gratiana* 19 (1976):123–46.
44. *Acta* 3.36; cf. "Praefatio scriptoris" 1.
45. Romain Roussel, *Le pèlerinage à travers les siècles* (Paris: Payot, 1954), 30.
46. *Acta* 3.36.
47. Kenneth Hurlstone Jackson, *A Celtic Miscellany: Translations from the Celtic Literature* (Cambridge, Mass.: Harvard University Press, 1951), 148, cited by Zacher, *Curiosity and Pilgrimage*, 55 n. 61; Jonathan Sumption, *Pilgrimage: An Image of Mediaeval Religion* (London: Faber & Faber, 1975), 96, and on Rome as not availing, 289–90. The original is in *Thesaurus palaeohibernicus*, 2:296, cited by Constable, "Opposition to Pilgrimage," 129.
48. Zacher, *Curiosity and Pilgrimage*, 54; J. G. Davies, *Pilgrimage Yesterday and Today: Why? Where? How?* (London: SCM, 1988), 85–86, 46; Sumption, *Pilgrimage*, 256–61.
49. Gaudenzio Boccazzi, "La curiosité du voyageur au XVIe siècle: Ou l'art d'apprendre et de se parfaire par les voyages," in *La curiosité à la Renaissance*, ed. Jean Céard (Paris: Société d'édition et d'enseignement supérieur, 1986), 49–62 on Rabelais and Montaigne.
50. Bartolomé Cairosco de Figueroa, "Peregrinación," cited by Hahn, "Peregrinatio," 15.
51. *Acta* 4.38; 3.35–36.
52. Ibid. 2.13.
53. See Sumption, *Pilgrimage*, 168.
54. *Acta* 3.19; 2.18; 3.35–36; 4.38–39; 4.40; 4.42; 4.42–43.
55. See Sumption, *Pilgrimage*, 185.
56. *Acta* 5.49, 50.
57. See Sumption, *Pilgrimage*, 208.

58. *Acta* 5.53; 6.54; 6.56; 6.57; 6.63; 8.73–75.

59. Raymond of Capua, *Vita* 1.4, in *Acta sanctorum*.

60. *Acta* 8.76–77; 8.84.

61. See Piero Boitani, *Chaucer and the Imaginary World of Fame*, Chaucer Studies, 10 (London: D. S. Brewer, 1984), 97–98, 131–34 passim.

62. *Acta* 9.87; 9.89; 9.90; 9.91; 10.93; 10.95; 11.100; "Deliberatio de paupertate."

63. Petrarch, *Epistolae familiares* 13.4.20, 23, 25.

64. Sumption, *Pilgrimage*, 122–25, citing "Veneranda dies" in *Liber s. Jacobi* 1.17; 208, 168, 265, 160.

65. Peter Burke, *The Historical Anthropology of Early Modern Europe: Essays on Perception and Communication* (Cambridge: Cambridge University Press, 1987), 72–73.

66. *Acta* 6.56.

67. *Exercitia spiritualia*, pp. 148, 260–62.

68. Lester K. Little, "Pride Goes before Avarice: Social Change and the Vices in Latin Christendom," *American Historical Review* 76 (1971):16–49.

69. Howard, *The Three Temptations: Medieval Man in Search of the World* (Princeton, N.J.: Princeton University Press, 1966), 54, citing at 45 Gregory the Great, *Homiliae* 1.16.2. Since medieval allegory was not empirically discrete, Christ's temptation to jump from the pinnacle of the temple not only could be related to vainglory, but also to avarice, as a curiosity about corporeal abilities, 50.

70. Origen, *In Matthaeum* 15.18.

71. *Vita Antonii* 40.

72. *Exercitia spiritualia*, p. 246.

73. *Acta* 4.38.

74. Jerome, *Epistolae* 22.25; *Select Letters of St. Jerome*, trans. F. A. Wright (New York: G. P. Putnam's Sons, 1933), 109.

75. Bernard of Clairvaux, *De gradibus humilitatis et superbiae* 10, cited by Zacher, *Curiosity and Pilgrimage*, 25. See also *Ancrene Riwle* 2. For a Spanish example of the rape of Dinah see detail, Pamplona bible, 12th century, Amiens, Bibliothèque municipale, MS lat. 108, fol. 20v; reproduced in Diane Wolfthal, "'A Hue and a Cry': Medieval Rape Imagery and Its Transformation," *Art Bulletin* 75 (1993):44, fig. 5.

76. Thomas J. Heffernan, *Sacred Biography: Saints and Their Biographers in the Middle Ages* (Oxford: Oxford University Press, 1988), 142.

77. See Guido Ruggiero, *The Boundaries of Eros: Sex Crime and Sexuality in Renaissance Venice* (New York: Oxford University Press, 1985), 89–108, without reference to Loyola.

78. Ladner, "Homo viator," 236 n. 14, citing Augustine, *Sermo* 14.4.6; 80.7; 177.2; 178.8; *Tractatus in evangelium Iohannis* 40.10; Gregory the Great, *Moralia in Iob* 8.54.92.

79. *Acta* 9.91.

80. Fabri, *Evagatorium*, 2:68–69.

81. See also the Hill of Virtue in Jan David, S.J., *Veridicus christianus*, Antwerp, 1601. Reproduced in Samuel Chew, *The Pilgrimage of Life* (New Haven,

Conn.: Yale University Press, 1962), fig. 138. Three men ascend on hands and knees, while a fourth tumbles down, a hill crowned with the seven virtues.

82. See Chew, *Pilgrimage of Life*, 147–48.

83. Howard Rollin Patch, *The Other World According to Descriptions in Medieval Literature* (New York: Octagon, 1970), 7–10, 34–35, passim.

84. Gregory the Great, *Dialogi* 4.37–38. For the bridge in Dante's pilgrimage see Theodore Silverstein, "Dante and the Legend of the Mi`rāj: The Problem of Islamic Influence on the Christian Literature of the Otherworld," *Journal of Near Eastern Studies* 11 (1952):89–112, 187–97.

85. *Acta* 9.91.

86. Gregory the Great, *Dialogi* 4.37; *Dialogues*, trans. Odo John Zimmerman (New York: Fathers of the Church, 1959), 241.

87. Françoise Joukovsky, *La gloire dans la poésie française et néolatine du XVIe siècle (Des rhétoriquers a Agrippa d'Aubigné)*, Travaux d'humanisme et Renaissance, 102 (Geneva: Droz, 1969), 343–47.

88. *Acta* 4.42.

89. Detail of the Creation mosaics, 13th century, vestibule, S. Marco, Venice. Reproduced in Francis Klingender, *Animals in Art and Thought to the End of the Middle Ages*, ed. Evelyn Antal and John Harthan (London: Routledge & Kegan Paul, 1971), 255, fig. 159.

90. Guillaume de Deguileville, *Pèlerinage de vie humaine* 19069–232, cited by Hagen, *Allegorical Remembrance*, 92–93. The pilgrim and the sea of the world, London, British Library, MS Cotton Tiberius A.7, fol. 52v, cf. fol. 58, reproduced, figs. 41, 42. Also reproduced from the Spanish translation by Vinçente de Maçuelo in *Pelerinage de la vida humana*, 309, fig. 12.

91. Holloway, *Pilgrim and the Book*, 61.

92. Augustine, *Confessiones* 7.5.7; trans. Bourke, 168. For other patristic literature on the topic see Hugo Rahner, *Symbole der Kirche: Die Ekklesiologie der Väter* (Salzburg: Muller, 1964), 239–564. For development of this topic see Boyle, "Cusanus at Sea: The Topicality of Illuminative Discourse," *Journal of Religion* 71 (1991):180–201.

93. Boyle, "Prudential Augustine," 137–41, 144–48. For the comparison of life to a voyage at sea see Campbell Bonner, "Desired Haven," *Harvard Theological Review* 34 (1941):49–67; and for the development of the topic, Boyle, "Cusanus at Sea."

94. *Acta* 4.43–44.

95. Fabri, *Evagatorium*, 1:144; *Felix Fabri (Circa 1480–1483 A.D.)* trans. Aubrey Stewart, The Library of the Palestine Pilgrims' Text Society, vol. 7–10, 2 vols. in 4 (London, 1893–97), 1:160.

96. *Acta* 4.44.

97. John Demaray, *The Invention of Dante's "Commedia"* (New Haven, Conn.: Yale University Press, 1974), 11–14.

98. *Acta* 4.44–45

99. See Holloway, *Pilgrim and the Book*, 129, 141, citing *Mandeville's Travels*, 71–72.

100. *Acta* 4.45; cf. Fabri, *Evagatorium*, 1:237.

101. *Acta* 4.45.

102. Roussel, *Pèlerinages*, 31–32.
103. *Acta* 4.47.
104. Fabri, *Evagatorium*, 1:64; trans. Stewart, 1:49.
105. *Acta* 4.47–48
106. Victor Turner and Edith Turner, *Image and Pilgrimage in Christian Culture: Anthropological Perspectives* (New York: Columbia University Press, 1978), 11.
107. For the Mount of Olives as the site of the ascension see among many sources Jerome, *Epistolae* 108.12.1; Fabri, *Evagatorium*, 1:387–89, cf. pp. 382–83.
108. See G. W. Pigman III, "Versions of Imitation in the Renaissance," *Renaissance Quarterly* 33 (1980):9–22.
109. Fabri, *The Wanderings of Felix Fabri*, 2 vols. (New York, 1975), 1:4, cited by Davies, *Pilgrimage Yesterday and Today*, 67.
110. Fabri, *Evagatorium*, 1:402–4.
111. *Exercitia spiritualia*, p. 372.
112. Paulinus of Nola, *Epistolae* 49.14; 31.4, cited by Sumption, *Pilgrimage*, 91; *The Letters of Paulinus of Nola*, trans. P. G. Walsh, Ancient Christian Writers, 35, 36, 2 vols. (Westminster, Md.: Newman, 1966; New York: Newman, 1967), 2:273, 129–30.
113. Jerome, *Epistolae* 47.2; 58.3, cited by Davies, *Pilgrimage Yesterday and Today*, 80; *Epistolae* 58.2, cited by Zacher, *Curiosity and Pilgrimage*, 54; Constable, "Opposition to Pilgrimage," 126.
114. Erasmus, *Enchiridion militis christianae*, in *Opera omnia* (Leiden), 5:38; *The Handbook of the Christian Soldier*, trans. Charles Fantazzi in *The Collected Works of Erasmus* (Toronto: University of Toronto Press, 1988), 66:82.
115. Pico della Mirandola, *Oratio de dignitate hominis* 11; *The Renaissance Philosophy of Man*, ed. and trans. Ernst Cassirer et al. (Chicago: University of Chicago Press, 1948), 229.
116. Robert Southwell, S. J., *Mary Magdalens Funeral Teares*, p. 67. See in general Marjory E. Lange, *Telling Tears in the English Renaissance*, Studies in the History of Christian Thought, 70 (Leiden: E. J. Brill, 1996).
117. Davies, *Pilgrimage Yesterday and Today*, 67.
118. Eugene F. Rice, Jr., *Saint Jerome in the Renaissance*, Johns Hopkins Symposia in Comparative History, 13 (Baltimore, Md.: John Hopkins University Press, 1985), 103–4, citing Laudivio, *Vita beati Hieronymi*, fol. 4v; Fabri, *Evagatorium*, 1:237–40.
119. *Exercitia spiritualia*, pp. 352–53.
120. St. Peter's Denial, mosaic, S. Apollinare nuovo, Ravenna. Rembrandt, St. Peter's Denial, Rijksmuseum, Amsterdam. Reproduced in E. H. Gombrich, "Action and Expression in Western Art," in *Non-Verbal Communication*, ed. R. A. Hinde (Cambridge: Cambridge University Press, 1972), 383, figs. 7a, 7b.
121. Fabri, *Evagatorium*, 1:261.
122. First published in 1560, but manuscript copies were widely circulating in Roman ecclesiastical circles by 1559, according to Mario Praz, "Robert

Southwell's 'Saint Peter's Complaint' and its Italian Source," *Modern Language Review*, 19 (1924):287.

123. For the poetry of tears see Terence Cave, *Devotional Poetry in France, c. 1570–1613* (Cambridge: Cambridge University Press, 1969), 249–66.

124. Nancy Pollard Brown, "The Structure of Southwell's 'Saint Peter's Complaint,'" *Modern Language Review* 61 (1966):3–11; Praz, "Southwell's 'Saint Peter's Complaint,'" 273–90.

125. Brown, "Structure of 'Saint Peter's Complaint,'" 5, citing G. J. Spykman, "Attrition and Contrition at the Council of Trent," Ph.D. diss., University of Amsterdam, 1955, 161, with reference to *Canons and Decrees of the Sacred and Oecumenical Council of Trent* 14.4.

126. *Acta* 6.54–57; 8.73.

127. Boyle, "Fools and Schools: Scholastic Dialectic, Humanist Rhetoric: from Anselm to Erasmus," *Medievalia et humanistica* 13 (1985):173–79.

128. See Howard, *Three Temptations*, 54–55.

129. Vergil, *Aeneid* 173–97, citing 180–3; *Virgil*, trans. H. Rushton Fairclough, 2 vols. (Cambridge, Mass.: Harvard University Press, 1947), 1:409.

130. Chaucer, *House of Fame* 1376–85.

131. Joukovsky, *Gloire dans la poésie*, 498–515, 601–5, citing at 603 Cesare Ripa, *Iconologia, overo Descrittione dell'imagini universale cavate dall'antichità et da altri luggi* (Rome: Gio. Giogliotti, 1593), p. 73; and see for glory as flight, Joukovsky, *Gloire dans la poésie*, 330–32. Chew, *Pilgrimage of Life*, 181–83, citing *Bocace de la Genealogie des dieux* (Paris: Verard, 1498), fol. Xiiv. For surveys of fame see Boitani, *Chaucer and Fame*; Achatz Freiherr von Müller, *"Gloria bona fama bonorum": Studien zur sittlichen Bedeutung des Ruhmes in der frühchristlichen und mittelalterlichen Welt*, Historische Studien, 428 (Husum: Matthiesen, 1977).

132. *Acta* 1.10. Italics mine.

133. *Acta* 4.45, 47.

134. *Acta* 6.54; 4.41.

135. "Praefatio scriptoris" 3.

136. See Ernstpeter Ruhe, " 'Les plumes du paon et le mouton assimile' : Zum Problem der Originalität im Mittelalter," in *Mittelalterbilder aus neuer Perspective: Diskussionsanstösse zu "amour courtois," Subjectivität in der Dichtung, und Strategien des Erzählens*, ed. idem and Rudolf Behrens, Beiträge zur romanischen Philologie des Mittelalters, 14 (Munich: Wilhelm Fink, 1985), 194–209.

137. *Epistolae* 15; *The Collected Works of Erasmus*, trans. R. A. B. Mynors and D. F. S. Thomson (Toronto: University of Toronto Press, 1974), 1:20–21; cited in Boyle, *Erasmus on Language and Method in Theology*, 50.

138. Helen Nader, *The Mendoza Family in the Spanish Renaissance, 1350 to 1550* (New Brunswick, N.J.: Rutgers University Press, 1979), 138–39.

139. *Acta* 4.41.

140. See Sumption, *Pilgrimage*, 185–86.

141. *Acta* 4.41; 5.49; 5.51; 6.55. For stripping a man of his clothes as divesting him of honor see Thomas V. Cohen, "The Lay Liturgy of Affront in Sixteenth-Century Italy," *Journal of Social History* 25 (1992):857–62.

142. Fabri, *Evagatorium*, 2:475.
143. *Acta* 6.57; 6.59; 6.62; 7.64, citing Terence, *Andria* 635.
144. *Acta* 5.50; 8.84.
145. General examen, *Constitutiones* 2.3.44.
146. *Exercitia spiritualia*, pp. 294–98.
147. *Acta* 8.83. Cf. Raymond of Capua, *Vita* 2.4; 2.2; Fabri, *Evagatorium*, 1:246–47.
148. *Acta* 4.41–42, 43.
149. Fabri, *Evagatorium*, 1:114.
150. Quintilian, *Institutiones oratoriae* 8.6.67–68; 9.4.30; 9.4.44; 8.4.8; *The "Institutio oratoria" of Quintilian*, trans. H. E. Butler, 4 vols. (Cambridge, Mass.: Harvard University Press, 1933–1936), 3:267.
151. *Acta* 7.72; 5.51; 6.60; 7.67; 7.79.
152. Sumption, *Pilgrimage*, 67, 102.
153. *Acta* 7.71.
154. For the phenomenon see A. Y. Syrkin, "On the Behavior of the 'Fool for Christ's Sake,'" *History of Religions* 22 (1982):150–72.
155. *Exercitia spiritualia*, pp. 260–62.
156. *Acta* 7.65.
157. Aristotle, *Rhetorica* 1410a; *The "Art" of Rhetoric*, trans. John Henry Freese (New York: G. P. Putnam's Sons, 1926), 393.
158. David Summers, "*Contrapposto*: Style and Meaning in Renaissance Art," *Art Bulletin* 59 (1977):336–61, citing Aristotle, *Rhetorica* 1410a, and Leonardo da Vinci, *Trattato della pintura* 271.
159. Martin Luther, *De servo arbitrio*, p. 287, cited by Boyle, *Rhetoric and Reform: Erasmus' Civil Dispute with Luther*, Harvard Historical Monographs, 71 (Cambridge, Mass.: Harvard University Press, 1983), 46–47.
160. *Acta* 6.58–62; 7.64–71; 9.86; 10.93; 11.98.
161. Julio Caro Baroja, "Honour and Shame," in *Honour and Shame: The Values of Mediterranean Society*, ed. J. G. Peristiany (Chicago: University of Chicago Press, 1966), 101–3.
162. *Acta* 6.59.
163. Cited by Julian Pitt-Rivers, "Honour and Social Status," in *Honour and Shame*, 35.
164. *Acta* 10.96.
165. Turner and Turner, *Image and Pilgrimage*, 11. The theological foundation of this book is not "orthodox Catholic," as stated, but Pelagian: "On the one hand, the believer is plied with graces by God; on the other, he continually exerts his free will by accepting [sic] or rejecting them," 30. See also Edmond-René Labande, "*Ad limina*: Le pèlerin médiéval au terme de sa démarche," in *Mélanges offerts à René Crozet*, ed. Pierre Gallais and Yves-Jean Riou, 2 vols. (Poitiers: Société d'études médiévales, 1966), 1:283–91.
166. *Ephemeris*, passim; *Exercitia spiritualia*, pp. 218–20.
167. See A. J. Vermeulen, *The Semantic Development of "Gloria" in Early-Christian Latin*, Latinitas christianorum primaeva, 12 (Nijmegen: Dekker & van de Vegt, 1956), 110–14; on virginity, 96–97, 99, 100.
168. Maurice Carrez, "La gloire de Dieu: Etude des diverses notions de glo-

Notes to Chapter 4

ire dans les écrits de l'ancien testament et du judaisme," Lic. thesis, Faculté libre de théologie, Paris, 1957, 11, 13, 19, 197–98. See also idem, *De la souffrance à la gloire: De la "doxa" dans la pensée paulinienne* (Neuchatel: Delachaux & Niestlé, 1964); Mauritius Steinheimer, *"Doxa tou Theou": Die "doxa tou Theou" in der römischen Liturgie*, Münchener theologische Studien, 2, systematische Abteilung, 4, (Munich: Karl Zink, 1951), 33–59.

169. See G. Celio, Glory of the Cross. Reproduced in Howard Hibbard, "*Ut picturae sermones*: The First Painted Decorations of the Gesù," in *Baroque Art: The Jesuit Contribution*, ed. Rudolf Wittkower and Irma B. Jaffe (New York: Fordham University Press, 1976), pl. 26; Mary, queen of martyrs, and SS. Andrew, Peter, Paul, Catherine, and Stephen in martyrdom, pls. 18a-21b. The interpretation is mine. For glory as a winged goddess see Joukovsky, *Gloire dans la poésie*, 601. Cf. the painting of Glory as a nude young girl on the ceiling at the Villa d'Este. Reproduced in David Coffin, *The Villa d'Este at Tivoli*, Princeton Monographs in Art and Archaeology, 34 (Princeton, N.J.: Princeton University Press, 1960), 58–60 and fig. 72.

170. Vermeulen, *Semantic Development of "Gloria,"* 54–95.

171. *Acta* 10.98–99.

172. *Acta* 12.101.

173. *Exercitia spiritualia*, e.g., pp. 200–2.

174. *Acta* 2.27; 4.44; 4.48; 11.98.

175. *Acta* 4.44.

176. For the equator see Dante, *Purgatorio* 4.79–84, and Demaray, *Invention of Dante's "Commedia,"* 82.

177. Jerome, *Epistolae* 108.12.5. For the importance of symbolic baptism in the Jordan during pilgrimage, and as imitated at Compostela, see Sumption, *Pilgrimage*, 128–30. See also *Exercitia spiritualia*, pp. 254, 462.

178. Ambrose, "Splendor paternae gloriae" 3.5, *Hymni* and passim. See also Vermeulen, *Semantic Development of "Gloria,"* 156–63; Franz J. Dolger, *"Sol salutis": Gebet und Gesang im christlichen Altertum* (1925, rpt.; Münster: Aschendorff, 1972), 379–410.

179. *Speculum perfectionis* 119, in *The Little Flowers of St. Francis, The Mirror of Perfection, St. Bonaventure's Life of St. Francis*, trans. Hugh McKay (New York: Dutton, 1910), 294. See Francis of Assisi, "Canticum fratris solis vel laudes creaturarum" 3–4.

180. Dante, *Paradiso* 23.28–39.

181. Boyle, *Petrarch's Genius: Pentimento and Prophecy* (Berkeley and Los Angeles: University of California Press, 1991).

182. E.g. Richard of St. Victor, *In Apocalypsim Joannis libri* 1.4.

183. See Joukovsky, *Gloire dans la poésie*, 328–30, 347–63.

184. *Acta* 10.93

185. Stephen F. Ostrow, "The Sistine Chapel at S. Maria Maggiore: Sixtus V and the Art of the Counter Reformation," Ph.D. diss., Princeton University, 1987, 26; idem, *Art and Spirituality in Counter-Reformation Rome: The Sistine and Pauline Chapels in S. Maria Maggiore* (Cambridge: Cambridge University Press, 1996).

186. *Acta* 10.94

187. Francis Rapp, "Les pèlerinages dans la vie religieuse de l'occident médiéval au XIVe et XVe siècles," in Freddy Raphaël et al., *Les pèlerinages de l'antiquité biblique et classique à l'occident médiéval* (Paris: Paul Geuthner, 1973), 120–38.

188. See Demaray, *Invention of Dante's "Commedia,"* 22, 86.

189. Jean Gagé, *Apollon romain: Essai sur le culte d'Apollon et le développement du "ritus graecus" à Rome des origines à Auguste* (Paris: E. de Boccard, 1955), esp. 426–27, 499–516, 585–94, 673–74.

190. Dolger, *"Sol salutis,"* esp. 336–79; idem, *Die Sonne der Gerechtigkeit und der Schwarze: Eine Religionsgeschichtliche Studie zum Taufgelöbnis* (1919; rpt. Münster: Aschendorff, 1970), esp. 100–41, citing at 2 Jerome, *Commentariorum in Amos prophetam libri* 3.6.14.

191. André Grabar, *Early Christian Art: From the Rise of Christianity to the Death of Theodosius*, trans. Stuart Gilbert and James Emmons (New York: Odyssey, 1968), 92–93.

192. Adolphe N. Didron, *Christian Iconography: The History of Christian Art in the Middle Ages*, trans. E. J. Millington, 2 vols. (New York: Frederick Ungar, 1965), 1:35.

193. Ibid., 80–81 and pl. 74; B. M. A. Ghetti et al., *Esplorazioni sotto la confessione di S. Pietro in Vaticano*, 2 vols. (Vatican City: n.p., 1951), 1:38–42 and pls. 10–12; Jocelyn Toynbee and John W. Perkins, *The Shrine of St. Peter and the Vatican Excavations* (London: Longmans, Green, 1957), 72–74, 116–17, pl. 32.

194. Hans Henrik Brummer, *The Statue Court in the Vatican Belvedere* (Stockholm: Almquist & Wiksell, 1970), 222–26. For another Apolline image see the fresco in the second Tiburtine room in the Villa d'Este at Tivoli. Coffin, *Villa d'Este at Tivoli*, 63–64 and fig. 80. For the continuity of solar magery later in the papacy of Pope Sixtus V (1585–90) see Corinne Mandel, "Starry Leo, the Sun, and the Astrological Foundations of Sixtine Rome," *Revue d'art canadienne/Canadian Art Review* 17 (1990):17–39.

195. Plato, *Respublica* 7.532; *The Dialogues of Plato*, trans. Benjamin Jowett, 2 vols. (New York: Random House, 1937), 1:791.

196. At Delphi the Pythia drank from the Castalian springs before uttering Apollo's oracles, and they became a sacred font of poetic and prophetic inspiration. Pierre Amandry, *La mantique apollinienne à Delphes: Essai sur le fonctionnement de l'oracle* (Paris: E. de Boccard, 1950), 134–39; and for the spring Cassotis, Georges Roux, *Delphes: Son oracle et ses dieux* (Paris: Belles lettres, 1976), 136–45. It was characteristic of the Apolline sanctuaries that all were important hydraulic installations. René Ginouves, *Balaneutikē: Recherches sur le bain dans l'antiquité grecque* (Paris: E. de Boccard, 1962), 327–44.

197. Plato, *Phaedo* 99d-100a.

198. *Exercitia spiritualia*, p. 186.

199. See Louis Réau, *L'iconographie de l'art chrétien*, 6 vols. (Paris: Presses universitaires de France, 1955–59), 3-2:673; F. Werner in *Lexikon der christlichen Ikonographie*, ed. Engelbert Kirschbaum, 8 vols. (Rome: Herder, 1968–76), 6:569–71; Ricardo García Villoslada, in *Biblioteca sanctorum*, 12 vols.

(Rome: Istituto Giovanni XXIII nella Pontificia università lateranense, 1961–68), 6:674–705.

200. See Adolf Katzenzellenbogen, *Allegories of the Virtues and Vices in Mediaeval Art: From Early Christian Times to the Thirteenth Century* (London: Warburg Institute, 1939), 55.

201. Herrad of Hohenbourg, *Hortus deliciarum*, fol. 201v, pl. 114.

202. See Réau, *Iconographie de l'art chrétien*, 3–2:673; *Lexikon der christlichen Ikonographie*, 6:569–71; *Biblioteca sanctorum*, 6:702.

203. Chew, *Pilgrimage of Life*, 251–52, citing its reproduction in René Fülöp-Miller, *The Power and Secret of the Jesuits*, trans. F. S. Flint and D. F. Tait (London: G. P. Putnam's Sons, 1930), pl. 8. The description of the engraving is mine, for the peacock has been overlooked. On peacocks and vainglory see also Chew, *Pilgrimage of Life*, 82–83, 93, 95–98.

204. Reproduced in Joseph M. Gasol, *Manresa: Panorama d'una ciutat* (Manresa: Montañà, 1971), 49. Also reproduced from J. de Mesa/A. Collaert, *Vita beati patris Ignatii* (Antwerp: C. Galle, 1610), nr. 3 in Ursula König-Nordhoff, *Ignatius von Loyola: Studien zur Entwicklung einer neuen Heiligen-Ikonographie im Rhamen einer Kanonisationskampagne um 1600* (Berlin: Gebr. Mann, 1982), Abb. 85.

205. Cornelius I. Galle, Ignatius in solitude tormented by serpents, Etterbeek, Biblioteca della Società dei P. P. Bollandisti, 17th century. Reproduced in *Biblioteca sanctorum*, 7:683. Also reproduced from Rubens/Barbé, *Vita beati p. Ignatii* (Rome, 1609), nr. 12 in König-Nordhoff, *Ignatius von Loyola*, Abb. 411. See also Abb. 432 and 520, in which the snake has a woman's head, while Loyola in Jesuit garb grips a rosary and a staff—the attributes of St. Anthony the hermit in Matthias Grünewald's painting for the Isenheim altar—but without anguish. In Abb. 521 and 522 the serpent is an ordinary snake.

206. Several scenes of Mary thus appearing to him in a grotto were portrayed. Gerard Seghers, Vision of St. Ignatius of Loyola, Wallraf-Richartz Museum, Cologne. Reproduced in Horst Vey, "Gerard Seghers: A Vision of St. Ignatius Loyola during the Writing of the Rules of the Jesuits," *Master Drawings*, 2 (1964):pl. 17 and see 268–71. Gerard Seghers, Tableau painted for the Jesuit College at Gand, engraved by Schelte at Bolswert; Jeronimo Espinosa, 1653, Provincial Museum, Valencia; Valdès Leal, 1674, Provincial Museum, Seville. Réau, *Iconographie de l'art chrétien*, 3–2:675.

207. Quintilian, *Institutiones oratoriae* 5.10.20, 21–22; trans. Butler, 2:213.

208. See David Carrasco, *Quetzalcoatl and the Irony of Empire* (Chicago: University of Chicago Press, 1982), 60; as morning star, 30–32, and other celestial phenomena. Carrasco does not consider Pettazoni's fundamental research.

209. *Exercitia spiritualia*, p. 194.

210. For the classical comparison see Michael O'Loughlin, *The Garlands of Repose: The Literary Celebration of Civic and Retired Leisure: The Traditions of Homer and Vergil, Horace and Montaigne* (Chicago: University of Chicago Press, 1978), 87–88.

211. *Acta* 10.99.

212. Cicero, *De oratore* 2.39.162.

213. Quintilian, *Institutiones oratoriae* 7.10.14–15, trans. Butler, 3:171; 8.pr.28–30, trans., 193.

214. See Michael Baxandall, *Painting and Experience in Fifteenth-Century Italy: A Primer in the Social History of Pictorial Style*, 2d ed. (Oxford: Oxford University Press, 1988), 145–47, citing Leon Battista Alberti, *De pictura*.

215. Summers, *Michelangelo and the Language of Art* (Princeton, N.J.: Princeton University Press, 1981), 60–64.

216. Walter Kaiser, *Praisers of Folly: Erasmus, Rabelais, Shakespeare* (Cambridge, Mass.: Harvard University Press, 1963), 3.

217. Deguileville, *Pèlerinage de vie humaine* 22510–18, cited in Hagen, *Allegorical Remembrance*, 110.

218. Augustine, *De civitate Dei* 11.23; *The City of God*, trans. Gerald G. Walsh and Grace Monahan (Washington, D.C.: Catholic University of America Press, 1952), 222.

219. Anne Bradstreet, "The Author to her Book."

Primary Sources

The principal text is Luis Gonçalves da Câmara, *Acta patris Ignatii*, ed. Dionisio Fernandez Zapico and Candido de Dalmases, S.J., Monumenta historica societatis Iesu, 66 (Rome: Monumenta historica societatis Iesu, 1943). Cited texts of Loyola are his diary of 1544-45, *Ephemeris*, in *Constitutiones societatis Iesu*, ed. Arturo Codina, S.J., 86-158, Monumenta historica societatis Iesu, 83 (Rome: Borgo S. Spirito 5, 1934); the related "Deliberatio de paupertate", ibid., 78-81; the *Constitutiones*; his *Exercitia spiritualia*, ed. Joseph Calveras, S.J., Monumenta historica societatis Iesu, 100 (Rome: Institutum historicum societatis Iesu, 1969); *Epistolae et instructiones*, Monumenta historica societatis Iesu, 7 (Madrid: Gabriel Lopez del Horno, 1903). Translations are mine.

Aelian. (*De animalibus*). *On the Characteristics of Animals*. Ed. A. F. Scholfield. 3 vols. Cambridge, Mass.: Harvard University Press, 1971-72.

Alain de Lille. *De fide catholica. De sex alis cherubim*. In *Patrologia latina* 210:305-430, 266-80.

Albert the Great. *Liber animalium*. Ed. Hermann Stadler. Beiträge zur Geschichte der Philosophie des Mittelalters, 15-16. 2 vols. Münster: Aschendorff, 1916-20.

Alberti, Leon Battista. *Opere volgari*. Ed. Cecil Grayson. 3 vols. Bari: Giuseppe Laterza & Figli, 1960-73.

———. (*De pictura*). (*De statua*). *On Painting and On Sculpture: The Latin Texts of "De pictura" and "De statua"*. Ed. Cecil Grayson. London: Phaidon, 1972.

Aldrovandi, Ulysse. *Delle statue antiche, che pertutta Roma, in diversi luoghi, et case si veggono*. Hildesheim: Georg Olms, 1975.

———. *Orinthologiae liber decimustertius*. Bologna: Io. Bapt. Bellagambam, 1600.

———. *Serpentum, et draconum historiae, libri duo*. In *Opera omnia*, 10. Bologna: C. Feronius, 1640.

Alfonso X. *Cantigas*. Madrid: Catedra, 1988.

———. *Las siete partidas*. Madrid, 1807.

Alvares, Francisco. *Verdadeira informação das terras do preste João das Indias*. Ed. Augusto Reis Machado. Divisão de publicaçãos e biblioteca: Agência geral das colonias, 1943.

Ambrose. (*Hymni*). *Hymnes* . Ed. Jacques Fontaine and Jean-Louis Charlet. Paris: Cerf, 1992.

Ancrene Riwle. *The English Text of the "Ancrene Riwle": "Ancrene Wisse", Edited from Ms. Corpus Christi College, Cambridge 402"*. Ed. J. R. Tolkien. Early English Text Society, 249. London: Oxford University Press, 1962.

Angela of Foligno. (*Librum de vere fidelium experientia*). *Le livre de l'expérience des vrais fidèles*. Edited by M.-J. Ferré. Paris: E. Droz, 1927.

Anglo-Norman Lapidaries. Ed. Paul Studer and Joan Evans. Paris: E. Champion, 1924.

L'Apocalypse de Saint-Sever: Manuscrit latin 8878 de la Bibliothèque nationale (XIe siècle). With descriptive notes by Émile-A. Van Moé. Paris: Cluny, 1942.

Apuleius. *Opera quae supersunt*. Ed. Rudolf Helm. 2 vols. Leipzig: B. G. Teubner, 1955.

Ariosto, Ludovico. *Orlando furioso*. Ed. Cesare Segre. Milan: A. Mondadori, 1976.

Aristotle. *Historia animalium*. Ed. A. L. Peck. 2 vols. Cambridge, Mass.: Harvard University Press, 1965–70.

———. *Metaphysica*. Ed. Werner Jaeger. Oxford: Clarendon, 1957.

Aristotle, Pseudo-. *De coloribus*. Ed. Carl Prantl. Leipzig, 1881.

Arnulf d'Orleans. *Allegoriae super Ovidii Metamorphosin*. In Fausto Ghisalberti, "Arnolfo d'Orleans: Un cultore di Ovidio nel secolo XII". In *Memorie del Reale istituto lombardo di scienze e lettere*, classi di lettere, scienze morali e storiche 24 (1932):157–234.

Arras, Jean d'. *Mélusine: Roman du XIVe siècle*. Ed. Louis Stouff. Dijon: Université, 1932.

Augustine. In *Patrologia latina*, 31–47.

———. *Confessionum libri tredecim*. Ed. Lucas Verheijen. Corpus christianorum series latina, 27. Turnhout: Brepols, 1981.

———. *Contra academicos, De beata vita, De ordine, De magistro, De libero arbitrio*. Ed. W. M. Green and K.-D. Daur. Corpus christianorum series latina, 29. Turnhout: Brepols, 1970.

———. *De civitate Dei*. Ed. Bernard Dombart and Alphonse Kalb. Corpus christianorum series latina, 47–48. 2 vols. Turnhout: Brepols, 1955.

———. *De sermone Domini in monte libros duos*. Ed. Almut Mutzenbecher. Corpus christianorum series latina, 35. Turnhout: Brepols, 1967.

———. *Quaestionum in heptateuchum libri VII*. Corpus christianorum series latina, 33. Ed. Johannes Fraipont. Turnhout: Brepols, 1958.

———. *Retractationum libri duo*. Ed. Almut Mutzenbecher. Corpus christianorum series latina, 57. Turnhout: Brepols, 1984.

Basil of Caesarea. *Regulae a Rufino latine versa*. Ed. Klaus Zelzer. Corpus scriptorum ecclesiasticorum latinorum, 86. Vienna: Hoelder, Pichler, Tempsky, 1986.

Primary Sources

Basil of Seleucia. (*Vita Theclae*). *Vie et miracles de sainte Thècle*. Ed. Gilbert Dagron. Subsidia hagiographica, 62. Brussels: Société de Bollandistes, 1978.
Beato de Liébana, miniature del Beato de Fernando I y Sancha (Codice B.N. Madrid Vit. 14-2). Ed. Umberto Eco. Parma: Franco Maria Ricci, 1973.
Benedict. (*Regulae*). *The "Rule" of St. Benedict in Latin and English*. Ed. Timothy Fry. Collegeville, Minn.: Liturgical Press, 1980.
Bernard of Clairvaux. *Opera omnia*. Ed. Jean Leclercq, H. M. Rochais, and C. H. Talbot. 8 vols. Rome: Cistercienses, 1955-77.
Bersuire, Pierre. *Opera omnia*. 3 vols. Mainz, 1609.
Bestiario Valdese. Ed. Anna Maria Raugei. Biblioteca dell' "Archivum Romanicum", 175. Florence: Leo S. Olschki, 1984.
Boccaccio, Giovanni. *Amorosa visione*. Ed. Vittore Branca. Florence: G. C. Sansoni, 1944.
———. *Decameron*. Ed. Charles S. Singleton. Baltimore, Md.: Johns Hopkins University Press, 1974.
Boethius, Anicius. *Philosophia consolationis, libri quinque*. Ed. Karl Buchner. Heidelberg: Carl Winter, 1947.
Bradstreet, Anne. *The Complete Works of Anne Bradstreet*. Ed. Joseph R. McElrath, Jr., and Allan P. Robb. Boston: Twayne, 1981.
Brisebarre, Jean. *Li restor du paon*. Ed. Enid Donkin. Texts and Dissertations, 15. London: Modern Humanities Research Association, 1980.
Caesarius of Hiesterbach. *Dialogus miraculorum*. Ed. Joseph Strange. 2 vols. Cologne, 1851.
Cairosco de Figueroa, Bartolomé. *Definitiones poéticos, morales, y cristianas*. In *Poetas líricos de los siglos XVI y XVII*, ed. Adolfo de Castro, 2:449-99. Biblioteca de autores españoles, 51. 2 vols. Madrid, 1857.
Calvin, John. *Opera quae supersunt omnia*. Ed. Eduard Reuss, Eduard Cunitz, and Johann Wilhelm Baum. Corpus reformatorum, 29-87. 59 vols. In 26. Brunswick: C. A. Schwetschke, 1863-1900.
Cancionero de Juan Fernandez de Ixar. Ed. José María Azáceta. 2 vols. Madrid: Consejo superior de investigaciones científicas, 1966.
Cardano, Jerome. *De subtilitate libri XXI*. Paris: Michael Fezandet and Robert Granion, 1550.
Cassian, John. *Collationes*. Ed. Eugene Pichery. Sources chrétiennes, 42, 54, 64. 3 vols. Paris: Cerf, 1955-59.
Castiglione, Baldassare. *Lettere del conte Baldassare Castiglione*. 2 vols. Padua, 1769-71.
———. *Il libro del cortegiano*. Ed. Vittorio Cian. 4th ed. Florence: Sansoni, 1974.
Castigos é documentos del rey don Sancho. In *Escritores en prosa anteriores al siglo XV*, ed. Pascual de Gayangos, 79-228. Bibliotheca de autores españoles, 51. Madrid: Rivadeneyra, 1912.
Cataneo, P. *I quattri primi libri di architettura*. Venice, 1554.
Catherine of Siena. *Il dialogo della divina Provvidenza, ovvero Libro della divina dottrina*. Ed. Giuliana Cavallini. Testi cateriniani, 1. Rome: Cateriniane, 1968.

———. *Le lettere di s. Caterina da Siena*. Ed. Piero Misciattelli with Niccolò Tommasèo. 6 vols. Florence: C/E Giunti-G. Barbèra, 1970.
Cavalca, Domenico. *Mirall de la creu: Versió catalana del segle XV, per Pere Busquets*. Ed. Annamaria Gallina. Els nostres clàssics, collecció A, 95–96. 2 vols. Barcelona: Barcino, 1967.
Celano, Thomas de. *Vita I s. Francisci. Vita II s. Francisci*. In *Legendae s. Francisci assisiensis*. In *Analacta franciscana* 10 (1941):1–260.
Chaucer, Geoffrey. *The Complete Works of Geoffrey Chaucer*. Ed. Walter W. Skeat. 2d ed. Oxford, 1899.
———. *The Text of the "Canterbury Tales"*. Ed. John M. Manly and Edith Rickert. 7 vols. Chicago: University of Chicago Press, 1940.
Cicero. *Cato Maior, de senectute*. Ed. J. G. F. Powell. Cambridge: Cambridge University Press, 1988.
———. *De inventione*. In *De inventione, De optimo genere oratorum, Topica*. Ed. H. M. Hubbell. Cambridge, Mass.: Harvard University Press, 1976.
———. *De oratore*. Ed. Augustus S. Wilkins. In *Rhetorica*, vol. I. Oxford: Clarendon, 1902.
———. *Orationes*. Ed. Albert Curtius Clark. Oxford: Clarendon, 1909.
———. *Topica*. Ed. H. M. Hubbell. Cambridge, Mass.: Harvard University Press, 1949.
Dante Alighieri. *La "Commedia" secondo l'antica vulgata*. Ed. Georgio Petrocchi. 4 vols. Milan: Mondadori, 1966–68.
———. *Il convivio*. Ed. Maria Simonelli. Bologna: Riccardo Pàtron, 1966.
———. *De vulgari eloquentia*. Ed. Pier Giorgio Ricci. 3d ed. Florence: Felice Le Monnier, 1957.
———. *Vita nuova*. Milan: Riccardo Ricciardi, 1980.
The Dead Sea Scrolls in English. Trans. G. Vermes. Harmondsworth, England: Penguin, 1962.
Della Casa, Giovanni. *Galateo, overo de' costumi*. Ed. Emmanuela Scarpa. Ferrara: Franco Cosimo Panini, 1990.
Diego de Estella. *Libro de la vanidad del mundo*. Ed. Pio Sagües Azcona. Madrid: Aranzazu, 1980.
Diogenes Laertius. *Vitae philosophorum*. Ed. H. S. Long. 2 vols. Oxford: Clarendon, 1964.
Dionysius the Areopagite [pseud.]. *Hierarchia caelestia*. Ed. Günter Heil. Sources chrétiennes, 58. Paris: Cerf, 1958.
Donne, John. *The Anniversaries*. Ed. Frank Manley. Baltimore, Md.: Johns Hopkins University Press, 1963.
Du Bellay, Joachim. *Oeuvres complètes*. Ed. Leon Seche. 3 vols. Paris: Revue de la Renaissance, 1903–10.
Ebreo, Guglielmo da Pesaro. *De practica seu arte tripudii: On the Practice or Art of Dancing*. Ed. Barbara Sparti. Oxford: Clarendon, 1993.
Emblemata: Handbuch zur Sinnbildkunst des XVI. und XVII. Jahrhunderts. Ed. Arthur Henkel and Albrecht Schöne. Stuttgart: J. B. Metzler, 1967.
Enchiridion symbolorum definitionum et declarationum de rebus fidei et morum. Ed. Heinrich Denzinger. 36th ed. Barcelona: Herder, 1976.

Erasmus, Desiderius. *Opera omnia.* Ed. Johannes Clericus. 11 vols. Leiden, 1703–6.
———. *Opera omnia.* Amsterdam: North Holland, 1971–.
———. *Epistolae.* Ed. P. S. Allen, H. M. Allen, and H. W. Garrod. 12 vols. Oxford: Clarendon, 1906–58.
Eschenbach, Wolfram von. *Parzival: mittelhochdeutscher Text.* Ed. Karl Lachmann. 6th ed. Berlin: G. Reimer, 1926.
Evagrius Ponticus. (*Logos praktikos*). *Traité pratique, ou le moine.* Ed. Antoine Guillaumont and Claire Guillaumont. Sources chrétiennes, 170–71. 2 vols. Paris: Cerf, 1971.
———. *Les six centuries des "Kephalaia gnostica".* Ed. Antoine Guillaumont. Patrologia orientalis, 28. Paris: Firmin-Didot, 1958.
Fabri, Felix. *Evagatorium in terrae sanctae, Arabiae, et Egypti peregrinationem.* Ed. Konrad D. Hassler. 3 vols. Bibliothek des Literarischen Vereins in Stuttgart, 2–4. Stuttgart, 1843–49.
Farsit, Hugues. *Libellus de miraculis Beatae Mariae Virginis in urbe Suessionensi.* In *Patrologia latina* 179:1777–1800.
Fiore di virtù. Rome, 1740.
Francis of Assisi. *Opuscula.* Ed. Cajetan Esser. Rome: Collegium S. Bonaventurae at Quarrachi, 1978.
Francisco Imperial, Micer. *"El dezir a las syete virtudes" y otros poemas.* Ed. Colbert I. Nepaulsingh. Madrid: Espasa-Calpe, 1977.
———. "Edición crítica del *Dezir a las syete virtudes.*" Ed. Archer Woodford. In *Nueva revista de filología hispánica* 8 (1954):268–94.
García de Salazar, Lope. *Las bienandanzas e fortunas: Codice del siglo XV.* Ed. Angel Rodríguez Herrero. 4 vols. Bilbao: Diputación de Vizcaya, 1967.
Gawain and the Green Night: A New Critical Edition. Ed. Theodore Silverstein. Chicago: University of Chicago Press, 1984.
Gerson, Jean. *Oeuvres complètes.* Ed. Mgr. Glorieux. 10 vols. Paris: Desclée, 1960–75.
Gesner, Konrad. *Historiae animalium.* Frankfurt: Ioannes Wechel, 1585–86.
Gonzalo de Berceo. *El libro de Alixandre.* Ed. Dana Arthur Nelson. Biblioteca románica hispánica, 4.13. Madrid: Gredos, 1979.
La gran conquista de ultramar. Ed. Pascual de Gayangos. Biblioteca de autores españoles, 44. Madrid, 1858.
La gran conquista de ultramar: The Text and Concordances of Biblioteca Nacional Manuscript 1187. Ed. Franklin M. Wallman and Louis Cooper. Spanish series, 22. Madison, Wis.: Hispanic Seminary of Medieval Studies, 1985.
Gregory of Nyssa. (*Vita Macrinae*). *La vie de saint Macrine.* Ed. Pierre Maraval. Sources chrétiennes, 178. Paris: Cerf, 1971.
Gregory the Great. *Dialogues.* Ed. Adalbert de Vogüé. 3 vols. Sources chrétiennes, 251, 260, 265. Paris: Cerf, 1978–80.
———. *Moralia in Iob.* Ed. Mark Adriaen. Corpus christianorum series latina, 143, 143a, 143b. 3 vols. Turnhout: Brepols, 1979–85.
———. *Registrum epistularum.* Ed. Dag Norberg. Corpus christianorum series latina, 140A. Turnhout: Brepols, 1982.

———. *XL homiliarum in evangelia.* In *Patrologia latina* 76:1075–1312.
Grosseteste, Robert. *"Le chateau d'amour" de Robert Grossetesste, évêque de Lincoln.* Ed. J. Murray. Paris: Champion, 1918.
Guazzo, Stefano. *La civil conversatione.* Vinegia: Salicato, 1584.
Guerrero, Francisco. *El viaje de Hierusalem (Seville, 1592).* Ed. R. P. Calcroft. Exeter: University of Exeter Press, 1984.
Guevara, Antonio de. *Libro aureo de Marco aurelio emperador y eloquentissimo orador.* Seville: Jacobo Cronberger Alemán, 1528.
Guicciardini, Francesco. *Opere.* Ed. Vittorio di Caprariis. Storie e testi, 30. Milan: Riccardo Ricciardi, 1961.
Guide du pèlerin de Saint-Jacques de Compostela. Ed. Jeanne Viellard. 4th ed. Mâcon: Protat Frères, 1938.
Guillaume de Deguileville. *"Le pèlerinage de vie humaine" de Guillaume de Deguileville.* London, 1893.
———. *"El pelerinage de la vida humana:* A Study and Edition". Ed. Maryjane Dunn-Wood. Ph.D. diss., University of Pennsylvania, 1985.
———. *The Pilgrimage of the Life of Man.* Trans. John Lydgate. Ed. F. J. Furnivall. Early English Text Society, 77. London: Kegan Paul, Trench, Trübner, 1905.
Heraclitus. *(Reliquiae). The Cosmic Fragments.* Ed. G. S. Kirk. Cambridge: Cambridge University Press, 1954.
Herodotus. *Historiae.* Ed. Carl Hude. Oxford: Clarendon, 1908.
Herrad of Hohenbourg. *Hortus deliciarum.* Ed. Rosalie Green et al. Studies of the Warburg Institute, 36. 2 vols. London: Warburg Institute, 1979.
Hesiod. *(Theogonia). Theogony.* Ed. M. L. West. Oxford: Clarendon, 1966.
Hildegard of Bingen. *Scivias.* Ed. Adelgundis Führkötter and Angela Carlevaris. Corpus chrisitanorum continuatio mediaevalia, 43–43A. 2 vols. Turnhout: Brepols, 1978.
Hilton, Walter. *Qui habitat.* In *Minor Works of Walter Hilton,* ed. Dorothy Jones, 113–68. London: Burns Oates and Washbourne, [1929].
———. *The Scale of Perfection.* Ed. Evelyn Underhill. London: John M. Watkins, 1948.
Historia de la linda Melosina: Edition, Study, and Notes. Ed. Ivy A. Corfis. Madison, Wis.: Hispanic Seminary of Medieval Studies, 1986.
Historia monachorum in Aegypto. Ed. A. J. Festugière. Subsidia hagiographica, 34. Brussels: Société des Bollandistes, 1961.
Homer. *Opera.* Ed. David B. Monro and Thomas W. Allen. 4 Vols. 2d and 3d eds. Oxford: Clarendon, 1919–20.
Horace. *Opera.* Ed. Edward C. Wickham and H. W. Garrod. 2d ed. Oxford: Clarendon, 1912.
———. *(Ars poetica). Horace on Poetry: The "Ars poetica".* Ed. C. O. Brink. Cambridge: Cambridge University Press, 1971.
Hugh of St. Cher. *Opera omnia in universum Vetus et Novum Testamentum.* 8 vols. Venice, 1703.
Huon de Meri. *Le Torneiment Antichrist.* Ed. Margaret O. Bender. Rev. ed. Romance Monographs, 17. University, Miss.: Romance Monographs, 1976.

Isidore of Seville. *Etymologiarum* [libri]. Ed. W. M. Lindsay. 2 vols. Oxford: Clarendon, 1911.
Jacopone da Todi. *Laude*. Ed. Franco Mancini. Rome: Giuseppe Laterza, 1974.
Jerome. *Commentariorum in Amos prophetam libri tres*. In *Opera, pars exegetica I/6*. Ed. Mark Adriaen. Corpus christianorum series latina, 76. Turnhout: Brepols, 1969.
———. *(Epistolae). Lettres*. Ed. Jerome Labourt. 6 vols. Paris: Belles lettres, 1949–58.
———. *Liber contra Vigilantium*. In *Patrologia latina* 23:339–52.
———. *Tractatus sive homiliae in psalmos, in Marci evangelium aliaque varia argumenta*. Ed. Germain Morin. Corpus christianorum series latina, 78. Turnhout: Brepols, 1958.
John of Garland. *Integumenta Ovidii: Poematto inedito del secolo XIII*. Ed. Fausto Ghisalberti. Messina: Giuseppe Principato, 1933.
John of Salisbury. *Policratici, sive, De nugis curialium et vestigiis philosophorum*. Ed. Clemens C. I. Webb. Oxford: Clarendon, 1909.
Juan de la Cruz. *Obras de san Juan de la cruz*. Ed. Silverio de santa Teresa. Biblioteca mística carmelitana, 10–14. 5 vols. Burgos: Monte Carmelo, 1929–51.
Juvenal. *Saturae*. Ed. J. D. Duff. Cambridge: Cambridge University Press, 1925.
Kempe, Margery. *The Book of Margery Kempe*. Ed. Sanford Brown Meech and Hope Emily Allen. Early English Text Society, 212. London: Oxford University Press, 1940.
———. *The Book of Margery Kempe 1436: A Modern Version*. Ed. W. Butler-Bowdon. London: Jonathan Cape, 1936.
Langland, William. *The Vision of Piers Plowman*. Ed. A. V. C. Schmidt. New York: E. P. Dutton, 1978.
Le lapidaire du quatorzième siècle. Ed. Is. del Sotto. Vienna, 1862.
Les lapidaires français du moyen âge des XIIe, XIIIe, et XIVe siècles. Ed. Léopold Pannier. Paris, 1882.
Latini, Brunetto. *Li livres du tresor*. Ed. Francis J. Carmody. University of California Publications in Modern Philology, 22. Berkeley and Los Angeles: University of California Press, 1948.
———. *Il tesoretto*. Ed. Julia Bolton Holloway. Garland Library of Medieval Literature, 2/A. New York: Garland, 1981.
Lena, Pedro Rodriguez de. *El passo honroso de Suero de Quinones*. Studien zur phantastischen Literatur, 2. Madrid: Fundación universitaria española, 1977.
Leonardo da Vinci. *Leonardo da Vinci's "Paragone": A Critical Interpretation with a New Edition of the Text in the Codex urbinus*. Ed. Claire J. Farago. Studies in Intellectual History, 25. Leiden: E. J. Brill, 1992.
———. *The Literary Works of Leonardo da Vinci*. Ed. Jean Paul Richter. 3d ed. 2 vols. London: Phaidon, 1970.
———. *The Notebooks of Leonardo da Vinci*. Ed. Jean Paul Richter. 2 vols. New York: Dover, 1970.
Letterae quadrimestres. 7 vols. Madrid: Augustinus Avrial, 1894–97. Madrid: Ibérica, 1920, 1925. Rome: A. Macioce & Pisani, 1932.

Liber s. Jacobi, codex Calixtinus. Ed. Walter Muir Whitehill. Santiago de Compostela: n.p., 1944.
Livy. *Ab urbe condita libri*. Ed. W. Wisenborn and M. Mueller. 10 vols. Berlin, 1873–88.
Lletres de batalla, cartells de deseiximents, i capitols de passos d'armes. Ed. Martin de Riquer. Els nostres classics, col. leccio A, 90, 98–99. 3 vols. Barcelona: Barcino, 1963–68.
Lombard, Peter. *Sententiae in IV libris distinctae*. 3d ed. 2 vols. Grottaferata: College of St. Bonaventure at Claras Aquas, 1971–81.
Longinus, Pseudo-. *Libellus de sublimitate*. Ed. D. A. Russell. Oxford: Clarendon, 1968.
Longuyon, Jacques de. *Les voeux du paon*. In John Barbour, *The Buik of Alexander*. Ed. R. L. Graeme Ritchie. Scottish Text Society, n.s., 12, 17, 21, 25. 4 vols. Edinburgh: William Blackwood for the Society, 1921–29.
López de Ayala, Pero. *Rimado de palacio*. Ed. Germán Orduna. Callana di testi e studi ispanici, 1, testi critici, 1. 2 vols. Pisa: Giardini, 1981.
Lorris, Guillaume de, and Jean de Meun. *Le "Roman de la rose" par Guillaume de Lorris et Jean de Meun*. Ed. Felix Lecoy. 3 vols. Paris: Champion, 1966–75.
Lucretius. *De rerum natura*. Ed. Cyril Bailey. 3 vols. Oxford: Clarendon, 1947.
Luis de Granada. *Guía de pecadores*. Ed. M. Martinez Burgos. Madrid: Espasa-Colpe, 1966.
Lull, Ramon. *Obres*. Ed. M. Obrador y Bennassar et al. 21 vols. Palma de Mallorca: Comissió editora lulliana, 1906–50.
———. *Libre de meravelles*. Ed. Salvador Golmés. 4 vols. Els nostres classics, col. lectio A, 34, 38, 42, 46–47. Barcelona: Barcino, 1931–34.
Luther, Martin. *Werke*. 58 vols. 1883. Reprint, Graz: Akademische, 1964–.
———. *De servo arbitrio*. In *Luthers Werke in Auswahl*, ed. Otto Clemen, 4:94–293. 6 vols. Berlin: Walter de Gruyter, 1960.
Mandeville, John. *Mandeville's Travels*. Ed. M. C. Seymour. Oxford: Clarendon, 1967.
Map, Walter. *De nugis curialium, Courtiers' Trifles*. Ed. M. R. James, rev. C. N. L. Brooke and R. A. B. Mynors. Oxford: Clarendon, 1983.
María de santo Domingo. *"Libro de la oración" de sor María de santo Domingo*. Ed. José Manuel Blecua. Madrid: Hauser y Menet, 1948.
La más antigua historia de Aranzazu (1648). Ed. Luis Villasante. Vitoria: n.p., 1966. Reprint from *Scriptorium victoriense* 12 (1965):74–173.
Mechthild von Magdeburg. *Offenbarung der Schwester Mechthild von Magdeburg, oder das fliessende Licht der Gottheit*. Ed. Gall Morel. Regensburg, 1869.
Mena, Juan de. *"Coplas de los siete pecados mortales", and First Continuation*. Ed. Gladys M. Rivera. Madrid: J. Porrua Turanzas, 1982.
Monumenta paedagogica societatis Iesu. Ed. Ladislaus Lukacs. Monumenta historica societatis Iesu, 92, 107. 2 vols. Rome: Institutum historicum societatis Iesu, 1965–74.
Morgival, Nicole de. *Le dit de la "Panthère d'amours"*. Ed. Henry A. Todd. Paris, 1883.

Mote, Jean de la. *Le parfait du paon*. Ed. Richard J. Cary. University of North Carolina Studies in the Romance Languages and Literatures, 118. Chapel Hill: University of North Carolina Press, 1972.
Nebrija, Antonio de. *Vocabulario de romance en latin: Transcripción crítica de la edición revisada por el autor (Sevilla, 1516)*. Ed. Gerald J. Macdonald. Philadelphia: Temple University Press, 1973.
Neckham, Alexander. *De naturis rerum*. Ed. Thomas Wright. London, 1863.
La "Nef des folles"—"Stultiferae naves" de Josse Bade. Reprint of 1st ed. Ed. Odette Sauvage. Grenoble: n.p., 1979.
Origen. *In Matthaeum*. Ed. Erich Klostermann. Griechischen christlichen Schriftsteller, 40. Leipzig: J. C. Hinrichs, 1935.
Ovid. *Metamorphoses*. Ed. O. Korn and H. J. Müller. 2 vols. In 1. Berlin: Weidmann, 1915–16.
Ovide moralisé. Ed. C. De Boer. 5 vols. Amsterdam: J. Müller, 1915–38.
Palladius. *The Lausiac History*. Ed. Cuthbert Butler. 2 vols in 1. Cambridge: Cambridge University Press, 1898–1904.
Paré, Ambroise. *De monstres et prodiges*. Ed. Jean Céard. Travaux d'humanisme et Renaissance, 115. Geneva: Droz, 1971.
(*Pastor Hermae*). *Das Hirt des Hermas*. Ed. Molly Whittaker. Griechischen christlichen Schriftsteller der ersten Jahrhunderts, 48. Berlin: Akademie, 1956.
Patrologiae cursus completus, series graeca. Ed. J.-P. Migne. 161 vols. Paris: Garnier, 1857–1912.
Patrologiae cursus completus, series latina. Ed. J.-P. Migne. 221 vols. Paris, 1800–75.
Peter the Venerable. *De miraculis libri duo*. Ed. Denise Bouthillier. Corpus christianorum continuatio mediaevalis, 83. Turnhout: Brepols, 1988.
Petrarca, Francesco. *Africa*. Ed. Nicola Festa. Edizione nazionale, 1. Florence: G. C. Sansoni, 1926.
———. *De secreto conflictu mearum curarum*. In *Prose*, ed. Guido Martellotti et al., 22–214. Milan: Riccardo Ricciardi, 1955.
———. *Le familiari*. Ed. V. Rossi and Umberto Bosco. Edizione nazionale, 10–13. 4 vols. Florence: Sansoni, 1933–42.
———. (*Rime sparse*). *Petrarch's Lyric Poems: "The Rime sparse" and Other Lyrics*. Ed. Robert M. Durling. Cambridge, Mass.: Harvard University Press, 1976.
———. (*Trionfi*). In *Rime, Trionfi, e Poesie latine*, ed. F. Neri et al., 481–578. Milan: Riccardo Ricciardi, 1951.
Petrus Alfonsi. *Die "Disciplina clericalis" des Petrus Alfonsi*. Ed. Alfons Hilka and Werner Soderhjelm. Heidelberg: Carl Winter's Universität, 1911.
Piacenza, Domenico. *De arte saltandi et choreas discendi*. Paris, B.N., Fonds it. 972.
Piccolomini, Alessandro. *Dialogo de la bella creanza de le donne*. In *Trattati del cinquecento sulla donna*, ed. Giuseppe Zonta, 3–69. Bari: Giuseppe Laterza & Figli, 1913.
Pico della Mirandola, Giovanni. *Opera omnia*. Ed. Eugenio Garin. 2 vols. Turin: Bottega d'Erasmo, 1970.

Plato. *Opera*. Ed. Ioannes Burnet. 5 vols. Oxford: Clarendon, 1900–1907.
Plautus, Titus. *Miles gloriosus*. Ed. Mason Hammond. Cambridge, Mass.: Harvard University Press, 1963.
Pliny. *Naturalis historia*. Ed. H. Rackham, W. S. Jones, and D. E. Eichholz. 10 vols. Cambridge, Mass.: Harvard University Press, 1938–42.
Plotinus. *Enneades*. Ed. Paul Henry and Hans-Rudolf Schwyzer. 3 vols. Brussels: Universelle, 1951–73.
Polanco, Juan de. *Chronicon*. Vol. 5. Madrid, 1897.
Prudentius. *Psychomachia*. In *Prudentius*, 1. Ed. H. J. Thomson. 2 vols. Cambridge, Mass.: Harvard University Press, 1949.
Quintilian. *Institutiones oratoriae*. Ed. Michael Winterbottom. 4 vols. Oxford: Clarendon, 1970.
Raoul de Houdence. *"Le songe d'enfer" suivi de la "Voie du paradis"*. Ed. Philéas Lebergue. 1908. Reprint, Geneva: Slatkine, 1974.
Raymond of Capua. *Vita s. Catharinae Senensis*. In *Acta sanctorum*. Ed. Joanne Carnandet. New ed. Vol. 12, 862–967. Paris, 1866.
Rhetorica ad C. Herennium. Ed. Gualterio Calboli. Bologna: Riccardo Pàtron, 1969.
Ribadeneira, Pedro de. *Catalogus scriptorum religionis societatis Iesu*. Antwerp: Io. Moreti, 1613.
———. *Vita nuova*. Ed. Domenico De Robertis. Milan: Riccardo Ricciardi, 1980.
Richard de Fournival. *"Li bestiaires d'amours" di maistre Richart de Fourneval e "li response du bestiaire"*. Ed. Cesare Segre. Documenti di filologia, 2. Milan: n.p., 1957.
Richard of St.Laurent. *De laudibus sanctae Mariae*. Inter Albertus Magnus, *Opera*, 36. Ed. Augustus and Aemilius Borgnet. 38 vols. Paris, 1898.
Richard of St. Victor. *Benjamin minor*. *In Apocalypsim Joannis libri*. In *Patrologia latina* 196:1–64, 683–888.
Ripa, Cesare. *Iconologia, overo descrittione di diverse imagini cavate dall'antivchità, e di propria inventione*. 1603. Reprint, Hildesheim: Georg Olms, 1970.
Rodríguez de Montalvo, Garci. *Amadís de Gaula*. Ed. Juan Manuel Cacho Blecua. 2 vols. Madrid: Catedra, 1987.
Rolle, Richard. *The "Incendium amoris" of Richard Rolle of Hampole*. Ed. Margaret Deanesley. Manchester: Manchester University Press, 1915.
———. Transcript of Cotton Titus C.XIX, fols. 92b-117b. Appendix B of Mary Felicitas Madigan, *The "Passio Domini" Theme in the Works of Richard Rolle: His Personal Contribution and its Religious, Cultural, and Literary Context*. Elizabethan and Renaissance Studies, 79. Salzburg: Institut für Englische Sprache und Literatur, 1978.
Ronsard, Pierre de. *Oeuvres complètes*. Ed. Gustave Cohen. Paris: Gallimard, 1950.
Rovere, Francesco della [Pope Sixtus IV]. *L'orazione della Immacolata*. Ed. Dino Cortese. Padua: Centro studi antoniani, 1985.
Ruiz, Juan. *Libro de buen amor*. Ed. Manuel Criado de Val and Eric W. Naylor.

Classicos hispanicos, 2.9. Madrid: Consejo superior de investigaciones cientificas, 1972.
Salutati, Coluccio. *De seculo et religione*. Nuova collezione di testi umanistica inediti o rari, 12. Florence: Leo S. Olschki, 1957.
Salvian. (*Epistolae*). *Oeuvres*, vol. 1, *Les lettres, Les livres de Timothée à l'église*. Ed. Georges Lagarrigue. Sources chrétiennes, 176, 220. 2 vols. Paris: Cerf, 1971-75.
Sanchez de Vercial, Climente. *Libro de los exenplos por A. B. C.* Ed. John Esten Keller. Madrid: Consejo superior de investigaciones científicas, 1961.
Seneca. *Opera quae supersunt*. Ed. Friedrich Haase. 3 vols. In 2. Leipzig, 1852-53.
———. *Naturales quaestiones*. Ed. Thomas H. Corcoran. 2 vols. Cambridge, Mass.: Harvard University Press, 1971-72.
Seuse, Heinrich. *Büchlein der ewigen Weisheit*. Ed. Georg Hofmann. Deutsche mystische Schriften, 1. Düsseldorf: Patmos, 1966.
Sextus Empiricus. *Opera*. Ed. Hermann Mutschman, rev. Jürgen Mau and Karl Janácek. Leipzig: B. G. Teubner, 1958-62.
Le songe du castel. Ed. Roberta D. Cornelius. In *Publications of the Modern Language Association* 46 (1931):321-32.
Soranus. *Gynaeciorum libri IV, De signis fracturarum, De fasciis, Vita Hippocratis secundum Soranum*. Ed. Johannes Iberg. Corpus medicorum graecorum, 4. Leipzig: B. G. Teubner, 1927.
Southwell, Robert, S.J. *Marie Magdalens Funeral Teares*. Delmar, N.Y.: Scholars' Facsimiles & Reprints, 1975.
Sulpicius Severus. (*Vita s. Martini*). *Vie de saint Martin*. Ed. Jacques Fontaine. 3 vols. Sources chrétiennes, 133, 134, 135. Paris: Cerf, 1967-69.
Teresa of Avila. *Libro de la vida*. In *Obras completas*, ed. Otger Steggink and Efren de la Madre de Dios, 28-89. 2d rev. ed. Madrid: Biblioteca de autores cristianos, 1967.
Theodolphe d'Orleans. *De ordine baptismi*. In *Patrologia latina* 105:223-40.
Thesaurus palaeohibernicus. Ed. Whitley Stokes and John Strachan. 2 vols. Cambridge: Cambridge University Press, 1901-3.
"*A Treatis of Discrescyon of Spirites*" and "*A Pistle of Discrecioun of Stirrings*". In "*Deonise Hid Divinite*" *and Other Treatises on Contemplative Prayer Related to "The Cloud of Unknowing"*. Ed. Phyllis Hodgson. London: Early English Text Society, 1955.
Vergil. *Opera*. Ed. R. A. B. Mynors. Rev. ed. Oxford: Clarendon, 1954.
Vita Antonii. In *Patrologia graeca*, 26:835-978.
Vita Danieli. In Ignazio Guidi, "Vie et récits de l'abbé Daniel, de Scété (VIe siècle): Texte copte publié et traduit", *Revue de l'orient chrétien* 5 (1900).
La voie d'enfer et de paradis: An Unpublished Poem of the Fourteenth Century. Ed. M. Aquiline Pety. Washington, D.C.: Catholic University of America Press, 1940.
Volucraires. Ed. Hartmut Kleinedam. In *Zeitschrift für romanische Philologie* 86 (1970):1-21.
Voragine, Jacob de. *Legenda aurea*. Ed. Th. Graesse. 2d ed. Leipzig, 1850.

Whiterig, John. *The Monk of Farne: The Meditations of a Fourteenth-Century Monk*. Ed. Hugh Farmer. London: Darton, 1961.
Xenophon. *Memorabilia*. Ed. Carl Hude. Leipzig: B. G. Teubner, 1934.
Zarathustra. *The Hymns of Zarathustra*. Trans. Jacques Duchesne-Guillemin and M. Henning. Boston: Beacon, 1963.

Index of Subjects

abstinence, 37, 50, 75–76, 84. *See also* fasting
affectivity, 37–38, 40, 85, 87, 90, 148
agonism, 25, 32, 38, 40, 41, 58, 59, 62, 64, 78, 91, 145
Alcalá de Henares, University of, 168
Amazons, 47
animal, 9, 45, 53–54, 63, 77, 108, 109, 110, 116, 120, 121, 123, 139, 158, 162, 180, 181
anonymous works: *Ancrene Riwle*, 246 n. 75; *Cloud of Unknowing*, 126; *Cursor mundi*, 192 n. 110; *Emblemata*, 231 n. 137; *Fiore di virtù*, 123–24; *La gran conquista de Ultramar*, 213–14 n. 175; *Guide du pèlerin de Saint-Jacques de Compostela*, 107; *Historia monachorum in Aegypto*, 200 n. 122; *Liber s. Jacobi*, 145, 159; *Pastor Hermae*, 38; *Poema de mío Cid*, 189 n. 55; *Physiologus*, 117; *Rhetorica ad C. Herennium*, 189 nn. 44, 45; 198 n. 49; *Salernitan Questions*, 45; *Songe du castel*, 32; *Speculum perfectionis*, 178; *Testament of the Twelve Patriarchs*, 120; *Vita Danieli*, 210 n. 119; *Volucraires*, 227 n. 85
antithesis, 116, 141–42, 146, 173
Aránzazu, 54–55, 59
assumption, 41–42, 134, 175
autobiography, 1–3
avarice, 159–60, 119, 161

Basques, 24, 25, 60, 61, 63, 91, 107, 110–111, 113

begging, 29, 69, 156–60, 161, 162–63
Benedictine rule, 19, 88
bestiary, 116, 117, 140
blood, 63, 92, 93, 130–31, 133, 176. *See also* purity of blood
bridge, 161–62
Burgos, 50–51, 55, 56–57

caballero, 67, 170
capital vices, 84, 110, 117, 119–21, 154, 159
Carthusians, 50–51
castle, 32, 41
cell, 77–78
chastity, 39, 41–42, 45, 47, 59, 60–61, 75, 92, 140, 176
cherubim, 102–4, 106, 107, 111, 115, 116, 126, 176
chivalry, 23, 26, 27, 31–32, 33, 34, 36, 37, 61, 62, 64, 66–67, 83, 114–15, 138, 145
choice of Hercules, 2, 24, 25, 59, 63, 83, 86, 129, 139
circumcision, 63, 176
clarity, 5–7, 8, 10, 21, 25–26, 33–34, 101, 136, 142, 175–76
clothing, 65, 66, 67, 68, 71–72, 73–75, 113, 114, 122, 123, 129, 170–71
color, 6, 10, 94, 101, 109, 110, 111, 117–18, 141–444
comedy, 11, 22, 24, 48, 149
composition, 9, 10
confession, sacramental, 24, 28, 30, 58, 65–66, 76–77, 84, 85, 87–88, 89–90, 91, 120, 167

Constitutiones, 12, 18, 19, 20, 21, 64, 73, 83, 158, 171, 177–78, 181
convert, 61, 62, 64, 174, 177
courtesy, 14, 18–21, 26, 31–32, 71–72, 143, 150, 172
crucifix and crucifixion, 85–86, 101, 109, 129, 130–31, 135, 140, 142, 143, 144, 164, 176
curiosity, 19, 89, 97, 141, 155–56, 160, 167, 168

dance, 32, 57–59, 145
date, 22, 55, 59, 85
delay, 5, 11–12, 13–14, 15, 16, 17, 50
devil, 37, 43, 52, 58, 76, 81, 82, 84, 104–6, 108–10, 111, 116, 118, 120, 123, 124–26, 130, 133, 135, 141, 143, 145, 146, 154, 160, 163, 180, 181
diary, 92, 129, 176, 182
discernment of spirits, 36–38, 58, 63, 69, 76, 84, 101, 108, 109–10, 116, 126, 127, 135, 139–40, 143, 145, 168
Dominicans, 64, 77, 87, 92, 96, 133, 134, 171, 174
dream, 39, 40, 95, 153

epideictic rhetoric, 1, 3, 17, 22, 39, 70, 78, 95, 145, 148, 151, 170, 173, 174, 177, 178, 184
Espinosa de los Monteros, 55
Essenes, 38
Eucharist, 92, 93
Exercitia spiritualia, 3, 9–11, 19, 40, 45, 93, 119, 120, 159, 160, 166, 167, 171, 173, 176, 177, 178, 180, 181, 182, 183

facility, 177, 182–83
fame, 1, 7, 27–28, 32, 67, 69, 83, 90, 114, 124, 138, 158, 168–69, 172, 173
family, 51–53, 54, 59, 61, 67
fasting, 75, 83–84, 126, 171
flying serpent, 100–1, 110–11, 121, 141, 181, 182. *See also* peacock
fool, 127, 141, 173, 183
fortune, 64

garden, 5, 17, 25, 48, 57, 112, 118, 128, 134, 152–53
gesture, 18, 19–21, 28, 31–32, 46, 53, 58–59, 68, 80–81, 145–46
Gesù, the, 93, 135, 176
glory, 27–28, 30, 41–41, 50, 102, 106, 112, 121–23, 128, 138, 139, 140, 141, 163, 169, 176–77, 181
guide, 40–41, 100, 97–98, 153, 165

hagiography, 3, 7, 13, 16, 33, 35–36, 39, 41, 44–45, 47, 48, 49, 52, 66–67, 68, 69–70, 75, 78–79, 83, 95–96, 97, 108, 135, 145, 157, 158, 160, 169, 172, 174, 175, 183–84
hair, 70–73
honor, 22, 26–27, 60–61, 62–63, 64, 67, 71–72, 74, 85, 87, 90–91, 122, 123, 138, 146, 149, 159, 160–61, 169, 173, 174–75
humility, 19, 88–89, 122, 141, 159, 173

illusion, 98–99, 127, 128–29, 136, 140, 143
illustration, 99, 101, 130, 134, 136–37, 139
image, 39–40, 45–46, 54–55, 57, 59–60, 85, 139, 156
imagery, 8
imagination, 33–34, 35, 36, 37, 38, 39, 40, 45–46, 153, 158, 178
imitation, 4–5, 7, 8, 14, 35, 36, 37, 38, 74, 95, 130, 133–34, 136, 139, 148, 150, 158, 165–67, 170
immaculate conception, 41, 56, 57, 58, 60, 63, 92–93, 134
infamy, 72, 81, 90, 98–99, 157, 159, 173, 174
Inquisition, 33, 40, 62, 69, 96, 171, 172, 173–75
introduction, 14–19
invention, 9, 10
irony, 98–99, 141, 163
Islam, 61, 105, 112

Jerusalem, 37, 38, 50–51, 53, 74, 148, 149, 155, 164–67, 179
Jesuits. *See* Society of Jesus
Jesuit Rule. *See Constitutiones*
Jews, 131
John the Baptist, feast of, 28, 29, 58
Judaism, 105

lameness, 28–33, 42–44, 47, 51, 54, 59, 70
Las Machorras, 56
law, 61, 71–72, 90, 99, 146, 173
light, 38–39, 47, 93–94, 100, 125, 129, 130, 135–35, 142, 143–44, 160, 161, 179
literacy, 7, 33, 47–49, 89, 131, 133, 134, 135, 140, 168, 180–81

Manresa, 59, 67, 69, 99–101, 110, 150
manuscript illuminations, 68, 103–5, 112, 131, 135, 169
martyrdom, 29, 30–31, 93, 122, 176, 177

memory, 2, 4, 7–10, 12–13, 15, 18, 19, 29, 34, 48, 59, 65, 84, 89, 93, 99, 123, 145, 148, 150, 168, 169, 170, 175
military and military imagery, 22, 23–24, 25–27, 29, 32–33, 51, 58, 91, 95, 113, 145, 160, 172, 181
mirror, 1, 2, 4, 16, 17, 24, 33, 72, 117, 121, 127, 130–31, 132, 137, 139, 140, 141, 144, 148, 183. *See also* water
modesty, 15–16, 17, 19, 21, 72
Montserrat, 65, 67
Mount of Olives, 165–66, 167
multicephalism, 105, 107
Muses, 41, 101
Muslims, 61, 62

name, 147–50, 168, 176
Neoplatonism, 17, 94, 109, 151, 163
nominalism, 49–50, 109

ocular motif, 102–8, 111, 117, 124, 126, 135, 140, 168–69, 181
orality, 7

painting, 6, 10, 11, 73, 135–36, 142, 143–44, 183
paintings, 2, 39–40, 59, 68, 81, 85–86, 87, 93, 111, 112, 115, 126–27, 135, 167, 176–77
Pamplona, 2, 22, 24, 25, 28, 44, 62, 112, 174
papacy, 24, 28, 62, 114, 153, 174, 177, 178, 179, 180
Paris, University of, 49–50, 59, 113–14, 158, 168
peacock, 31, 111–20, 121, 123–24, 126–27, 129–30, 135, 136, 139–41, 143, 145, 163, 168, 170, 176, 180, 181
penance, 37, 38, 50, 51, 70, 90, 95, 167, 171
perpetual virginity, 60, 61, 62, 63, 92, 134
perspective, 143–44
pilgrim and pilgrimage, 9, 10, 24, 25, 28, 32, 38, 53, 55, 56, 59, 60, 66, 70, 74, 141, 144–45, 146, 148, 149, 150–53, 155–56, 157, 158, 161–62, 163–65, 171, 173, 175, 178, 183
pinnacle, 77–78, 79, 82–83, 171
place, 7–10, 32, 88–89, 137, 150, 161, 176, 178, 181–82
Pléiade poetry, 179
pride, 81–82, 119, 120–21, 122, 128, 130, 140, 141
prudence, 1, 8, 24, 89, 95, 125, 140, 159, 164, 173, 180–81
purity of blood, 62–63, 64, 91–93, 174–75, 176

Pythagorean Y, 86

Qurān, 61

rape, 60, 128, 160–61
Ripoll bible, 151
romance literature, 9–10, 27, 28, 34–35, 41, 61, 62, 64–65, 114, 138–39, 149, 151, 160, 173
Rome, 2, 28, 59, 148, 150, 155, 174, 179–80

S. Maria Maggiore, 56, 134–35, 179
Santiago da Compostela, 25, 30, 60, 148, 153
scrupulosity, 66, 76–77, 78, 79, 80, 82, 83–84, 85, 86, 87, 156
sexuality, 41, 42–43, 44–47, 60–61, 96
sloth, 11, 79–80, 84, 124
Society of Jesus, 1, 3, 12, 16, 24, 28, 43, 54, 57, 63, 64, 89, 90, 91–93, 120, 153, 158, 169, 170, 174, 176, 177, 179, 180, 181, 182. See also *Constitutiones*
Spiritual Exercises, 158, 168
stargazing, 49–50, 81–82, 153, 132, 136, 180
Stoicism, 30, 72
stylite, 78
suicide, 80–81
sun, 25, 117, 125, 131, 136, 137, 143, 177, 178–80
surgery, 28, 29, 30

tears, 14–15, 17–18, 29, 66, 67, 68–69, 85, 87, 89, 90, 91, 129, 167, 177, 182
temptations, three, 51–52, 82–83, 141, 156
tetramorph, 102–3, 104, 107–8, 135, 169, 176
travel, 2, 8–10, 23–24, 53, 60, 64, 149, 152, 154, 155–57, 159, 160–62, 164, 170, 172
Trinity, 85–86, 88, 90, 91, 92, 93, 94, 105, 145, 150, 177
troubadour poetry, 23, 27, 34, 36

vainglory, 14–15, 16, 17, 19, 21, 22, 24–25, 26, 30, 31, 32, 36, 38, 50, 51, 67–68, 69, 71, 72, 74, 78–79, 82, 95, 96, 97, 98, 120, 121–24, 128–29, 132, 139, 140, 141, 145, 146, 147, 148, 149, 154–55, 156, 159, 163, 168, 170, 171, 172–73, 174, 180, 182
vision, 6, 17–19, 20–21, 40, 45, 83, 100, 102, 123, 127, 129, 130, 136, 140, 141, 144, 160, 180. *See also* ocular motif

visionary literature, 40–41, 62, 102, 123, 128, 138, 141, 151–52, 153, 155, 162–63
visions, 25, 39, 46, 84–85, 93–95, 96, 97, 98, 100–101, 119, 136, 140, 142, 158, 164, 169, 175–76, 177, 178, 179, 180
visuality, 6, 7, 8, 9, 10

water, 29, 43, 94, 100, 101–2, 107, 127, 129, 130, 133, 136, 137–39, 144, 161, 163–64, 180
wild man, 54, 70, 170
woman, 60–61, 71, 72, 75, 92, 95–97, 137–38, 150, 160–61

youth, 5, 22–24

Zoroastrianism, 38

Index of Persons

Achilles, 25, 37
Adam, 19, 43, 44, 82, 100, 124, 151, 152, 155, 163
Aelian, 193 n. 122, 229 n. 111
Aeneas, 43, 86
Alain de Lille, 115, 148, 153, 221 n. 22
Albert the Great, 45, 92, 111, 117, 118, 168
Alberti, Leon Battista, 10, 46, 142, 143, 183
Aldrovandi, Ulisse, 110, 111, 117–19
Alexander the Great, 114, 120–21
Alfonso X, 42, 53–54, 90, 98–99
Altdorfer, Albrecht, 81
Ambrose, 178
Angela of Foligno, 131
Anthony, Abbot, 44, 48, 70, 108, 109, 160, 253 n. 205
Anthony of Padua, 118
Apollo, 101, 131, 179, 180
Apuleius, 214 n. 185
Argos, 6, 108, 111
Ariosto, Ludovico, 152
Aristotle, 14, 44, 83, 92, 117, 139, 141–42, 183, 250 n. 158
Aristotle, Pseudo-, 142
Arnulf d'Orleans, 128
Athanasius, 225 n. 60
Augustine, 1–2, 3, 11, 17, 23, 27, 28, 30, 34, 35, 36, 42, 45, 46, 48, 50, 69, 72–73, 77–78, 82, 94, 106, 110, 112, 122, 124, 130, 131, 139, 139–40, 141, 151, 154, 155, 161, 163–64, 184

Baal, 102
Bade, Josse, 119
Barbara, Saint, 113–14
Bellay, Joachim du, 102, 163
Benedict, 119
Benning, Simon, 112
Benvenuto di Giovanni, 115
Berceo, Gonzalo de, 120–21
Bermejo, Bartolomé, 86, 103, 105, 210 n. 122
Bernard of Clairvaux, 19, 43, 82, 88–89, 125, 135, 153–54, 155, 160
Bernardino of Siena, 17
Bes pantheos, 102–3, 107, 111
Boccaccio, Giovanni, 152, 163, 169
Boethius, 40–41, 117, 153
Bonaventure, 120
Bonaventure, Pseudo-, 120, 190 n. 59
Borgia, Francis, 5, 57
Borrassà, Luis, 108
Bosch, Hieronymus, 116, 117, 231 n. 135
Botticini, Giovanni, 115
Breughel, Pieter, the Elder, 117
Brisebarre, Jean, 114
Buonarotti, Michelangelo, 71
Buoncompagno of Signa, 98
Burgkmair, Hans, the Elder, 114, 208 n. 76

Caesar, Julius, 147
Caesarius of Hiesterbach, 42, 209 n. 92
Cairosco de Figueroa, Bartolomé, 156
Calvigero, Francisco, 182
Calvin, John, 124
Cardano, Jerome, 117

Cassian, John, 41, 120
Castiglione, Baldassare 16, 26, 31, 53, 74
Catherine of Alexandria, 113
Catherine of Siena, 112, 132-33, 158, 172
Cavalca, Domenico, 74, 83
Celano, Thomas de, 36
Celio, 176-77
Chaucer, Geoffrey, 26, 49, 95, 115, 149, 169
Chavero, Alfredo, 182
Cicero, 7, 8, 9, 11, 14, 15, 16, 17, 18, 27, 30, 136, 183, 188 n. 35, 189 n. 44
Cid, the. *See* Díaz, Rodrigo
Cisneros, Ximenez de, 168
Codretto, Annibal de, 13
Coler, Johann, 201 n. 147
Collaert, A., 181
Columbini, Giovanni, 47-48, 134
Cosmas and Damian, Saints, 112
Courcy, Jean de, 155
Coxie, Michael, 126-17
Crivelli, Carlo, 115

Dante, 6, 25, 35, 44, 76, 100, 105, 107, 140, 148, 153, 164, 178, 106, 244 n. 26, 247 n. 84, 251 n. 176
David, Jan, 247 n. 81
Della Casa, Giovanni, 31, 154
Destorrents, Ramón, 230 n. 125
Díaz, Rodrigo, 62, 150
Diogenes Laertius, 202 n. 170
Dionysius the Areopagite [pseud.], 106, 140
Domenico de Piacenza, 32
Dominic, Saint, 35, 36, 52, 77, 133, 150
Don Carlos, 31
Donne, John, 43
Dürer, Albrecht, 126

Eck, Johann, 88
Ephraeum Syrus, 113
Epictetus, 72
Erasmus, 4, 6, 20, 21, 22, 31, 38, 47, 48, 49, 51, 54, 70-71, 73, 74, 86, 113, 129, 134, 154, 154-55, 166, 168, 170, 195 n. 27, 202 n. 158
Eschenbach, Wolfram von, 32, 64, 189 n. 55
Escobar, Andreas de, 88
Evagrius Ponticus, 78, 82, 84, 86, 120, 121-22, 154
Eyck, Jan van, 112, 115
Ezekiel, 102, 103, 106, 107, 108, 176

Fabri, Felix, 10, 149, 156, 164, 165, 166, 167, 171, 172

Faria, Baltasar de, 150
Farinator, Matthias, 119
Farsit, Hugues, 42
Ferdinand II, 95, 96
Ferrer, Jaume, II, 105
Ferrer, Vincent, 17
Fisher King, 43
Fra Angelico. *See* Giovanni da Fiesole
Francis of Assisi, 3, 35, 36, 52, 68, 131, 133, 150, 178
Francisco Imperial, Micer, 138

Gabriel, Archangel, 115
Galle, Cornelius I., 181
García de Loyola, Lope, 63
García de Salazar, Lope, 63, 91
Gawain, 41, 114
George, Saint, 111
Gerson, Jean, 97, 122
Gesner, Konrad, 227 n. 86, 231 n. 138
Ghirlandaio, Domenico, 112
Giotto, 81
Giovanni da Fiesole, 115
Goes, Hugo van der, 115
Gonçalves da Câmara, Luis, 2, 4-5, 7, 8, 11-21, 23, 24, 39, 40, 55, 57, 58, 66, 67, 83, 85, 89, 90, 101, 150, 158, 165, 168, 169-70, 174, 177-78
Gozzoli, Benozzo, 115
Gregory the Great, 44, 82, 103, 112, 120, 151, 160, 161, 162-63, 201 n. 138, 212-13 n. 155
Grien, Hans Baldung, 126
Grosseteste, Robert, 41
Grünewald, Matthias, 108, 127, 253 n. 205
Guardia, Gabriel, 85-86
Guazzo, Stefano, 117
Guerrero, Francisco, 190 n. 59
Guevara, Antonio de, 54
Guglielmo Ebreo da Pesaro, 32, 58-59
Guicciardini, Francisco, 26
Guillaume de Deguileville, 2, 66, 119, 144, 153, 163, 183-84
Gutenberg, Johannes, 144

Hadrian IV, 150
Hawkwood, John, 26
Henry of Ostia, 232 n. 147
Heraclitus, 18
Hercules, 2, 28, 30, 70, 145-46, 155
Herodotus, 149
Herrad of Hohenbourg, 181, 221 n. 22
Hesiod, 189 n. 43
Hildegard of Bingen, 106
Hilton, Walter, 125-26
Hippocrates, 45
Homer, 25, 27, 68-69, 150

Index of Persons

Honorius of Autun, 155–56
Horace, 25, 32–33, 182, 194 n. 21
Hugh of St. Victor, 47
Huguet, Jaume, 108, 231 n. 127
Huon de Méri, 62, 151–52

Isidore of Seville, 23, 98, 110, 111

Jacob, 43, 45
Jacopone da Todi, 131
James, Saint, 157
Jerome, 10, 35, 41, 68, 124, 133, 134–35, 160, 165, 166, 167, 178, 179–80
Jiménez, Miguel, 105
John Chrysostom, 70, 106
John of Dambach, 31
John of Garland, 128–29
John of Salisbury, 128
John the Baptist, 46
Joseph, Saint, 161
Joubert, Laurent, 45
Juan de la Cruz, 37
Juliana, Saint, 145
Juno, 111, 115, 118, 140
Juvenal, 182

Kempe, Margery, 81, 149

Laínez, Diego, 13, 64
Langland, William, 119, 153
Latini, Brunetto, 31, 74, 111
Laudivio, 167
Laurent, Friar, 81
Lefevre d'Etaples, Jacques 38
Leonardo da Vinci, 21, 34, 81, 130, 135–36, 142, 143–44, 154, 173, 201 nn. 139, 142
Liberius, 56
Lippi, Filippo, 115
Livy, 194 n. 21
Longinus, Pseudo-, 143
Longuyon, Jacques de, 114
López de Ayala, Pedro, 120
Lorris, Guillaume de, 112, 128, 152, 153
Lucian, 117
Luis de Granada, 34
Lucretia, 81
Lucretius, 142, 143
Lucy, Saint, 100
Lull, Ramon, 26, 27, 53, 89–90
Luther, Martin, 1, 79, 87, 88, 173

Macrobius, 39
Maçuelo, Vincente de, 244 n. 27
Maestro de Mart de Torres, 229 n. 103
Maestro de Rubió, 230 n. 125
Malherbe, 167
Mancinellus, Julius, 117–18

Mandeville, John, 149, 164
Marcus Aurelius, 190 n. 62
Marcus of Orvieto, 126
María de santo Domingo, 96, 97
Martin of Tours, 68, 148
Martini, Simone, 115
Martorell, Bernat, 115, 224 n. 46
Mary Magdalen, 70, 167
Mary the Egyptian, 48
Masaccio, 135
Masolino, 135
Master of St. George, 224 n. 48
Maximillian I, 114
Mechthilde of Magdeburg, 113
Memmi, Lippo, 230 n. 117
Mena, Juan de, 121, 138
Mesa, J. de, 181
Mestre de Glorieta, 105
Meun, Jean de, 112, 128, 131, 145–46, 152, 153
Michael, Archangel, 105, 115, 116
Montaigne, Michel de, 19, 46, 47, 50, 54, 67
Moor, the, 60–62, 63, 64, 90, 92, 150, 159, 160, 174
Mote, Jean de la, 114
Musonius, 72

Nadal, Jerónimo, 5, 12, 13, 15, 16–17, 177
Nájara, Duke of, 51, 59, 150, 156
Narcissus, 127–29, 131, 133, 138
Nebrija, Antonio de, 214 n. 175
Nebuchadnezzar, 71
Neckham, Alexander, 128

Ocozias, 81
Onuphrius, 70
Oppian, 117
Orcagna, 105
Origen, 106, 160
Orozco y Berra, Manuel, 182
Ovid, 32, 111, 117, 128, 169, 214 n. 185

Palladius, 41, 76, 78–79
Paolo Veronese, 135
Paré, Ambroise, 46, 201 n. 150
Parzival, 32, 64–65, 95
Paschasius Radbertus, 134
Passavanti, Jacopo, 208 n. 85
Paul IV, Pope, 13, 62
Paula, 10, 178
Paulinus of Nola, 166
Pencz, George, 208 n. 76
Penelope, 11
Perez de Guzman, Fernan, 233 n. 156
Perugino, 87

Peter, Saint, 28–29, 87, 89, 134, 150, 167, 173
Peter Lombard, 82, 87, 120, 168
Peter of Limoges, 144
Peter the Venerable, 51, 201 n. 138
Petrarca, Francesco, 4, 40, 44, 48, 50, 72, 131, 158, 169, 173, 178, 191 n. 83
Petrus Alfonsi, 64
Philo, 106
Piacenza, Domenico de 32
Pico della Mirandola, Giovanni, 166–67
Piero della Francesca, 131
Plato, 49, 136, 136–37, 161, 180
Plautus, 24, 190 n. 64, 195 n. 28
Pliny, 117
Plotinus, 94, 137, 163
Plutarch, 19, 127
Polanco, Juan de, 64
Politziano, Angelo 17
Polyphemus, 48–49, 95
Pomponzaai, Pietro, 201 n. 150
Prester John, 13, 54, 95
Prudentius, 66, 81, 173
Pyrgopolinices, 24, 25, 95

Quintilian, 7, 8, 10, 17, 18, 21, 25, 33–34, 46, 81, 98, 99, 136, 145, 172, 178, 181–82, 183; 189 nn. 44, 46; 191 n. 91; 196 nn. 48, 50; 197 n. 62, 212 n. 138, 218 n. 249

Raoul de Houdence, 151
Raphael, Archangel, 115
Raymond of Capua, 133, 158, 172
Raymond of Peñaforte, 87, 120
Rayner, Saint, 68
Rebello, Jacobus Lupi, 217 n. 227
Ribadeneira, Pedro de, 181
Ricci, Matteo, 13
Richard of St. Laurent, 92
Richard of St. Victor, 47, 125, 178–79
Ripa, Cesare, 169, 195 n. 30
Rodriguez de Lena, Pedro, 197 n. 56
Rodriguez de Montalvo, Garci, 34, 65, 69, 138–39
Rolle, Richard, 126
Ronsard, Pierre de, 102, 163
Roscius Gallus, Quintus, 11
Rubens, Peter Paul, 111
Ruiz, Juan, 30–31, 65, 71, 121, 129, 197 n. 56
Rutebeuf, 151

Salutati, Coluccio, 213 n. 202
Salvian, 147
Sanchez de Vercial, Climente, 65–66, 77, 206 n. 75
Saul, 81

Scaliger, Julius Caesar, 110, 117
Scotus, John Duns, 87
Sebastian, King, 13, 20
Seghers, Gerard, 181
Seneca, 4, 8, 49, 72, 101–2, 170
Seneca, the Elder, 81
Serra, Jaume and Pere, 85
Seuse, Heinrich, 132
Severus, Sulpicius, 147
Sextus Empiricus, 143
Shakespeare, William, 139
Sixtus IV, 57
Sixtus V, 252 n. 194
Socrates, 20
Solis, Virgil, 169
Sophocles, 196 n. 43
Soranus, 45
Soto, Domingo de, 168
Southwell, Robert, 167
Spenser, Edmund, 119
Stefano di Giovanni (Sassetta), 209 n. 102

Tansillo, Luigi, 167
Tasso, Torquato, 117
Terence, 46, 171
Teresa of Avila, 44–45
Thales, 49, 51
Theophrastus, 117
Thomas à Kempis, 156
Thomas Aquinas, 8, 80, 82, 92, 106, 120, 122, 155
Tosses, 87
Triani, Francesco, 213 n. 170
Trotaconventos, 30–31, 95

Venus, 43
Vergil, 43, 153, 165, 168–69, 202 n. 174
Vincent of Beauvais, 233 n. 149
Vio, Tommaso de, 96
Virgin Mary, 10, 39–40, 41–42, 44, 47, 52, 54–55, 56–57, 58, 59, 60, 61, 63, 65, 66, 67, 83, 85, 87, 89–90, 92–93, 100, 109, 112, 114–15, 115, 116, 118, 127, 129, 130, 140, 141, 142, 150, 153, 159, 160, 161, 166, 175, 176, 177, 178, 179, 181, 217–18 n. 243
Voragine, Jacob de, 77, 100

Weinsberg, Hermann von, 201 n. 147
Weyden, Rogier van der, 69, 115, 190 n. 59
Whiterig, John, 131–32

Xavier, Francis, 175
Xenophon, 186 n. 5, 194 n. 14

Compositor:	Impressions Book and Journal Services, Inc.
Text:	10/13 Sabon
Display:	Sabon

www.ingramcontent.com/pod-product-compliance
Lightning Source LLC
Chambersburg PA
CBHW021655230426
43668CB00008B/634